"Tell Them We Are Singing for Jesus"

MERCER
UNIVERSITY PRESS

Endowed by
TOM WATSON BROWN
and
THE WATSON-BROWN FOUNDATION, INC.

"Tell Them We Are Singing for Jesus"

The Original Fisk Jubilee Singers and
Christian Reconstruction,
1871–1878

Toni P. Anderson

Mercer University Press
Macon

MUP/H785

© 2010 Mercer University Press
1400 Coleman Avenue
Macon, Georgia 31207

First Edition.

Books published by Mercer University Press are printed on acid free
paper that meets the requirements of American National Standard for
Information Sciences—Permanence of Paper for Printed Library
Materials.

Mercer University Press is a member of Green Press initiative
(greenpressinitiative.org), a nonprofit organization working to help
publishers and printers increase their use of recycled paper and
decrease their use of fiber derived from endangered forests. This book
is printed on recycled paper.

Anderson, Toni P., 1957-
    Tell them we are singing for Jesus : the original Fisk Jubilee Singers
and Christian reconstruction, 1871-1878 / Toni P. Anderson. -- 1st
ed.
    p. cm.
Includes bibliographical references and index.
ISBN 978-0-88146-112-1 (hardback : alk. paper)
1. Jubilee Singers—History—19th century. 2. American Missionary
Association—History—19th century. 3. Choirs (Music)—United
States—History—19th century. 4. African American singers. I. Title.
ML421.J77A54 2010
782.42162'96073006076855--dc22
                                                          2010001203

Contents

154725

Acknowledgments

This work reflects a long labor of love that stretches over many years. I first began to research the Fisk Jubilee Singers as a doctoral student years ago at the prompting of Wayne J. Urban, one of my professors. I was familiar with the ensemble and aware of its importance in American music history and the development of black higher education, but never expected to find such a treasure trove of data waiting to be unearthed and explored. I am grateful to Dr. Urban for launching me on a remarkable journey of scholarly and personal growth.

The material for this work was gathered primarily from two special collections: the Fisk University Franklin Library, Special Collections; and the Amistad Research Center at Tulane University. I am especially thankful to Beth Howse, the librarian/archivist at the Fisk University Special Collections and a descendant of Ella Sheppard Moore, for her generous help, insight, and friendship over the years. Ms. Howse's graciousness made my many research trips to her institution delightful events, each one offering new material I had not seen previously, as some of the material to which I was granted access had yet to be fully catalogued. I am grateful to Ms. Howse and her staff for their assistance with my varied requests and questions.

I also extend my thanks to Brenda Square at the Amistad Research Center, Tulane University, for her expert help on many phases of this project. There are many other reference librarians who assisted my research and to whom I am indebted. My deep appreciation goes to Arthur Robinson of LaGrange College Library for his patience and expert assistance in finding sources. I am equally grateful for the help given by Charlene Baxter and Mary Lou Dabbs at LaGrange College. Thanks also go to Raymond Wilson from the Portage County Historical Society, Cynthia Gaynor of the Reed Memorial Library, Judy Proffitt of the Noxubee County Library, and Lisa Pillow of the Ohio State University Library for research assistance. I also benefited from the help of the staffs at the British Newspaper Library at Colindale, the British National Library at St. Pancras, the Tennessee State Archives, the Moody Bible Institute, the Auburn Avenue Archives, the Moorland-Spingarn Research Center, and the Limestone County Archives.

I am indebted to my home institution, LaGrange College, for a summer grant to work on the research phase of this project and a sabbatical leave during which to complete the writing. My deep appreciation goes to my colleagues in the music department, who graciously assumed many responsibilities and kept things running smoothly in my absence: Lee Johnson, Debbie Ogle, Mitch Turner, Anne Duraski, Pat Callaway, and Ann Sellman. I also benefited from the help of Christiane Price, who spent considerable time translating portions of German reviews. Thanks also go to Katherine Roberts, my student research assistant, who read through microfilm, made photocopies, and did countless miscellaneous chores.

This work builds upon the research of other fine scholars to whom I am deeply indebted. I relied heavily on Joe Richardson's history of Fisk University and the American Missionary Association's work in the South to inform the conceptual framework of this book. Other scholars of the Jubilee Singers have contributed to my understanding of the ensemble's significance; three deserve mention here. Doug Seroff provided me invaluable assistance in the early phases of my work, shared some of his own research, and offered feedback on mine. Andrew Ward's book on the ensemble appeared shortly after my dissertation, providing rich historical context I found informative. He also graciously shared portions of his research with me, for which I am indebted. Sandra Graham's dissertation followed, examining the Jubilee Singers' contribution to the emergence of the concert spiritual. Her musicological research is a valuable addition to scholarship.

My sincere and humble thanks go to those who read through portions of this manuscript during its various stages of development. At the top of the list is my husband, Chuck, who patiently reviewed multiple versions of the manuscript and offered his critical assessment and editorial suggestions. In addition, I am most grateful to Wayne Urban, Linda Buchanan, Marva Carter, Dwight Thomas, Ann Sellman, and Pat Callaway, whose helpful questions and comments were critical to the completion of this book. I particularly thank the editors at Mercer University Press for their contribution to this work.

Various research trips turned into exciting adventures because of the company of special people who were willing to combine work with play. My sister-in-law, Mary Catherine Passmore, did the tedious job of reconstructing the Jubilees' concert itinerary. My mother, Lois Passmore, read through British newspapers, pausing only to comment on advertisements she found humorous. Erin, my daughter, was my frequent research buddy over the years, creating happy memories I will always cherish. She also read through portions of the manuscript and her imaginative comments were most helpful. Special thanks go to Linda Buchanan, who shared early research trips with me and never tired of my endless discussions about the Jubilees.

Finally, this project would not have happened without the constant love and affection of my family. Thank you, Chuck, Erin, Wes, and Brian, for your gifts of humor, which brightened the dreary times, and for your unwavering belief in me. Your encouragement, along with the unflagging support of other family members and friends far too numerous to list, inspired me to stay the course. I extend my heartfelt thanks to you all.

Preface

Voice of a ransomed race! Sing on
Till Freedom's every right is won
And slavery's every wrong undone![1]

The story of the Fisk Jubilee Singers reads almost like a fairy tale. That a group of nine young men and women fresh from slavery, voices trumpeting the songs of their ancestors, could capture the attention of the world is indeed remarkable. With rich, sonorous tones, these African Americans sang with dignity and artistry, heralding the songs of freedom, justice, and hope for a better world. Their songs tugged at the hearts of their audiences, chipping away at prevailing stereotypes, and thus contributing to a national discourse of what a post-Civil War America should be. In the case of the Jubilee Singers, music framed the social dialogue and became a conduit for the powerful public expression of African-American possibility.

The ensemble was the musical creation of George Leonard White, the white treasurer and choral director of Fisk University, established at the close of the Civil War by the American Missionary Association (AMA) for freedmen's education. On 6 October 1871, he and his troupe set out on a quixotic mission to raise money through concerts and thereby salvage their institution on the brink of financial failure. Within three months of the troupe's inception, the ensemble adopted the name "Fisk Jubilee Singers" and came under the authoritative umbrella of the AMA. From that moment until the close of its third campaign in July 1878, AMA employees set the vision, goals, and campaign strategy of the ensemble while also overseeing the troupe's social obligations and daily operations. The individual singers in the company were under contract with the AMA and considered partners in the association's grand efforts to revolutionize American society.

The AMA was formed in 1846 by leading New England abolitionists who were largely dissatisfied with the silence of other missionary organizations on the subject of slavery. Prior to the Civil War, the association sponsored missionary works in various foreign lands, and through its home department, sent missionaries into a few areas in the Midwest, Kentucky, and North Carolina.[2] At the close of the Civil War, the association stepped up its efforts against slavery's effects with a major focus on providing education to emancipated slaves. The largest among relief organizations, the AMA was the first to enter the freedmen's education movement and the last to leave.[3]

The association engaged in a work that historian Joe Richardson aptly labeled "Christian Reconstruction," a large-scale liberation effort that recognized the consequences of slavery upon both the outward and inward person. It was not enough to these abolitionists to provide material resources; true freedom must include liberation of the soul and mind. "Education and Christianity—and they only can solve the problem; not education alone, not Christianity alone, if such a thing could be, but Education and Christianity combined; - an educated Christianity," was the association's rhetoric. Therefore, the AMA sent missionary-teachers into the South bringing benevolent relief, the textbook, the Bible, and the "New England Way" in hopes of educating, elevating, and evangelizing freedmen. Such efforts, they believed, would transform African-American men and women into productive citizens ready to participate fully in the mainstream of American society. The schools they founded would become the "ganglia or nerve-centers from which will radiate in every direction Christian influences."[4]

This book explores how the ideals of the AMA's Christian Reconstruction worldview governed every aspect of the Jubilee Singers' historic seven years of fundraising campaigns (1871–1878) and influenced the lives of its individual members. It is neither an exhaustive historical chronology nor a musicological analysis, but rather a study of the ideological forces that spawned, shaped, and gave meaning to the Fisk Jubilee Singers, whose remarkable success in turn solidified Fisk University's organizational identity and purpose. The company was more than a musical ensemble that won the hearts of the Western world, although this alone was a significant accomplishment worth consideration. Neither was it merely a vehicle for raising money for Fisk University, although this goal dominated most of its campaigns. At times, the AMA relied on the Jubilee Singers' fundraising capability to offset some of its other pressing needs, reallocating the funds they earned for the construction of Fisk's new Jubilee Hall to other causes.

And though the ensemble became an authoritative and outspoken voice for civil rights, the AMA considered this outcome a welcomed part of the company's overall Christian ministry. First and foremost, the AMA perceived the Jubilee Singers as co-laborers in its great missionary endeavor to change American society, and it is this aspect of the ensemble's raison-d'être that is the primary focus of this book. They were living ambassadors of the AMA's Christian Reconstruction ideals and testimonials to what its formula of religion-plus-education could accomplish.

This Christian Reconstruction worldview, then, provides the lens through which this research examines the Jubilee Singers' story and their significance in American history. From its inception, the AMA's educational work in the South involved both blacks and whites united for a common cause. The Jubilee Singers enterprise was a microcosm of this kind of partnership. By placing the ensemble on the Western world's concert stages, the AMA subjected its ideology to public scrutiny. Could its particular brand of freedmen's education produce the results they claimed?

Collectively and individually, the Jubilee Singers became a public demonstration of what the AMA hoped to achieve. Therefore, the company's managers carefully guarded the public and private aspects of the business enterprise and its participants. The ideals of Christian Reconstruction—true freedom, equality, and recognition of human dignity—were tested daily as blacks and whites learned to live and work together. Victorian codes of conduct interlaced with Christian standards of morality were the AMA's boundaries for behavior and the benchmarks for success in the social arena. Any public triumph over caste prejudice in either the public or private spheres of life that the Jubilee Singers enjoyed was used by the AMA to validate the moral superiority of its Christian Reconstruction beliefs.

Because this is a story about human beings and their ideas, it is fraught with foibles and virtues, triumphs and tragedies. Musical, missionary, ministry, and mercenary motives coexisted and struggled for preeminence. Each person associated with the campaigns—whether black or white, administrator, agent, or musician—brought to the experience a unique perspective on the company's mission and his or her role in the organization. The diversity of participants in this partnership complicated daily operations and sometimes made the ensemble's road to success a bumpy one.

In a very real sense, this is a story about the search and struggle for freedom: emancipation from slavery; liberation of the mind, soul, and spirit; social and political equality; and jubilee songs that trumpeted freedom's arrival. Freedom for all was the AMA's ultimate goal; Christian Reconstruction was its roadmap to achieve it. Without divine intervention, believed the proponents of this ideology, any efforts to transform human beings, and ultimately American society, were woefully incomplete.

Within a short time, 6 October 1871, the day the Jubilee Singers embarked on their first fundraising mission, became a celebrated holiday at Fisk University commemorating the supreme efforts made by this small band of vocalists to ensure the survival of the institution. Eloquent speeches, appearances by original members of the troupe, and the singing of Negro spirituals kept the history of the Jubilee Singers alive and transformed their exploits into the stuff of legend. The faith and determination underlying the troupe's inauguration, and the adversity they endured before achieving success, provided a gripping story that contributed to Fisk University's institutional pride and collective memory, creating an emotional bond between faculty, students, and alumni. Within a decade, Fisk University had established its reputation as a respected institution for black higher education with an unwavering commitment to a classical education designed to develop African-American leaders. The self-denial, dedication to civil rights, pursuit of excellence, and sense of responsibility for racial uplift that characterized the original Jubilee Singers campaigns permeated the atmosphere of Fisk University, in turn influencing the institution's values and giving it a sense of purpose that sustained the college through tumultuous decades ahead.

A word about the text is in order here. I have relied heavily on individual voices as I find each one's perspective and word choices not only fascinating to read, but the most authentic way of telling the story. In transcribing original documents, it was often difficult to determine whether the author intended a dash, comma, or period. I have made judgments to the best of my ability that may disagree with other scholars. The reader should rightly assume that odd capitalizations, and occasional misspellings or grammatical errors reflect the original sources.

I have also made generous use of AMA official publications and correspondence between its employees (including the Jubilee Singers), as these documents are replete with religious jargon and reveal how this language was well understood and frequently used by all involved with the company, regardless of one's personal devoutness. Theirs was a Christian Reconstruction world in which certain principles and codes of behavior were shared by the broader evangelical community on both sides of the ocean. Data suggest that everyone associated with the Jubilee Singers affirmed the AMA's Christian tenets at some level and attempted to abide by those standards.

Last, in a spirit of candor, I offer a few words about potential biases. I developed an intense fondness for my subjects from the moment I encountered them almost fifteen years ago. As a vocal artist, I appreciated the Jubilee Singers' remarkable talent and celebrated their hard-earned success. My tenure as a professor has been equally divided between two liberal arts institutions, during which I have toured with hundreds of students across the United States and abroad. I know firsthand how tensions can surface and hard feelings abound, and therefore I must admit my sympathies for George White and the company. Perhaps I judge the characters and institutions in this story less harshly than would another observer. Nonetheless, in telling and interpreting the Jubilee Singers' remarkable story, I have made every attempt to be fair.

---

[1] John Greenleaf Whittier, *Anti-Slavery Poems: Songs of Labor and Reform* (1888; rep., New York: Arno Press, 1969) 268. This stanza is the last one of a poem entitled "The Jubilee Singers."

[2] *History of the American Missionary Association: Its Churches and Educational Institutions Among the Freedmen, Indians, and Chinese* (New York: S. W. Green, Printer, 1874) 3–5. In 1854, the AMA had seventy-nine commissioned missionaries in West Africa, Jamaica, the Sandwich Islands, Siam, Canada, and Minnesota through its Foreign Department. By the following year, they had sent 110 missionaries to Kentucky, North Carolina, and a few Midwestern states, such as Kansas. The missionaries in the South primarily engaged in preaching the gospel and establishing schools. The AMA felt that their presence stood as an "unequivocal testimony against Slavery" (5).

[3] Clara Merritt DeBoer, *Be Jubilant My Feet: African American Abolitionists in the American Missionary Association 1839–1861* (New York and London: Garland Publishing, Inc., 1994) 4.

[4] Joe M. Richardson, *Christian Reconstruction: The American Missionary Association and Southern Blacks, 1861–1890* (Athens and London: University of Georgia Press, 1986) 19–22; "Thirtieth Annual Report of the American Missionary Association—1876," 10, American Missionary Association Archives (hereafter cited as AMAA).

Pencil sketch of the original site of Fisk School, from a photograph taken in 1866.
Fisk School was incorporated on 22 August 1867 as Fisk University.
Courtesy of the Fisk University Franklin Library Special Collections.

RULES AND REGULATIONS

OF THE

FISK UNIVERSITY

NASHVILLE, TENN.

In order to aid students in the proper division of their time, and the right employment of their energies, the following *Rules and Regulations* have been adopted. All students, therefore, on entering the Institution, are expected to acquaint themselves with them.

I. To attend promptly and cheerfully all the prescribed exercises of the Institution, unless for good and sufficient reasons excused.

II. To observe neatness and order, both in person and in the arrangement of books, desks and other furniture, in and about their private rooms, the school-room, and on the grounds.

III. To rise promptly at the ringing of the *first bell;* and to observe quiet and good order in their private rooms, in the school-rooms and on the school-grounds during ·hours of study.

IV. To retire at or before ten o'clock at night; and to see that all lights in their rooms are extinguished, and fires properly secured *before* retiring.

V. Students boarding on the grounds will not leave them on any·occasion without the knowledge and consent of the Principal, or some authorized person.

VI. They are expected to attend Chapel service every morning, Wednesday afternoon lecture and regular services on the Sabbath at the Chapel of the University.

VII. Students are not allowed to visit each other's rooms during hours of study, or after nine o'clock at night, nor to be absent from their rooms after that time

VIII. Ladies and Gentlemen are not allowed to visit each other, strangers or friends, under any circumstances, at their private rooms. All interviews must be public and in presence of a Teacher.

IX. The use of ardent spirits, tobacco in any form, and all games of chance are strictly forbidden, at all times and in all places, while connected with the Institution.

X. Students are expected to abstain at all times and in all places, from profane, indecent or indecorous language or allusions, to be kind, courteous and polite to one another and to strangers, and respectful and obedient to instructors.

XI. To prevent losses and needless expenditures, all Students boarding on the grounds, on entering the Institution, are required to deposit all their money with the Treasurer who will give them a receipt, and to draw upon him as they may have need.

PENALTIES.

The willful violation or evasion of any of the above Rules or Regulations, will subject the offender to reprimand, suspension or expulsion, according to the nature of the offense and the character of the offender.

HOURS OF STUDY:

IN WINTER.

A. M. from 5 1-2 to 7, and from 8 1-2 to 12 M.   P. M. from 1 to 4, and from 6 1-2 to 9.

IN SUMMER.

A. M. from 5 1-2 to 7, and from 8 1-2 to 12 M.   P. M. from 2 to 5, and from 7 1-2 to 9.

During which times Students are expected to be in their private rooms, or in the school-rooms engaged in studies.

JOHN OGDEN.

APRIL 4TH, 1868.   *Principal, and President Board of Trustees.*

Rules and regulations governing student conduct at Fisk University, 1868. Courtesy of the American Missionary Association Archives, Amistad Research Center, Tulane University.

Professor Adam Knight Spence, principal of the Fisk School from 1870 to 1875. Spence continued to serve as professor of Greek until 1900. Courtesy of the Fisk University Franklin Library Special Collections.

The parlor of Adam Knight Spence where the original Jubilee Singers often gathered as students to sing and share spirituals. Courtesy of the Fisk University Franklin Library Special Collections.

Erastus Milo Cravath became the first president of Fisk University in 1875 and joined the Jubilee Singers on their third campaign as manager. He served as Fisk's president for twenty-five years. Courtesy of the Fisk University Franklin Library Special Collections.

George Leonard White, the founder and director of the original Fisk Jubilee Singers, 1871–1878. Courtesy of the Fisk University Franklin Library Special Collections.

The original nine members of the Jubilee Singers in early 1872. Seated, left to right: Eliza Walker, Benjamin Holmes, Ella Sheppard, Jennie Jackson, Greene Evans, Minnie Tate. Standing, left to right: Thomas Rutling, Maggie Porter, Isaac Dickerson. Courtesy of the Fisk University Franklin Library Special Collections.

THE JUBILEE SINGERS.—REV. HENRY WARD BEECHER AS THE MANAGER OF A NEGRO MINSTREL TROUPE.—EXTRAORDINARY ATTRACTIONS AT PLYMOUTH CHURCH, BROOKLYN, WEDNESDAY, JANUARY 3, 1872.—SEE PAGE 18.

Cartoon mocking the Jubilee Singers in concert at Henry Ward Beecher's Plymouth Church on 3 January 1872. The caption reads, "The Jubilee Singers. Rev. Henry Ward Beecher as the manager of a Negro minstrel troupe. Extraordinary attractions at Plymouth Church, Brooklyn, Wednesday, January 3, 1872." Courtesy of the Fisk University Franklin Library Special Collections.

Handbill advertising the Jubilee Singers in concert at Steinway Hall, 14 January 1873. Courtesy of the Fisk University Franklin Library Special Collections.

Anthony Ashley Cooper, seventh earl of Shaftesbury, whose patronage of the Jubilee Singers successfully introduced the troupe to London's most influential citizens. Courtesy of the Fisk University Franklin Library Special Collections.

Crystal Palace as it appeared when the Jubilee Singers performed there in July 1873 for the National Temperance League's annual fête. Over 53,000 people attended portions of the event. The facility was destroyed by fire in 1936. Reproduced by permission of English Heritage. NMR.

Reverend Charles Haddon Spurgeon, the renowned
pastor of London's Metropolitan Tabernacle and a
supporter of the Jubilee Singers. Courtesy of the Fisk
University Franklin Library Special Collections.

C. H. Spurgeon's church, Metropolitan Tabernacle, c. 1870, where the Jubilee Singers performed in July 1873 to an estimated crowd of 7,000. All but the building's front portico and
basement were destroyed by fire in 1898. Reproduced by permission of English Heritage. NMR.

Painting of the Jubilee Singers commissioned by Queen Victoria, ca. 1873, now housed in Jubilee Hall on the Fisk University campus. Females, left to right: Mabel Lewis, Minnie Tate, Ella Sheppard, Jennie Jackson, Maggie Porter, America Robinson, Georgia Gordon. Males, left to right: Greene Evans, Isaac Dickerson, Thomas Rutling, Benjamin Holmes. Courtesy of the Fisk University Franklin Library Special Collections.

The Jubilee Singers, third campaign, 1875–1878. Seated, left to right: B. W. Thomas, Julia Jackson, Ella Sheppard, Georgia Gordon, America Robinson, Thomas Rutling. Standing, left to right: Maggie Porter, Frederick J. Loudin, H. D. Alexander, Jennie Jackson.Courtesy of the Fisk University Franklin Library Special Collections.

Dwight L. Moody, evangelist. The Jubilee Singers participated in many of Moody's revival services in England and Scotland between 1873 and 1875.
Reproduced by permission of the Moody Bible Institute.

Ira B. Sankey, the noted soloist who participated with D. L. Moody in his revivals. Courtesy of the Fisk University Franklin Library Special Collections.

Alleinige Inseraten-Annahme
bei Rudolf Mosse
Annoncen - Expedition
für sämmtliche Zeitungen
Deutschlands
und des Auslandes.

Beiblatt zum Kladderadatsch.

Insertions-Gebühren
für die
4-gespaltene Nonpareill-Zeile
oder deren Raum
1 ℳ = 1 ½ Gr.

in Berlin Jerusalemerstraße 48, Hamburg, Frankfurt a. M., Stuttgart, Breslau, Leipzig, Dresden, Halle, Cöln, London, München, Nürnberg, Prag, Wien, Strassburg, Zürich, Basel.

Nr. 57. Drittes Beiblatt.   Berlin, den 16. December 1877.   XXX. Jahrgang.

Ein schwarzer Anschlag.

Man bitte doch von den Jubiläum-Sängern ein einfaches Quartett in Berlin zurückbehalten. Für Hochzeiten, Kindtaufen und sonstige Freudenfeste reichen wir ja mit unseren Sängern. Wie festlich aber müßte es sein, wenn wir fortan für ernste Feierlichkeiten auch ein schwarzes Quartett besäßen!

Artist representation of the male members of the Jubilee Singers that appeared in a Berlin newspaper, 1877. The handwriting on the left is America Robinson's: "See Mr. Loudin with his air of self satisfaction, Mr. Thomas intent on his music not yet fully acquainted with the songs. While Tom is lost to everything but the power of song. Alexander maintains his personal dignity." Courtesy of the Fisk University Franklin Library Special Collections.

A young Ella Sheppard reunited with her half sister, Rosa, c. 1867.
Courtesy of the Fisk University Franklin Library Special Collections.

Ella Sheppard, George L. White's talented and loyal musical assistant. Courtesy of the Fisk University Franklin Library Special Collections.

Ella Sheppard Moore (center) with her family seated on the steps of the home they built across from Fisk University. To the left are her sons, George Sheppard and Clinton Fisk Russell. To the right is her husband, George W. Moore, and mother, Sarah Hannah Sheppard. Courtesy of the Fisk University Franklin Library Special Collections.

George Washington Moore, who married Ella Sheppard in the parlor of George and Susan White on 20 December 1882. Courtesy of the Fisk University Franklin Library Special Collections.

Ella Sheppard Moore (bottom right) and the Fisk Jubilee Club she trained, c. 1900. Courtesy of the Fisk University Franklin Library Special Collections.

Frederick J. Loudin, c. 1877, joined the
Jubilee Singers for its third campaign and
eventually toured the world with his own
company. Courtesy of the Fisk University Franklin
Library Special Collections.

Jubilee Hall was built on a twenty-five acre site that was formerly Fort Gillem. The dedication for the new building occurred on 1 January 1876, while the Jubilee Singers were still on
tour in England. Courtesy of the Fisk University Franklin Library Special Collections

"Otira," the home F. J. Loudin built in Ravenna, Ohio, and named after a gorge in New Zealand. Reproduced by permission of the Portage County Historical Society.

Loudin filled his Ravenna home with wood and treasures gathered during his world travels. Reproduced by permission of the Portage County Historical Society.

Frederick J. Loudin and his wife Harriet in their later years. Reproduced by permission of the Portage County Historical Society.

Chapter 1

The Roots of Christian Reconstruction:

The American Missionary Association and

Fisk University

The operations of the American Missionary Association are based on these evangelical views. It cannot, it will not, divorce education from religion. Its schools must be pervaded by religious influence, and its religious efforts with these people must be educational. The garments we give, the asylums we found, the schools we open, the churches we plant, must all be in one Name, and, for one object—the physical, intellectual and religious elevation of this long crushed people to the high plane of a Christian civilization.[1]

The signing of the Emancipation Proclamation in January 1863 launched a new era in American race relations. Loosed from the legal bondage of slavery, nearly two million African Americans now faced the daunting challenge of discovering how to exist in a society that offered only a few friends and plenty of foes. The path to acceptance as equal members of society was laden with racist attitudes regarding African Americans' moral, social, and intellectual potential. Moreover, Victorian ideals that had long defined social respectability and acceptable personhood in the dominant white society now became the benchmarks for whether or not blacks "fit" in the mainstream of American life. Emancipation was only the beginning of a long and arduous journey toward full equality and societal inclusion.

Northern benevolent societies committed to abolition prior to the Civil War quickly stepped up to assume the task of preparing freedmen for participation in a "civilized" society. Good intentions, though not always perfect practice, motivated their efforts along with an unwavering belief in the rightness of their cause. Most prominent among the benevolent societies was the American Missionary Association (AMA), called by one historian a "society whose reputation was won as a leader in the education of the freedmen."[2]

The story of the Fisk Jubilee Singers is inseparable from that of the AMA. Further, the values and ideals that formed and sustained this musical ensemble find their root in the association's espoused worldview. As founder of Fisk University, the AMA provided leadership and vision for the institution along with missionary teachers who were firmly committed to its cause. A sense of divine mission and call permeated the Fisk campus, and it is therefore not surprising to find similar sentiments undergirding the Jubilee Singers operation. Three months into the first campaign, the AMA assumed official sponsorship and broadened the company's mission. More than a mere fundraising enterprise for a single institution, the leadership viewed the musical ensemble as an extension of its larger work and the members as ambassadors not only of Fisk University, but also of the AMA. To fully appreciate who the Jubilee Singers were, collectively and individually, first requires an understanding of this powerful and influential missionary organization and its leaders.

Formation of the AMA

The spirit of crusade and reform that permeated New England throughout the second half of the nineteenth century was due in part to the "Second Great Awakening," a religious revival that swept much of the United States in the 1820s. The leading evangelical revivalist was Charles Grandison Finney, a fiery young preacher whose conversion experience in 1821 drastically changed the course of his life. Finney's series of successful revivals in the Western Reserve brought him national attention and paved the way for services he held in New England between 1827 and 1832. Finney stressed each person's choice to repent of sins and the need for Christians to apply their faith to daily living. Winning converts was his primary goal, but Finney also emphasized that moral reform would lead logically to social reform as Christians surrendered unconditionally to God's will. To Finney, an important outward sign of one's inward spirituality was the degree to which a Christian engaged selflessly in evangelical and benevolent efforts to impact the world.[3] Finney's message influenced the lives of thousands of Americans, many of whom were important figures in the founding and early history of Fisk University: Arthur and Lewis Tappan, George Whipple, Erastus Cravath, and Adam Spence.

In this climate of spiritual reflection and renewal occurred several historical events that significantly influenced the AMA's formation, the first of which was the Lane Seminary rebellion of the 1830s. The Cincinnati seminary existed in part due to the benevolence of Arthur Tappan, who had pledged to pay the salary of Lyman Beecher, the seminary president, for as long as he could. Arthur and his brother, Lewis, had made their fortunes as silk merchants and were radical leaders in the antislavery movement. In deference to Arthur's abolitionist sentiments, Lane Seminary had admitted one African-American student, but was otherwise relatively quiet on the subject of abolition. In March 1834, a series of "debates" (actually prayer and sermon sessions) on the issue resulted in several of the students denouncing slavery and putting their new convictions into practice. The trustees were somewhat alarmed at this turn of events and threatened to expel the students. Unrepentant, the "Lane rebels" refused to adopt a compromising stance.

To the Tappan brothers, the incident demonstrated the trustees' ambivalence on the slavery issue, evidence that Lane Seminary and Lyman Beecher were not fully committed to ridding the nation of this terrible "sin." Arthur Tappan was unwilling to concede any ground on the abolition issue, choosing instead to board the intransigent students near Cincinnati and begin looking for a new home for his scholars. Several months later he had still failed to find an educational institution that shared his religious and reform convictions when he had a fortuitous visit from the Reverend John Shipherd.

Shipherd, a Presbyterian minister, had come to the Western Reserve in 1833 and formed a nucleus of scholars committed to simplicity, devotion to church and school, and intense interest in missionary causes. His dream of using this core group to establish an educational institution needed financial backing, and he hoped Arthur Tappan would catch the vision. Tappan did, but insisted on adding his own ideas to the school's philosophical framework: commitment to moral reform (in particular, antislavery), freedom of speech on all reform issues, and guaranteed entrance of African

Americans. He was also adamant about hiring Charles Finney as the head of the theological division and guaranteed his salary. Tappan saw in the new institution a home for the wayward "Lane rebels" and a place in which to nurture future generations in pious living and concern for humanity.[4]

The new Oberlin Collegiate Institute quickly became the center of Western abolitionism. George Whipple, co-founder of the AMA and a "Lane rebel," was a product of the school. Finney's spiritual influence was strengthened at the institution when he became the president of Oberlin in 1852. The school furnished scores of missionaries who served the AMA in various foreign fields and hundreds of "Yankee teachers" who filled posts throughout the South. From its inception until 1860, 90 percent of the AMA's workers were former Oberlin students.[5]

A second historical event that awakened public consciousness on the slavery issue was the *Amistad* case of 1839. West Africans who had been illegally enslaved by Spanish slave traders rose against their captors while in Cuban seas and succeeded in killing most of the crew. They wanted to sail back to Africa and ordered the remaining Spaniards to direct the way. The sailors managed to chart a zigzag route, traveling east during the day but guiding the ship north at night, until the schooner landed near Long Island where it was boarded by United States Navy Lieutenant Commander Thomas R. Gedney. He seized the *Amistad*, took the Africans to jail, and charged them with crimes of murder and piracy.

The case caused quite a stir with the public and instantly won the sympathies of abolitionists. Reverend Simeon S. Jocelyn, Reverend Joshua Leavitt, and Lewis Tappan voluntarily formed a committee to care for the Africans and provide them with legal counsel. John Quincy Adams argued the final case before the Supreme Court and won freedom for the Africans in March 1841, two years after their capture. The members of the Amistad Committee felt their responsibility to the Africans could not be relinquished until they had safely returned them to their native land. Within a year, they raised the necessary funds and finally sailed the Africans to Sierre Leone, the homeland of most, along with three missionaries from Oberlin. With monies largely furnished by Arthur Tappan, the Mendi Mission in West Africa was formed, and came under the supervision of the AMA within a few years of its existence.[6]

The *Amistad* case galvanized public opposition to slavery and fueled the antislavery cause. It occurred at a time when religious leaders were beginning to encourage personal responsibility for social reform, and where progressive intellectual thought complemented such convictions. Moral, political, religious, and social forces merged to create an environment where men and women of either religious or secular persuasion fought against society's ills. Another significance of the *Amistad* case was that it brought together influential men with like minds and religious convictions, such as Jocelyn and the Tappan brothers. By appealing to Oberlin for missionaries for the Mendi Mission, these men strengthened their ties to an institution that would come to play a major role in the life of the AMA. In fact, within a few short years, these same men would join their efforts to create the missionary organization.

The AMA owed its existence in large part to Lewis and Arthur Tappan's growing irritation with American Christianity's failure to adopt an uncompromising stance on slavery. Various missionary organizations in which the Tappan brothers participated continued to accept members and donations from Southern slave owners, a fact that offended the Tappans' abolitionist sensibilities. The frustrated brothers therefore initiated a move to create a new organization that would conduct missionary evangelism in an unadulterated manner. They gathered other like-minded abolitionists who shared their dissatisfaction and on 3 September 1846 formed the AMA. The founders included prominent abolitionists who assumed influential leadership positions within the organization: George Whipple, in charge of foreign missions; Simeon Jocelyn, responsible for domestic missions; and Lewis Tappan, treasurer and policy-maker in the executive committee. Three missionary organizations that had previously existed—the Union Missionary Society (formerly the Amistad Committee), the Committee for West-India Missions, and the Western Evangelical Missionary Society—ceased operating independently and merged their missions and funds into the AMA, recognizing the benefits that such a union offered.[7]

Of all the Christian missionary organizations that embraced the challenges presented by millions of freed slaves, the AMA was arguably the most influential. As early as 1861, association personnel followed upon the heels of the Union Army, bringing relief, education, and religion to refugee slaves with the goal of transforming former slaves into productive, full citizens. It was certainly a lofty aim, testing the conviction, endurance, and pocketbooks of its membership. By 1868 the association sponsored over five hundred agents in Tennessee and its border states, who in addition to their benevolence work were outspoken voices for civil and political rights for former slaves. Its sheer volume of activity positioned the AMA as the dominant benevolent society in the South. In 1867, for example, seventy-six of the eighty-four freedmen schools in Georgia were founded and maintained by the organization.[8]

Membership in the AMA was open to "any person of evangelical sentiments who professes faith in the Lord Jesus Christ, who is not a slaveholder or in the practice of other immoralities." The inclusion of the evangelical clause served to exclude Unitarians and helped distinguish the society's Christian abolitionist stance from that of the William Lloyd Garrison clique.[9] Publicly, the association called itself an independent, nonsectarian, nonecclesiastical organization, but in practice, the leadership and most of the membership were from the Congregational Church. All of the AMA founders were Christian abolitionists with years of experience in the antislavery movement.[10]

Lewis Tappan was the most influential of the AMA's founders and took the lead in its formation. As a committed believer in Charles Finney's message, Tappan refused to give only lip-service to his ideals, choosing rather to put his personal convictions into practical action. His energy and commitment were infectious, and though he was not the president of the association, he was able to sway the organization in a direction that conformed to his own way of thinking. Although he resigned his position in the AMA in 1865, he remained a powerful voice for radical social reform until his death in 1873. Tappan and his fellow founders can be credited with giving the AMA clear goals and steadfast, unswerving direction during the early years of its existence. After Emancipation, their ideal of a society devoid of social prejudice continued to be the model for which the association strived.[11]

Perhaps Tappan's greatest contribution to the internal structure of the AMA was his instigation of a system of district secretaries responsible for collecting funds in designated regions. One district secretary who played a prominent role in the history of Fisk University and the Jubilee Singers was

Erastus Cravath. The AMA assigned him to the Cincinnati office in 1866 and gave him the responsibility of establishing schools in the South. Born to abolitionist parents, Cravath grew up seeing fugitive slaves cared for in his home at a time when such action was liable to a fine of $1,000 for each offense. In 1850, he attended New York Central College, a small school founded by abolitionists that admitted African Americans and had one black professor. A year later, he enrolled at Oberlin where he trained as a minister and joined the Congregational Church. For awhile he served a church in Ohio, and then became a chaplain in the Union Army, taking part in the Atlanta campaign. Cravath felt called to some form of work in the South, a call fulfilled when he entered the service of the AMA. In 1875, Cravath assumed the presidency of Fisk University and held that position for twenty-five years. Also that year, he assumed business control of the Jubilee Singers and traveled with the company until it disbanded in 1878.[12]

Tall and dignified with his bushy beard and round spectacles, Erastus Cravath exuded a quiet demeanor, but firm and authoritative leadership. He was described by one admirer as "majestic" and had a reputation throughout Nashville for being an honest and astute businessman. Indeed, he proved quite able in dispersing the slim funds available for AMA schools throughout his district while also lending wise counsel to help manage the various temperaments of his missionary leaders and teachers. His task as district secretary was certainly not an easy one, and with limited funds and high expectations from those under him, he often had to make difficult decisions. Cravath proved cautious and somewhat slow in his decision-making (a reality that would evoke irritation in some of his subordinates), but resolved and firm once the decision was made. Emotion and intellect, Cravath believed, must always be tempered by reason. "The man who has perfect understanding, huge intellect, an iron will and tender feelings, but who is lacking in judgment, may for a time appear to succeed, but finally he will be a failure," he once remarked.[13]

Tappan and Cravath, along with the other founders of the AMA, shared similar ideologies and a firm commitment to the antislavery stance of the AMA. Both men also adhered to the Charles Finney brand of Christianity with its emphasis upon personal dedication to Christ, social reform, and evangelism. Their vision and firm leadership defined the mission and overall culture of the respective institutions they led. The philosophical underpinnings of the association's founders had a rippling effect, influencing the officials, teachers, and eventually the students who entered AMA schools.

True equality under the law and full rights of citizenship for African Americans were the AMA's ultimate aims, but the leaders were convinced this could be accomplished successfully only through religious and educational training that prepared former slaves for society's demands. Thus, they eagerly embarked on a mission "to elevate, educate and evangelize an ignorant and downtrodden people" and thus establish a secure, moral, and prosperous nation. With determination and a sense of divine call, they proclaimed their intent to "improve, without distinction of race or color, the condition of the people of the South in industry, education and morality." The AMA leadership was convinced that this noble goal could not be achieved without the principles of evangelical religion shaping their efforts. They concluded that an education including Christian religious instruction was the most effective means for achieving the highest state of civilization. Therefore, AMA teachers faithfully carried with them "the Word of God and evangelical religion" so that the new nation might become a "civilization based upon religion, & not [a] civilization *without* religion."[14]

Elevate, educate, and evangelize were inseparable goals to the AMA; to leave out one was to jeopardize the success of the other two. The AMA insisted that elevating each person individually and a society collectively required both a regimen of education by which to transform the mind, and evangelization for the conversion of the soul. Education alone was insufficient to accomplish the task of bringing freedmen up from the "bottom niche in the scale of American civilization."[15] Intellectual development must concur with one's spiritual growth for effective social uplift, believed AMA leaders. Christian abolitionists sought freedom from sin as well as from slavery, believing that only through personal regeneration could any person, black or white, become all that God had intended. It was not enough to bring physical relief to former slaves, or to educate the mind alone, or even to fight the political battle for civil rights, though the AMA vigorously engaged in all of these efforts. Without spiritual transformation, the ideologues of Christian Reconstruction felt their emancipated brothers and sisters in Christ would lack the character traits and moral training necessary for full and effective participation in mainstream society.[16]

The term "Christian abolitionist" was one that AMA leaders proudly adopted for themselves, believing that work among the freedmen was nothing short of the highest missionary calling, an act of self-sacrifice for the sake of the gospel. Here was a "long crushed people" in desperate need of spiritual regeneration, physical relief, education, and social assimilation so that they might be elevated to the "high plane of a Christian civilization." Therefore, they reasoned, it was only right to link educational efforts with religious training, and all for the purpose of social equality and reform. "What, then, is the great lever for the lifting up of races?" asked the *American Missionary*, the organization's monthly journal. "Christians, answer unhesitatingly—the Gospel!"[17]

The AMA proposed to instill in African Americans the necessary skills and values to ensure an educated citizenry, not only for the salvation of their souls but also for the survival of the nation. "Every reflecting person must admit that we cannot afford to cherish in the Republic a class to whom shall be denied the boon of education," argued one author writing for the AMA's journal. Had not history shown that "religion and education have been most intimately blended in every instance in which nations have attained greatness—moral and material?"[18] By merging religion and education, the AMA hoped to right the wrongs of slavery, conquer racial discrimination, and prepare the nation's new members for the rights and privileges of citizenship.

Ironically, the AMA's call for participation in its Christian Reconstruction activity often employed rhetoric riddled with racist language and thinking common of the time. One sermon delivered at the association's 1872 annual convention warned how critical it was for Christians to engage in missionary activity, for African Americans would not remain as "docile and impressible and tractable as now." The speaker continued: "They are as yet overflowingly grateful, recognize us of the North as their deliverers, give us their supremest confidence, and are eager to have us become their teachers and counselors in their new estate of freedom. We can hence do almost anything with them that we wish. They are eager, likewise, to learn; and ten thousand schools opened among them to-morrow would be thronged." Fear for the supremacy of Protestantism was also at stake, urged

9

the speaker, as Catholics were actively engaged in similar benevolent work and African Americans might be drawn to a religion replete with "pictures and dresses and music and gaudy trappings and showy ceremonies." "If they [African Americans] should join the papists or communists or infidels, farewell to the republic. The day that witnessed that compact would see the Mene Tekel written on its walls, and its glory forever departed."[19] The language of this speech reveals not only the underlying fears that may have motivated many who answered the AMA's missionary call, but also shows how fine was the dividing line between influence and control. The proponents of Christian Reconstruction had a shared understanding that effective assimilation of emancipated slaves into mainstream society required that they embrace Protestant ethics, values, and morals.

Contributing to the AMA's Southern work was the Bureau for Freedmen's Affairs (commonly called the Freedmen's Bureau), established by the federal government in 1865 for the purpose of attending to all matters relating to refugees and freedmen, including the supervision and management of abandoned and confiscated lands in the former Confederate states. With such a vague and broad description of duties, one historian remarked that the "Bureau could be largely the creature of the commissioner's own imagination."[20] General Oliver O. Howard was Lincoln's choice for commissioner, and though not a professing abolitionist, he was nonetheless a Congregationalist, the denomination most closely aligned with the AMA. His strong friendship with many AMA leaders such as Whipple and Cravath positioned the organization to receive sympathetic treatment from the bureau. Despite criticism by other denominations that he was displaying favoritism, Howard gave substantial support to AMA endeavors, channeling bureau funds into construction and repair costs, travel expenses for teachers, and even subsidies for teacher salaries. One scholar estimated that the AMA received over half a million dollars from the Freedmen's Bureau during the agency's existence.[21]

European friends and allies also supported the AMA's cause, thanks in part to the success of association representatives who vigorously campaigned throughout England to gain the favor of the Congregational Union of England and Wales and the General Assemblies of Scotland. By 1874, the

AMA estimated it had received over a million dollars in money and hundreds of barrels of clothing and blankets in response to these efforts. The European connections the association made early in its existence later figured significantly in the success of the Jubilee Singers.[22]

The AMA owed much of its distinction, though, to the qualified missionary teachers who gave their lives for the cause of freedmen's education. Both black and white AMA missionaries traveled south to establish schools and bring relief to freedmen. The significant presence of African Americans within the rank and file of the AMA attests to the organization's commitment to its espoused philosophy of racial equality.[23] The number of teachers and missionaries commissioned by the association grew from 250 in mid-1865 to over 500 by 1868. By June 1867, more than 38,000 students were involved in day and night classes and 18,010 pupils in Sabbath schools established in local churches.[24] Ella Sheppard, a founding member of the Jubilee Singers, recalled that the Sunday-school classes she attended in her childhood "were practically spelling classes in which the blue back speller figured as the text book," indicating how Sabbath schools were as devoted to literacy as they were to spiritual instruction.[25] The association's self-published history in 1874 lists the following seven colleges founded and supported by the AMA: Berea College, Hampton Institute (now University), Fisk University, Atlanta University, Talladega College, Tougaloo University, and Straight University (now Dillard). The cost of such a large-scale educational effort was enormous, expending nearly two and a quarter million dollars during the AMA's ten years of work among the freedmen.[26] One historian calculated that by 1893, the AMA had spent more than twice what the Freedmen's Bureau did during its entire existence.[27]

The AMA teachers who came to the South met willing pupils eager to learn. African Americans firmly believed that education was essential for racial uplift and had long pursued literacy, often surreptitiously under the unknowing gaze of the plantation master. After Emancipation, they sought educational opportunities openly and eagerly. "Suddenly, as if at the sound of a trumpet, a whole race that had been slumbering for centuries...awoke and started off one morning to school," noted Booker T. Washington.[28]

When escaped slaves first poured into Virginia's Fortress Monroe in 1861, General Butler issued a dictum declaring them "contraband of war," which allowed the Union Army to provide relief and protection. In 1862, the number of escaped slaves in Western Tennessee was so large that General Ulysses S. Grant ordered his army chaplain, John Eaton, Jr., to establish a massive program of contraband camps throughout the Mississippi Valley. Over the next three years, Eaton maintained charge of a constantly expanding contraband camp system that included access to education. His quarterly report in 1865 stated that 7,360 pupils with an average attendance of 4,667 were enrolled in fifty-one schools manned by 105 teachers.[29]

Literacy, long denied, was a mark of freedom to African Americans and a treasure eagerly sought regardless of age. One Freedmen's Bureau inspector estimated in 1866 that there were at least 500 "native schools" in operation, many in places where Northern benevolent societies had yet to visit. The freedman's faith in the magic of education led to the accepted notion that "anyone devoted to his books was on the road to freedom; anyone ignorant of books was on his way back to slavery."[30] So strong was the thirst for learning that men, women, and children of all ages crowded into the many crude school houses that sprang up across the South. Booker T. Washington was part of the swelling wave of eager learners. He later recalled, "Few people who were not right in the midst of the scenes can form any exact idea of the intense desire which the people of my race showed for education. It was a whole race trying to go to school. Few were too young, and none too old, to make the attempt to learn."[31]

The association keenly recognized both the enormity and the seriousness of the task it had undertaken. Therefore, AMA officials refused to choose teachers casually. They carefully screened each applicant to determine whether or not the candidate possessed the requisite skill, character, and consecration needed for the work. Through their official publication, the *American Missionary,* the AMA defined the qualifications necessary for the job:

> 1. Missionary spirit. …No one should seek, accept, or be recommended for an appointment who is not prepared to endure hardness as a good soldier of Jesus Christ…to subordinate self to the cause and acquiesce cheerfully in the directions and supervision

of those who have the matter in charge.... None should go, then, who are influenced by either romantic or mercenary motives; who go for the poetry or the pay; who wish to go South because they have failed at the North.

2. Health. The toil, the frequent hardships, the tax of brain and nerve...will justify us in giving an appointment to no one, not enjoying good health. This is not a *hygienic* association, to help invalids try a change of air, or travel at others' expense.

3. Energy. The service demands not only vigorous work as laid out and required by others, *in the school room*, but a disposition and ability to find something to do beyond these prescribed items—to set oneself to work—to seek to do good for Christ and his poor...

4. Culture and Common Sense. It is a mistaken and mischievous idea, that "almost anybody can teach the Freedmen." Nowhere is *character*, in the school and out of it, more important....

5. Personal habits. Marked singularities and idiosyncrasies of character are specially out of place here. Moroseness, or petulance, frivolity or undue fondness for society, are too incompatible with the benevolence, gravity, and earnestness of our work, to justify the appointment, or recommendation, of any exhibiting such traits....

6. Experience. As a general rule only those should be commissioned, or recommended, who have had experience in teaching, and whose experience, especially as *disciplinarians*, has been crowned with marked success.[32]

The criteria almost seemed aimed at dissuading rather than persuading volunteers. Nonetheless, hundreds answered the AMA's call and met the approval of its executive committee.

The AMA was forthright in its assessment of the difficult task before these missionaries. Those who flooded into the South often faced social ostracism, financial and physical hardship, and at times physical danger and death. Teacher reports sent back to AMA headquarters often spoke of Southern hostility: "...we are made to feel constantly that we are in the 'enemy's country.' Much of the opposition seems to arise from the non-education of the whites themselves. They are just beginning to feel their own deficiency in this respect, and it mortifies them to see the negroes receiving advantages which they and their children have never enjoyed."[33] Indeed, most Southerners bitterly resented the presence of the "Yankee school m'arms." Many openly agreed with the sentiment expressed in this editorial from the *Norfolk Virginian* of 2 July 1866:

> The "negro schoolmarms" are either gone, going, or to go, and we don't much care which, whereto, or how…indeed, we may say that we care very little what land they are borne to, so not again to "our'n".… We congratulate our citizens upon a "good riddance of bad baggage" in the reported departure of these impudent missionaries. Of all the insults to which the Southern people have been subjected, this was the heaviest to bear.[34]

Persecution was often the lot of a missionary, reasoned the AMA; therefore, only the strongest and most dedicated candidates should apply. The applicant must consider him or herself first and foremost a missionary, one who could endure hardship and sacrifice material gain for the sake of the gospel, leave friends and family and identify with those of another race, and willingly "bear the cross" and confront the evils of racism without flinching. "We want the best," announced the AMA, for "the cause demands—is worthy of it."[35]

The hardships of the job took their toll on many, and though the AMA asked for teachers who felt called to be "life missionaries," there was a high turnover among personnel. Not all enjoyed the life of a missionary or were physically equal to the task. Others found that a year or two in the South helped "expiate their guilt" and they returned home. Occasionally, the AMA dismissed or reassigned teachers for a variety of reasons, ranging from teaching ineffectiveness to fractious behavior. But the majority of missionaries persevered despite adversity, men and women whom W. E. B. DuBois, a graduate of Fisk University, revered as "apostles of human culture."[36]

Southern hostilities were so intense that many missionaries could not find lodging and often resorted to living in the school facilities or boarding with local African Americans.[37] In the case of freedmen's education, the situation proved advantageous for it easily fostered a learning environment that extended beyond the schoolroom to include decorum, manners, and general rules of behavior. Northern missionary teachers believed that the

Victorian values that dominated middle-class white society formed the morally superior blueprint for constructing a civilized society and needed to be taught if their pupils were to become the kind of citizens they desired. Therefore, AMA teachers blended their daily instruction with social messages geared to encourage the cultural assimilation of this new segment of society.[38]

The "New England Way" was as important to learn as one's ABCs. Rules of behavior in Victorian society were well prescribed, and knowing "how to be" and "what to do" was essential if one wished to walk the upward road. Daily lessons encouraged attributes such as thrift, industry, morality, charity, cleanliness, and humility.[39] American Victorians were convinced that these were the characteristics of a self-controlled person, and if all could become self-controlled, the world would be an orderly place. By both precept and deed, teachers emphasized the virtues of hard work, "serious" behavior, delayed gratification, efficient use of time, and self-improvement. The AMA sought teachers who not only embodied these personal characteristics but could effectively inculcate them in their new charges.

The task of promoting virtue and social responsibility was shared by higher education institutions of this era, but assumed deeper meaning for those missionary educators associated with freedmen's education. For the Christian abolitionist, Victorian values were natural by-products of Christianity and indicators of a life that had been transformed spiritually. Continued self-improvement enabled one to be of better service to God. Essential to the AMA's mission was discipling their young wards not only in the understanding of biblical truth, but also in the knowledge of how to apply that truth to their daily lives. For the proponents of Christian Reconstruction, salvation was the first step toward righteous living.

Most Victorians were completely convinced, even a bit smug, about the superiority of their beliefs. Intense self-righteousness certainly characterized Christian abolitionists, thus many scholars have levied legitimate charges of paternalism and acculturation against the missionary movement. Yet one must also consider that the AMA missionaries' actions to impose their ethics, values, and morals came at great personal cost. For hundreds of missionary teachers, working for freedmen's education was sacrificial service in the earnest, albeit imperfect, pursuit of equality for African Americans.

15

The missionary movement, notes one historian, marks the "point in history when Negroes began to be exposed to basic elements of the white man's values on a mass basis."[40] Because teachers interacted intimately and on a daily basis with Southern blacks—teaching, socializing, and often living together—they were a potent force for acculturation. In the words of W. E. B. DuBois, this was the gift of the missionary teacher: to bring "not alms, but a friend; not cash, but character." He remembered fondly his years at Fisk University and the close association he had with such officials as Erastus Cravath and Adam Spence. DuBois viewed the missionary effort as the "finest thing in American history, and one of the few things untainted by sordid greed and cheap vainglory." He held the teachers and their efforts to instill character and culture in high esteem:

> The teachers in these institutions came not to keep the Negroes in their place, but to raise them out of the defilement of the places where slavery had wallowed them. The colleges they founded were social settlements; homes where the best of the songs of the freedmen came in close and sympathetic touch with the best traditions in New England. They lived and ate together, studied and worked, hoped and harkened in the dawning light. In actual formal content their curriculum was doubtless old-fashioned, but in educational power it was supreme, for it was the contact of living souls.[41]

Despite the imperfections that characterize any human effort, the daily interactions between young Fisk students and many of their missionary teachers seemed to have left a lasting, positive impression. Like DuBois, many of the students who participated in the Fisk Jubilee Singers benefited from the tutelage and lifelong friendships they made with professors at Fisk, men and women who left indelible imprints upon their lives.

The AMA's educational efforts multiplied during the 1870s. By then, several of their higher education institutions such as Fisk had college classes and university status. In addition to preparing teachers, the AMA recognized that they must also develop educated black leaders prepared to lead the African-American race:

> We dare not plan to reduce our educational force. We shall indeed do less, directly, for common schools, but we shall do more, indirectly, by preparing teachers for them. The States, or the national government, will yet plant common schools in the South. We can help and hasten, by training in our normal schools and colleges, the army of teachers that will be needed. We

will also help in a still broader way. No people can rise without leaders, and as these Freedmen toil up the steep ascent, they need the inspiring call and example of those of their own race who can guide them upward. Our institutions are preparing, on a large scale, those who shall act as leaders, in the various walks of life—ministers, teachers, intelligent farmers, mechanics, business and professional men.[42]

AMA officials also realized that the crusade for an egalitarian society would not be short-lived. While they never relinquished their belief in the ability of African Americans, association personnel nonetheless began to feel that the legacy of slavery had deep roots that could not be eradicated overnight. The leaders reasoned that their "hopes for the future of this race must lie in the children born to freedom." [43] A formula of time, education, and hope became the creed of those AMA officials hoping to achieve political and social equality for African Americans.[44]

The AMA was one of the most progressive voices for social equality of its time, never retreating from its pursuit of equal rights for all. In the midst of intense Southern hostility, it continued to uphold the ideal of a society free from caste and prejudice, and refused to relinquish its belief that the twin emphases of religion and education could rectify social ills. In assessing its first decade of progress after the Civil War, the association noted that the "real difficulty lies so deep that it remains almost untouched; it is in the ignorance and degradation of the blacks and the prejudices and hatreds of the whites—in other words it is in the *minds and hearts* of men." AMA leaders felt that the nation had too often applied external remedies to an internal problem. The failure of political Reconstruction efforts reconfirmed for AMA leaders the rightness of their Christian Reconstruction ideology. The ultimate battle for freedom was not to be won by "legal restraints or party victories, but by education and the Gospel," declared the association.[45]

Founding of Fisk University

It was in this atmosphere of radical Christian missionary fervor that Fisk University was born. AMA field agents Edward P. Smith and Erastus Cravath, charged with scouting out the best locations for educational institutions, determined that Nashville would be an ideal spot for a black institution of learning. Not only was it Tennessee's capital, but its central location could attract students from surrounding border states. Moreover, it had a large population of African Americans, and the city was a "point of great business, social and political importance."[46]

In its beginning, the founders envisioned a school that offered instruction from grades primary through "normal," a term used to designate vocational training for future teachers. The AMA firmly believed that preparing qualified teachers who would in turn bring instruction to the masses was a critical component to racial uplift. However, their vision extended beyond a normal department. Eventually, they hoped to advance the institution to university status, thus providing the full spectrum of educational privileges enjoyed by whites. Smith and Cravath presented their plan to John Ogden, superintendent of the Freedmen's Bureau in Tennessee, who caught the vision and promised bureau funds for the project.[47]

The search for a site was an early lesson in Southern racial prejudice, for most landowners would not sell once they discovered that the establishment of a freedmen's school was the buyers' intent. A unique opportunity arose when the federal government expressed a desire to relinquish its Union hospital facilities west of the city. General Clinton B. Fisk, serving then as the assistant commissioner in charge of the Freedmen's Bureau in Tennessee, arranged for the transfer of the buildings to the AMA. However, the land upon which the hospital barracks sat was owned privately and priced at $16,000. Since the AMA lacked sufficient funds to acquire the land, Ogden, Cravath, and Smith pledged personal notes for the first installment, thus making the freedmen's school possible.[48]

The Fisk School, named after General Clinton B. Fisk, officially opened on 9 January 1866.[49] John Ogden resigned his position with the Freedmen's Bureau to become the school's first principal. Within two months, Fisk enrolled five hundred scholars in the day school and one hundred in a night class, ranging in age from seven to seventy. By the end of 1866, the school boasted a day enrollment of approximately 1,000 and some within Nashville's white community recognized it as a "power in the city." Ten teachers aided Principle Ogden in offering daily instruction.[50]

The original school facilities were quite primitive. Helen Morgan, one of Fisk's earliest teachers, recalled that a soldier's blanket provided the rug for her room. Her furnishings included a hospital cot, small wardrobe, washstand, table, and a "very small, very unmanageable stove" for which she was grateful since the students' rooms were unheated. A common "family sitting room" for the females provided a place for monitored social interaction, and a couple of assembly rooms and recitation rooms constituted the classrooms. A dining room, kitchen, store room, and laundry room completed the facilities. Despite its "Spartan-like" austerity, visitors and friends were impressed with the cleanliness and neat appearance of the school.[51]

Fisk officials reasoned that providing board for their students would create a situation whereby the missionary teachers could consistently model and reinforce the solid Christian values they felt their students needed. They held, as did all Victorians, that the home was the single most important institution in American society, an orderly, safe haven where one prepared for a useful life. By emphasizing this "cult of domesticity," Victorians upheld mothers as the guardians of morality and the agents through which cultural values were transmitted. Christian abolitionists were quick to state that slavery had denied African Americans any hope of a normal home life, resulting in moral degradation and degeneration. Those who had suffered the most, they noted, were black females upon whom the world had "so long trampled upon and despised." Therefore, attending to the home, particularly by raising a "standard of Christian womanhood," was an important strategy for lifting the race.[52]

In 1867, around thirty female students from outside Nashville boarded at Fisk. This living arrangement allowed female missionaries to provide the "proper" home life they felt these young girls needed. "We are now educating under the two-fold influences of a daily Christian family life, and an enlightened educational and domestic training, a body of young women, who will be shining lights on every hill in our fair Southern land." Teachers began to notice how boarders as opposed to non-boarders acquired more quickly the manners, morals, and habits they hoped to instill. Therefore, they decided to enlarge their boarding department so that more students "might be under good home influences." Within three years, the number of boarders living in Fisk's "home" increased to about forty, a number that more than doubled by 1871.[53]

The boarding department quickly grew to accommodate males as well, requiring rules and regulations not only to keep their students appropriately busy, but also to manage relationships between the sexes. School officials established strict codes of behavior and a highly regimented schedule through which to govern their students' daily lives. Fisk University officials required its boarders to maintain neat and orderly rooms, study from 5:30 to 7:00 a.m., attend "promptly and cheerfully" all classes, study again from 6:30 to 9:00 p.m., and retire by 10:00 p.m. Males and females could not enter each other's private rooms and visits between sexes had to be publicly monitored.[54] Such rigid regulations were common to most American liberal arts colleges of this time. Laurence Veysey noted that "an overriding spirit of paternalism infused the American college of the mid-nineteenth century," an era in the history of American higher education that he termed "discipline and piety."[55]

Besides academic study and daily chores, nearly all the teachers and students living at Fisk engaged in relief work and evangelistic efforts throughout the city. The emphasis on religious instruction nurtured a pious atmosphere at Fisk. Classes and faculty meetings opened with prayer and students attended required chapel services and prayer meetings. Teachers and officials confidently expected conversions and proudly included them in their annual reports to the AMA headquarters. The 1871 report claimed that, "of the 99 pupils who share the blessings of the 'Home,' 32 have become Christians this year; 41 were already professors of religion…and 26, as far as it is known, are still unconverted." The unconverted, the report explained, had been in the home "but a short time," suggesting the author's belief that the close relationships between teachers and pupils and the overall influence of a Christian home life would eventually move the remaining "unconverted" to professions of faith. Fisk officials took heart in the "many scenes of deep interest" that occurred throughout the year and the "sensible presence of the Lord" that they felt.[56]

Some of the first missionary teachers at Fisk were especially instrumental in determining its religious character. Principal John Ogden fanned the religious flame of the fledgling school, rejoicing in students' spiritual growth as much as their academic progress. Henrietta Matson, one of the school's most ardent spiritual matriarchs who arrived at Fisk in 1869 and remained there for thirty-eight years, gladly reported in 1870 that a great revival had swept through the campus. Conversions were so frequent that most of the current student body professed a faith in Christ. Reverend Henry S. Bennett, a professor of theology and Fisk pastor from 1867 to 1894, was responsible for the supervision and training of future African-American ministers. Bennett was well loved by many Fisk students not only for his spiritual guidance, but also for his sunny disposition, which set him apart from the other more serious and solemn teachers.[57]

Equally influential in molding Fisk's religious character was Adam Spence, who assumed leadership of the school in 1870. He remained for thirty years, taking the institution through its development from a normal school into a college during the five years he served as principal. A Scotsman by birth, Spence grew up in an extremely religious family who immigrated to the States when he was three years old. Two of his brothers became ministers and two sisters married ministers, much to the delight of Spence's mother. His father died while Spence was still in his teens, leaving the family severely strapped for income. He attended the preparatory department of Oberlin where he met and developed a lifelong friendship with Erastus Cravath, future AMA district secretary.

Spence harbored hopes of becoming a minister but grew discouraged by his rhetorical teacher's continual criticism of his speaking voice. On graduation day, he received an offer for a teaching post at the University of Michigan as a Greek professor, an event he later described as "providential." But Spence was dissatisfied with the secular nature of the institution and thought it restricted his religious work. Equally important to intellectual learning was spiritual regeneration, Spence believed firmly, and both must occur to achieve the greatest personal growth.[58] He was a model Christian abolitionist, with strong morals, character, evangelical zeal, and a serious approach to life. Years later when Jubilee Singer America Robinson learned that her boyfriend, James Burrus, hoped to pursue a professorship, she cautioned him from becoming as sedate as his mentor. "Don't ever get like Prof. Spence," she urged. "Deliver me from such as he. I do not want to be afraid to laugh."[59] In spite of his serious and pious nature, Spence's uncompromising stance on behalf of freedmen won him the admiration and affection of many Fisk students.

In 1870, the earnest young Spence gladly accepted the "divine call" to serve as principal of Fisk University, a position made possible in part because of his friendship with Cravath.[60] His devotion to scholarship and spirituality made him an ideal candidate for both Fisk and the AMA's missionary work in the South. Firmly committed to building up a "university free to colored people," Spence was thrilled with Cravath's mid-year inspection of the school: "Mr. Cravath expresses himself as highly pleased with the appearance of the school and thinks it is on the whole in a better condition than ever before. While there are some minor details in which he suggests improvement he thinks the examinations better than any previous ones and says he has more hope of its growing into a university."[61] Spence eagerly embraced the idea of beginning collegiate level instruction and is credited with having established its Greek department.[62] An avid learner, Spence later joined Nashville's Greek club where he gathered with other like-minded scholars and pored over pages of Greek at a sitting.

Spence's religious passion for Fisk University equaled his dedication to scholarship. "The religious feature of the institution is very prominent and is to me most delightful," he wrote.[63] His letters to his mother, Elizabeth Spence, are full of references to the religious work in which Fisk teachers and students engaged. They held prayer meetings and open air revivals in the city, conducted house-to-house solicitations for Sunday school, held campus meetings for Bible reading and prayer, and regularly visited the sick. "We are standing for a principle and beginning a work of vital importance," Spence proudly wrote home.[64]

The musical interest that characterized Fisk from its earliest beginnings also proved a good match for Adam Spence. He had taken up the violin as a boy, but his mother considered the young man with whom he played to be an "unfit associate" and quickly put a stop to the friendship. Spence later met an accomplished musician who introduced him to instrumental and sacred music classics. In college, he joined a vocal club dedicated to singing Palestrina's masses and soon his love for music rose to a passion. In his early twenties, however, Spence had an experience he referred to as a "second conversion," after which he gave up music for fear that he "loved it too much." At this time, he resolutely laid aside his musical dreams and decided to pursue an academic career. Arriving at Fisk, Spence was thrilled to learn that music, especially singing, permeated the campus life. Here he was introduced to the Negro spiritual, a genre he held in high regard throughout the remainder of his life.[65]

Unfortunately, Spence's dedication to education and evangelization was not matched by strong administrative skills. Neither did his solemn and somewhat timid nature make him especially adept at dealing with the constant complaints of disgruntled and overworked Fisk teachers. Finances were tight and expenses increased with the organization of a collegiate department. The school managed to stay afloat by pinching pennies and requiring its instructors and boarders to endure inadequate heat and poor food. The difficult conditions and close quarters made the "family atmosphere" of the school tense and prone to pettiness. "Everybody knows everything about everybody," Spence complained to his mother.[66]

Perhaps his most difficult rival was Fisk's treasurer, George Leonard White, a man of equally strong religious convictions who possessed a more forceful personality. White was born in 1838 in Cadiz, New York, where he attended public school until the age of fourteen. At the age of twenty, he became a teacher in Ohio and the director of a choir known throughout the area for its excellent concerts. White joined the "Squirrel-Hunters" in 1862 to fight in the defense of Cincinnati and then enlisted in the Seventy-Third Ohio Infantry Regiment. Subsequent military battles took him to areas in Tennessee. After the Civil War, he remained in Nashville to work as an agent for the Freedmen's Bureau and to lend assistance to freedmen's schools. He began teaching music at the nearby Fisk School where he met and later married Laura A. Cravath, Erastus Cravath's younger sister. In 1868, White took on the extra duties of serving as Fisk's financial steward, a position some claimed was granted only because of his familial connections to Cravath. As a full-time employee, White's duties included financial oversight of the institution and instruction in vocal music and penmanship.[67]

George White was a towering six feet, four inches high, his large and lanky frame easily enveloping a doorway. He had a head of thick black hair that joined a coarse, heavy beard and mustache. Dark, bushy eyebrows framed his piercing blue eyes, completing his powerful and authoritative presence. White was a strong leader, opinionated, and unwavering in his commitment to high principles, Christian morals, and the AMA's missionary cause. The missionary spirit that would characterize the Jubilee

Singers campaigns was introduced by White, who personified the traits the AMA expected in any "good soldier of Jesus Christ." "To do hard work, go to hard places, and submit, if need be, to hard fate," as well as to cheerfully "subordinate self to the cause" should characterize any soul willing to embrace the life of a missionary for freedmen's education, stated the AMA.[68] When White answered the call to service, he entered into the work with complete self-abandonment and fervency. He was a man who trusted in God literally, said Mary Spence, Adam Spence's daughter. She later recalled White saying that "if the Lord told him to jump through a wall, it was his part to jump and the Lord's to put him through."[69] Any work that White felt was God-inspired was one worth his entire heart and soul, regardless of the immensity of the task or the cost to his personal or family life.

Such devotion to a cause and the self-sacrifice it required were integral to White's understanding of Christianity. Having a faith that found practical expression in social action appealed to White, inspiring him to become an abolitionist, volunteer to fight for the Union cause, and stay behind in Nashville to labor for freedmen's education. His personal temperament, characterized by passion and tenacity, led him to embrace these activities with the wholehearted dedication of a crusader. The difficulty of the task before him seemed only to strengthen his resolve.

White was also extremely loyal and paternalistic toward his students, especially those who participated in his chorus, often calling them "his children." His sacrifice and self-denial for their well-being earned their respect. "He loved us very, very near," recalled one.[70] Fisk students remembered him as a man of great courage, generosity, and faith. But private letters exchanged between Fisk teachers reveal that some considered White to be inflexible, blunt, demanding, and somewhat arrogant. His commanding personality threatened Spence, who felt that White had far too much control at Fisk. Stubborn, gruff, and often uncompromising, George White was a difficult opponent for the meek and mild Professor Spence.[71]

Bickering characterized the relationship between White and Spence. White complained to Cravath that he was forced to "buy more & better" because Adam Spence and his wife were difficult to please. "They call for this change & that change in food—as in other things—in my despair I have bought & bought & bought."[72] He was equally disgruntled with Spence's management style, telling Cravath that the university had a "very superior working force" but sadly lacked a leader with "brains—ideas - & force."[73] For his part, Spence accused White of being "a schemer...ambitious for himself and the institution." To his mother he complained, "He is a man of no education obtained from books. He is gruff, and often impolite and Kate thinks he has an especial il [sic] will to her."[74] Both were somewhat correct in their accusations of each other. Adam Spence, the scholarly gentleman, was a much better professor than presidential leader, whereas George White's resolute belief in himself and his ideas often made him headstrong and obstinate.

Such was the cast of characters who set the stage for the formation of the Fisk Jubilee Singers. These were men and women whose strong convictions led them to attempt seemingly insurmountable tasks. They were Victorians convinced of their values and mores, abolitionists ready to battle injustice, missionaries willing to endure sacrifice for the cause of Christianity. They traveled south to teach, preach, mold, influence, and suffer if need be for the sake of a higher cause, namely freedom: politically, spiritually, and socially. Paternalism, short-sightedness, personality and cultural clashes, along with human frailty, tainted the purity of their efforts. Yet the ideals of Christian Reconstruction remained the guiding force as the missionaries for freedmen's education struggled to create a new American society void of slavery's ills.

Chapter 2

The Birth of the Jubilee Singers:

Vision, Mission, and Divine Blessing

> It is further agreed that the Jubilee Singer's movement shall be conducted as a Christian missionary enterprise...to the promotion of the interests of Christ's kingdom.[1]

A prominent feature of the early years of Fisk University was its emphasis on musical instruction, attributed largely to the presence of George White. He was not a professional musician; in fact, he had very little musical training and made no pretensions about being a vocalist. What he lacked in formal education, he made up for in his sheer love of music, perhaps instilled by his father who had played in a nonprofessional band.[2] Moreover, he possessed rare musical instincts, a keen sense of musical effect, and great charisma as a director. He was an exacting taskmaster, requiring hours of rehearsal to achieve the sound he desired. Nonetheless, his students gladly gave half their noon hour and all their spare time to study music with White.[3]

By spring 1867, White's chorus had progressed sufficiently to perform a concert in Nashville's Masonic Hall, earning approximately $400. In his 1874 history of Nashville's black schools, G. W. Hubbard noted that the concert was a "brilliant success, the building being crowded, and the audience most enthusiastic. Many of the best citizens of Nashville were present, and expressed themselves highly pleased with the quality of the music and the accuracy of its rendering."[4]

The next year, White requested additional funding from the American Missionary Association (AMA) headquarters for musical instruction at Fisk. He wrote to E. P. Smith, the AMA's general field agent, for copies of Bradbury's *Anthem Book* and other similar collections, stressing that access to such music would help "keep up & improve the choir, as is thought best to do." He further argued the overall effect music could have on developing Fisk's religious services:

> We have a prospect—at the opening of our new chapel to build up a good congregation—and to retain with us many of our students who never attend our worship now. To do this we shall have to do our part well—not that we depend on our own efforts to accomplish the work—only as a means under God's blessing & direction of accomplishing it. If we fail now in building up a good congregation—which we never had heretofore—by any neglect or shortsightedness on our part—it will be long before another such opportunity will occur.

Teaching their students standard sacred music had far-reaching effects, White noted. Many of their day students were introducing the tunes they learned at Fisk in their own Sunday schools.[5]

Music instruction at Fisk took a leap forward when White engaged Ella Sheppard, one of his capable music students, as a teacher of instrumental music. She arrived at Fisk in September 1868, and it did not take long for White to notice her musical skill. Within a year, he sought her services. "A music teacher has been engaged and will be on the ground this week," he informed AMA agent E. P. Smith. "If she is the right sort of stuff I shall hope to raise some money by a concert or two after a while."[6]

Apparently Cravath suggested that White curtail his emphasis on musical instruction. Nonetheless, White continued training his choir during the early months of 1871 in spite of Cravath's advice:

> Contrary to your direction—but by request of the faculty my singing class is kept up—meeting the first half hour after school—as our regular work—we have been preparing the Cantata of Esther the Beautiful Queen—which is now about completed and we contemplate singing it two nights about the first of March, at Masonic Hall - one half of the proceeds to be given to the managers of the Colored Peoples Fair Grounds. We concluded that it would win their regard - & aid them in a very good work—and that we should realize as much in giving them half—as we should in keeping the whole & "going it alone"—We hope to make *something*.[7]

Ella Sheppard was already hard at work learning the music and drilling singers for this latest production. *The Cantata of Esther* by William Bradbury ran for two days in March 1871, a lavish production performed in costume with piano accompaniment. To White's satisfaction, the concert was a glowing success and well received by the Nashville community. "To say that all who attended these concerts were delighted, is not sufficient to express the pleasure evinced by those who listened to the representation," stated a local critic.[8] General Fisk also expressed his congratulations: "I have been greatly rejoiced to learn of your prosperity and read with much interest of your triumphant music performance in *Masonic Hall*. That *was* a triumph worth recording."[9]

Though grateful for the income the concert generated, Adam Spence was even more pleased with the positive impression it made on the community. "A fine concert given entirely by colored people is a new thing. It encouraged the colored people themselves and tends to lift them into respect with others. Examinations in Greek, Latin & the like cannot be appreciated [as] a concert can. We must do some thing to keep before the people. This I think was a good way to accomplish that." Spence nonetheless tempered his enthusiasm by also acknowledging that the production had taken "a world of labor" and interrupted the students' studies. "And I think it drew our minds somewhat from religious things," he confessed.[10]

While White's concerts earned praise for their musicality and a few dollars towards the institutional coffers, they could not stem the rapidly escalating financial crisis at Fisk. The institution received some scholarship money from the Peabody Fund and assistance from the Freedmen's Bureau for construction and building repairs, but operational funds were sadly lacking.[11] White found he could no longer pay local debts for food and fuel. The old hospital barracks, designed as temporary buildings, were falling apart. Ella Sheppard later recalled the dilapidated condition of the ladies' dormitory, originally the site of the army hospital's morgue. "The wind whistled around and groaned so fearfully that we trembled in horror in our beds, thinking the sounds were the cries of lost spirits of the soldiers who had died in them," she wrote.[12] A worried White struggled to make ends meet, but the crisis deepened. "I am thinking that *some thing will have to be done*," wrote the frazzled treasurer to his brother-in-law, Erastus Cravath.[13]

White's Idea of a Concert Tour

As the financial situation at Fisk University deteriorated rapidly throughout the 1870–1871 academic year, White began to scheme of ways to keep the institution afloat. The primary motivation for his early concerts was to help promote Fisk University in its efforts to boost enrollment and establish its reputation. The small profits these concerts earned, however, triggered White's imagination as to the fundraising possibilities of a singing group. The success of the *Cantata of Esther* had prompted some to suggest that White organize a company comprised of his best singers. "Much is being said about having a company of Singers," he told Cravath. "I have nothing to say—only there can be a first-class company prepared…and I am willing to do what seems to be best for the school & Association."[14]

Meanwhile, grumbling among the Fisk faculty only escalated as the financial situation worsened. "We missionaries are not angels," Adam Spence confessed to his mother.[15] "We have never had one half the complaints & fault finding which we have had this year," White glumly reported. The sorry state of the buildings forced him to spend money on repairs, and the complaints about food only multiplied. "I believe half our quarrels and trouble arise from sour stomachs," White wryly told Cravath.[16] Indebtedness was at an alarming $2,000 with no hope of additional income in sight. Creditors demanded their pay and some of Fisk's best teachers began to consider employment elsewhere. As the only income-generating projects had been White's few public concerts, he became increasingly convinced that launching a concert tour held promise. He therefore appealed to Cravath to consider the idea, outlining the possibilities of his plan and stressing that there were "elements of *great Success* in the scheme as talked up by our friends here who are pushing it."[17]

Cravath and the other AMA secretaries, however, were skeptical of the idea. Nothing like this had ever been attempted before by the AMA, and the novelty of White's proposed enterprise seemed too uncertain. But White, the "dreamer of dreams," was persistent.[18] His Christian faith, strong-willed nature, and visionary tendencies made him take hold of the seemingly risky idea of launching a concert tour with as much determination as he and other AMA members had shown when they entered into freedmen's education. After having co-labored with others whose life choices could also be labeled as actions of blind faith, White found it difficult to understand why these same people now hesitated to fully embrace what appeared to him as clear direction from God. Fisk's financial status forecast impending institutional death, and it seemed to him that the university needed something akin to a miracle if it were to stay alive. How could the AMA leaders not see the hand of providence at work in the formation of this especially gifted ensemble?

> A talented company—with the parts well balanced...cannot be gathered every day. If the company that has [unclear word] come together this year should slip away from us I should never expect to get their equal together again—without great labor and expense.... A company of twelve persons has naturally come together—without special effort on our part—which has all the essential elements of a *first class* concert troupe.... I don't believe their equal in *natural talent* could be gathered in a year's travel.[19]

Moreover, argued White, the students were "in a situation to give their time to such an enterprise." And had not his local concerts turned a small profit? While touring with a smaller ensemble might be a novel idea, as "nothing of the kind was ever put before the public North," White considered this a fact in their favor rather than a deterrent to the project. AMA officials' inability to recognize the rarity of such a collection of talent or realize the real pecuniary potentials of the "concert business" may have seemed to White a glaring lack of vision and spiritual faith.[20]

Since he needed funds with which to board and clothe his future performing troupe, he began tapping potential donors, beginning with the school's namesake, General Clinton B. Fisk. He asked Fisk to lend his assistance in two ways: "to aid this enterprise first by aiding me in raising the Special funds for the support and equipment of the Company— Secondly by so shaping your business that you can give a few days or weeks when we start to making it a grand triumphant success." About three or four hundred dollars would be sufficient, advised White. "Will you not help me in raising the money, and in putting the thing through?" he pleaded. "If I commence it I wish to make it a grand success."[21]

General Fisk's response was somewhat indifferent, saying only he would consult Cravath about the idea.[22] At the heart of the matter for AMA leaders were three fundamental questions that needed answering before they could wholeheartedly lend their endorsement. First, how would Christian audiences react to such a musical troupe? Americans had seen black faces onstage primarily in the minstrel shows that were an extremely popular form of theatrical performance at home and in England. Both black and white entertainers participated in these derogatory depictions of African Americans, blackening their faces with burnt cork. Respectable society criticized this form of entertainment and considered it vulgar.[23] And since the target community for this fundraising effort were religious folks, a group AMA leaders considered a "better class of people," one "having too much principle or taste to accept the popular entertainments that come within reach," officials had reason to think an African-American choral ensemble would hardly be the best choice to represent the association's cause.[24]

The second burning question was a spiritual one: was the project divinely blessed? The leaders of the AMA were men of action willing to take risks for great causes, but they also acknowledged providential guidance in decision making. If spiritual blessing rested on this venture, they were willing to step out in faith and support it. However, no one could agree that White's plan actually was inspired of God; instead, it seemed completely foolhardy.

The third issue was financial. Launching a concert tour could possibly be costly not only in dollars but in damage to the association's reputation. Even Cravath wondered whether or not the undertaking was as potentially lucrative as White suggested:

> About the concerts—I am in doubt. It does not seem to me that the time has come to attempt a tour in the north yet. I should fear for the pecuniary success. It seems to me that this can be done to great advantage during the vacation. Arrange for a series of concerts in Nashville and perhaps in a few places in GA & KY. If a series of concerts could be made to pay expenses I should approve this plan most heartily. As a movement in the interests of education it would pay…. So far things of this kind are rarely successful in the north that it seems to me too uncertain a thing.[25]

In spite of his own trepidation, Cravath promised to "bring the subject of a trip north before all the officers" of the AMA.

White's colleagues at Fisk also had mixed feelings about the viability of the project. Though none had qualms about the ensemble's musical excellence, some shared the AMA leaders' concerns about the start-up costs for launching a company and fears over whether or not this kind of investment would actually yield a profit. Fisk University certainly did not have the money to underwrite the project, and such a chancy experiment could only deepen the school's debt and move the institution one step closer to closure. Further, many expressed similar feelings as the AMA leaders over how Northern audiences would respond to this novel company. Adam Spence's letter to Cravath in April 1871 sums up the various thoughts among the Fisk faculty regarding White's proposed tour:

> I find there is a general feeling of opposition to the scheme although have had no faculty meeting on the subject. A good many think it beneath the dignity of our institution to be represented by a strolling band of singers, or negro minstrels as they term it. Some fear the success of the thing as a musical performance, some financially and others that it would not even get us the interest nor wish. Then again it is viewed from the stand point of its effect on the institution directly, tending to dignify musical talent too much, and the singers themselves, turning them temporarily and perhaps permanently from their studies, dissipating their minds and lowering their piety, as many of them are Christians.

In spite of these concerns, Spence admitted, the institution had to find money somehow. The abundance of musical talent at Fisk seemed to be a divine gift through which they might address their needs. He had no reservations about the musical quality of the group ("they do sing admirably") but wished the ensemble could perform throughout the summer months and not during the academic year. Of one thing he was certain: the troupe would need the AMA's endorsement if it hoped to succeed.[26]

Spence's letter did not seem to settle the AMA secretaries' minds one way or another. White was disappointed but so certain of providential guidance that he continued training his singers throughout summer 1871 despite the doubts of those who viewed his efforts as foolishly ideal. "From our Enemies much is said that tends to dishearten the class," White reported to Cravath, and the students felt "very much disheartened and depressed on account of the failure of the Association to support the troupe."[27] He also warned that a few private gentlemen who had heard the ensemble offered to assume management of it as a private business venture. "I am well assured that it will be taken up as a private speculation, and put through, if it is not used by the school," White warned Cravath. "Two or three gentlemen have said to me that they would furnish money to pay the expense and direct the profits—or assume the loss as the case might be." White needed the AMA to act soon lest he lose his best talent to enticing businessmen with deep pockets ready to finance a new venture.[28]

Bills continued to mount through summer 1871 and White could no longer hold off creditors. He told Cravath the only way he would remain at Fisk University would be in the capacity of concert manager. "I am satisfied whether I go on a tour or not...it will not be best for the School or for me to remain here another year in the same relations...that I have had," he wrote. White was willing to "do the concert work," but the circumstances of the institution, both financially and interpersonally, were more than he could bear.[29]

The students were also restless, tired of rehearsing in the summer heat when they were "used heretofore to much more freedom." Both he and the students were weary of waiting for a final word from the AMA headquarters and fearful that their hard summer's work would be in vain. "It will about kill them...if they don't go," White cautioned Cravath.[30] Rather than lose the opportunity to use his group to the advantage of Fisk, White finally announced he was going to launch the company without official sanction from the AMA. "I have with the advice of friends here, decided to make the trial trip at all hazards," he told Cravath.[31]

Cravath's response was disheartening. "I have been unable to bring the Secretaries of the AMA to the point of assuming the responsibility of the concert," he wrote in late August and suggested that White consider abandoning his plans.[32] Spence, sensitive to the AMA's continued hesitation, agonized over whether or not White's idea was truly God-inspired. Neither had General Clinton Fisk changed his mind "about the success of the 'new departure.'" Undeterred and unwilling to yield to the skeptics, White informed Cravath in September 1871 that "rather than go back on what we have done, I shall risk it, and go to Louisville & Cin. week after next and make preparation—and go up with the troupe as soon thereafter as I can." In response to General Fisk's inability to catch the vision, he remarked that he was trusting "in God and not in General Fisk." And to the timid Spence's concerns about God's leading, White characteristically retorted, "Of course it is of the Lord; it is as plain as day" and prepared his company for departure.[33]

White assumed great personal risk with this decision as his entire reputation lay in the success or failure of this endeavor. Though Cravath finally admitted he had "a fair amount of faith" that the concert business might yield a profit, he was unable to convince the AMA secretaries of the same. "It seems to them to involve too heavy an expense to launch it & that the success is too uncertain to make it safe for this Association to undertake it," Cravath informed White. Though he had not "the strength of body and mind...to take any care or responsibility in connection with this concert," Cravath nonetheless gave a hundred dollars of his own toward the effort.[34]

Adam Spence speculated on how much of the plan was of God and how much was simply the result of White's stubbornness. "Mr. White does not give up the concerting scheme yet," he wrote to his wife in September 1871. "He is very persistent you know."[35] To his mother, he confided that there were "those who are praying it may fail." Among the naysayers was Henrietta Matson, Fisk's most religious matriarchal figure and a great spiritual support to Adam Spence. Her lack of confidence that God's hand was truly guiding this enterprise no doubt contributed to his own cautiousness.[36] Then, too, launching the company had come at a great cost and Spence was left to manage the risk to the institution:

> Every dollar was raked and scraped to go.... So now we have no money, no steward, no treasurer. It requires some courage to face the situation which I now have to do.... If money does not come in we will soon have nothing to eat.... I am glad at all events that this music is to be tested and the thing settled in one way or the other. I don't care much which. If that is the Lords [sic] way may it succeed if not may it fail.... He [White] is to be gone if he succeeds at all about four weeks. Then he will go for a longer time if it seems best. Meanwhile, you see, I am left in the lurch.[37]

Though Spence and Cravath eventually acquiesced to White's determination to proceed with the "concert business," their support was weak at best. In the end, the responsibility for the success or failure of the tour lay with White, who remained firm in his resolve. "I am confident that the expectations of the most sanguine will be *more* than realized," he reassured Cravath.[38]

White's choice to use his musical ensemble as a missionary enterprise on behalf of Fisk University and the AMA, rather than a business venture for personal profit as had been offered to him by gentlemen in Nashville, had internal repercussions. One effect of this decision was that it reinvigorated the company's commitment to a cause despite the doubt and criticism from those White thought should be his partners. It also unified the ensemble and deeply impacted the members' conviction regarding the mission. Theirs was a seemingly foolhardy leap of faith, but White reasoned that the cause warranted such action. Six years had passed since slavery had been abolished and public interest was starting to wane. To renew awareness and realize a profit, White told General Fisk they would first "melt" the audience with their music, and "while they are *melted squeeze them.*"[39] He was confident that the power of their singing would tug at the hearts and generosity of their listeners.

Though White was sure of his company's musical preparedness, other obstacles remained. He had not raised the advance money they needed and the singers were poorly clad for Northern winter climate. No one owned an overcoat or wrap, so Fisk instructors divided their clothing between the students. As a result, recalled Ella Sheppard, the troupe's attire looked like "Joseph's coat of many colors and styles."[40] The odds were against White and his small band of singers. He would have to act as business manager and advance agent in addition to maintaining his musical responsibilities. Yet he and a few Fisk instructors also believed that their hopes for the survival of the institution rested with the small group of eleven. If they failed, Professor Spence glumly noted, they would have to get home as best they could.[41]

In spite of the dismal prospects for success, and without AMA endorsement, White turned his eyes North and departed with his company on 6 October 1871. He left behind his ailing wife and two small children in the attendance of a nurse, considering the sacrifice necessary for the cause before him. The AMA secretaries responded to White's actions with a "wait-and-see" attitude. Success would indicate heavenly approval; failure would validate the wisdom of their cautiousness. Time would tell.

Guarded to the end, Principal Spence offered a somewhat lukewarm prayer of consecration as the troupe departed: "O Lord, if this thought comes from Thee, prosper the going out of these young people. Care for and protect them, and bring them back to us bearing their sheaves with them, and we shall give Thee the glory."[42] One can only wonder how George White judged his faint-hearted colleague's mixed blessing. He had never felt confident that the institution would survive under Spence's leadership. "We are weak now for the want" of a dynamic leader "and shall grow weaker," White warned Cravath just weeks prior to his departure.[43] To him, Spence seemed woefully incapable of providing the kind of leadership necessary to take the institution forward, thereby making the success of his venture all the more critical to the survival of Fisk University.

Defining the Mission: The First Months of Travel

White's inaugural company consisted of his trusted musical assistant Ella Sheppard and nine additional singers. Benjamin Holmes, tenor, was an enterprising and remarkably astute young man whose cleverness had once earned him the title of a slave who "knew too much." Thomas Rutling's golden tenor voice was described by the local press as "by far the best tenor voice ever heard in Tennessee." Maggie Porter, one of the company's most colorful personalities, thrilled audiences with her extraordinary soprano voice. She was joined by Jennie Jackson, granddaughter of a slave and personal body servant of General Andrew Jackson, whose voice was described as "remarkable, possessing much power."[44] Fun-loving, mischievous, and flirtatious Isaac Dickerson, bass, brought high spirits to the company in contrast to the sober, industrious, and politically-minded Greene Evans, who also sang bass. Eliza Walker carried the alto along with little Minnie Tate, only fourteen years old. The young Tate astonished audiences with the "pure rich contralto tones she poured forth to the delight of all who heard her."[45] Ella Sheppard accompanied the troupe on piano, guitar, and/or organ, rehearsed the group, and often sang soprano. Phebe Anderson, soprano, left the group within a few weeks of its start due to her father's impending death, reducing the total number of the musical ensemble to nine. Mary Wells, principal of an AMA school in Alabama, agreed to travel as governess, bringing along her eight-year-old ward, George "Little Georgie" Wells. The precocious youngster often amused audiences with improvised songs, dances, or humorous recitations.[46]

The company's first performance in Cincinnati was a happenstance event. Upon their arrival, the troupe decided to visit the exposition in town. When they reached the musical department, George White asked Ella Sheppard to begin playing the piano. In a short time, a large crowd had gathered and White saw an opportunity to gain public exposure for his troupe. As they began to sing, the crowd grew. The audience was both amazed and entertained by the talent of this company of African Americans, surprised at how different these musicians were from the stock caricatures they had seen portrayed on the minstrel stage.[47]

The Reverends Halley and Moore, local Congregational ministers, met with White, listened to his ensemble, and agreed to open their churches to him. The singers gave several performances across Cincinnati and in nearby towns over the next few days, drawing sizeable crowds and positive praise, but failing to receive offerings sufficient to offset expenses. In Chillicothe, the troupe received its first earnings (just under fifty dollars), which they donated in an act of Christian self-sacrifice to the city's relief fund for victims of the great Chicago fire.[48]

On 17 October 1871, the troupe returned to Cincinnati eager to present its first public performance with an admission fee in a formal concert hall. General admission was fifty cents and reserved seats were seventy-five cents. While "dense audiences" attended the church-sponsored performances, recalled Ella Sheppard, only a "slim audience greeted our paid concert in Mozart Hall."[49] Nonetheless, the press was generous in its praise, noting the "sweetness of the voices, the accuracy of the execution, and the precision of the time." Minnie Tate was "worthy of no ordinary commendation" and Jennie Jackson's rendition of the famous Southern melody, "Old Folks at Home," elicited equal admiration. While the group took pride in knowing that they were perhaps the first African-American ensemble to ever perform on the Mozart Hall stage, they were nonetheless disappointed in the concert's meager income.[50] Once again, they barely met their expenses. It seemed that curiosity drove the public into church meetings where giving was optional, but as yet the troupe lacked the wide reputation to command a paying audience.

White was encountering the kind of audience skepticism that the AMA secretaries had feared. The religious community was generally suspicious, if not outright opposed, to any form of theatrical entertainment, but all the more wary of supporting anything that might possibly be associated with the minstrel shows:

Was there not so much odium attached to negro concerts, as represented in burnt cork minstrels, that people of taste and character did not think it becoming to rush in crowds to a paid concert given by negroes. And again, may there not have been a prejudice that led people to be uncertain whether or not they were in their senses if they found themselves ready to pay liberally to hear a few songs from a class of poorly clad untutored colored students?[51]

Only by establishing a clear distinction between his company and any form of popular entertainment could White hope for success. Unless they distanced themselves from minstrelsy, the public might be confused about their mission.

Hesitation to embrace the ensemble was quite evident among many of the ministers to whom White appealed. His request for an opportunity to appear in their praise meetings or sing in their Sabbath schools was frequently met with "coolness, amounting often to indifference and sometimes to suspicion." Even staunch supporters of the AMA were loath to accept this "new agency for raising funds." Fearful of sharp backlash from their congregants, pastors were reluctant to "let the Singers into their choirs, and if they gave them use of their churches for a praise meeting, they sometimes showed a strong inclination to take their own seats among the audience and near the door!" stated J. B. T. Marsh, author of one edition of the Jubilee Singers history.[52]

In light of such wary behavior by some hosting ministers, and given that they were novices, it is not surprising that the singers experienced performance anxiety. Each concert was before a new, unknown audience whom they eagerly wanted to please. Sometimes their insecurity showed. G. D. Pike, AMA secretary and author of two company biographies, noted that Isaac Dickerson's knees knocked together so violently during his first rendition of the "Temperance Medley" that it sounded like chattering teeth. "The whole class were said to have been trembling for him," he reported. At another concert, Thomas Rutling attempted to accompany himself on the piano, but was so frightened that he played in one key and sang in another, an act Pike described as an unsuccessful experiment. Unwilling to accept defeat, White made Rutling start the piece again and again until he got it right.[53] Their youthfulness and inexperience did not help matters. "We were nothing but a bunch of kids," recalled Maggie Porter, most between the ages of fourteen and nineteen, with only the faintest hint of the polished performers they were to become.[54]

Lack of a distinctive repertory contributed to the troupe's rocky beginning. During these early days, the company had yet to establish the Negro spiritual as the main staple of its programs, performing instead "white man's music," mostly popular tunes, sacred anthems, and patriotic songs. White interspersed a few spirituals at times throughout the evening, but they were hardly the featured items.[55] No doubt White felt compelled to match his troupe's ability against the leading vocalists of the day in comparable musical selections. The students were just as eager to "show what they could do and how they could do it," Maggie Porter recalled. Performing "slave songs" did not appeal to the students as these songs represented their former life. They feared that offering them publicly might degrade their people.[56]

> It was our own expectation at that time to sing the more difficult music— composed by educated and talented artists, and our practice consisted chiefly in rehearsing these pieces. It was not common for us to spend much time singing slaves song—the tendencies of the freedmen being to leave them behind in the grave of slavery—indeed some seemed almost to regard them as signs of their former disgrace to shun them as one would the prison clothes of the days of his incarceration. We did not realize how precious they would be held by those who had prayed for us, and with us till we were delivered from slavery, & how these were the genuine jewels we brought from our bondage. It was our fear that the colored people would be grieved to have us expose the ignorance & weakness incident to the days of their degradation—not know that our songs would be regarded as born of God— and sweet & touching as angels lifes [sic] might sing.[57]

Years later, Adam Spence admitted that he, too, initially resented the students performing slave spirituals publicly for fear that these songs smacked of the "olden time of slavery." When news reached him that the Jubilee Singers had sung spirituals in their Cincinnati concert, he believed they were "letting down the tone of their enterprise."[58] In time, public demand and White's persuasion helped both the Jubilees and Spence feel comfortable with the repertory change.

Not only did their initial programming provide little distinctiveness for the group, they also lacked a name by which to identify themselves. "A band of negro minstrels will sing in the Vine Street Congregational Church this morning," stated one of the earliest press advertisements. "They are genuine negroes, and call themselves 'Colored Christian Singers.'"[59] The press often referred to the troupe as the "Colored Students from Fisk University," at least linking them with their institution, but were less consistent in describing their performances. Was the ensemble offering a praise meeting, missionary service, or concert? Were they attempting ministry, entertainment, or both? White's attempt to clearly portray the group as a musical missionary enterprise in the service of Fisk University and the AMA while avoiding the negative connotations of the minstrel shows was a difficult task indeed.

In hindsight, it is remarkable that the group survived the first few months at all. The identity of the company and its purpose were ill-defined at best, which only handicapped efforts to establish its reputation. Effective marketing critical for financial success was nearly impossible as the work rested solely with White, who had neither the time nor the financial resources to adequately advertise his troupe. He frequently had to rely on the generosity and good graces of ministers to take out notices in the local dailies. More often than not, White left the company in the chaperone of Miss Wells and the able musical hands of Ella Sheppard to travel ahead and press for favors, secure appointments, and work out performance details. "Sometimes Mr. White goes *one* way and two of the young men *another* to have notices given of our coming to each of the places," Ella Sheppard informed Adam Spence, "while we poor girls remain at some other place to wait their return. It is a very tiresome work yet we are not tired or weary nor discouraged."[60]

Most troubling to White was the fact that the company had yet to turn a profit. Collections either barely covered expenses or left the group with campaign debts. Hotel lodging, when they could secure it, amounted to almost twenty-six dollars a day; advertisements cost around twenty-five to fifty dollars per concert; halls rented for approximately seventy-five dollars per night. White often was forced to make an earnest appeal to the audience for money to cover their expenses and railroad fare to get them to their next appointment. It seemed that just enough funds came in to keep the company alive, but nothing more.[61]

In the midst of these discouragements, the company discovered that they possessed one compelling tool in their favor: their singing. "Such music is indeed 'beauty unadorned,'" stated the *Cleveland Herald*, "and fairly captivates the listener."[62] Audiences seemed especially moved by the few spirituals peppered throughout the program and demanded to hear more. "They have sung at *praise meetings* the old fashioned religious music and with great effect," Spence wrote to his mother. "People have applauded waved handkerchiefs cheered & wept."[63] White encouraged Ella Sheppard to arrange more spirituals for the company, which required the students to spend time recalling the slave songs and even more rehearsal time to prepare them for public performance. Within a few short months, said Ella Sheppard, "a program of nineteen numbers, only two or three of which were slave songs, was inverted," much to the delight of their listeners.[64] This gradual repertoire change was a significant step forward in solidifying their musical identity and providing a distinctive marketing niche to set them apart from other choral groups.

White worked feverishly to gain as many appearances as he could. The troupe spent October and November singing in various churches throughout Ohio, always receiving large praise for their performance if not large remuneration. In late October they sang before the Presbyterian Synod in Springfield, Ohio to much acclaim. What was supposed to be a half-hour performance was extended upon demand to an hour. "To say that the Synod and visitors were highly pleased with the simple and yet grand and beautiful music which they furnished would be superfluous," noted one Ohio paper. "At the close of the songs the audience testified their delight in a vociferous, heartfelt and decidedly unclerical manner, with hands, feet and voices."[65] "Many were so roused," recalled Ella Sheppard, "they could not refrain from rising and acknowledging *we had converted* them and stirred their hearts in the interest of general education in the South."[66] The Synod passed a resolution endorsing White and his company and took up a small collection totaling $105. Still, the company was not earning enough to send home much-needed resources to Fisk. "They have been received very favorably…in Cincinnati and elsewhere in Ohio," Spence told his mother, but also noted that "the thing is still an experiment."[67]

By the second week of November, just one month into their travels, White's ensemble had performed over twenty times. They had sung in praise meetings at various churches, appeared in Sabbath schools, and given a few performances in public concert halls. The students quickly observed how a notice that the "Fisk U[niversity] students will sing at such a church" generated a capacity crowd. Ella Sheppard estimated the attendance at the Congregational Church in Delaware to be near 1,600.[68] The numbers were encouraging, yet did not translate into ample profits. While the Christian community readily approved of the missionary cause of White's songsters and obviously enjoyed their singing, they seemed unsure of whether or not their financial endorsement of the troupe was a safe and respectable response.

In mid-November, White gained an appearance before the National Council of Congregational Churches meeting at Oberlin. He thought that perhaps the ministers and laymen present would respond favorably to his troupe's cause and offer their support to arrange future concerts. In short, he desperately needed a change in fortune and hoped this would be a turning point for the company. It was, although White would not feel the far-reaching effects of that evening for yet another month. The singers enthralled the delegates, who took a collection of $131 and offered much needed encouragement to the fainthearted group. But the most important outcome of this performance was its impact upon a few key people in the crowd. Reverend Thomas K. Beecher heard the singers that day for the first time and was so impressed that he invited them to his church in Elmira, New York. Beecher was the brother of Henry Ward Beecher, arguably the most popular and influential pastor in America. The friend the company made that evening in Thomas Beecher would prove to be one of the most important connections of their initial campaign. Also seated in the audience were two AMA secretaries who both lent their enthusiastic support of White's plan to work his way to New York, just the kind of encouragement White sorely needed to keep pressing forward. However, the man who stepped forward to volunteer his services as advance agent, G. Stanley Pope, probably received the heartiest welcome from the weary George White. Pope was a member of the Oberlin Theological Seminary and a former AMA missionary. His willingness to assume the duties of advance agent for a few months eased the immense strain White had been under and allowed him to focus once again on making excellent music.[69]

Whatever joy their performance before the Congregational Council may have generated for the troupe was sorely tested in the next two weeks. Again the singers found that crowds came to hear them perform at Sabbath meetings, but failed to turn out for a paid concert. In Cleveland's Case Hall, a disheartened White rose to inform the audience that he "believed he was called of God to bring these students North to awaken an interest in behalf of their race" but he was unable to meet expenses. It was Saturday night and he had insufficient funds to pay for the hall, no money to board his troupe for the weekend, and no rail fare to take them to their next performance in Columbus. One gentleman wrote a check for $100 on the back of his program and a few others gave cash. It was enough to keep the company going.[70]

A few nights later, a small crowd showed up for their concert at the Columbus Opera House and White instantly knew the income would certainly not cover their expenses. They would be lucky if they broke even. White's discouragement permeated the company. In the slim audience that evening was a friend from home, Reverend Henry Bennett, a Fisk University trustee and the students' well-loved pastor whose AMA church was one many of the Jubilees attended. He met with the company after the concert to hear their concerns. Real obstacles were ahead: concerts were not turning a profit, the students were ill-clad for the approaching winter weather, and debts continued to mount both for the campaign and the institution they had left behind. They were at a crossroads and decided to hold a prayer meeting to determine whether or not they should continue.[71]

The next morning, George White met his company "with a glowing face." He announced that he had spent the night in prayer and had decided upon a name for the group. "Children," he said, "it shall be Jubilee Singers in memory of the Jewish year of Jubilee."[72] The Year of Jubilee, described in the twenty-fifth chapter of the book of Leviticus, was part of the law given by Moses. Every fifty years, Israelites were required to observe the Year of Jubilee and follow its conditions for release from slavery, redemption of property, and care of the land. White and many AMA officers felt a strong kinship between the biblical account of the Jewish nation's struggle for freedom and the Christian Reconstruction work in which they were now engaged on behalf of African Americans. The Levitical provision for freedom appealed to White's theology of how spiritual truth should find practical social expression. *"Let my people go,"* cried the old Negro spiritual, and White was doing his best to answer the call in his own way. He could think of no better name for his ensemble than one that resonated with a biblical call for freedom. "The 'Jubilee'—or 'year of Jubilee' has been talked of and sung so much in connection with this change," White told Cravath, "that I can think of no expression, or word that so nearly gives the idea, as 'the Jubilee Singers,' and submit it as the result of my effort to get a name."[73]

Everyone in the company seemed pleased with the name for it lent dignity to the group. They felt they were engaged in a noble cause that required a noble name; the "Jubilee Singers" both embodied the freedom message and evoked the religious associations that appropriately represented their mission. Ella Sheppard and others believed that the name was truly inspired. At the "usual family worship that morning there was great rejoicing," she reported.[74] "I feel that our enterprise will, it must, be a success," wrote a renewed Benjamin Holmes to Adam Spence, "for God is with us and has given us favor in the sight of the people."[75]

Gradually, the distinctiveness of White's group was taking shape. As the "Jubilee Singers," the company began establishing an identity that clearly differentiated them from the "negro minstrels" with whom the press often associated them. The name's biblical connotation helped remind audiences that this musical ensemble was not simply another group of entertainers, but musicians with a religious purpose and reason for singing. The subtle change of repertoire throughout October and November to feature mainly spirituals began to give them a unique musical identity. No popular ditties, ballads, or comedic songs of the minstrel stage characterized this troupe. Rather, they sang a new song: deep, heartfelt musical expressions of slave life, unfamiliar to many Northern ears. The purpose and performance style of the Jubilee Singers were slowly evolving.

White felt there was one element for success that still needed much work: advertising. He keenly felt his lack of a finely tuned marketing strategy by which to promote his company. Two difficult months of touring without making a profit had taught him just how critical it was to effectively publicize the ensemble. His company desperately needed a marketing hook with which to capture the public's attention. In late November, White wrote Cravath suggesting a promotional concept that capitalized on a sense of history, advertising the company's "peculiar position before the people, as standing on the border between the 'old & the new'—reaching back, as they do, in their experience and memory into the *old*—being actively identified with the work of the '*new*'—and looking forward with hope to a future full of promise." Slavery may have been abolished, but much work was still ahead. "Please do what you can to stir up a public sentiment ahead of us through the papers and churches—How would it do to print a *circular* setting forth the fact regarding the class, and the enterprise…and distribute either through some newspaper—or send direct to churches for distribution? or both."[76] White knew that performance mediocrity did not account for his troupe's inability to realize a profit; glowing press reviews and commendations from ministers testified to the company's musical excellence. He had witnessed firsthand how the Jubilee Singers' rich harmonies could carry "the people into ecstasies of sympathy and pleasure."[77] What he still lacked, however, was the endorsement and tangible support of prominent Christian leaders, especially the officers of the AMA, to give the enterprise momentum and help popularize their concerts. He was certain that lack of effective management was the remaining obstacle to great success. Though the company continued inching its way toward New York, Cravath's response to White's frequent letters offered no hope that the AMA officers would change their minds about embracing the mission. "If your letter is an index of the feeling of the Secretaries," he woefully wrote to Cravath, "I have not the slightest hope of success."[78]

Pesky troubles continued to nag at White and his Jubilee Singers as they advanced toward New York. Ella Sheppard became so ill that the doctor advised she return to Nashville. "Mr. White declined to act upon this advice," recalled Pike, "believing that God meant his company should move North, pianist and all." Within twelve hours, Sheppard reported to Spence, she was somewhat better and proceeded on with the company, trusting that no further health complications would force her departure. Concert proceeds continued to barely meet expenses and provide travel costs for the next leg of the journey. G. Stanley Pope's service as advance agent helped to generate interest in the company, but there were still many details to a successful campaign that required attention. White was forced to become proficient at begging and borrowing, both for money to purchase coats for his singers and for lodging in the various cities in which they sang.[79]

The apparent failure of the mission weighed heavily on White. As of yet, Fisk University had not realized a cent from his risky fundraising campaign. Spence had been forced to pick up White's duties as treasurer but was proving to be a very poor fiscal manager. The institutional accounts were in complete disarray, for which White admitted partial responsibility:

> I am wretched that you—or those at the School should be so much embarrassed by my failure. I have no excuses to make—or apologies—I will stand all that comes—I have done my duty. The accounts were left in the shape they were because you failed to send a man to take my place. Perhaps you could not. Neither could I work miracles. I have no resource here for the payment of Fisk University debts. If you can at any price raise money to relieve the pressure there—and forward it at once—I will settle it at some rate *personally* next week—when I hope to reach N.Y.[80]

White wrote to a worried Adam Spence that money would arrive within ten days. "How he expects to accomplish this, I do not know," a disbelieving Spence told his mother. "Thus far the concert troupe has just been paying expenses."[81] True, the company had nothing to show for its efforts thus far; nonetheless, White maintained stubbornly that what the AMA considered as a foolish venture had potential yet to be fully realized. "I have shown that with proper management," he insisted to Cravath, "there is even more power for good in it than I had claimed."[82]

Validation: New York and Henry Ward Beecher

By the first week of December, the company finally reached the state of New York for a series of concerts prior to arriving in the city and the headquarters of the AMA. In Elmira, they sang at Reverend Thomas K. Beecher's church, fulfilling the invitation he had offered when he heard them in Ohio. Once again, their performance earned generous praise from the local press. The concert "was altogether the most satisfactory entertainment we have attended in many a year," noted the *Elmira Daily Advertiser.* "The entertainment, purely as an entertainment, is worth twenty times the price of admission, and the object is one which deserves the encouragement and patronage of every good and benevolent man."[83] A delighted Beecher sent the company on its way with a warm letter of commendation to hand to his brother, Henry Ward Beecher, when they arrived the following week in Brooklyn.

.Such avid praise from those who heard the ensemble, thought White, ought to sway the AMA officers' opinion of his company's mission. Still, the officers remained as uncertain about lending their endorsement as they had been from the onset. White interpreted their hesitancy as utter cowardice and poured out his irritation to his brother-in-law:

> There is enough in the papers now it seems to me—to warrant at least a public endorsement of the enterprise by the offices of the Association—and a recommendation of the troupe to the people. I was disappointed in the article in the Missionary—as there was no cordial commendation of the work—An announcement was made that such a craft was afloat—and that *somebody else* had been brave enough to speak a good word for it.[84]

"My judgement is that the sooner we get a hearing in Brooklyn or Boston," mused White, "the sooner we shall get out of the woods." Arriving in New York City armed with glowing endorsements from prominent ministers should be the arsenal he needed to open doors. Two grueling months of work had produced little results, White admitted, but "now influences will begin to reach out before us again." To Professor Spence, he expressed hope: "We have been in the wilderness two long, weary months and are just coming to see light ahead." It had been a struggle, he admitted, one that he had endured alone:

> I have had to fight my way single handed—and make a public sentiment in our favor, under the most adverse and crushing circumstances—about the only help I have had from those who ought at least to have said "Godspeed"—has been severe cold criticism on the enterprise and a continual pointing to its difficulties—and the probability of a failure. The officers of the Association have not used as much influence in our favor as the Methodists in Delaware or the Presbyterians in Springfield. I have read the article in the Missionary Magazine. There is no cordial hearty commending of the enterprise to the people—but a mere statement that such a doubtful craft has been launched—and an implied "we shall see."[85]

Despite the lack of AMA support, White and his company held fast to the belief that their mission was divinely inspired. The suffering they had endured thus far was a testing of their faith, one that neither he nor the students wanted to fail. "All the young people are well and happy," White told Spence, "notwithstanding the fearful trial through which we have pressed.... You will hear from the 'Jubilee Singers'—more frequently now."[86]

Spence, however, was more inclined to share the wariness of the AMA officers. The success of White's venture, he believed, fully depended "upon the divine guidance and blessing" of God rather than upon the bullheaded actions of White. Spence felt that he alone was "in charge of the University in its hours of peril," and without divine intervention in a most miraculous way, he could not see how the company's fortune would change.[87] He confided his doubts to his mother:

> Tomorrow they are to arrive in New York...their success or the lack of it then will probably decide the fate of the enterprise. If they make they go on, if they fail they get home if they can. Let us pray that all may be right. The Lord seems to give them favor with the people but the outgos are great. So many people to lodge and feed at hotels and transport to say nothing of their time. Still they are doing great good and their "praise meetings" are most highly spoken of. They are attended with immense enthusiasm, tears of joy and gratitude at the sight of such a band of singers once in slavery. But unless the hearts of the benevolent and wealthy are opened to give liberally the thing as a financial scheme must fail.

The company's religious influence gladdened Spence's heart, and he could not discredit the spiritual good that might be accomplished. But demanding creditors were breathing down his neck and they were "almost out of food" at Fisk. "Mr. White went abruptly," he complained to his mother, "leaving all things just as they happened to be." Spence needed money desperately and time was running out.[88]

The Jubilee Singers arrived in New York City on 4 December 1871. Hotel rates proved to be highly unreasonable, so AMA secretaries Erastus Cravath, E. P. Smith, and Gustavus Pike took them into their private residences where they lived for the next six weeks.[89] True to White's expectations, it was indeed in New York that the company's fortune took a drastic turn. The change began when Reverend George Whipple, senior secretary of the AMA, contacted Henry Ward Beecher and asked him to allow the singers to perform in one of his church meetings.

Beecher was at the height of his ministerial career. His success did not rely on his physical appearance, for observers admitted there was nothing particularly striking about his looks. One contemporary described him as "medium height, with heavy body and brawny shoulders, large head and broad face, features regular, but none of them strongly marked, ruddy complexion, and hair somewhat gray, indicating a man a little past the meridian of life, in full health and vigor, with a well-developed physique."[90] What attracted crowds was his effective and unique preaching. Beecher did not dwell on theology and abstract truths as his predecessors had done but delivered down-to-earth sermons that spoke to the concerns of daily human life. He did so with simplicity, charm, and natural expression people found appealing.

The great orator was completing his twenty-fifth year as pastor of the prestigious Plymouth Church in Brooklyn and was one of the most sought-after Christian lecturers in the country. "As it is said of the Savior, so of him; the common people, as well as the rich and the learned, hear him gladly," noted one observer. When city authorities were once debating how to raise money for a good cause, one had dryly observed: "Obtain the Academy of Music, secure the services of Henry Ward Beecher, and you will get all the money you want."[91] Making a friend of Henry Ward Beecher could only play to the Jubilee Singers' favor.

Having already heard good reports of the Jubilees from his brother, Thomas, Beecher gladly granted Whipple's request to have the ensemble perform at one of his popular Friday evening prayer meetings.[92] White knew their performance that evening was a critical one that could possibly make or break the company. AMA Secretary G. D. Pike, who was hearing the troupe for the first time, recalled the visual impression they made: "A motley group! The girls, dressed in water-proofs, and clothed about the neck with long woolen comforters to protect their throats, stood in a row in front. The young men occupied positions closely in the rear, the class standing solid, as they term it, in order to secure the most perfect harmony."[93] White bent his six-foot frame, got down on his hands and knees, crawled in front of the group with a pitch pipe in order to give the first note, and the ensemble began to sing.[94] "I shall never forget the rich tones of the young men as they mingled their voices in a melody so beautiful and touching I scarcely knew whether I was 'in the body or out of the body,'" recalled Pike, instantly captivated.[95] Beecher later recalled that the audience was as "still as death," and by the second song, tears had begun to flow freely. For twenty minutes, the Jubilee Singers kept the audience spellbound with their songs.[96]

Their final number was "Steal Away," a song that would soon become their signature piece: "Steal away, steal away / Steal away to Jesus / Steal away, steal away home / I haint got long to stay here." "I often feel my heart quicken when I recall myself for the first time standing before the vast audience in Rev. Henry Ward Beecher's church," recalled Maggie Porter, "and again hear my voice tremble as I attempted to lead 'Steal Away to Jesus.'"[97] For this number, White employed the full spectrum of dynamic contrast, with a powerful forte in the verses ending with a double pianissimo on the final cadence of the chorus. The effect was mesmerizing.

As the last sound floated away over the hushed audience, reported Porter, an enthralled Henry Ward Beecher "was on his feet, and with his hands in his pockets he brought out five dollars and told everybody to follow suit."[98] The singers were already making their way down from the loft, but Beecher would not let them go so easily. Pike described how Beecher called them back before the people and announced that this was "but a foretaste, in hearing and in giving"—the Jubilee Singers would be back to sing again.[99] Within a few days, he opened Plymouth Church for their concert and charged a fifty-cent admission fee. "That was our start," declared Maggie Porter. "From that time on we had success."[100]

It is not surprising that Henry Ward Beecher was attracted to the Jubilee Singers. His contemporaries described him as imaginative, poetic in thought, and eloquent in language.[101] The spirituals captured Beecher's inquisitive, artistic mind immediately and their profound simplicity seemed to resonate with his soul. He described hearing in them the "inarticulate wails of breaking hearts made dumb by slavery...in short, the inner life of slave hearts, expressed in music." Beecher's message of a personal Christ who befriended all men in all times and in all circumstances found living expression in the young people standing before him singing, "Oh, how I love Jesus." Everything about the Jubilee Singers struck his fancy, from their novel songs with their quaint phrases, to their uncompromising stance for freedom and equality.[102]

Beecher's Friday evening services drew large crowds and enjoyed regular press attention. It therefore did not take long for the word to spread and for the public to respond to his encouragement to give "a hearty welcome" to this company. "The concert of the Jubilee Singers in Plymouth Church," stated one Brooklyn daily, "was one of the greatest treats we have ever had."[103] The house was almost filled, noted the reviewer, and he predicted a capacity crowd at the troupe's next performance. Another remarked, "Their singing last evening was excellent, some of it very remarkable, and the whole entertainment was regarded by all present as a success."[104] However, not all reviewers were as positive in their assessment of the Jubilee Singers. The morning after a second concert at Beecher's church, the *New York Herald's* column labeled the company as "Beecher's Negro Minstrels" and included a wood cut that portrayed the company with the stereotypical features associated with the caricatured prototypes of the minstrel shows. "It has not yet been announced whether the next performance at Mr. Beecher's theatre will be comedy, opera, or melodrama," ridiculed the paper. Yet White and his troupe were learning that even negative press, "while it did not warmly commend, yet largely advertised the performance" and "served to spread tidings of them, without influencing good people against them."[105] Audiences continued to grow until the halls were packed, and the company was "received with the wildest enthusiasm." "In each city where we appeared a perfect furore of excitement prevailed," recalled Ella Sheppard.[106] Henry Ward Beecher's commendation was just the kind of high-profile endorsement that White needed to turn the tide of sentiment in their favor. The troupe was on its way.

For the next six weeks, the Jubilee Singers appeared in concerts throughout New York and New Jersey. Prominent ministers welcomed them into their services and warmly sanctioned their performances as respectable entertainment. No longer did nervous ministers hide near the back doors fearful of their congregants' response. Instead, they worked vigorously to entice people to turn out for the Jubilees' concerts in full force, and their efforts were rewarded. The public scrambled to gain entrance, filling halls to capacity, leaving scarcely a space "where a person could hang on, so great was the pressure of the multitude."[107]

Witnessing the large audiences and the public excitement the singers were generating, the "wonderful spiritual effect of the slave songs," and especially the funds that were beginning to pour in, the executive committee began realizing the potential of using White's company to both support and advance the AMA cause. Though they had withheld initial endorsement, they now believed the troupe was an unexpected avenue through which to forward their work and began soliciting prominent churches to host the Jubilee Singers. "Providentially there has been developed in connection with our educational work in Fisk University, Nashville, Tenn., a remarkable power of song," announced the association's December issue of the *American Missionary*.[108] The journal also included newspaper reviews of concerts the company had performed in Ohio. In its January publication, the AMA further endorsed the company:

> The year of jubilee has come to the bondmen of the South, and why should not the voice of their songs resound throughout the land? God has given them a gladness of heart, and an unsurpassed sweetness of voice that cheered them even in the house of their bondage, and now that they are redeemed from their captivity, it is fit that heart and voice should find joyous utterance. Those sweet voices are beginning to be heard.... We heard them twice before the Council in Oberlin. It is not needful that we eulogise those performances. Many abler pens have done this. But it is becoming in us to say that the friends of the American Missionary Association then present were filled with gladness as they witnessed the deep impression made on that Council, by those touching and artless songs. It was the most effective appeal that could be made in behalf of that struggling race and of the efforts of the Association to assist them.[109]

The AMA printed and distributed a "circular calling for $20,000 for Fisk University," Spence told his mother.[110] At last, the AMA secretaries seemed to have awakened to what White had said all along: his company was a novel enterprise with which to capture public sentiment and solicit funds. "We have proven the power of the music," an elated White informed Spence, "even to the conversion of Mrs. Cravath - & the officers of the AMA, Bro. Pike included."[111]

January was far different from the previous three months of struggle. Suddenly, everyone seemed eager to lend a hand to the Jubilee Singers enterprise. White was much relieved, especially because the company was finally earning profits with which he could address the financial woes at

Fisk. "I will pay just as fast as it is wise," he wrote to Spence in late December, assuring him that success was only a matter of time.[112] By the middle of January, he was able to make good on his word, sending his first sizeable installment to alleviate Fisk's most pressing financial needs.

Henry Ward Beecher began urging a New England tour in the belief that a handsome sum might be gained by presenting the Jubilee Singers at lyceums.[113] He was willing to use his persuasion to help secure engagements and offered to send a letter of warm support to James Redpath, head of the Boston Lyceum Bureau. "They will charm any audience sure," he gushed.[114] Dr. Theodore L. Cuyler, pastor of Lafayette Avenue Presbyterian Church, hosted them at his church and sent a warm endorsement to the *New York Tribune:*

> I never saw a cultivated Brooklyn assemblage so moved and melted under the magnetism of music before. The wild melodies of these emancipated slaves touched the fount of tears, and gray-haired men wept like little children.... Allow me to bespeak, through your journal...a universal welcome through the North for these living representatives of the only true, native school of American music. We have long enough had its coarse caricature in corked faces: our people can now listen to the genuine soul music of the slave cabins, before the Lord led his "children out of the land of Egypt, out of the house of bondage."[115]

The letter appeared in several papers, quickly spreading the word about the troupe and its authentic folk music. Concert proceeds increased dramatically, and by the first of February the company was nearly debt free and hoped to start earning at least five hundred dollars above expenses per week. "We are now an institution almost completely out of debt and our financial horizon has cleared up wonderfully," a gleeful Spence wrote to his mother. "Our singers are still prospered and meet with great enthusiasm and some money besides expenses."[116]

Divine Blessing

White considered the company's first few months of hardship as validation of spiritual direction. Suffering had proven to him that he and his company were indeed exercising true missionary service. He felt they had answered a divine call, persevered under the most trying of circumstances, received spiritual fortification at their darkest moment, fought for a worthy cause, and eventually defeated the odds. It had been a genuine battle, White acknowledged, one that had undeniably tested their character and willingness to sacrifice all for the cause of Christ. Ella Sheppard agreed: "We spent many long weary weeks working, toiling in tears and prayer before a single ray appeared to encourage us." In her letter to Spence, Sheppard attributed the company's success in large part to the spiritual fortitude of George White. "Many times would we have given up in despair had it not been for our noble friend Mr. White. He, in the midst of suffering, cheered us on our mission saying 'he had to [sic] much faith in God to fail in so great a work.'"[117] For his part, White shared the praise with the young singers in his company: "We have had a fearful struggle—the 'Jubilee Singers' ought to be immortal in name. They have stood the test nobly."[118]

Beecher's support and the subsequent positive ripple effect it had on local ministers helped others within the AMA to concede that perhaps God had approved of White's venture all along. The Jubilee Singers were drawing large crowds who seemed spiritually moved by their performances. Moreover, funds were pouring into the AMA coffers. The association officers perceived these two outcomes as evidence of providential blessing. While the leadership gladly welcomed the funds generated for the work at Fisk University, they preferred to emphasize the spiritual aspect of the Jubilee Singers in promoting the company. "They are being felt by the churches as a spiritual power," the monthly journal reported, "warming and quickening religious worship."[119] Adam Spence was also grateful for the troupe's religious influence, but equally thankful for the company's financial success. "We have another $500 to pay off old debt," Spence happily informed his mother. Once installments started arriving at Fisk, Spence concluded to his mother that "the Lord prospers the troupe."[120]

Were it not for Beecher's endorsement and had not the AMA finally assumed supervision of the Jubilee Singers, it is highly doubtful that the company would have survived. Christian evangelicals were careful not to endorse any semblance of entertainment; an African-American musical troupe was highly suspect. This community needed the approval of significant Christian voices to validate the Jubilee Singers' cause as righteous, their patronage as respectable, and the troupe's concerts as an acceptable blend of ministry and entertainment.

Perhaps White could have successfully launched the troupe as a private enterprise, but doing so was contrary to his true desire. He had always felt that the company was an "appointed agency of God" for the salvation of Fisk University. He knew the musical possibilities of his ensemble and had accurately forecast that a management team with a developed marketing strategy could make the enterprise profitable. The last three months of unprecedented success had vindicated White from all previous charges of unrealism and nullified whatever doubts may have lingered in the minds of the skeptics. White was grateful for the change of heart among his colleagues, even though it had been hard earned at great personal risk to himself and his reputation. "The 'Jubilee Singers' are doing good work. It has been a terrible struggle to get to a point where we could *touch bottom*— but we have conquered—and shown that there is all in the enterprise which we have claimed and even more of real spiritual power." Success brought its own potential pitfalls, though, and White requested that Spence pray for them that they "may be humble."[121]

Humility, however, would have to rest side by side with White's latest grand vision. Already, he imagined a new building made possible with funds raised by the Jubilees. Once debt-free, White was ready to take the field again and earn money for the university's first boarding and general classroom building to which he already assigned a name: Jubilee Hall. Since the company was actually earning a profit, White's vision of a building was easier for Spence to adopt with genuine eagerness. Less worried about the future, a more confident Spence piously wrote his mother: "No doubt it is our Christian duty as well as privilege to not be worried about the future. There do seem to be prospects of our getting aid through the 'Jubilee Singers,' and 'Jubilee Hall' does not seem to be so impossible after all. The topic is winning great sympathy and some money toward the $20,000 called for by the AMA for a building."[122] In late January, a triumphant White sent Spence another $500 toward debt and related the news of their concert before a 2,000-member audience in Boston's Music Hall. "It was a perfect success in every point. Mr. Redpath said he had never seen a Boston audience more enthusiastically moved.... I shall 'salt down' now for the new building."[123]

The crisis moment for Fisk University was past. Debts were quickly being met as the Jubilee Singers' fame spread and concert proceeds mounted. The bleak "financial horizon" had "cleared up wonderfully," a somewhat amazed Adam Spence wrote his mother.[124] White confidently told Spence that Fisk University would soon "begin to rise again."[125]

Chapter 3

"Doing the Work of the Master"

Developing a Campaign Strategy for

Christian Missions

...the singers will go forth confident that they are doing the work of the Master and that He will signally crown with his blessing their efforts in the future as He has in the past...[1]

The New England tour launched in spring 1872 marks the point where the American Missionary Association (AMA) became intimately involved in managing all aspects of the Jubilee Singers enterprise. The troupe's success in New York assured the leadership that there was real gain, tangible and intangible, to be had through the Jubilee Singers. The AMA leadership now agreed with White that the work of the entire association, not just Fisk University, could benefit from the exposure and publicity afforded by this remarkable musical ensemble.

AMA officers had accurately forecast that using a student musical ensemble for fundraising could present some real challenges. They needed the troupe to earn ample profits while maintaining its Christian ministry focus and without endangering the reputation of either Fisk University or the AMA. As managing a concert troupe was a new experience for all involved, an evolutionary process began with the launch of the 1872 New England campaign that eventually culminated in a well-defined mission, public image, daily operational systems, and governance practices with which to guide the ensemble. By May, the managers felt they had a workable blueprint with which they could achieve their financial goals without risking the Christian Reconstruction principles defining the AMA's educational and ministry efforts.

The New England Campaign of 1872

A few changes in personnel occurred prior to the beginning of the 1872 New England campaign. Mary Wells returned to her post at Trinity School in Athens, Alabama, taking with her young Georgie Wells, whose contribution to the performance "was not quite appropriate compared with the general high standard of the company's singing."[2] George Stanley Pope, who had served as advance agent since early December 1871, chose to return to Oberlin after the Connecticut concerts were concluded along with his wife, Catherine Koontz Pope, who had held the role of governess. She was replaced by Susan Gilbert, an AMA teacher from North Carolina, and George G. Shelton became the new advance agent.[3]

Administratively, the most important addition to the team was the Reverend Gustavus D. Pike, an AMA district secretary who joined the enterprise as business manager. From the first time he heard them at Beecher's church, Pike became one of the Jubilee Singers' most devoted fans. White once referred to him as "the most enthusiastic champion the Singers have."[4] What Pike initially intended as a short stint with the company developed into a travel commitment that spanned two years and two continents.[5]

Prior to the AMA's sponsorship, White was forced to attend to all the various demands of a concert tour, serving as advance agent, porter, ticket seller, advertising agent, as well as musical director. Pike felt this was certainly no way to run a successful business:

> Those familiar with enterprises of the kind understand that to do a profitable business, it is necessary to have a business manager, who lays out the routes, visits or corresponds with editors and public men, and arranges the general plan of the campaign. Then an advance agent goes forward and puts these plans in operation. A treasurer pays bills, sells or takes tickets, and provides for details; while the musical director arranges programmes, drills the chorus, and answers the ten thousand inquiries of admiring friends.... Financial success is not achieved without an intelligent and experienced faculty, and a host of allies, who must be induced to co-operate at the right moment; otherwise ever so popular a company would fail to pay expenses.[6]

What Pike had to offer was a multitude of connections within the evangelical community and an astute business sense. He wasted no time in applying both to the company's operations.[7]

An enhanced, systematic marketing strategy was Pike's first objective for the New England tour. "We found we had the goods," he noted, "and what remained was to bring them in, in a business-like way, to market." His first job was to ensure that their concerts were well publicized. His advance agent, Shelton, "worked the field" ahead of the company, gaining the support of respected ministers and flooding the town with promotional materials by adopting four basic advertising strategies: 1) notices placed in the local papers and religious publications; 2) posters placed in public buildings; 3) slips, or "dodgers," filled with testimonials delivered to private residences and stores; and 4) prepared notices to be read in the local churches.[8] Endorsements by their prominent clergy friends brought credibility to the ensemble. "They will charm any audience, sure," gushed Henry Ward Beecher. "Our people have been delighted with them." "Do you be sure to go and hear them, no matter what the weather is," urged John Henry in a letter published in the *Congregationalist.* "You'll be sorry forever if you don't."[9] Statements of support from such respected individuals were so influential that suddenly "every one, apparently, wished to serve the enterprise," claimed Pike, "and many prominent men gave their services in making the stay of the Singers pleasant and successful."[10]

His second task was to motivate the public to attend the ensemble's concerts. Generally, the Jubilee Singers first appeared on Sundays in the most prominent churches in the cities they attended, an act which he felt afforded them "a wonderful prestige." Pike sought the patronage of the city's distinguished citizens to lend dignity to the enterprise and boost audience attendance. His efforts were successful, and the Jubilees' popularity began to climb, as did profits. In one week they grossed almost $4,000, a vast difference from the income they had earned in fall 1871.[11] Merchants gave material goods with which to furnish the future Jubilee Hall: clocks, silverware, gas fixtures, books, personal valuables, pledges to supply rooms, and a Winsted memorial bell "with the names of the singers cast upon it" to adorn the new building's tower.[12] "They are evidently up on the top wave of enthusiasm," Spence told his mother. She replied that it certainly seemed to have been a "heaven directed plan" that the company "went out to sing." "Let us 'thank God and take courage,'" said a grateful Spence. "I have been more hopeful of late."[13]

The format for the New England concerts continued the pattern White established during his first trial months: introductory remarks by influential local sponsors, followed by singing interspersed with speeches explaining the Jubilee Singers' mission and its relation to the work of the AMA. As the campaign continued, some newspapers began criticizing the frequent speeches, leading Pike to concede that perhaps "on some occasions these remarks were too elaborate." However, he countered, they "were not *showmen.*" The main objective of any concert was to advance the AMA cause, albeit a different approach from the association's past attempts. While Pike recognized that many people attended for the sole purpose of hearing the singing, engaging in entertainment was certainly not the troupe's purpose. On the other hand, he reasoned, why not take advantage of the public spotlight now cast upon the Jubilee Singers? "We believe we should have been derelict in duty if we had not availed ourselves of a few moments to communicate facts," Pike remarked, "while the Singers were winning so many golden opinions."

> We knew full well that a large majority of those who gathered to hear singing knew but very little, if anything, about the work of the American Missionary Association; and that by hearing slave songs, they got no knowledge of facts, any more than they would by listening to mocking birds.... God had given us the ears of the multitude, who needed to be informed and brought into co-operation with the work. I sought, therefore, to popularize this part of our programme.[14]

For Pike, the concerts were primarily an avenue through which to advance missionary work. "We were out to promote the cause of Missions, not like an organ-grinder, to gain a livelihood," he remarked.[15]

The zeal with which Pike delivered his lengthy and fervent speeches about the AMA's work sometimes unsettled the press. One critic described the Jubilee Singers' entertainment as "most agreeable and excellent," but felt Pike's remarks were a "good deal less harmonious than the rest of the programme":

> He assured the audience that the Jubilee Singers had been repeatedly solicited to come to Troy, but had now come at a loss of $50. Troy, too, as

he piously suggested, had not done much lately for the freedmen.... He thought the audience would be glad to know, also, that the tour of the Jubilee Singers had been successful; that they took in $1,050 last night at Springfield, and would go back to Nashville with the $20,000 which they started to raise. The audience *were* glad to learn these things. They were much more pleasant to hear than the general tenor of Mr. Pike's remarks; but how the Jubilee Singers could appear to an audience of even six or seven hundred, and actually lose money, we understand with difficulty, and only by a childlike faith in Rev. J. D. Pike, rather than by any effort of our mere carnal reason.[16]

Given the company's operating expenses, Pike's remarks about concert costs were undoubtedly true. This critic, however, certainly did not appreciate the public rebuke.

Chiding audiences for their lack of substantial giving was a tactic both Pike and White employed at times. At the close of a four-concert run in Boston, White told the packed house at Tremont Temple that net receipts for the Boston performances were less than a single concert in the little town of Winsted, Connecticut. Again, the press quickly reacted. "I cannot say I thought the taste very good that would induce a manger to make such a reflection upon those whom he was soliciting to patronize his entertainment," rejoined the writer of an editorial to the *Boston Daily Advertiser*. He suggested that the company simply do away with speeches as they offered nothing new beyond what was already printed in their programs. "The nine singers told their own story by their appearance and their songs, far better than any one else could tell it for them."[17] The correspondent for the *Congregationalist* agreed, saying the managers' speeches were "quite out of place." "These colored minstrels tell their own story and that of the American Missionary Association perfectly well without help, and far more impressively than with it."[18] However, such commentary fell on deaf ears, and speeches expounding the cause and mission of the AMA remained a prominent part of the company's performance format.

Additional revenue from the New England concert tour accrued from effective efforts to reduce campaign expenses. AMA officials used their influence to gain reduced fares for transportation, lodging, and hall rentals. In Waterbury, they succeeded in securing special trains for patrons in outlying areas coming to concerts. "The Superintendent of the Naugatuck

Railroad, followed the example of the President of the New Haven, Hartford, and Springfield Railroad, and gave us half fare," Pike proudly reported. The AMA leadership had no compunction about pressuring business owners for discounts. They felt their cause was just and purely benevolent, and therefore corporations and individuals ought to lower prices so that the company might reach its goal of $20,000. Pike and the other agents working for the Jubilee Singers enterprise proved to be accomplished lobbyists whose talent for cutting expenses contributed significantly to the company's financial return.[19]

Sale of Jubilee Singers merchandise helped satisfy the public's curiosity while also generating revenue. White had photos printed of the Jubilees that sold for ten cents apiece, and engaged Theodore F. Seward, editor of the *New York Musical Gazette*, to notate the slave songs for publication, a task which proved to be a real challenge. The Jubilee Singers' musical renditions of the spirituals not only seemed to defy accurate description, but also musical notation. "Some of the phrases and turns are so peculiar that they might be supposed to be incapable of exact representation by ordinary musical characters," observed one critic.[20] Western European notation had no tools with which to capture certain vocal nuances characteristic of the ensemble's singing. Nonetheless, Seward tackled the task zealously and had his transcriptions ready for purchase at twenty-five cents each by early spring.[21] Upon examination, Thomas Rutling, one of the company's original members, claimed that the respected music scholar had "made so many errors…that the singers did not recognize their own songs."[22] Even so, the twenty-eight page collection, *Jubilee Songs: As Sung by the Jubilee Singers of Fisk University*, sold rapidly, spreading the Negro spiritual across America and padding the building fund. "The hills and valleys, the parlors and halls, all over the regions where we traveled, were vocal with the melodies of the Singers," pronounced Pike.[23] "The songs of the slave have become songs of jubilee," declared one New York critic. "As we have taken the freedmen into our national life, so may we take profitably to the expression of that life in this music which they bring."[24]

In addition to developing an effective campaign strategy, the New England tour also marked the Jubilee Singers' transition from a fledgling musical troupe to a professional ensemble. Concerts throughout New England that spring were described as one "continuous ovation." Critics praised their voices "of superior power and sweetness" and their blend in "exquisite harmony." "Rarely are an equal number of persons in any one choir or chorus endowed with such full and pleasantly modulated voices," exclaimed one daily.[25] "Neither the opportunity to aid in the noble object which brings these Jubilee Singers among us, nor the rare opportunity to hear them ought to be neglected by anyone who can attend their concert," proclaimed another reviewer.[26] With time, experience, and enthusiastic audience reception, the Jubilee Singers began to lose their performance jitters and command the stage with authority.

Pike considered the company's performance at New Haven, Connecticut as one of their most successful concerts. The singers were "almost obliged to march on the heads of the people to reach the pulpit," he recalled. The hall was filled far in advance of the troupe's arrival, and many audience members had to stand until the final notes of the evening had drifted away. Henry Ward Beecher was scheduled to lecture on the same night that the Jubilee Singers were performing in New Haven. However, public demand for tickets to the musical concert was so great that the sponsors were compelled to cancel Reverend Beecher's lecture. "Probably no one was more delighted than Mr. Beecher," alleged Pike, "to see the day had come when colored students in New Haven could rival the foremost lecturer and preacher in the land in calling out an audience."[27] "New life" had come into the troupe, said Ella Sheppard, and they "sang as if inspired." "We feel that we must have the $20,000 before we come home," another Jubilee wrote home to Adam Spence, "and we by the help of God intend to have it."[28]

All indicators seemed to forecast certain success. Residents of Bridge-port, Connecticut practically made history in their enthusiastic response to an upcoming Jubilee Singers performance. Never had there been "so great a sale of reserved seats in the city as had transpired that week in anticipation of our concert," recorded Pike. A subsequent appearance in Norwich provided the largest collection they had ever received at a Sunday service. The audience applauded so loudly and gave so generously that Pike felt as though the company was "riding on a comet" of good will.[29]

Immense, enthusiastic audiences were especially gratifying to the company and duly reported with pride to the Nashville family. "Our concerts are so well attended that many are doomed to stand," Ella Sheppard told Professor Spence. The New Haven hall that held 2,500 had nearly every seat filled and concert requests continued to pour in: "*Oh such a grand success.* Mr. White is receiving dispatches every day from different cities—wanting us to come there—people come from twenty to fifty miles to hear us—in some cities excursion trains were run and are going to run to the places where we sing—the people seem to be perfectly frantic about the 'Jubilee Singers.'" Sheppard hoped that their success would not have a negative affect upon the members of the troupe. She asked for Spence's prayers that the company "may feel all the more humble to our *Leader* above for this glorious success." It was an attitude that was becoming increasingly difficult for some to maintain, she admitted, for the Jubilee Singers were "petted and loved and flattered" by almost everyone they met.[30]

Concert requests began flooding in, leading Pike to draft standard instructions in a leaflet entitled "How to Do It" for those wishing to host the Jubilee Singers in their town.[31] "Citizens of cities and towns wishing to hear the Jubilee Singers of Fisk University, Nashville, Tenn., are invited to consider the following suggestions," began the guide. Pike then presented four points with lengthy explanations and examples from previous concerts for potential hosts to emulate. First, anyone wishing to host the Jubilees needed to send a written request. The sample letter he provided demonstrated how several influential citizens of one town were united in their request to host the ensemble and offered free lodging at a good hotel. Second, the prospective hosts needed to prepare a plan for "working up" the concerts. Pike suggested the action of John Backup, Esq. of Boston, who pulled together a committee of town citizens to sell tickets in their respective churches, as an excellent model to follow.

The third consideration was where to host a concert. "The Jubilee Singers enterprise is purely benevolent," Pike reminded prospective hosts. Therefore, he encouraged them to secure a church with a large seating capacity (800 to 1,000 persons) whose officers were willing to offer the facility for free. At the very least, the cost of lighting should be the only venue expense. The last point referred to ticket prices. Pike stated that the

Jubilees were grossing an average of $500 per concert, which he admitted might seem large at first glance. However, he reminded potential hosts that the company's earnings were "little when compared with the amount needed to secure for the perishing African who is stretching out his hand to God, the facilities for carrying the gospel to scores of millions of that race. The price paid for a ticket can be regarded in part as a contribution for the Freedmen." Hosting the Jubilee Singers in concert should be viewed as partnering with the AMA in its missionary work. Therefore, asked Pike rhetorically, "Is it not both generous and just that all suitable efforts be put forth to secure a profitable Concert at all such places as the Jubilee Singers are invited to give entertainments?"[32]

These guidelines became the criteria Pike used to determine which concert requests they should accept. Notes written by field agents on the sides of financial records from this period indicate that the managers generally rejected those invitations where the hall or church seated less than 1,000 people. They also denied those letters of request from clergy unwilling to sell tickets.[33]

Selectivity on the part of the managers did not seem to have a negative effect on the company's success. A flurry of almost nightly concerts occurred from mid-March until May stretching from Rhode Island to Maine. Vast crowds turned out and demanded encore after encore to which the Jubilee Singers willingly obliged. They also yielded to public requests for repeat performances in certain towns. A second matinee concert at Tremont Temple in Boston garnered $1,235, which at that point in their campaign, reported Pike, was the "largest amount, exclusive of in-kind gifts, ever received at a single entertainment." The following Sunday, the company appeared at a temperance meeting held at Boston's Park Street Church. Though the weather was stormy, the hall was so full that "every inch of standing room seemed to be taken."[34] Interspersed throughout the program were several temperance melodies, including "Wine is a Mocker," whose lyrics from Proverbs 20:1 became the theme song of the Temperance movement.[35] A duet between Ella Sheppard and young Minnie Tate introduced the tune and the rest of the members joined in on the chorus. Pike described the audience response as "perfectly electrical" and told of one clergyman who clapped his hands "with an energy that I fear would have put to blush the fathers who stood where he did during the early history of this venerable church." The audience would not quiet down until a collection was taken.[36]

Unfortunately, the appreciation the company earned onstage was not always matched by equal respect outside the concert hall. More often than not, the Jubilee Singers battled discriminatory practices from proprietors of public establishments. Such was the case when they arrived in Newark, New Jersey after a series of glowing successes in Connecticut. The Newark proprietor thought he was lodging a minstrel company and "when he discovered that they were the genuine article, and not the imitation, he promptly drove them into the street," reported the *New York Independent.*[37] When word leaked out about how they had been treated, Newark citizens "vented their just censure upon the proprietor," reported Pike, and some of the hotel's boarders left immediately. City officials took advantage of public sentiment to "pass an ordinance opening the city public schools to colored children."[38]

Incidences such as this one heightened the Jubilee Singers' awareness that popularity gave them some leverage when dealing with widespread discrimination in America. "It was to be part of our mission," wrote Ella Sheppard, "if not to remove at least to ameliorate" such prejudice.[39] Likewise, the AMA began to appreciate this new emerging aspect of the Jubilee Singers' mission: the troupe could be powerful voices for civil rights that carried weight and respect. "So it would seem that God had chosen these Jubilee Singers, not only to *enjoy* but to *suffer* for the benefit of the race they represent," wrote Pike.[40] America was casting favorable eyes toward these newly freed men and women, providing a unique opportunity for them to address unjust social distinctions. The press noticed this as well: "It has fallen to the lot of these young persons to perform a most valuable service for their race. Jubilee Hall, which will stand at Nashville, as the memorial of their success, will represent but a small part of the work they have accomplished. Their best achievement is what they have done to conquer the old prejudice against color, and to win a kindlier regard and a more generous sympathy for the people whom they represent."[41] The Jubilees understood that they were singing ambassadors not only for Fisk University and the AMA, but also for the uplift of their people. Their success could be interpreted as a victory for all African Americans.

On 2 March 1872, the troupe left for a quick excursion to Washington, DC to support a bill pending in Congress concerning the transfer of federal lands to Fisk University. By this time the company had raised $10,000 and expected another $4,000 by the first of May with which to begin construction of Jubilee Hall.[42] After visiting several Washington sites, they returned to Howard University to receive the good news that they had gained an audience before the President of the United States, Ulysses S. Grant. The following morning, Grant warmly welcomed them at the White House. "And these are the 'Jubilee Singers' I have read so much of," he said. "I am very interested and hope you may have a glorious success." At his request, they sang a spiritual:

When Israel was in Egypt's land,
Let my people go;
Oppressed so hard they could not stand,
Let my people go.
Go down, Moses, way down in Egypt land,
Tell ole Pharaoh, Let my people go.

The Jubilee Singers' rich tones poured forth this freedom message in the highest hall of the land. The stirring spiritual had seemed to work magic on previous audiences: one critic informed the public that hearing this "most inspiring" melody alone was "worth the admission fee."[43] President Grant also expressed his delight, and after a tour of the White House, the Jubilees returned to Howard University where a reception was waiting for them.[44]

Before heading back to New England, the Jubilee Singers gave their final New York concert in Steinway Hall on 8 March 1872, a stunning affair presented before a packed house. The stage was full of clergy and other distinguished guests who offered profuse speeches of commendation at various points throughout the evening. Among the dignitaries was General Clinton B. Fisk, who admitted that he was hearing the company for the first time. "I trust these dusky Singers will continue to move the masses, by their indescribable power," he proclaimed to thunderous applause, "until they have sung a dollar out of the pocket of every man, woman and child in this broad land." Reverend William Adams, pastor of the Madison Avenue Presbyterian Church, remarked on the "peculiar indignities" to which the company had been subjected at various points in their sojourn. Though they may have often felt they were "rolling through an unfriendly world," he declared, borrowing a phrase from a spiritual in the Jubilees' repertoire, "I wish to say to them, that they are here surrounded by a cordon of Christian sympathies and respect.... I bless God for these scenes of Jubilee."[45]

Successful concerts continued throughout April, and on 2 May 1872, the Jubilee Singers said goodbye to their Northern friends and set out for home. Careful management had earned the company an additional $12,000 in less than two months. Their goal had been accomplished: Fisk's debts were under control and they were returning with the proposed $20,000 plus numerous gifts. A joyous welcome awaited them at Fisk. "They had gone forth weeping, but returned, bringing their sheaves with them.... Those who had scoffed at them when going forth, venerated them now," claimed Pike.[46] The company's astonishing success engendered intense pride in the Fisk family and the African-American community. Hope for a brighter future permeated the campus.

The Jubilee Singers remained at home for only one week before returning North to accept a personal invitation by Patrick Gilmore, the flamboyant bandmaster, to participate in his World's Peace Jubilee held in Boston's Coliseum.[47] The event was an immense affair touting a twenty-thousand-voice choir, two thousand instruments, and field artillery. The eighteen-day extravaganza, closing on 4 July 1872, attracted national and international attention and drew crowds as large as forty thousand.

Gilmore had scheduled the Jubilee Singers to appear in a rendition of "The Battle Hymn of the Republic." George White correctly forecast that the orchestra would play the selection in the key of E flat, a key that would pitch the melody extremely high for singers. "Hence, in order to be heard satisfactorily by the vast audience," recalled Ella Sheppard, the Jubilees had to "enunciate with perfect accuracy of pitch and purity of tone every word and every part of a word in a key three half steps higher than usual."[48] For several weeks, White would raise the pitch a little higher during their daily drills until his ensemble could sing the piece with ease.

Finally, the performance day arrived. The Hyers Sisters, two African-American singers from Sacramento, California, were to sing the first verses with the Jubilee Singers taking the final verse. Having established their reputation in an 1867 debut recital in their hometown, the Hyers Sisters had set off on a transcontinental tour in 1871, which included this appearance for Patrick Gilmore's extravaganza.[49] According to Ella Sheppard, the sisters failed to anticipate the key change and "found themselves obliged greatly to strain their voices and unable to sing their parts satisfactorily." The director had asked White's ensemble to join in on the chorus, but they chose instead to reserve all their energies for their solo moment. The Jubilee Singers entered on the third verse—"*He hath sounded forth the trumpet*"—their clear, distinct, powerful voices astounding the crowd: "The audience of forty thousand people was electrified. Men and women arose in their wild cheering, waving and throwing up handkerchiefs and hats. The twenty thousand musicians and singers behind us did likewise. One German raised his violincello and thwacked its back with the bow, crying 'Bravo, bravo!' and Strauss, the great composer, waved his violin excitedly. It was a triumph not to be forgotten."[50] Amid waving handkerchiefs and hats tossed high in the air, the crowd cheered and shouted, "The Jubilees! The Jubilees forever!"[51]

The success of this event symbolized the professional transformation of the Jubilee Singers. Ten months earlier, the fledgling company had set out with ambitious goals and labored under grueling circumstances with little chance for success. Now they stood alongside hundreds of fellow musicians and before thousands of appreciative fans. Whatever doubts the singers may have harbored about their musicality were laid to rest. They had rivaled some of the best performers in America and had risen to claim their title as first-class entertainers.

The end of the spring 1872 campaign marked an equally remarkable transformation in the troupe's business practices. Ten months earlier, White functioned as both musical director and business agent, scrambled to secure concert dates, and was sometimes reduced to begging for lodging and travel. Now the Jubilee Singers received multiple concert requests, which Pike and his field agents carefully screened, choosing only those invitations that would guarantee a sizeable profit. AMA sponsorship lent respectability to the fundraising venture and kept the troupe's progress before a wide audience. Pike supervised field agents to handle advance work, established sound business principles that jibed with the AMA's philosophy of Christian missions, and promoted a respectable, untarnished public image of the Jubilee Singers that would appeal to all audiences. The result of these efforts was that the company met its fundraising goal within a short concert season, thereby securing the future existence of Fisk University while bringing unexpected advertisement to the AMA and its work.

Pike's ability to enlist the patronage and participation of the prominent ministers within his wide network of clergy friends was largely responsible for the welcomed change. Their endorsements galvanized public interest, shaped positive public opinion, and as a result, elevated the company's popularity. Ministers helped reduce concert costs by eliminating venue charges, providing free hotel accommodations, assisting with promotion and marketing, and reducing transportation fees. Sale of merchandise developed by the AMA boosted the coffers while contributing to the troupe's popular appeal.

Pike applied his business expertise to every level of the company's operations, from how to handle promotion and marketing to establishing clear fiscal boundaries for accepting concert requests. Guiding his efforts was his dedication to the AMA's vision of Christian missions. Applying strong business principles to this new fundraising venture was his way of contributing to the association's work in freedmen's education. Therefore, Pike was determined to strike an appropriate balance between entertainment and Christian ministry, and thus raise money. His leadership brought results. Internally, the Jubilee Singers had evolved into a well-run business enterprise with effective marketing and promotional strategies. Externally, the troupe enjoyed the approval of the Christian community as partners in the AMA's missionary work in the South.

Convinced that White's ensemble was a God-given tool with which to win friends and gain support for their work, the AMA leadership began to look toward the future. In its September issue of the *American Missionary*, the association stressed the Jubilee Singers' spiritual beginning, emphasized its Christian ministry purpose, and set new goals:

> ...few except Mr. White and the singers felt certain in October last, when the little company started from the institution Northward, that the movement was in the line of God's purposes, and therefore designed to large success. It was not therefore possible definitely to settle methods and plans of work. It must be left to the development of God's providences to determine the length of time that the singers should remain in the field, and

to His blessing upon their labors as to the amount of money they should raise. They had volunteered for the concert season of one year, and it was thought that in this time the net sum of twenty thousand dollars ought to be raised. As has been announced, this sum was raised and stood to the credit of Fisk University the 1st of May 1872. Of course, this is but a small portion of the money required to erect the permanent buildings which are needed for the institution. The success of the past year has vindicated the confidence felt by Mr. White and the singers in their movement, as the instrumentality appointed of God to establish beyond question the permanency of Fisk University.... It has, therefore, been felt by the singers themselves, as well as by the trustees and faculty of the institution and the officers of the Association, that they should be continued in the field for at least another year, and it is hoped that they will be able to raise from fifty to sixty thousand dollars.[52]

The AMA used proceeds from the New England tour to eliminate Fisk University's debt and purchase a twenty-five acre tract for the institution's new site. Projected costs for Jubilee Hall were $50,000, funds AMA officials hoped would come from the new touring efforts of the Jubilee Singers.[53]

The association announced that Gustavus Pike would continue as the Jubilee Singers' business manager, commissioned to "reach with concerts or missionary meetings, the largest number of places practicable." They further assured their readers that the troupe would "sing the same music and represent the same interests." As the company had enjoyed remarkable success and "universal favor" in its New England tour, declared the AMA officers, the Jubilee Singers could begin this new campaign "confident that they are doing the work of the Master and that He will signally crown with his blessing their efforts in the future as He has in the past." No longer hesitant to link its name with the Jubilee Singers, the AMA leadership sanctioned the troupe as equal partners in the association's work. "We, therefore, commend the Jubilee Singers, the University they represent, and the educational interests of their race, especially as under the fostering care of the American Missionary Association, to the churches and to the public."[54]

Chapter 4

Broadening the Campaign Goals:

Africa, Affinity Groups, and Revival Services

> To establish permanently a University for the colored people of the South, to educate the teachers of their schools and the pastors of their churches, and thus to lift up the race in this country and to turn a tide of Christian civilization to the shores and into the heart of Africa, is the object of the Jubilee Singers, the purpose of Fisk University, and the grand aim of the American Missionary Association.[1]

With the Jubilee Singers' reputation well-established and sound business practices in place, the managers began considering ways of expanding the troupe's influence and fundraising potential. They took advantage of connections with other Christian ministries of which the American Missionary Association (AMA) approved—temperance and benevolent societies, the YMCA, revival movements, etc.—further sealing the ensemble's identity as a missionary endeavor working not only for the advancement of Fisk University, but also for the greater good of humanity. The Jubilee Singers found their participation with these various Christian charities and ministries to be mutually beneficial: their novelty and rising fame swelled attendance at these events, while their contribution to various causes enhanced the company's repute. Over time, the ensemble was known both for its acts of Christian service as well as its excellent musicianship.

As the managers looked to potential new audiences abroad, they redefined or developed fresh ministry goals for the company compatible with changing trends in the Christian community. For their European travels, they advanced the cause of African missions, which extended the company's purpose and gave the work of Fisk University, and consequently freedmen's education, new importance. The Jubilees also participated extensively with D. L. Moody's revival work throughout England and Scotland. These additional ministry activities demonstrate the extent to which the Jubilee Singers evolved from a musical ensemble raising funds for Fisk University to a professional troupe representing not only the AMA's work in freedmen's education, but also its broader ministry goals.

Preparing for the Second Campaign: May 1872–May 1873

White and his company spent summer 1872 in Acton, Massachusetts resting and rehearsing for a second campaign scheduled to begin in the fall. Anticipating increased public demand, he drafted new singers from Fisk and reorganized the troupe into two companies. Concerts throughout the fall, however, proved disappointing and White became increasingly convinced that there was little financial gain in keeping two companies afloat. For one thing, several private companies fashioned after the Jubilee Singers had sprung up and were a source of continual frustration to White. One called "The Canaan Jubilee Singers" merited his investigation. Rumor had it that the troupe claimed to be raising money to help endow higher education institutions not only for African Americans, but others in need of education. Neither their musicality nor their management impressed White. "They get what favor they do get because people think they are the Fisk J.S.," White reported. "I have no fear of their doing much but they ought to be prevented from humbugging the people if possible."[2]

Presidents of other black higher education institutions also took notice of the Jubilee Singers' immense success and some quickly began organizing their own choral groups modeled after the company. Hampton Institute's president, General Samuel Armstrong, secured Thomas P. Fenner to establish a music department. Within six months, he trained and launched the Hampton Singers, an ensemble that eventually claimed its own measure of respect for its renditions of spirituals. Following the Hampton Singers were groups from Tuskegee and Utica Institutes, helping to establish a strong choral tradition among black higher education institutions.[3]

These unexpected competitors threatened the financial success White and Pike hoped to achieve in the States. Therefore, at the suggestion of Henry Ward Beecher and other friends, the company cast its eyes toward

Europe for new territory in which to perform.[4] The English Christian community had long espoused antislavery and temperance causes and its current fascination with African missions mirrored the AMA's desires for the continent.[5] Moreover, the AMA had connections with several highly esteemed British clergymen, philanthropists, and missionary societies. Perhaps the time was ripe for the Jubilee Singers' appearance across the sea.

In January 1873, White disbanded the two small ensembles and reorganized one eleven-member group, which included seven members of the original company: Ella Sheppard, Maggie Porter, Jennie Jackson, Minnie Tate, Thomas Rutling, Isaac Dickerson, and Benjamin Holmes. Missing from the original group was Phebe Anderson, who had left the company soon after its start because of her father's impending death. Also absent were Eliza Walker and Greene Evans, both of whom had decided to give up "jubileeing" and remain in Nashville. Josephine Moore, pianist, and Henry Morgan participated in one of the two small companies White had commissioned during the autumn months of 1872, but their services were no longer needed once he scaled down the operation to feature just one company.[6]

The new additions to his reorganized company introduced four remarkable talents, one of whom was Georgia Gordon. White had invited the petite young woman to join the original group of 1871, but an altercation between the director and his headstrong soprano became so intense that he not only banned her from the group but also threatened to dismiss her from Fisk.[7] Appeals from other Fisk faculty members managed to keep Georgia in school, and by the second campaign, White had patched up his differences with the talented singer. She remained a Jubilee Singer throughout the rest of the company's seven historic years of tours.

Edmund Watkins, bass, came to Fisk University after a short stint at Talladega College. His name appears in the 1871–1872 university catalog as a student in the college preparatory division.[8] Julia Jackson, contralto, also entered Fisk in 1871 as a member of the normal school's first-year class.[9] She found such pleasure traveling as a Jubilee Singer that she once told Cravath, "As for my part I enjoy our practice hours so much that I imagine all the others feel the same way about them as I do."[10] The final new member of the company was a powerful young contralto White heard while the troupe was vacationing in Acton, Massachusetts. Mabel Lewis was studying voice at nearby Worcester and came to audition for the company at the insistence of her foster parents. Though she was not enrolled at Fisk, White was so taken by her ability to "balance one hundred and fifty girls" that he hired the robust singer on the spot.[11]

The second campaign marks the first time that salaries were awarded to the participants of the Jubilee Singers. Those who had labored in the first campaign had done so without pay. By 1873, newcomers to the company received $500 for ten months of work plus board and transportation.[12] An 1874 diary entry of Ella Sheppard's indicates that the AMA promised a $200 bonus if the company's net proceeds exceeded $25,000.[13] By 1876, salaries for the Jubilee Singers increased to a range of $700–$1000, depending on length of prior service with the company.[14] These were substantial salaries when compared to the average income of Fisk instructors and other AMA employees. In 1874, one female missionary teacher at Fisk earned the meager salary of $15 per month. By 1915, the average salary was slightly less than $780 per year and the head of what had then become Fisk's highly regarded music department earned only $622 annually. The AMA did not have a uniform pay scale, so salaries differed greatly between schools and positions. In 1876, G. Stanley Pope, the AMA employee who served as White's first advance agent, earned $1,500 per year but furnished his own house and board, while a female teacher at Talladega, also an AMA institution, received $120 plus room and board for her eight months of teaching.[15]

However, pecuniary gain, either to the individual singers or their managers, was never the aim of the AMA. Rather, participation in the Jubilee Singers enterprise was ultimately viewed as service to the association's overarching missionary cause. Contracts clearly stipulated that each member was "to do faithfully and conscientiously the work" that would further "the interests of Fisk University and the American Missionary Association." Doing the work of a Jubilee Singer meant taking on the mantle of a missionary, as the fourth clause of their contract specified: "It is further agreed that the Jubilee Singer's movement shall be conducted as a Christian Missionary enterprise, and that strict regard shall be had in all public duties and private conduct to the usefulness of the enterprise, to the American Missionary Association and Fisk University as *Christian Institutions*, and in general to the promotion of the interests of Christ's kingdom."[16] Though the demands of "jubileeing" were great, they paled in comparison to the vast needs remaining for the freedman, reasoned AMA officials. "Slavery was a crime whose expiation must be by suffering and self-denial," stated the association's April 1872 journal. Three stages marked the era: slavery, emancipation, and regeneration. This third stage, now upon them, required "Christian toil and self-denial."[17] White took this charge seriously and worked unceasingly for the cause. "Mr. White as usual is bent on advertising freedmen work and building up Fisk University," Pike informed Cravath in January 1873, "and will neither spare himself or family in furthering these objects."[18] White expected no less from his company of singers.

The Jubilee Singers spent spring 1873 giving successful farewell concerts throughout the North, which garnered another $20,000 for the AMA treasury. Anticipating an even greater success abroad, the managers began advance work for the company's arrival in London, gathering letters of introductions and testimonials from governors, leading religious divines, and other dignitaries. Mark Twain commented, "I heard them sing once, and I would walk seven miles to hear them sing again."[19] A glowing letter commending the Jubilee Singers' Christian work and business practices poured from the pen of Henry Ward Beecher:

> Their success has been wonderful. Already they have raised more than forty thousand dollars in America—all of which is put into buildings. Every brick thus is, as it were, a musical note. You may venture upon receiving this corps with the utmost confidence. The managers are men of good sense, integrity, and of devoted piety. We are not ashamed to send this band to our British brethren, and we are sure that their music will strike a chord which will vibrate long after their songs shall cease.[20]

The renowned Scottish novelist George MacDonald wrote a letter of introduction to the Reverend Henry Allon, the influential Congregational pastor of London's Union Chapel. "There is something inexpressibly touching in their wonderfully sweet round bell voices," he wrote. "I pity any one present who discovers that he has forgotten his handkerchief."[21]

Armed with flattering endorsements and anticipating a bright future, Pike and his assistant, Reverend James Powell, traveled a month ahead of the company to secure concerts. Meanwhile, the seasoned Jubilee Singers prepared for departure to England.

England and African Missions

"Considering the Missionary object of our Work, will you allow me to ask...if you will kindly give the following notice next Sabbath from your pulpit," read the opening to the advertisement Pike provided pastors.[22] He strongly felt that stressing the missionary aim of their work was critical to success in England. Pike was an ardent champion of African missions and believed that the Christian English society would enthusiastically embrace the Jubilee Singers if they felt the company was supportive of this cause. "I judge it would be hard to interest Englishmen in Freedmen for America's sake—or for the Freedmen's sake—but they will give for Africa," he told Cravath.[23]

England had outlawed the right to own slaves in 1807 and abolished the slave trade in 1834. In the following decades, a flurry of missionary activity sprang up as the British Christian community founded numerous societies to take the gospel to lands under imperial British rule. The adventures of the famed missionary explorer David Livingstone, published in 1857, thrust the "dark continent" of Africa into the limelight, capturing the imagination of all Englishmen. By the late 1800s, England was embroiled in an intense competition with France and Germany to acquire African land and thus extend the British Empire, as well as missionary activity aimed at Christianizing African people and transplanting its version of a moral, civilized society.[24]

Pike noted that the English gave approximately $300,000 per year for the "conversion of Africans," some of which came from the Freedmen's Aid Society of Great Britain, the English auxiliary to the AMA. This organization was led by the Right Honorable Earl of Shaftesbury, Anthony Ashley Cooper, the eldest son of the Sixth Earl of Shaftesbury, a man described by Pike as "the foremost philanthropist in the world" and a strong supporter of African missions.[25] British hearts would open to the Jubilee Singers, Pike reasoned, if only they could be shown the "intimate relations between the Christian education of the Freedmen and the evangelization of Africa." He insisted that the message of their campaign should be that they were raising money "for the education of Freedmen because they are *Africans,* and as such might become missionaries to Africa, or on the plea that there was greater hope of supplying missionaries for Africa from among the exslaves than otherwise." Such an idea would have popular appeal among the British, Pike argued.[26]

Cravath and the other executive secretaries agreed. Confident that the Jubilee Singers would "touch the British heart in a very soft place," the AMA sent their singing ambassadors off to conquer new lands. "The foundation of the Jubilee Hall has been laid with American greenbacks," stated the *Congregationalist.* "Let the superstructure be raised by English gold."[27]

The company left by steamer for England on 12 April 1873. The trip across the ocean was a novel experience for all of these young people. "The great floating house, our home for eleven long days," recalled Maggie Porter, "stands out alone in my first impressions of Ocean Steamer and the OCEAN." Despite instructions on how to manage an ocean voyage, most were dreadfully sick. Porter was ill for five days and marveled that she lived to tell about it. "I can see the young girls of the company now as they must have looked to our fellow-passengers," she later wrote, "each one wearing a calico wrapper with head bound up in long woolen scarfs [sic], creeping cautiously to her deck chair, prepared to be sick. Of course we were sick!"[28]

While the individual singers battled sea sickness, the managers wrestled with the question of what would be the most appropriate and effective strategy for raising money in England. Most of their British clergy friends suggested giving free concerts and taking a collection at the end, but the singers' experiences in America had shown that this approach often yielded large and appreciative audiences but little profit. A second option was to give concerts with an admission charge in public halls exclusively, but Pike felt they needed the assistance of influential clergy to succeed in England, and like their American counterparts, many within the British religious community also considered concert attendance a base form of entertainment. All things considered, Pike determined that success for the Jubilee Singers would rest on three things: concerts "on neutral grounds" to avoid denominational rivalry, admission fees substantial enough to turn a profit, and cooperation of the entire religious community. They would especially need the support and liberal giving of those whose personal theologies were aligned with the AMA cause.[29]

London Premier: Lord Shaftesbury and the Freedmen's Aid Society

Good fortune greeted the company from the moment they arrived on English soil, helped in part by letters of introduction that had opened the way for the company's advance agents to call upon the Earl of Shaftesbury prior to their arrival. Born in 1801, Shaftesbury was a tall, stately gentleman of extreme aristocratic bearing, who by his own admission was prone to melancholy and hypersensitivity. He had spent the previous thirty years of his life as a champion of the poor and underprivileged members of British society, lending his influence to numerous societies working for these causes. The Refugees, Bands of Hope, the Society for the Prevention of Cruelty to Animals, the YMCA, and various Sunday Rest Societies, Shoe-black Brigades, Ragged Schools, and Bible societies comprise just a partial list of benevolence agencies that benefitted from his support. Shaftesbury considered himself an Anglican evangelical and brought a decidedly religious zeal to his efforts to conquer injustice, chairing countless meetings and delivering literally hundreds of speeches with a brilliance that revealed his inner passion. "I cannot speak unless on conviction...I can say nothing but what I feel," Shaftesbury wrote, "and my feelings frequently get the better of me."[30]

Shaftesbury was over seventy years of age when he met the Jubilee Singers for the first time and was by then a well-recognized and respected voice in all levels of British society. When Pike asked if he would sponsor the Jubilee Singers' first concert in England, he gladly agreed to host a private concert in London's Willis's Rooms, St. James, on 6 May 1873. The auspicious occasion served as a "fine introduction to the English public," noted *The Christian World*.[31] The Reverend Dr. Healy, corresponding secretary of the Freedmen's Aid Society, later remarked that success would have been doubtful without Shaftesbury and the organization's endorsement, "and in this I feel this Society has done no little service."[32]

Launching the Jubilee Singers under the auspices of Shaftesbury and the Freedmen's Aid Society immediately set the religious tone of their work and made a clear connection to the shared vision of African missions. "It should be remembered that this movement is emphatically a religious one, being promoted by the American Missionary Association," one newspaper told its readers. "Special attention is given at the 'University' to the training of missionaries, and who shall say that it may not lead in the end to the evangelization of Africa."[33]

Pike was extremely pleased that so many of England's religious elite and social dignitaries attended the inaugural performance. "The more I understood the methods of the English," he later recalled, "the more I came to appreciate the vast importance of securing the patronage of the pious nobility in furthering a benevolent enterprise." Writing to Cravath, Pike positively reported, "I do think a good deal can be done over here if the field is well worked."[34]

The Duke and Duchess of Argyll were present at the company's inaugural London concert and requested that the company visit them at their private residence. The Jubilee Singers traveled to Argyll Lodge the following day. To their surprise, the duke announced he had invited Queen Victoria and expected her arrival any moment. Ella Sheppard recalled the awkwardness of their first encounter with royalty:

> A messenger beckoned us to follow him. We were led in haste into a spacious drawing-room, elegantly furnished (all over, it seemed), and left alone for a few moments. We quietly stood gazing upon the exquisite objects all about us, occasionally exchanging a nod or whisper of admiration, until we discovered at the other end of the room, some distance off, a stout, ruddy-faced lady sitting, simply dressed in black, and at her feet sat a young girl simply attired. We bowed slightly as we would to any stranger, and became silent, thinking it odd that they should sit in the middle of the room. A moment later, and a slight noise beyond the lady caused us to look again that way. The Duke of Argyle, the impersonation of dignity and astonishment, had entered, looking as though he wondered that the floor had not swallowed us; but before we could realize the cause, he had advanced, and, bowing extremely low, addressed the lady as "Your Majesty!" and began introducing us. Some of us, at least, had always thought of Queen Victory as young and beautiful, clothed in royal robes, crowned, and with scepter in hand. That matronly looking lady, dressed like ordinary mortals, Queen Victoria! contradicted our conception of a queen. Our faces must have reflected something of this astonishment, and a sense of the ludicrous must have struck Her Majesty and us simultaneously, for ripple

after ripple flitted across her flushed motherly face and ours, and she and we, for a moment, were convulsed with laughter.[35]

Their appearance before Queen Victoria did not escape the notice of the British press. "It is remarkable that this company of negro singers should have vaulted at once to the highest circles in the land."[36] Pike later described this unexpected performance as evidence of God's blessing: "We had embarked on an untried career, upon a foreign shore; we had sped our way, borne on the bosom of ten thousand prayers, and resting on the arms of sympathy and of great love. The gates had been opened, and obstacles removed, with the same power by which the 'walls of Jericho fell down.'" To him, the Jubilee Singers had entered the "land of promise" and now needed only to "wait on the Lord, and to be of good courage."[37]

Grassroots Efforts

Pike also knew success in London would depend heavily on what happened at the grassroots level and therefore sought the support of a couple of England's leading ministers: Dr. Henry Allon, pastor of London's Union Chapel; and the Reverend Newman Hall, the Congregational minister of Surrey Chapel. Both offered to host paid concerts in their facilities, an unusual practice for British clergy, thus setting a precedent for other ministers to follow. When Charles Haddon Spurgeon, renowned pastor of the Metropolitan Tabernacle, agreed to have the singers participate in one of his evening services, their acceptance into the religious community was complete. Spurgeon offered the tabernacle for a concert a few nights later and four thousand people arrived within ten minutes of the doors opening. "The whole concert was a succession of triumphs," recalled Pike.[38]

Requests for the Jubilee Singers began in earnest. The introduction by the Freedmen's Aid Society "furnished a very suitable background" for the company's launch, noted W. E. Shipton, Secretary of the City of London YMCA.[39] The Reverend Dr. Healy, corresponding secretary for the Freedmen's Aid Society, agreed. Relationship with this noble missionary society "at once placed them upon high vantage ground," he told Cravath. "If they fail in their noble enterprise, it will not be attributable to British coldness."[40] Ministers wrote to offer their churches free of charge or use their influence to gain access to a public hall, "gas included," and pledged their influence to "stir up Christian friends to go and support them."[41] However, according to Pike, their British friends were shocked to learn that he hoped to earn at least £100 per night. They informed him that no benevolence agency had ever raised that kind of money in England. Individuals or patrons who sponsored concert series never expected to make much more than expenses. Admittedly, "star singers" earned a living by their craft and "low minstrel companies" made money by catering to the "vulgar tastes of people," Pike explained, but no musical ensemble of pious mission had earned as much profit as he anticipated. He and White hoped their efforts in England would not be in vain.[42]

Meanwhile, Reverend Allon arranged for the troupe to perform at the Congregational Union's annual dinner, an event that hosted over six hundred of Britain's leading Congregational ministers. Similar to the company's experience at Oberlin at the start of the first campaign, this appearance before such a gathering of ministers led to many promises of cooperation. "The applause was so hearty," Pike later wrote, "I fear the brethren might think me discourteous if I should make known to the public how enthusiastic it was."[43] The assembled clergy responded so fervently that near pandemonium ensued:

> The venerable body of divines forgot their dignity, swung their hats, waved their handkerchiefs, and in some cases caught up the plates from the table (for it was just after dinner) and shook them with screaming accompaniments, in the air.... "Take up a contribution, take up a contribution—pass around the hat," were shouts that came from all parts of the house. Such a scene of confusion is seldom witnessed.... It was only after a vigorous pounding of the table and repeated assurances from the authorized chairman, that a collection would be taken that order was restored.[44]

They received an equally animated reception a few days later when they performed at the annual meeting of the Freedmen's Aid Society. The Jubilee Singers' appearance had been well advertised and crowds thronged the hall long before the scheduled meeting time. When the company rose and sang "John Brown's Body," the audience could contain its enthusiasm no longer and responded with a thunderous ovation, throwing handkerchiefs and hats into the air. "And thus," reported one newspaper on the event, "closed one of the most successful gatherings of the year."[45]

England's National Temperance League also sought the Jubilee Singers' assistance in its work. Since its inception, the AMA had claimed to be an anti-slavery, anti-caste, anti-rum, anti-tobacco organization. At any social event the Jubilee Singers attended, reported Ella Sheppard, the managers made sure the hosts understood that their "glasses must be turned down."[46] The National Temperance League, learning that the singers were "thorough teetotalers," considered them as allies in its cause and eagerly hoped to enlist their assistance. Pike willingly accepted the invitation for the company to perform at the league's annual soiree. "Every hole and corner was crammed," noted the press:

> ...and even the domestics left the kitchen and the scullery when the magnificent Jubilee voices of the singers were heard echoing through the hall. It is rarely waiters display an interest in what is going on around them. On Monday even they relaxed, and in spite of starched cravat and rigid collar, were heard to say the singing was beautiful.... Every eye, upstairs and down, was turned in one direction. Every ear was strained to catch the liquid melody that now came hushed and gentle as the soft sigh of a summer night, and anon thundered along clear and loud as a clarion call to victory and joy.[47]

When the sponsors announced that the singers were "water drinkers," the crowd's excitement rose and would not abate until a "collection was improvised on the spot."[48] In addition to the offering, the league arranged for free use of the Crystal Palace's opera house for a concert and handled the entire advertisement for the event.[49]

Although the Jubilees' appearances at religious annual meetings had favorably launched the company into the British Christian community, the troupe still had too few paid concerts to meet its fundraising goals. From May to August 1873, social engagements filled the singers' schedule but there were barely enough concert dates to meet expenses, which were significantly greater in London than in New York. Many residents left the city during the hot summer season, thus making an earnest fundraising effort impractical. "The demand for Singers is great but we cannot more than make expenses by singing twice a week," Pike wrote, and informed Cravath not to expect "money from England before October."[50] He knew that making the enterprise profitable required "consecrated economic hard work," which meant almost nightly concerts and little time for rest. "The papers and pictures are 'sowing the seed,'" said Pike, but "it is only 'hearing that is believing' in this Jubilee Singing business." Pike felt he must somehow endear the company to the wider public in order to gain momentum for the enterprise. In September, England's "concert season," they would commence a full-scale effort, he informed Cravath.[51]

An important change in the troupe's advertisements occurred during this time. Early in the company's tenure, White had referred to his students' performances as "praise services" in an attempt to set a religious tone for their work. Pike called the Jubilee Singers' appearances "Missionary Association Meetings" during which the ensemble conducted a "service of song," employing a label widely used for religious meetings primarily comprised of singing that sprang up in the evangelical fervor of the mid-1800s.[52] American press reviews, however, interchanged the terms "concert" or "entertainment" in their descriptions of the Jubilees' performances.[53] When the troupe traveled to England in 1873, Pike provided prospective hosts with a sample press release clearly stating that the Jubilee Singers would give a "Service of Song." Many British newspapers adopted this description, a label that extended the scope of the singers' work beyond musical performance to clearly imply religious activity.[54]

The Jubilees' performance schedule changed dramatically beginning in August 1873. "Mr. White is hopeful and says he will sing five times a week next month," wrote Pike. "There is money to be made and no mistake over here if one can only command the situation."[55] In addition to church services and paid concerts, the Jubilee Singers appeared at breakfasts for the poor, Sunday schools, hospitals, orphanages, prisons, and private bedsides of the sick and invalid. Their support of worthy causes, while not earning money directly, gained them favorable press attention and increased their celebrity, thus endearing them to the public and subsequently improving audience attendance.[56] "They have gone in and out of the churches, Sunday-schools, and mission rooms singing for Jesus," later reported the Reverend H. T. Robjohns of Newcastle. "Such service to souls and Christ have opened wide the people's hearts and the Jubilees have just walked straight in, to be there enshrined for evermore."[57]

Though they enjoyed the favor of the religious community and the general public, Pike felt he must also capture the attention of the wealthy who could afford the higher ticket prices he wanted to charge. He became convinced of this when he received a letter from W. E. Shipton of the YMCA discussing the matter:

> I will be very frank in telling you what I think on this subject. Your friends are chiefly connected with one section of the community—Chapels, School-rooms, and such like places have been open to you, and you have also taken your chance with the general public at the places which you have hired; but you have hardly yet had an opportunity of laying hold of the upper Middle Class—the people who have most to give, and whose influence, drawn into your region, would be most influential. These persons are represented chiefly on our Platform, and in the better places of our lecture Hall, and I hoped…that by your acceptance of my proposition, these persons might be added to the list of your sympathizers, and that so a way should be opened for Concerts or gatherings in regions which you have not yet touched.[58]

The advance work done by ministers preceding their concert in Sunderland assured Pike that Shipton was right. Their hosts arranged for Mr. J. Candlish, a member of Parliament, to preside as chair and successfully persuaded various leading clergymen to allow their names to appear as patrons on advertisements. "This gave a dignity to the movement," declared Pike, "besides making an impression that it was an affair of the better class of people."[59] Victoria Hall was completely filled, "every hole and corner being crammed, and hundreds having to go away owing to the closing of the doors."[60]

This positive result persuaded Pike that he now had a fundraising template for the Jubilee Singers' overseas operations: participation in worthy causes to win recognition, cooperation of reputable ministers to "harvest the field," patronage by Britain's elite to gain prestige, and adequate admission fees to turn a profit. In developing fundraising and promotional strategies, he and White grappled with tensions that inevitably arise between issues of Christian ministry and fundraising methodology. Within the first few months of the British campaign, the managers had settled upon a fundraising formula that was both productive and consistent with AMA values. Isaac Dickerson's letter home to the AMA main office summed up the end to which all their activities led: "Tell them we are 'Singing for Jesus' trying to serve him where ever we go."[61]

Participation with D. L. Moody

Along with the arrival of the Jubilee Singers to British soil in fall 1873 came the revival team of Moody and Sankey. Dwight L. Moody, a former shoe salesman turned evangelist, had first visited England in 1867. The short visit profoundly impacted the young preacher. He visited YMCA facilities, Sunday schools, prayer meetings, and worship services throughout England, Scotland, and Ireland in a mere four months, delivering sermons with a blunt disregard for British propriety that both shocked and delighted audiences. During this visit, Moody often attended services conducted by his spiritual idol, Charles Haddon Spurgeon, whose preaching had a marked influence on him. Between his first visit and 7 June 1873, the day he returned to England with his singing partner Ira Sankey, Moody underwent an intense period of spiritual growth. Close associates remarked that a "divine energy" and a "Spirit-led" purposefulness now characterized D. L. Moody's ministry.[62]

The story of this revival team's introduction to England has a similar ring to that of the Jubilee Singers. Small audiences attended the Moody revival services until the respected, dignified Baptist pastor, F. B. Meyer, warmly commended the team and helped "break the ice" among clergy. Almost immediately, doors opened to these relatively obscure Americans.[63] Successful revival meetings in York led to an invitation to preach in Sunderland, and then in Newcastle where Moody met the Jubilee Singers for the first time.

According to Pike, Moody's revival services "helped pave the way" for the Jubilee Singers, but both may have mutually benefited from each other's presence in England.[64] London's welcome of the Jubilee Singers in May 1873 prior to Moody's arrival may have helped prepare British audiences for the new style of singing that Ira Sankey's gospel songs presented. The Jubilee Singers also entered Scotland a full two months prior to the Moody and Sankey team, giving Scots a taste of informal religious music from America. Most Scottish churches adhered to Puritan forms of worship that considered music an unneeded adornment. Congregational singing, the use of the Psalter, and rare use of the organ (if used at all) defined most worship services. Generally, Scottish churches eschewed choral singing as mechanical and too secular for church. That these congregations would warmly embrace either the Jubilee Singers or the Moody/Sankey revival team was rather remarkable.

Historian Lyle Dorsett relates a prophecy by a well-known and respected Scotsman named R. S. Candlish given shortly before his death and right before the arrival of both Moody and the Jubilee Singers. The old saint said that Scotland was about to experience "a great blessing" from God that the people should be careful to receive. He warned, though, that it would come "in a strange fashion."[65] The prophecy could have easily applied to either Moody or the Jubilee Singers as both groups held services that were far from traditional. Uneducated and untrained, Moody preached plainly, utilizing his uncanny gift for storytelling. In a natural, unaffected manner, he called all people regardless of station in life to dedication to Christ:

> He had learned to preach simply, —let us rather say he had not learned to preach otherwise; and in the unaffected language of nature, uncorrupted by the fastidious culture of the schools, he spoke face to face with men; and they heard him. Sprightly and vivacious, with a touch of humor as well as pathos, direct and pointed in his appeals, urging to an immediate decision, and feeling his dependence of the Spirit of God, he compelled all classes to acknowledge that he was a man of power.[66]

His partner, Ira Sankey, was famous for his passionate delivery of gospel tunes, often accompanied by a harmonium. The catchy and memorable melodies of the gospel songs were a strong contrast to the formal hymns of the church and appealed to the masses. Many left a Moody service humming phrases from Sankey's simple songs under their breath.[67]

The Jubilee Singers were equally novel, both in appearance and musical style. The simplicity of the spiritual's language with its repetitive phrases also made the words and tunes easy for listeners to recall. It is also likely that the earnest, emotional delivery that characterized the Jubilee Singers' performances prepared audiences for the deep feeling Sankey brought to his solos. Both groups helped convince the Christian community, especially in Scotland, that the gospel could be conveyed through the medium of music.

For their part, the Jubilee Singers benefited from the revival fire simmering in England and Scotland that Moody's preaching helped flame. News about Moody's unusual revivals spread quickly across parts of Northern England where the Jubilee Singers had yet to appear. It seemed that people were spiritually ready for something different; the arrival of both the Jubilee Singers and D. L. Moody was timely. The stateliness and formality of church worship services seemed dull in comparison to either a Jubilee Singers concert or a Moody revival service. "The Christian community," observed Dorsett, "was ripe for new soul-stirring music that spoke to the hearts of that generation."[68]

The Reverend H. T. Robjohns arranged for the singers to perform in one of Moody's meetings in Newcastle, the town where the revivalist's work had its first substantial response. When Moody first heard "Steal Away to Jesus," said Pike, the Jubilee Singers "stole his heart and led him at once to appreciate the power of their music for good."[69] The troupe members were equally impressed with Moody's humility and unpretentiousness. Jubilee Singer Mabel Lewis spoke of the easy, unassuming way in which he approached his audiences: "Mr. Moody came in as [if] unconcerned, took off his coat and said, 'Friends, I have some good news to tell you. Do you know that Christ died for you?' There were such hard-looking faces, but before he got through you could see them soften. You could see that they felt it."[70] Moody's earnest preaching affected Lewis spiritually as well. Reared a Catholic, she was converted during the Jubilee Singers' participation in these services.

The Newcastle meetings were the first time the Jubilee Singers shared the platform with D. L. Moody, but not the last. After Newcastle, both teams parted ways, later joining in Edinburgh for a series of December meetings. The Jubilees sometimes sang as many as six times a day to crowds so large that many "were obliged to leave for want of accommodation."[71] The AMA gladly relayed the details of the Jubilee Singers' association with the Moody revivals to its readership, saying "this has been a spiritual benefit to the Singers themselves, and a means of usefulness to others."[72]

The Jubilees once happened upon one of Moody's revival services and decided to attend unannounced. Arriving late, they found seats in the packed audience in the upper gallery. At the close of the prayer time, they began to sing spontaneously: "There are angels hovering round / To carry the tidings home." "The effect was wonderful and most impressive," thought Ella Sheppard. It seemed almost as if angels had descended upon the service. The Reverend Robjohns agreed: "It was like a snatch of angelic song heard from the upper air as a band of celestials passed swiftly on an errand of mercy."[73]

According to one observer, the presence of the Jubilee Singers and the Moody/Sankey revival team in Scotland left a lasting impression on that country's Christian community in two important ways:

> It would seem, from the reports lately received from Scotland, that the movement for improved congregational singing has derived a mighty impetus from the contemporaneous visits of the Jubilee Singers and Mr. Sankey.... Fortunately, the transatlantic visitors who have so wonderfully stirred the heart of Scotland have at the same time impressed the Scotch mind with the conviction of the eminent use of music for the holiest purposes, and a well-informed writer, noting the quick work that has been made of national prejudices as to hymn singing and the use of an accompaniment, expects henceforth to find church choirs much more numerous, better trained, and more full of devout feeling than formerly. The same witness also notes that a lesson has been learned as to public prayer from the recent revival services, which have shown how much more specific it ought to be.... These two reforms in the important matters of praise and prayer would suffice to show that the visit of the American Evangelists to Scotland is destined to make an abiding and most salutary effect on that country...[74]

Between the Jubilee Singers' concert appearances and Moody's revival services, every major city in Scotland came under the influence of these "transatlantic visitors." Literally thousands of Scots turned out to hear the Jubilee Singers and the heartfelt preaching of D. L. Moody.

Effective Ambassadors of the AMA

On 31 March 1874, Pike and White brought the extraordinarily successful Great Britain campaign to an official close with a farewell concert at London's Exeter Hall. Night after night, the Jubilees had given their "service of song" in churches and halls throughout England and Scotland. In addition, they appeared at the annual meetings of such religious associations as the Freedmen's Aid Society and the National Temperance League, spoke often at Sunday schools or prayer meetings, and participated frequently in the Moody and Sankey revival services. While some criticized the appropriateness of their religious music, few questioned the cause or dedicated missionary service of this band of songsters. Pike and White had successfully sealed the reputation of the Jubilee Singers as ambassadors of the AMA. "They represent in general the interests of the great work of the American Missionary Association among the Freedmen, and are in themselves an illustration of the value of emancipation, and the subsequent efforts to elevate the emancipated," read a prepared statement.[75]

A speech given by one of the Jubilee Singers during the farewell concert clearly illustrates how the company had maintained its commitment to advancing freedmen's education and the overarching ministry goals of the AMA:

> You have nobly responded to our appeal for £6,000 and have given us £10,000, and we feel sure that the foundation of Jubilee Hall, which was laid last spring with American greenbacks, will be capped with British gold. (Laughter and cheers).We hope in that University a noble work will be accomplished. We hope that we who live in the Southern States of America will be able to prove to you that we are worthy of the liberty which, through the influence of good people, and by the blessing of God, we now enjoy. (Cheers). We hope that men and women will be educated there who shall go to Africa—that country which has so long been in bondage and sin—and carry the glad tidings, and tell Africa that there is a God for them. We ask you, as we leave you, that you will remember us in your sympathies and prayers to God, that we may be successful in the work which we have undertaken. By the assistance of the good people of England and America, and by our own efforts, we hope by the blessing of God to get, before many years, even Africa to praise God and serve him as you do. (Applause).[76]

The message was clear: every dollar given to the Jubilee Singers in support of Fisk University was an investment in the evangelization of Africa.

At the close of the concert, Lord Shaftesbury, their loyal friend and patron who had introduced them to British society, rose to offer his commendation of the Jubilee Singers' work:

> Did you observe these people singing to you the songs of their captivity that the prayer came from their hearts to God to keep them "from sinking down"? He has not only kept them from sinking down, but raised them in his mercy; and now they stand before you fit to compete with the very best of all the human race. (Cheers.) There is a noble self-denial and patriotism

exhibited by these young people who were recently groveling in slavery unfit to be accounted members of the human race. See how the moment the pressure was removed they have come forth and have been the means not only of exalting themselves but all their brethren who have been so long trodden down in the lowest depths of human misery.

Shaftesbury pledged the "affection and respect" of all of England to the young Jubilee Singers and offered them a blessing. To the audience, he announced: "They come before you and ask your sympathy, you give it, and England and America are united on behalf of the down-trodden and afflicted members of the African race." Amid cheers and applause, he shook the hands of each Jubilee Singer as they departed the stage.[77]

Return to Revival Work: May 1875

In spring 1875, White suggested that the AMA commence the company's third campaign by rejoining the Moody and Sankey revival team in London: "Moody and Sankey are to be in London April, May & June. If the Singers reach London in time to work somewhat in co-operation with them, we can greatly aid them in their meetings and they can benefit us. The Jubilee Singing fits in nicely in the wake of their meetings. I don't mention that as making merchandise out of Revival meetings, but in *doing good* we get good, and it is worthy of thought in our plans."[78] White's suggestion appealed to the AMA leadership, who began attending to the details.[79]

The Jubilees returned to London in May 1875 for their final European campaign, arriving just in time to appear at the annual meeting of the Freedmen's Mission Aid Society. According to Ella Sheppard, the company received an invitation from Moody to participate in his afternoon service at the Haymarket Opera House less than an hour after their arrival. Moody and Sankey were in the closing months of their revival campaign and gladly welcomed the aid of the Jubilee Singers. "It seemed our duty to turn aside from concerts to help win souls," wrote Ella Sheppard. Newcomer Jubilee Singer Frederick J. Loudin agreed with her assessment, announcing to one crowd that the singers' decision to participate in Moody's revival meetings in deference to their regular mission "was prompted by a sole desire to aid in the good work of saving souls."[80]

For the next month, the company sang daily to audiences of ten or twelve thousand at the revival meetings held in London's East End.[81] "Oh such a mass of beings," noted Ella Sheppard, "10,000 and more gathered to learn of Jesus." A fifteen-year-old girl who had been converted in one of the meetings stopped Sheppard in the street to tell her how the Jubilees' songs had inspired her soul. "Oh what couldn't the Jubilee Singers do if they were only in the spirit to do it," Sheppard reflected. "We are surely being led by a divine hand."[82]

Whether conversions happened because of the singing or the preaching was difficult for Ella Sheppard to tell. "One man…said that he went to hear the preaching, but the singing had saved his soul," she related.[83] It seemed to Sheppard that Reverend W. Hay Aitken, one of the local ministers who preached at several of these services, was intimidated by the possibility that the Jubilees' singing was drawing more people than his preaching. Rather than relying on their managers to decide what songs best fit the sermon text, Reverend Aitken insisted upon choosing their repertory himself. "[He] has seemed afraid and jealous of us from the evident fact that it is our *singing* which brings the people in such numbers, not the gospel—well this seems true for until we came the hall had not ever been more than a fourth full since Mr. M & S [Moody and Sankey] left. This fact seems to irritate him exceedingly."[84] Crowds came by the thousands and the overflow so filled the streets that the Jubilees found it almost impossible to make their way into the hall. "Such a sight!" wrote Sheppard in her diary. "No doubt they said to their own hearts that they were going to 'hear the Singers' but I earnestly believe it was the *gospel truth* their souls really sought. Anyway— thank God—they did hear the gospel and in a way both by preaching and singing."[85]

The singers' sacrificial assistance in the Moody revival meetings did not escape the attention of the press. The AMA printed several newspaper excerpts in its September issue, including the following: "The way in which these American (or African?) friends have stuck to their posts at Bow-road Hall is beyond all praise, though we feel assured they seek not the praise of men, but the glory of God, in the redemption of their fellows. Still, we hope their generous devotion will not be forgotten when they follow anew the more immediate object of their mission."[86] According to Marsh, "nothing could have better prepared the way for their special work, nothing could have better prepared them for it, than these revival labors." As most of the religious publications carried reports of their participation in the London revivals, the "great Christian heart of England" opened gladly to receive the Jubilee Singers, boosting attendance at their subsequent concerts.[87]

Moody closed his London revivals with a service at the conference hall at Mildmay Park on 12 July 1875. A few days later, he sent his thanks to White and the company for the "valuable help in the evangelistic work" they had freely given. "Night after night they have sung the gospel at the Bow-road Hall, at the East-end, to tens of thousands...and much blessing has been the result."[88] Moody gave an autographed Bagster's Bible bound in Russian leather to each Jubilee Singer, a gift that held special spiritual meaning for Ella Sheppard: "I prize it greatly for many reasons—one because *he* gave them which makes it worth its weight in gold—for this gift will ever call up thousands of such glorious and beautiful associations—such associations as lift one away from earth right up to the Master."[89] Moody encouraged the company in its Christian endeavors, saying he believed there was "no better way of evangelizing a nation than through its own sons, who have been brought to Christ." Fisk University's efforts to uplift the "long downtrodden African race" would no doubt result in future missionaries being sent to Africa as "heralds of the cross." He therefore advised White to "keep prominently before the public that the singers are missionaries" in order to help raise funds.[90]

Pike needed no reminding. During his entire tenure as business manager, he constantly strived to keep the Jubilees' missionary identity at the forefront of public consciousness. His tireless efforts had produced results. By 1875, the Jubilee Singers enterprise had evolved into a well-run operation. It enjoyed a wide reputation for musical excellence and a solid public image as a company of missionary workers dedicated to the AMA's overarching Christian Reconstruction goals: freedmen's education, evangelism, social change, and missions.

Livingstone Missionary Hall

The evangelization of Africa remained central to the Jubilee Singers' stated mission throughout the troupe's tenure. Their final campaign to Great Britain in 1875 included many repeat appearances in those towns where they had enjoyed prior success. The handbills advertising their return assured supporters of the continued quality of their concerts and firm commitment to missions:

> While five of the old Singers have felt obliged, for varying personal reasons, to retire, these vacancies have been happily filled, and the Company has suffered no loss of strength or distinctive character. They expect to give better concerts than ever before; they hope to make them well worth all they shall cost those who attend them. And their ardent desire is that these little sums, so small singly as to be scarcely felt by those who pay them, may be so large in the aggregate as to make Fisk University not only a great power in the education and elevation of their own people in America, but, through their missionary labours, in the final evangelization of Africa and the islands of the sea.

The handbill also included an excerpt from Lord Shaftesbury's welcome given prior to the singers' performance at the annual meeting of the Freedmen's Aid Society. He commended their "holy cause" on behalf of their race in America and their efforts to "send missionaries of their own color to the nations spread over Africa." [91]

While the Jubilee Singers crisscrossed Great Britain raising money, construction was underway on Jubilee Hall. It was finally completed and dedicated on 1 January 1876 as an instructional and residential facility. Now, the AMA leadership had an opportunity to place before the public a new construction project—Livingstone Missionary Hall—to be erected with subscription funds in the sum of £10,000 solicited by the Jubilee Singers. [92] The idea of a companion building on the Fisk campus devoted to missionary training appealed to British sympathies. "The project of erecting Livingstone Missionary Hall, to be dedicated to the training of Missionaries to follow up the work of the great explorer, has been received with much favour by the friends of this work in Great Britain," stated one British daily, "and upwards of one hundred shares—one thousand pounds—have already been subscribed." [93] On both sides of the ocean, newspaper reports hailed the Jubilee Singers for having "turned the eyes of the Christian world to Fisk University as the source of supply for both missionaries for Central Africa and teachers of the Southern States. Indeed, in the work of elevating the coloured people of America, and of Christianizing the millions of Africa, Fisk University promises to play an important part." [94] General Fisk, present at the singers' concert in Banbury, informed the audience that "everyone who contributed £10 became one of the founders of the Livingstone Missionary Hall, and their names would be enrolled and preserved in the records of the University." Each donor would help further the grand work Livingstone had begun.[95]

Fisk University's commitment to African missions was tangibly realized when four of its students pledged their lives to missionary service at the AMA's Mendi Mission in Sierra Leone: Albert P. Miller, Andrew E. Jackson, and their two brides, one of whom was the former Jubilee Singer Ella Hildridge. These Fiskites were the first African Americans in a long line of white missionaries the AMA had sent to the continent. The Jubilees sent a warm letter of blessing to the four: "We have prayed and labored long for this day, and now, thank God, our prayers are being answered.... You are our first band of missionaries at the outpost of the American Missionary Association in the land of our forefathers. May the light of God so shine in your hearts that its reflected rays shall be a balm to those who may come to you, to be healed and taught of God."[96] Sixteen had already lost their lives while serving in Africa, but this fact did not deter Miller. Recognizing the physical dangers, he nonetheless declared that "we are not too busy ourselves so much about the *falling*, but we are to see about the *standing*, at the post of duty, only waiting till He calls."[97]

From the time the Jubilee Singers returned to Great Britain in 1875 until their last concert on German soil in 1878, the managers kept the troupe's commitment to African missions at the forefront of their public image. The cause was as much appreciated by German audiences as it had been by British ones. "God is preparing among these four million blacks to carve out his instrument in order to lead the people of Africa so that his kingdom will come for and through them," declared one daily.[98] Another German reviewer lauded the Jubilees for using their songs as a victorious tool with which to conquer foreign lands. Using phrases popularized by David Livingstone, the reviewer praised the singers for remembering the "homeland of their fathers" and working sacrificially to "take the 'Good News' to the people 'of the dark hearts.'"[99]

Ambassadors of Christian Reconstruction

When the AMA assumed sponsorship of the Jubilee Singers enterprise in 1872, it proclaimed unabashedly that the musical troupe was dedicated to "doing the work of the Master."[100] This was a commission the managers took seriously and impressed upon the members of the Jubilee Singers. Every concert, church service, religious meeting, and even social event was conceived within the broader context of ministry. As a result, they successfully cast Fisk University as a quality higher education institution committed to the Christian Reconstruction goals of elevating, educating, and evangelizing former slaves who would, in turn, help transform the world for the better.

The men and women who were first students at Fisk University prior to joining the Jubilees had been taught to view the world through Christian lenses. Those who had never enrolled at Fisk quickly learned that this perspective permeated every aspect of the concert campaigns. As Jubilee Singers, company members were expected to give practical expression to the AMA's evangelical Christian ideals. Though not all company members shared an equal passion for missionary service, they all certainly understood the Christian circles in which they operated, the religious jargon that defined and interpreted their actions, and the evangelical theology that flavored their work.[101]

The AMA's gospel message of spiritual renewal had always been coupled with an outward expression of social reform. Supporting the ministry aims of the AMA, therefore, was not difficult for the individual members of the Jubilee Singers as the association's work blurred the distinctions between Christian evangelicalism and social activism. If carefully balanced, ministry could coexist with entertainment; political and social concerns rested alongside religious ones. For the young men and women who comprised the Jubilee Singers, representing the Christian Reconstruction goals of the AMA translated into actions that not only helped others, but offered empowerment to themselves and their race as well.

Chapter 5

Artistry and Refinement:

Gaining Public Acclaim

Their artistic accomplishments do away with the assumption that Negroes are not capable of any culture.[1]

The public spotlight cast upon White's musical ensemble gave Fisk University and the American Missionary Association (AMA) international exposure. Consequently, the association's ministry philosophy and efforts to transform society were open to investigation and analysis on both sides of the ocean. The leadership felt the stakes were high, as much of white America would judge the intellectual and cultural possibilities of the African-American race based on their own interpretation of these young musicians and the perceptions of others. If African Americans were to successfully assimilate into mainstream society, AMA leaders felt they must demonstrate convincingly that they were capable of meeting the criteria by which whites judged a well-bred and cultivated person.[2]

The standards for what constituted culture were similar between America and Europe and derived largely from Victorian values. Victorianism defined how a person was to be and what a person should do, and set the criteria for what signified middle-class status. While many ethnic groups comprised the fabric of American society and exercised their own traditions and social customs, the set of values, beliefs, and attitudes characteristic of Victorian culture dominated the public's collective thinking, creating a sense of homogeneity between people groups in terms of what was considered appropriate social behavior.[3] AMA personnel not only firmly believed in the moral correctness of Victorian values, but also felt that conformity to these prevailing codes of conduct would prepare African Americans as social equals.[4]

By the turn of the century, a distinct educational perspective historian Laurence Veysey termed "liberal culture" had emerged, bringing aesthetic, moral, emotional, and social connotations to the definition of culture. A cultured person would display high artistic and literary taste and an appreciation for beauty; make choices from a wellspring of emotional depth and moral character; and demonstrate refined, polished social behavior. Advocates of liberal culture held fast to the idea that the civilized, genteel tastes shared by the educated bourgeoisie would permeate society and trickle down to change the masses.[5]

This educational mindset is reflected in the rhetoric of the AMA and the founders of Fisk University.[6] Famed Fisk graduate W. E. B. DuBois wrote that the founders' goal from the onset was to encourage "adequate standards of human culture and lofty ideals of life" in order to raise up educated, respectable African-American leaders who could in turn influence and elevate others of their race.[7] Fisk University was a higher education institution committed to the principles of a classical education; its instructors strived to create well-rounded scholars with an appreciation for and keen understanding of what constituted beauty. The missionary teachers confidently proclaimed that hard work and perseverance would enable any man or woman to throw off the shackles of ignorance and develop the intellect, moral character, and refinement of person needed to succeed in life. The light of intellect and the warmth of spirituality would raise former slaves to the "high plane of Christian civilization."[8]

Fisk University sought every means possible to convince white Americans that African Americans were their equal. The institution frequently sponsored public events to demonstrate the caliber of its educational methods and their students' remarkable progress. The recitations, debates, speeches, and entertainments the university hosted were applauded by the local press and became avenues through which Fisk teachers could prove to the Nashville community the intellectual and cultural capacity of African Americans.[9] This idea of showcasing student progress as an indication of the race's capabilities took on larger meaning, and even a sense of urgency, with the rising fame of the Jubilee Singers. Every aspect of the company was under constant scrutiny by the public, from its concert programming and onstage deportment to its offstage activities. Success of the fundraising enterprise, therefore, depended heavily on earning approval of the Jubilee Singers' repertoire and excellent musicianship, and winning public trust in regards to their character.

The Jubilee Singers' Repertoire: The Negro Spiritual

Scholars credit the Jubilee Singers with introducing the Negro spiritual to the wider Western world and elevating it to a lofty position of respect. Spirituals were not the mainstay of the Jubilee Singers' programs in the company's first few months on the road.[10] However, the fervent emotional response of audiences to the few spirituals White inserted in his early programs forced a reevaluation and gradual change in the company's repertoire to feature spirituals almost exclusively. This genre of music was unfamiliar to most Americans and Europeans. It was not until the early decades of the 1800s that the texts of slave songs began to appear sporadically in periodicals and books. The first printed anthology of plantation songs, *Slave Songs of the United States,* became available to the public in 1867.[11] By then, says musicologist Eileen Southern, the term "spiritual" had wide usage and referred to songs used for multiple purposes: spirituals for religious services; spirituals for "jes' sittin' around"; and those used to accompany the "shout," a religious ceremony derived from African ritual dance.[12] The "shout" involved worshippers dancing in a circle with shuffling feet that were barely lifted from the floor, accompanied by the singing of a spiritual.[13] The song lyrics and melodic lines were simpler for those spirituals used as accompaniment so that the rhythmic elements of the dance remained prominent. Repetitious refrains that were almost chants, hand clapping, and the percussive sounds of shuffling feet contributed to a hypnotic effect that propelled the ceremony forward into a state of religious ecstasy. Spirituals were not restricted solely to the shout, but were also sung outside of this ceremony where they retained their rhythmic features.[14] "The slaves, when singing, kept time with the foot or by swaying the body," explained Jubilee Singer Thomas Rutling, "and there was no rallentando until the last bar but one.... Therefore, whoso sings these songs must keep strict time."[15]

As spirituals were born in bondage and shaped under the realities of oppression, they were powerful expressions of the collective consciousness of slaves. John Wesley Work, a professor at Fisk University in the early 1900s and a performer/scholar of spirituals, called them songs of life.[16] Rather than creations in response to life experiences, they were musical manifestations of life itself. The poignant pains of sorrow and the joyous heights of ecstasy found expression in these slave songs. Frederick Douglass, the great orator for freedom, said that spirituals were musical prayers to God: "They were tones, loud, long and deep, breathing the prayer and complaint of souls boiling over with the bitterest anguish. Every tone was a testimony against slavery, and a prayer to God for deliverance from chains."[17] Scholar Earl E. Thorpe carries this thought further, saying that the spirituals' creators believed in the power of prayer and what we now know as spirituals were originally musical expressions pouring forth from the soul, prayers sung aloud. Such singing enabled slaves to persevere in the face of suffering and promoted mental well-being.[18] Jon Michael Spencer posits that spirituals may have evolved from the preaching event in black worship, a byproduct as it were of the reciprocal relationship characteristic of the preacher's extemporaneous melodious delivery of the text accompanied by audience tonal response.[19]

Samuel Floyd's research explores how African-American music reflects an authentic African cultural memory that informed the musical and performance practices of black musicians. "Whatever its nature and process," states Floyd, "cultural memory, as a reference to vaguely 'known' musical and cultural processes and procedures, is a valid and meaningful way of accounting for the subjective, spiritual quality of the music and aesthetic behaviors of a culture."[20] Frederick Loudin's explanation for the performance power of the company of Jubilee Singers he managed later in his life supports this concept. Though he acknowledged the value of talent and training, he appealed to social memory as the primary source of his ensemble's pathos:

> We admit frankly that such music was born only after contact with civilization. It certainly could not have existed in the progenitors or the Negroes in Africa. But it may be questioned whether it was mere contact with Anglo-Saxon civilization which brought out such results. *We incline to think that it was experience of sorrow which envolved the hidden music of the African's soul* (his italics). Every one who has heard these Jubilee Singers has felt the strong pathos in their sacred songs in particular.... But the seed must be in the soil, ere any external environment can effect it. In the same

way it is sufficient for our purpose that the musical capacity was there. Genius needs external conditions for its development; but that fact does not prove its evolution from bygone generations.[21]

Paul Allen Anderson finds a similar theme in the writings of W. E. B. DuBois, who saw this body of religious folk music as containing both the ancient moorings and the future aspirations of enslaved Africans. "Music offered itself to DuBois's imagination as not only a haunted site of memory but as an energizing site of utopian anticipation," he writes.[22]

Messages of freedom and equality are woven throughout the body of spirituals, often in coded phrases that carried double meaning. Consider the following spirituals: *"Go down, Moses, Way down in Egypt's Land, Tell ole Pharaoh, "Let my people go!"* and *"The gospel train is coming, I hear it just at hand... Get on board, children, For there's room for many a-more."* Such tunes spoke not only of eternal release from bondage, but were calls for escape to freedom here on earth as well.[23] Though spirituals wore a mask, notes Jon Michael Spencer, they did so freely, thus becoming "authentic and audacious" expressions of protest against oppression.[24] As songs of rebellion, the spirituals communicated physical liberation from slavery as well as spiritual release, and an overriding sense of ultimate universal justice. Spirituals sustained slaves through the bitterness and brutality of their existence, connecting them to their African heritage and reminding them that deliverance, freedom, and justice were the real messages of the Bible.[25]

Satisfying Musical Expectations

When George White first overheard his students singing spirituals, he was instantly drawn to the music. His "soul understood and responded" to this body of music, claimed Spence's daughter, Mary. "He believed not only that the 'Jubilee Songs' expressed the highest possible spiritual fervor, but that they were capable of receiving the highest possible culture."[26] Mary Spence's use of the phrase "highest possible culture" assumes a clear distinction between low culture and high culture, or put another way, a difference between primitive art and cultivated art. To her, the spirituals sung by the young Fisk students needed altering—refinement or polishing, if you will—before presentation before audiences if they were to meet prevailing standards of "culture." Even G. D. Pike commented on White's "superior skill and taste in teaching companies of our students in the south how to sing their old slave songs in the best possible manner."[27] From his perspective, the way in which Fisk students initially sang the spirituals was molded and transformed under White's guidance into something "better."

It is clear that White and his contemporaries felt that the performance of spirituals needed to conform to a shared set of rules that governed Western European music making before they could be worthy of consideration as art. Therefore, he engaged Ella Sheppard to arrange choral versions of spirituals, and together the two rehearsed the ensemble, aiming for precision and flawless choral blend: "The blending of the voices of the company was perfect. Not one voice was even to be heard as distinct from the others in the *ensemble* singing, but each one was to hear every one else when he was singing.… He insisted on perfect enunciation of words, so that every syllable could be heard."[28] The consummate perfectionist, White would not rest until his group produced a pure, unified vocal tone, regardless of the dynamic level, with resonant power that could send the sound to the farthest reaches of the hall. When he believed his singers were losing focus during rehearsal, or failing to connect their thoughts with the meaning of the text, he would bellow out, "Do you believe that?"[29] To aid expression and musical interest, he encouraged extreme dynamic contrast for effect, as in "Steal Away to Jesus." Their impressive performance of this spiritual received a vivid description from the critic of the *Tonic-Sol-fa Reporter*:

> It was sung slowly. The first chords came floating on our senses like gentle fairy music, and they were followed by the unison phrase "Steal Away—to Jesus," delivered with exquisite precision of time and accent; then came the soft chords and bold unison again, followed by the touching, throbbing cadence, "I haint got long to stay here." Next follow the loud, lofty trumpet call in unison, "My Lord calls me; the trumpet sounds it in my soul, I haint got long to stay here." But it seems as though the angels also were speaking to the sufferer, for we hear again those beautiful chords, delivered with double *pianissimo,* whispering to the soul, "Steal away to Jesus."[30]

First a collective whispered prayer, and then a thunderous chorus proclaiming deliverance, the Jubilee Singers' dramatic performance of "Steal Away to Jesus" left a powerful and lasting impression. According to Mary

Spence, their rendition of this number "commanded the attention of every audience" and conquered even the "most critical enemy."[31]

Musical excellence demanded performance perfection, White reasoned, and therefore he drilled his ensemble incessantly. "He would keep us singing…all day until he was satisfied that we had every soft or loud passage to suit his fastidious taste," recalled Georgia Gordon. "We sometimes thought him too exacting, but we who are left know too well that our success was through the rigid training received at his hand."[32] White never relinquished his daily drills, recalled Maggie Porter. "Mr. White believed if the machinery of throat and voice was to run well it must be daily overhauled and oiled."[33]

The end result of these rehearsed concert versions of spirituals, noted musicologist Samuel Floyd, was that the Jubilee Singers transformed the Negro spiritual into a "fine imitation of itself."[34] One listener described the troupe's performance as "a little toned down in fervor and pronunciation by the teaching which the vocalists have received," suggesting that the ensemble presented a refined version of the spiritual.[35] The following description of the Jubilee Singers given by John Sullivan Dwight, a well-respected Boston music critic of the era, also indicates a transformation of the spiritual that appealed to Western ears:

> By the severe discipline to which the Jubilee Singers have been subjected in the school-room, they have been educated out of the peculiarities of the Negro dialect, and they do not attempt to imitate the peculiar pronunciation of their race. They have also received considerable musical instruction, and have been made familiar with much of our best sacred and classical music, and this has modified their manner of execution. They do not attempt to imitate the grotesque bodily motions or the drawling intonations that often characterize the singing of great congregations of the colored people in their excited religious meetings.[36]

Comparisons between the Jubilee Singers and the Hampton Singers, a choral group formed in 1872 from Hampton Institute for similar fundraising purposes as the Fisk ensemble, also indicate the degree to which the Jubilees had concertized spirituals. Critics praised the Hampton Singers for their "faithful rendering of the original slave songs" and hailed the company for preserving the "*wail* which those who have listened to the singing on the old plantations recognize as the 'real thing.'"[37] Though the

Hampton Singers were perhaps "less cultured" than the Jubilees, noted John Sullivan Dwight, their performances were "more characteristic" of slave singing.[38]

The public was fascinated with the Jubilee Singers and their music. The words of these novel songs were unlike anything whites had ever encountered in their own religious services. Some described them as shocking, and yet filled with irresistible charm. One reviewer told readers that the lyrics of "The Gospel Train" were as "simple as that of the nursery": "The fare is cheap, and all can go, / The rich and poor are there, / No second-class on board the train, / No difference in the fare!" "And yet at these words, two thousand grown up men and women, laughed and cried, and rose to their feet and shouted for more," he reported.[39] Usually restrained and dignified Victorian audiences were so delighted by the Jubilee Singers' spiritual renditions that one critic thought "it was evident that had the audience been requested, they would have sung as heartily as the negroes.... Their simple and rude but soulful strains at times thrill every nerve of one's body, and make one feel like joining in the chorus."[40]

However, not all were positively swayed by the message of the spirituals or the Jubilee Singers' performance of these songs. One critic called their concert "profane and degrading," claiming that the company desecrated sacred objects and characters. "If 'professing Christians' tolerate such sheer profanity, and applause such burlesquing of sacred subjects," he declared, "in heaven's name let us hear no more of the immoral and irreligious tendencies of the stage."[41] The editor of the *Loomis Musical Journal* acknowledged the troupe's noble mission, but chided audiences who flocked after the Jubilee Singers for their woeful lack of artistic taste:

> Were it not for the fact that they are working for a noble cause, that of establishing a college for colored citizens of the South, we could not afford a word of encouragement for them. Their performance is a burlesque on music, and almost on religion.... We regret to see that, with about two thousand educated people in this civilized and enlightened city, the appreciation of music is at such a low ebb that they can enjoy the "singing" of these well-meaning but unmusical people.... But pardon us, good people: you enjoyed it simply because your knowledge of music is nearly as imperfect as that of the Jubilee Singers themselves, and on the same principle that an uneducated man prefers the illiterate prattle of his

associates to the well-defined and scholarly utterances of a Webster or an Everett.[42]

Such scathing reviews were rare. Generally, the Jubilee Singers enjoyed large, enthusiastic crowds and critical praise for their exquisite harmony and overall artistry.

Both negative and positive press reviews of the Jubilee Singers contain language that illustrates underlying racist assumptions held by many white Americans. Critics as well as the company's most loyal supporters often referred to the Jubilees' singing as "purely natural" or "rude and uncultivated," and ascribed a primitive simplicity to the spiritual. Words such as "quaint," "strange," "weird," "peculiar," "wild," and "grotesque" appear frequently, revealing racial undertones that reinforced Westerners' belief in "black difference" and fueled romantic fascination with the ensemble. According to Ronald Radano, such language infused the slave sound world with "special properties that tested the outer limits of the Western imagination" and assigned spirituals with the power to touch the deepest recesses of human emotion.[43] Puzzled critics did indeed question how these songs and the Jubilee Singers so profoundly moved listeners. Barely had the ensemble begun singing, said one observer, before a "breathless stillness" fell over the hall and tears began to flow, showing that the company's songs had "taken the heart." According to this reviewer, the source of their aesthetic appeal was that the Jubilee Singers sang with soul: "The very soul of music…lives and breathes in these simple songs."

> The first thing that strikes us in the singing of the Jubilee Singers is its intense earnestness. The subject of their song is to them a reality, something they have themselves realised, and not a mere sentiment or imagination; they feel the words, and therefore they sing the music. The words are very simple, usually they contain one striking idea. At first sight they may sometimes appear to be childish, if not irreverent, but to the singers they have a deep and vivid meaning.[44]

Reviews of the Jubilee Singers' concerts are filled with references to the "sympathetic power" of the spirituals and deep pathos of the troupe. Listeners seemed transported to a sublime spiritual level. Audiences wept, laughed, and demanded encore after encore.

Satisfying Visual Expectations

The AMA leadership recognized early on that musicality alone would not necessarily ensure the company's success. The evangelical community to whom White first appealed sought verification of the troupe's spirituality and validation of their respectability, factors that also mattered to the general public in its estimation of the troupe. Their audiences blended Victorian values with Protestant morals when judging the Jubilee Singers' cultural attainment. Therefore, White and the other managers carefully monitored the public presentation of the Jubilee Singers—visual details such as bearing and attire—in order to promote their image as gracious ladies and refined gentlemen. Dignified manner and conduct weighed heavily with both American and European audiences who expected moral, refined, and respectable behavior to accompany any talent worthy of their endorsement.

In order to win recognition as artists of the highest caliber, AMA personnel stressed the need for the Jubilees and their managers to maintain a certain elegance of manner appropriate to prevailing Victorian sensibilities. Attention to matters of respectability would distinguish the troupe's performances from other forms of "worldly entertainments" that were flagrant violations of the Protestant ethic. "The spirit of such amusements is manifestly adverse to the dignity, gravity, and usefulness of the Christian character," declared Catherine Booth, cofounder of the Salvation Army, in her treatise on this matter. Taking part in worldly amusements, she warned, led only to "lightness, foolish jesting...uproarious merriment and godless mirth," as well as possible backsliding.[45] Since adherence to rigid moral standards was the general practice of those who identified with the Christian evangelical community, the AMA knew that the Jubilee Singers' work would be severely compromised if this particular audience felt they were merely in the entertainment business.

The managers knew it was crucial for the company to disassociate itself with minstrel shows that had grown in popularity in America and Europe. To their credit, the troupe's stark difference from minstrelsy, both in appearance and performance, was perhaps the most striking aspect of the company that critics first noticed. These singers were not at all like the blackened faces seen in the minstrel shows, nor did their songs resemble those sung by the "Zip Coon" and "Jim Crow" caricatures popularized by this form of theatrical entertainment. Rather, the public called them a welcomed contrast to the negative portrayals of African Americans found in the minstrel shows and a more authentic presentation of black folk music. "These men, women and children are their proper interpreters. They surpass the hard-hearted mercenary imitators of their race, who, besmooched with burnt cork, have sung their songs for gain during all these years while the great struggle has been going on.... They are better singers—and doubtless more intelligent and better educated people—without doubt a hundred fold more moral and respectable."[46] European audiences were most familiar with the Christy Minstrels, a highly successful group organized in 1844.[47] After hearing the Jubilee Singers, critics recognized that minstrelsy was a gross distortion of slaves and original slave melodies. "The assumption of negro character and the negro *style* of singing by our present Christys is as false as the black on their faces," stated the *Tonic-Sol-fa Reporter*.[48] Another reviewer commended the troupe for programming none of the "conventional ditties" generally accepted as genuine Negro melodies. "The burnt cork negroes if they do not henceforward hide their diminished wigs, will surely take the hint," continued the writer.[49]

A Jubilee Singers concert was indeed a far cry from a minstrel show, with little fanfare or adornment that might distract from the singing. Instead, simplicity characterized both their music and concert etiquette. The company grouped close together onstage, "standing solid, as they term it," said Pike, "in order to secure the most perfect harmony."[50] Often they stood in three rows, shoulder to shoulder, and leaned their heads toward each other, listening carefully to one another for balance and blend.[51] The review of the singers' 1873 London premiere by the *Tonic-Sol-fa Reporter* provides a mini snapshot of how the troupe appeared onstage:

> The singers walk quietly on to the platform and fill the row of chairs at the back, one gentleman bowing as he takes his seat in response to the applause of the assembly. They are not so black as we expected, and they are not dressed in the gay colours which are falsely supposed to distinguish the negro taste. They are simply eleven young Christian ladies and gentlemen. They stand and arrange themselves in the front of the platform, in a phalanx three deep. They stand shoulder to shoulder, and with very close ranks.

They stand with head erect and somewhat thrown back, and looking upward or with eyes nearly closed. It is evident that the audience is nothing to them; they are going to make music, and listen to one another.[52]

Both White and Pike shunned any appearance of showmanship.[53] They focused instead on presenting finely executed music with great dignity, hoping to win public sympathy and support for the AMA and Fisk University.

The Jubilee Singers' thoughtful consideration of their visual presentation was quickly rewarded. Newspaper notices made it clear that a concert given by this African-American troupe was "an elevating, a refining, and remarkably delightful entertainment."[54] When describing the individual members, critics were as likely to report on the "modest yet self possessed manners" or "graceful and unassuming demeanor" as they were to praise their artistic ability. Speaking on behalf of the assembled audience, one minister declared that everyone had been "affected by the peculiar propriety of their [the Jubilee Singers'] deportment, in dress and address, in voice and manner."[55] Another reporter described how the company, dressed in "simple and pleasant clothing," proceeded into the auditorium "in well mannered and pleasing composure." Their appearance and conduct "won as much approval from the audience as their art," he remarked.[56] This visual first impression was a significant factor influencing audience opinion of the Jubilee Singers and their cultural sophistication.

Questions of Artistic Merit

Audiences' enthusiastic reaction to the Jubilee Singers' concerts prompted reflection on whether or not their performances qualified as "art." In short, was this music "high culture," appealing to one's loftiest sensibilities, or was this "low culture" as represented in the theaters and vulgar entertainment of the minstrel show? Further, were these African-American artists capable of delivering concert performances that met the highest standards of Western civilization?

The question was addressed by their fans in a variety of ways. Theodore F. Seward, who first transcribed the Jubilee Singers' repertoire of spirituals for public sale, pointed to the compositional structure of the spirituals in his argument for the artistic merit of the music. Though he held that the creation of the spirituals was the "simple, ecstatic utterances of wholly untutored minds," he nonetheless claimed that a thorough musical analysis revealed that the spirituals complied with accepted Western rules of musical structure and form:

> But I find that they are really and essentially beautiful, and have the right number of measures, fulfilling the law of structure; and that they also express wonderfully the words to which they are written; and thus they have that which the highest art aims at, and which it rarely reaches; and it has seemed to me that, coming as they do from minds having no knowledge whatever of the rules of art, and without culture, they must have sprung from something that is above us, of true inspiration.

Noting how the compositional structure of the spirituals fit accepted modes, and recognizing the Jubilee Singers' "immense power over audiences which include many people of the highest culture," Seward concluded that only a person "thoroughly encased in prejudice" would fail to recognize the superior artistic value of the spiritual.[57]

Listeners, including Mark Twain, appealed to authenticity as the source of the Jubilee Singers' power of expression and claim to distinction:

> I think these gentlemen and ladies make eloquent music—and what is as much to the point, they reproduce the true melody of the plantations, and are the only persons I ever heard accomplish this on the public platform.... I was reared in the South, and my father owned slaves, and I do not know when anything has so moved me as did the plaintive melodies of the Jubilee Singers. It was the first time for twenty-five or thirty years that I had heard such songs, or heard them sung in the genuine old way...for one must have been a slave himself in order to feel what that life was and so convey the pathos of it in the music.[58]

Henry Ward Beecher expressed similar thoughts after hearing the singers for the first time: "They make their mark by giving the spirituals and plantation hymns as only they can sing them who know how to keep time to a master's whip."[59] The spirituals represented authentic relics of slavery, and the Jubilee Singers' performance of them became for many a memorable aesthetic experience difficult to explain:

> No description is adequate to convey any idea of the strange attraction of these songs as sung by these people, most of whom were at one time slaves.

They are all pitched in a minor key, and have a wild, mournful, despairing undertone running through them, born only of intensest anguish, and of utter earthly hopelessness.... These weird melodies fairly drip with the blood and tears of whole generations of slave fathers and slave mothers, transmuted by some strange alchemy into music... They can only be appreciated by being heard.[60]

Critics also appealed to audiences' emotional response to defend the artistic value of the Jubilee Singers: "...but that they please the people let the applause they receive testify; that they touch the heart, let the tears which flow attest; that they call into play the better influences, let the experience of all who have heard them be the evidence."[61]

Often, supporters of the Jubilee Singers validated the company's artistic merit by contrasting them with established concert artists of the day. "The harmony of these children of nature and their musical execution were beyond the reach of art," boldly claimed Theodore L. Cuyler, pastor of Brooklyn's Lafayette Avenue Presbyterian Church. He felt the troupe's rendition of "Home, Sweet Home" put Jenny Lind's to shame.[62] Others made similar comparisons between the Jubilee Singers and classical artists gracing the concert stage:

If we should say these singers have done something for music as art, we suppose that the musical critics who write for the morning papers would wave us aside with silent contempt. Yet here is the fact, which we beg these gentlemen to account for as best they can. Their concerts have been crowded from the beginning to the end of the season by the most cultivated classes of New York and Brooklyn society; while Nilsson, and Parepa, and Wachtel, and Santley were dividing among them the honors which belong to the highest musical culture; while the town was reveling at the richest feast which has ever been spread before the patrons of artistic music, these uncultivated singers from the southern plantations came with their simple melodies, and gained attention and applause equal, at least, to that which has been given to the great artists.[63]

Remarked another, "Expression in music, which so many artistic performers lack, is preeminently characteristic of this troupe."[64] One New York critic argued that the operatic standards applied to other artists had no place in assessing these singers; rather, those who considered themselves true artists should quickly "undertake to find out what is the secret of their power."[65]

Others pointed to the elite citizens attending the Jubilee Singers' concerts as evidence of the ensemble's merit:

> Of the success of the company known as the Jubilee Singers our readers have doubtless heard. It is something extraordinary. If their success had been confined to small country villages, it might not have been so surprising. Or if large audiences in the great cities had been attracted a few times by a natural curiosity to hear a company of slaves sing the peculiar songs of their race, it would have been nothing strange. But it *is* strange and truly wonderful to see Steinway Hall filled to its utmost capacity, night after night, and to know that many of the audience have been present before— once, twice, thrice, in some cases attending every concert given by the Jubilee Singers in New York. It shows conclusively that the cause must be accounted for on other grounds than mere curiosity or a feeling of sympathy for a downtrodden race. It is undoubtedly to be found in the quaint, pathetic melodies, the "camp-meeting songs," the "spirituals," whatever be the name by which they are known, of which the programmes are mostly made up.[66]

Often, press reviews listed the names of distinguished persons who were present at concerts, suggesting that their patronage of the Jubilee Singers was indicative of the company's worth. For many, any evaluation of the ensemble's artistic attainment must take into account the immense popularity and warm reception the troupe enjoyed by both the general public and society's elite.

The Ultimate Test: Germany

During the seven historic touring years of the original company, the question of cultural and artistic value resurfaced each time new audiences encountered the Jubilee Singers. After their first concert in London, the respected music journal, *Tonic-Sol-fa Reporter*, announced: "Lord Shaftesbury said at the beginning that we must not expect artistic singing. But if the most delicate Expression, the most perfect unity of Attack, and a very beautiful Quality of voice are not artistic, what is?"[67] Similar sentiments were echoed in countless newspaper reviews, testimonials by clergymen, and comments from society's elite as the Jubilee Singers traveled in America and throughout Great Britain. Their melodies "both disarm and defy criticism" claimed Britain's *Lancaster Guardian*.[68]

As gratifying as positive commendations were, however, the troupe was understandably nervous when AMA officials suggested extending their fundraising efforts into Germany. Both America and England had long looked to Germany for cultural standards by which to judge the arts. Whether or not the Jubilees' musicianship would measure up or garner praise from those who could not understand their words was a question that haunted White. An opportunity to test the matter came while the ensemble was taking a much needed rest in Geneva, Switzerland in 1877. White decided to give a public concert at the Salle de la Réformation where neither the audience nor the chairman spoke or understood English. The house was packed and audience enthusiasm "rose to white heat." After the concert, Ella Sheppard confided in her diary that the evening was a "perfect success":

> The hall was about full—it is estimated to seat 4,500 and at least a good portion of that number could not understand of what we spoke or sang, yet we never appeared before a more enthusiastic audience. Indeed, they began to encore the first and through to the last piece.… Mr. White said we never gave a better concert. We felt so glad. This remark coming from him means a great deal. When *he* is satisfied, we know everybody else must be, therefore we felt unusually thankful.[69]

Sheppard and the other singers were surprised to discover how well the Swiss received their songs. When questioned, audience members responded that they did not need to understand all the words to *feel* the intent of the music. Their songs simply "filled their heart[s]."[70]

A second trial opportunity for the singers to sing for a non-English speaking audience arose when G. P. Ittman, Jr., a leading Christian businessman, invited the company to his homeland of Holland, pledging his services to make the trip a success. He proved as good as his word. Ittman formed local committees across the country that attended to all business matters regarding the concerts, and as a result, the two months the Jubilees spent in Holland yielded great results. Once again, royalty welcomed them, lavishing attention and honors upon the company. When they returned to England, the troupe brought back an additional $10,000 for the treasury and a readiness to attempt a German tour.[71]

White felt that the success of the company before German audiences would stand or fall ultimately on the merits of their singing.[72] The first opportunity to demonstrate their musicianship occurred shortly after their arrival in Potsdam. The Crown Prince invited the ensemble to appear privately at the "New Palace" on 4 November 1877, a "day long to be remembered," remarked Ella Sheppard. Royal carriages of white satin transported the Jubilees to the palace. They entered an elegant hall where the Crown Prince and Princess warmly welcomed them and introduced them to their children. After their performance of several spirituals, one of the royal party told Ella Sheppard that she had never before heard such perfect intonation and "could listen for hours" to the ensemble.[73]

The company's first public appearance in Germany occurred a few nights later when they performed at Berlin's Sing-Akademie.[74] Their interpreter revealed that several of Germany's most renowned music critics were sitting in the front row among an audience in full evening dress, jewels sparkling in the dim light. [75] "If we failed we would better pack our trunks and leave," said Ella Sheppard. "Then everything else forgotten, in a musical whisper, 'Steal Away' floated out so perfectly that one could not tell when it began," she recalled. "The astonishment upon the fixed, upturned faces of our critics told us that we had won; we were again at ease and did our best to maintain the good impression."[76] The profuse congratulations the Jubilee Singers received at the close of the evening convinced them they had passed this musical test.

For eight months, the Jubilee Singers gave successful German concerts. An article in the *Berliner Musik-Zeitung*, a journal known for its high critical standards, gave hearty endorsement to the ensemble's musicianship:

> What wealth of shading! What accuracy of declamation! Every musician felt then that the performances of these Singers are the result of high artistic talent, finely trained taste, and extraordinary diligence. Such a *pianissimo*, such a *crescendo* and a *decrescendo* as those at the close of "Steal Away" might raise envy in the soul of any choir-master.... Thus the balance turns decidedly in favor of the Jubilee Singers, and we confess ourselves their debtors. Not only have we had a rare musical treat but our musical ideas have also received enlargement, and we feel that something may be learned of these negro singers if only we will consent to break through the fetters of custom and long use.[77]

Other reviewers remarked on their well trained voices, "totally free of the bad habits" often criticized in other "European singers." Another praised their "purity, sure intonation, clarity of expression and ease of pronunciation" and unity of sound, as if "animated by one single spirit."[78]

Similar to other Westerners, German audiences assessed visual appearance and onstage demeanor when judging the cultural attainment of the Jubilee Singers and found the company's lack of ostentation appealing. The *Dortmund* pointed out the public's approval of the Jubilees' modest concert appearance: "The seven ladies had utmost simple clothing all in contrast to our present day concert singers who dedicate as much care to the combination of their wardrobe as to the order of their program."[79] Others praised the "quiet and inspiring simplicity of their presentation," their unpretentious manner, and "humble stage presence." By refraining from "crowd pleasing mannerisms," noted one review, the Jubilee Singers presented a stark contrast to the "arrogance and frivolous behavior" of other prominent artists gracing the stage.[80]

German critics applauded the educational and cultural heights to which these former slaves had risen: "The singers have demonstrated and proven what man, even if born as a despised slave, can accomplish by himself through seriousness, energy, and enthusiasm for the high goals of humanity."[81] Another stated: "These foreign and strange students have proven that colored people can satisfy in the art of singing even highest expectations."[82] Acknowledging their "honorable Christian behavior and their educated manners," one reviewer predicted that the Jubilee Singers' "cultural historical victory" would be "admired in the history of the Negroes for centuries to come."[83]

For the Jubilee Singers, success in Germany represented the crowning musical accomplishment of all their efforts. "Probably no band of singers ever captivated the hearts of the people as did this little band of ex-slaves, just emerged from the hands of their bondsmen," Georgia Gordon said proudly. "Does one wonder that the tears rolled down the cheeks of those who listened? What comes from the heart reaches the heart."[84] Ella Sheppard considered the German press reviews to be "some of the finest criticisms" the company received. "Each piece was analyzed," she noted and received a "favorable verdict" in all the press dailies.[85]

German praise was especially gratifying to the AMA, who had assured its constituency prior to the company's 1875 campaign that "the Singers and all who direct their movements, will seek earnestly and conscientiously to merit public favor and win success in their undertaking."[86] To AMA personnel, the approval of German audiences symbolized perhaps the highest affirmation possible of African-American cultural attainment:

It was a good thing to go up and down Germany singing Christian truth to multitudes who would have turned from it had it come in any other guise. Their visit was a revelation of the qualities and capacities of the negro to those who had known so little of him, that was in his favor. Listening to the Singers, thoughtful people said with surprise, "We could not take even our German peasantry and reach such results in art, and conduct, and character, in generations of culture, as appear in these freed slaves."[87]

The Jubilee Singers had effectively validated the association's claims that students under the influence of its educational institutions would demonstrate "refined tastes and worthier ambitions."[88] Since the harshest critics of the Western world had given their nod of approval to the company's cultured sophistication and sanctioned their music as high art, the AMA challenged any who would continue to question the cultural possibilities of the African-American race.

Chapter 6

"The Scar of the Dark Ages":

Social Standing in America and Europe

> Our nation, before it can honestly claim to be the land of the free...must
> see to it that public conveyances and places for entertainment...make no
> distinction whatever on account of race or color. Until that is settled, we
> must sit with a scar of the dark ages upon us.[1]

The Jubilee Singers' success on the concert stage did not automatically
translate into acceptance into other public and private spheres of American
life. Racism had deep roots that would not yield easily, and much of
American society was neither prepared nor willing to extend civil rights
fully. White Americans considered freedom their birthright; for the nation's
other citizens, freedom was something to be earned.[2] Therefore, the
American Missionary Association's (AMA) Christian Reconstruction work
on behalf of African Americans also included constant attacks on racist
attitudes and discriminatory practices that barred blacks from full
participation in American society.[3]

Outside the walls of Fisk University, the Jubilee Singers quickly
discovered that adopting prevailing social values and customs did not
necessarily ensure any change in their social standing in America.[4]
Emancipation may have altered their legal status, but did not amend the
distorted conceptions many whites held about blacks' personhood. The
Jubilees and their managers, therefore, engaged in an ongoing battle against
discrimination with rhetoric calling for equality in both the public and
private spheres of life. The contrast between American and European
acceptance of the group supported their stance. Generally, the racist
practices by American hotel proprietors and restaurateurs did not reoccur in
England, and the AMA lost no time in highlighting the disparity. And

while the Jubilee Singers were rarely the invited guests in American homes other than those with abolitionist sentiments or friends of their own race, in Europe, the singers received more social invitations than they had time to accept. "Abroad, we were entertained beautifully," claimed Mabel Lewis.[5]

The difference between American and European behavior toward the Jubilee Singers in both the public and private spheres of life provided illustrative material with which the AMA chastised America's racist practices and validated its Christian Reconstruction ideology. The association interpreted every public rejection of the Jubilee Singers as evidence of injustice leveled against all African Americans. Likewise, each triumph over discrimination was a celebrated victory for the entire race.

Confronting American Racism

The Jubilee Singers' first campaign in the States quickly demonstrated how prevalent racism was throughout their homeland, not just in the South. Northern establishments were as likely to refuse accommodations to them as Southern ones. Hotel managers often required the troupe to take its meals apart from the other white guests, and some railway stations turned them out of waiting rooms or refused to honor their first-class tickets. Much of America's popular print media still lampooned blacks for aspiring to be literate professionals. Many Northern newspapers printed racist cartoons with gross caricatures of African Americans, thus reinforcing stereotypes that were presented on the minstrel stage.[6]

The public humiliations they experienced form a dominant theme of the written recollections of the original Jubilee Singers. In 1911, over thirty years after their historic campaigns, Mabel Lewis recalled vividly the discrimination they endured in an article entitled "Some Hotel Experiences": "Shall I tell you about the different times when we were turned out of hotels because God took more pains with the making of our people than of others? Is it because He stopped to paint us and curl our hair that we have to suffer for these extra attentions that have been bestowed upon us? How many times we were refused accommodations in hotels, I cannot remember."[7] Maggie Porter was so traumatized by an experience at a railroad station in Nashville that she vowed never to return to Fisk or the South by train again. It was a promise she kept for fifty-one years.[8]

During the first campaign year, very rarely did the company find a first-class hotel willing to offer lodging. Often, they were forced to stay in run-down establishments with several members of the troupe squeezed together in just a few rooms. None of the principal hotels in Chillicothe, one of the company's first stops in 1871, would admit blacks. The proprietor of the American Hotel finally took the Jubilees in and gave up his bedroom to serve as their parlor, but refused to serve them meals with the other boarders. The troupe continued to face similar rejections. "There were many times when we didn't have a place to sleep or anything to eat," recalled Maggie Porter. "Mr. White went out and brought us some sandwiches and tried to find some place to put us up."[9] The students were often left behind at the train station while White trudged through the city seeking shelter for the group. Ella Sheppard remembered staying in a "condemned room over a porch so rickety" that they had to "lean to the wall to keep from falling." The young ladies found their room "so well occupied" that only a few slept "while the others slew the occupants."[10] When rooms were denied them, as was often the case, Porter recalled that White had no choice but to "go out to the ministers and the ministers would ask their members to let us stay in their homes."[11]

When the Jubilees began touring again in fall 1872, they found that neither the measure of fame nor success they had enjoyed the previous year abated the discrimination they had to endure. Mabel Lewis recalled being "kicked out of hotels and put in places where the beds were so filthy we had to sit up all night." "Was this in America or abroad?" asked her interviewer. "No, indeed, it was right here in 'My Country, 'tis of Thee,'" she replied.[12]

Lewis, who was of mixed parentage and reared in a white environment, found America's racist attitudes extremely offensive. One incident she recalled occurred in Elizabeth, New Jersey at a private boarding house. When the help learned that an African-American troupe had been admitted, they all walked off the job, leaving the work to the proprietor, his wife, and sister. He informed the company that he would take care of the rooms and that his sister had agreed to do the cooking. His wife refused to help at all. As they had arrived on a Sunday and had no engagements until Monday evening, the Jubilees asked if they could amuse themselves on the parlor piano:

The proprietor was perfectly willing. While we were singing we heard a great scuffling over our heads. I was frightened and looked out, and there at the head of the stairs was Mr. Proprietor tying Mrs. Proprietor with a clothes line to keep her upstairs, because she said, "I'm going to turn those niggers out of my house. I'm not going to have them pawing on my piano." The next morning he seemed to feel ashamed about what had happened the night before and tried to fix it up in some way. As we were about to leave he made the expression that he was very sorry for what had happened during our stay there, and whenever we came that way again we were welcome to stop at his house.

"Sometimes we were up and sometimes down," Lewis said wryly, "and sometimes flat upon the ground."[13]

In Columbus, Ohio, three guests left the dining hall when the Jubilee Singers appeared for breakfast. No hotel in Philadelphia was willing to accept them. In Washington, the Continental Hotel landlord asked the troupe to appear in the parlor "as little as possible" and had the members receive guests in his private parlor, which did not set well with the troupe at all. "It is extremely unpleasant to be under such a roof," wrote Ella Sheppard. "The hall through which we pass to enter our room is so offensive that we almost feel nauseated."[14]

One of America Robinson's first letters home includes a report of yet another disturbance between boarders over the troupe's presence in the hotel establishment:

A southern man was enraged because the proprietor took us in. A northerner asserted that if we had been refused admittance he would have taken his departure and told the southerner that he was a half "nigger" himself. The S- attempted to throw the papers at the N- so the N- struck him in the mouth with a chair. Many boarders threatened to leave. If the proprietor suffers materially we intend giving him a benefit concert. A man from your town would not take breakfast because we ate in the public dining room, he took his breakfast in the office.[15]

Life on the road demonstrated forcefully how unwilling white America was to share its public spaces with African Americans. In recounting their travels, Hinton Alexander wrote, "It is needless for me to attempt to describe the hatred and prejudice which confronted us. It was something terrible."[16]

This succession of humiliating rejections by commercial establishments was punctuated, at times, by a few notable public triumphs. Generally, local ministers and Christian supporters were the most vocal champions against prejudicial treatment of the Jubilee Singers, often spurred to action by the company's managers. When the American Hotel in Jersey City informed Pike that the "Jubille Singers can not be accomodated at his Hotel att all," Pike announced at the evening concert that perhaps it would have been disrespectable for the troupe "to lodge in a hotel that indulged in such miserable spelling." Enraged citizens unwilling to excuse the proprietor sent a few choice words of censure to the local papers.[17]

Sometimes the Jubilees were able to ignite public sentiment against American discriminatory practices and effect change. In Philadelphia, they performed in the Academy of Music, where less than three years earlier, officials had refused to allow a black United States senator to give an address. Now, pressured by influential local citizens, hall managers opened the facility to the Jubilee Singers. During the concert, Pike announced that no hotel would admit them, prompting the proprietor of the city's leading hotel to welcome the troupe to his establishment, the Continental. In its report of the incident to its readers, the *American Missionary* quoted the *Philadelphia Press*: "...after the noble example of the Continental, it may be doubted if any first-class hotel in our city will hereafter venture to close its wide doors against any lady or gentleman because of color."[18]

On a few occasions, the Jubilee Singers enjoyed a gracious welcome from American citizens. When they arrived in St. Johnsbury, Vermont, the Jubilees found bouquets of flowers awaiting them in their rooms, and more flowers with welcome notes arrived soon after. At Dartmouth College, President Smith and the professors expended great effort to treat the company well, escorting them to various points of interest connected with the institution.[19]

At other times, friends or supporters of the AMA rescued the company from the embarrassment of being denied public lodging by taking the Jubilee Singers into their private homes. Such was the case in New Haven, Connecticut. When the troupe was once again turned away because of their race, the managers decided against letting the matter pass unnoticed and made sure that the incident was reported in the local press. Public sentiment against "absurd and unjust colorphobia" flared.[20] Reverend E. L. Clark, pastor of the North Church, wanted to prove that the "good people" of New Haven strongly disapproved of the hotel's discriminatory practices. He made arrangements for the company in the private homes of many of the town's leading families who welcomed the Jubilees and entertained them as equals. They enjoyed the rare collection of art found in Reverend Clark's private residence and found themselves invited guests to outings. Similar actions were repeated throughout their New England travels, noted Ella Sheppard. "Hotels refused us, and families of highest social prestige received us into their homes."[21]

Fortunately, rejection by hotel proprietors was not universal. When the company arrived in Bridgeport, Connecticut, they found their rooms at the Sterling House "suitable for kings and princes" and were welcomed into the dining room at the usual hours. When asked if his boarders complained, the hotel proprietor staunchly replied, "I keep this hotel, sir." Having a hotel proprietor rise to their defense was so exceptional that Pike made sure to include the event in his chronicle of the company's first tour.[22]

Acts of kindness such as these earned the Jubilees' great appreciation. To their credit, they managed the harsh incidences with great aplomb. They chose to maintain a magnanimous spirit of gratitude for every small step towards full recognition of their rights, as Benjamin Holmes's letter home to Spence early in the first campaign attests:

> It is true we are not rec'd like the grand duke Alexis but then we are glad of it, for ours is an humble mission and we are sometimes willing to be ensconced in the 3rd or even 5th story of a 2nd class hotel if we cant do better. But in the whole when we allow ourselves to think seriously of our previous condition and our present acquirements we arrive at the conclusion that "we are willing to wait a little longer till the good time coming comes" when we can be received into first class without damaging their business.[23]

Holmes would have to wait until the company's arrival in England before experiencing the "first-class" treatment he deserved.

Welcome in England and Scotland

As the company prepared for its first ocean voyage to England in May 1873, the managers discovered that no American steamship would agree to take African Americans as passengers. Finally, Pike managed to secure them passage on the British "Batavia," where the singers were treated with respect. "The kindness of the captain and crew we shall never forget," recalled Ella Sheppard.[24] It was their first introduction to British hospitality.

Immediately upon arrival in Liverpool, the singers knew that life in England would be far different from that in America. Though they had made no previous arrangements, the managers of the Northwestern Hotel greeted the troupe "in the nicest manner" and provided them with the same accommodations as for "other passengers who were several shades whiter on the outside." Whereas in America the company sometimes paid "first-class price for second-class fare," Benjamin Holmes was pleased to find that here they were not assigned separate quarters from whites.[25] Pike noted that hotel managers throughout England and Scotland almost seemed to "pride themselves in showing kindness," reducing fares drastically in order to help the company financially. So many first-class hotels sought to lodge the group that Pike was fearful of offending those whose welcome they were forced to forego.[26]

The Jubilees' successful launch in London sponsored by Lord Shaftesbury, followed by favorable press coverage in most of the local dailies, assuaged doubts about their respectability and piqued British curiosity about this new troupe. "This introduction to the British public paved the way to countless invitations for concerts and social functions among Great Britain's distinguished people," noted Sheppard. The Duke and Duchess of Argyll were among the first to invite the company into their home at Kensington and introduce them to society's elite. Here, the singers found themselves engaged in free and pleasant conversation that at times turned rather amusing. "Our many shades of brown and black got us mixed up at times and, too, their English accent was so different from ours that at first we could not easily understand each other," reported Ella Sheppard.[27]

Pike, fearing that he might overextend the company's stay and thereby breach proper etiquette, sought guidance from a friendly guest whom he described as having the gift for "making everyone, from the smallest child to the Queen herself, happy and at home in her presence." The woman was Lady Augusta Stanley, wife of the dean of Westminster Abbey, who delicately prompted Pike in matters of propriety, including how to behave when Queen Victoria made her sudden unexpected visit to hear the Jubilees.[28] Lady Stanley's brother, Sir Frederick Bruce, served as the British Minister in Washington and had plied her with vivid letters detailing the Civil War and conditions of slavery, for which she developed an intense fascination. After meeting the Jubilee Singers at Argyll Lodge, she wasted no time in extending an invitation for them to visit the deanery at Westminster Abbey the next day. She supplied the Queen, with whom she corresponded frequently, a description of the event: "The black singers came to visit the Abbey yesterday and I undertook to lionize them in part—Your Majesty would have been amused to see an army of note books produced—greatly to my alarm, for I felt very shy when I found all my commonplace remarks taken down!! they are most intelligent and bright, poor things.—After we had left, they sang one of their Hymns in the Abbey and most beautiful it was..."[29] While Lady Stanley's curiosity about the Jubilee Singers was most likely stimulated by her brother's accounts of American affairs, the graciousness she extended to the troupe earned their gratitude. After singing "Steal Away to Jesus" at the tomb of "Bloody Mary" and chanting the "Lord's Prayer" at the tomb of Mary, Queen of Scots, the troupe returned to their hotel "feeling wiser for the ramble."[30]

These visits to Argyll Lodge and the deanery at Westminster Abbey marked the beginning of a whirlwind social calendar that characterized the singers' European campaigns. "The hospitalities we received in London were among the golden events of our lives," noted Pike.[31] Samuel Gurney, a former Parliament member and prominent in the Society of Friends, invited the company to visit his mansion in Regents Park. After escorting them on a three-hour excursion through the Zoological and Botanical Gardens of London, they returned to his home where Mrs. Gurney gave them a hearty welcome. They rested, wandered the mansion grounds, and enjoyed conversation with many Quaker friends who had been invited to meet the singers. Following dinner in the garden, the guests retired to the parlor and enjoyed further conversation, for as Benjamin Holmes remarked, "it seemed that the spirit had moved them to talk."[32]

Londoners wanting to make the acquaintance of the Jubilees were in abundance. "We meet continually in London dear friends who have used the influence of prayer in our behalf and now they rejoice with us that we are free," reported Benjamin Holmes, "and they are now praying for our elevation and enlightenment." There were so many invitations to tea that the company simply could not accept them all. "Week before last accepted and attended three," Holmes wrote, "this week, thus far, two, so you see we are not passing unnoticed." One invitation they did accept came from Mr. Heffers, a wealthy London merchant, who requested that the company spend a day with his family and friends. While playing croquet, his servants kept the troupe supplied with tea, coffee, lemonade, and cakes. Afterwards, they all retired to the parlor and "listened to very nicely executed vocal and instrumental music, and discoursed some of our music for the entertainment of our friends," related Holmes. Heffers then took Jennie Jackson's arm and led the group into the dining room where "the tables were groaning beneath the weight of the best the London market could produce in the way of meats, vegetables, fruits, pastry, wines, etc." After the meal, they returned to the parlor for a "pleasant *tete-a-tete* and good music" until carriages arrived to take them back to their hotel.[33]

Counted among their friends was the noted author George MacDonald, a relative of Adam Spence, who first met the Jubilee Singers in New York and was influential in persuading the company to travel to England. After hearing the ensemble sing for the first time, his wife wrote to their daughter, "I never heard anything so droll and fervid, so touching, so pathetic, so true." She described how "Papa sat with tears rolling down his cheeks." At the close of a second concert they attended, the family remained behind to converse with the troupe as the audience dispersed when suddenly the gas lights turned off. "All the same colour now!" jokingly called out one of the Jubilee Singers.[34] The MacDonalds invited the Jubilees to participate in their annual garden party on behalf of London's poor held at their residence on the banks of the Thames River. Before the curtain rose on the outdoor stage erected for the presentation of a play, they chanted the "Lord's Prayer" and sang other selections throughout the evening. "Mr. White and the Jubilee Singers were in their element," Pike claimed, "and never was a more grateful service rendered in England."[35]

Among the social invitations that most impressed the managers and the Jubilees were those that came from the Honorable William E. Gladstone, England's Prime Minister. The ensemble's first appearance at Carlton House Terrace, his London residence, was to provide musical entertainment for a lunch the Prime Minister hosted for the Prince and Princess of Wales, members of the royal family, and other distinguished guests.[36] The Jubilees arrived early and positioned themselves in a small alcove, partially hidden, where they could sing before lunch was served. Their singing took the guests by surprise. By request, they presented several more selections, including their version of "John Brown's Body," sung, said Pike, "with all the soul and power usually thrown into it by the singers":[37] "John Brown's body lies a mould'ring in the grave, / but his soul is marching on. / Now has come the glorious jubilee, when all mankind are free. / Glory, glory, hallelujah, when all mankind are free."[38] British audiences always seemed to come alive when the Jubilee Singers sang this tune. Contrary to Americans, the English threw hats and handkerchiefs into the air in animated appreciation, a response that greatly impressed the singers. "It sent a thrill through us to think that so many hearts beat in unison with ours on the subject of universal freedom," Benjamin Holmes remarked. "For in our own country there are many who think otherwise, and when we sang the same song there it was almost received with groans."[39] The luncheon guests that day received "John Brown's Body" enthusiastically, asking for an encore performance. "When we were through singing we took luncheon at the royal tables," reported Holmes, "bade Hon. and Mrs. Gladstone adieu and returned to our plain apartments (bearing with us our dignity)."[40]

Some invitations moved beyond the wish merely to hear the Jubilee Singers sing to a desire to know them personally. Prior to their appearance at the Prime Minister's luncheon, the company had rarely been invited to any event without being asked to perform. A note Pike received from the Prime Minister several days after their visit to Carlton House Terrace changed this reality. "It has occurred to me that perhaps they might like to breakfast with us, my family and a very few friends, but I would not ask this unless it is thoroughly agreeable to them," wrote Gladstone.[41] Pike was overwhelmed by the invitation and saw it as a symbolic change in the company's status.

If the Prime Minister of England can ask coloured people to sit at his table, can we not hope our loved country, where all men are born free and equal, where there is no aristocracy, where "high worth is elevated place," will sit in sackcloth for the abominations she hath done, till her wicked prejudices are taken away? I have ever felt that this event was worth as much to the coloured people the world over as the campaign cost us; and after it had transpired, I knew that our mission could in no case be reckoned a failure.

For Pike, this occasion marked a significant first for the Jubilee Singers. Rather than functioning as mere entertainers, they were being welcomed into a prominent home as friends. The invitation represented progress not just for these few African Americans, reflected Pike, but for the race as a whole. Perhaps the weary days of seeking hotel accommodations and passage on a steam liner were forever "remnants of the dark ages," he wrote.[42]

Neither did the special nature of this invitation escape the attention of the Jubilee Singers. Writing home, Benjamin Holmes happily pointed out that the company had been invited to eat, and *"Not to sing."*[43] Ella Sheppard's recollections of this event also reflect her delight that the Jubilee Singers "went as guests and were seated at table among other guests as distinguished as those on the previous occasion, and were royally entertained as guests."[44]

The breakfast was an extravagant affair. In addition to the fifteen-member party of the Jubilee Singers and the Gladstone family were several members of the nobility and other prominent citizens. Two breakfast tables adorned with flowers accommodated them, with the Jubilee Singers distributed evenly between guests at the tables. Reverend Newman Hall was in attendance and provided the New York *Independent* with a vivid and lengthy description of the event, drawing special attention to how the Jubilee Singers were treated as equals:

At the table where the dean and myself sat, Mrs. Gladstone, Miss Gladstone, and Mr. W. H. Gladstone were most assiduous in their kind attentions—not only seeing that the physical comfort of their negro guests was attended to, but conversing with them so constantly and pleasantly that they were quite at their ease. At the other table Lady Cavendish, acting for Mrs. Gladstone and seated side by side with her coloured sisters, diffused the same atmosphere of social geniality around. A number of liveried footmen ministered also to the wants of the guests, paying as much attention and deference to the coloured singers from Tennessee as to the titled ladies of the English aristocracy and to the untitled but no less noble lady whose guests we were. To English readers I should apologise for writing this way. My description would be severely criticized, as giving prominence to trifling courtesies which with us are matters of course. No one here, pretending to social refinement, would make the least distinction between the guests he might meet merely on the ground of colour, and no one would hesitate on that account to invite to his house any one otherwise suitable. I am told that there still exists in the United States some remnant of the old prejudice. This may be found, no doubt, amongst some of the ignorant and vulgar of our own land; and so also it would not be fair to infer that such prejudice is general in America because exhibited by some low-bred, unrefined and narrow souls. I fancy some of these were at Surrey Chapel the other Sunday morning, when the Jubilee Singers did me the honour of taking a little luncheon with some of my friends at Rowland Hill's parsonage. Some Americans had come to take my hand, and I asked them to join us. But when they entered the house, and saw our negro friends sitting down to table side by side with some English ladies, they looked surprised, stood awhile at the door, and then walked away down the street! I wish they had been present yesterday to see Mrs. Gladstone and her daughters, and the noble lords and ladies present, taking their negro friends by the hand, placing them chairs, sitting at their side, pouring out their tea, etc., and conversing with them in a manner utterly free from any approach either to pride or condescension; but exactly as if they had been white people in their own rank of life. And this not as an effort, nor for the show of it, but from a habit of social intercourse which would have rendered any other conduct perfectly impossible.[45]

After a guided tour through Gladstone's vast art collection, the guests returned to the drawing room where the Jubilee Singers offered to perform several selections, much to the Prime Minister's pleasure. He leaned forward in rapt attention, and when they had finished their last piece, exclaimed, "Isn't it wonderful? I never heard anything like it!"[46]

For the Jubilees, sharing their music on this occasion functioned as normal social activity between friends. Prime Minister Gladstone had engaged them in intellectual reflection and opened his home and private art collection to the Jubilee Singers with the same generosity of spirit he bestowed on his other guests. In return, they gave their music. Reverend Newman Hall, who had heard the ensemble before, thought their singing gained extra brilliance. "I never heard them sing…as they did yesterday," commented Hall. "It was not the music alone, but the features of the singers also which made it so impressive. They sang as beings inspired. Their whole forms seemed to dilate. Their eyes flashed; their countenances told of reverence and joy and gratitude to God."[47]

One notable British divine counted among their friends was the Reverend Charles Haddon Spurgeon. Like his counterpart in America, Henry Ward Beecher, Spurgeon had established his reputation as the foremost preacher in England. Pike referred to him as the "prince of his profession."[48] The son of a Congregational minister, Spurgeon chose to reject the traditions of his father and was baptized as an adult believer. He became the pastor of a Baptist church in New Park Street, Southwark, London, where his preaching drew such large crowds that the congregation decided to expand the chapel. During the construction phase, Spurgeon held services at the Exeter Hall. Upon its return to the renovated New Park Street, the congregation discovered that it had already outgrown its new facility. Finally, the church leaders decided to construct a grand tabernacle, which they christened the Metropolitan Tabernacle, an enormous facility that held six thousand people and functioned as a center for worship, education, and social activity. Spurgeon preached there from 1861 until just before his death.[49]

The British minister opened his Metropolitan Tabernacle to the Jubilee Singers based on their reputation alone. Before the fixed date, the company decided to attend one of Spurgeon's morning worship services, and waited afterwards in an adjoining room to meet the spiritual leader. The small crowd gathered with them asked if they would sing a song, a request they honored: "Oh, brothers, don't stay away, / For my Lord says there's room enough, / Room enough in the Heav'ns for you. / My Lord says there's room enough, don't stay away." Spurgeon was in the next room and overheard the singing. "I found tears coming in my eyes," he later reported, "and looking at my deacons, I found theirs very moist too." Casting convention aside, he asked the company to sing the same spiritual that evening as part of his sermon. Spurgeon introduced the ensemble to his congregation by proclaiming that "they preach in the singing; and may the Spirit of God send home this word to some to-night—some who may remember their singing if they forget my preaching."[50]

Prior to a repeat performance at the Metropolitan Tabernacle, Spurgeon and his wife invited the Jubilees to take tea at their residence. The troupe arrived at the station to find the minister waiting to escort them. They spent the afternoon playing croquet followed by a sumptuous dinner. When it was time to leave, the couple presented each member of the company with a book and donated eighteen volumes of Spurgeon's own work to the Fisk University library. A packed house of six thousand awaited them at the Tabernacle, and according to Benjamin Holmes, thousands more were turned away. The evening concert was a "succession of triumphs," crowed Pike. They answered encore after encore and the net proceeds were the largest they had yet received in London.[51]

Open doors in both the public and private spheres became the norm for the company's travel experiences in Europe. In Scarborough, they were welcomed by a high-flying flag and a grand reception. They took lodging with Mr. Whittaker, a member of the Town Council, at whose house "every attention was received."[52] When it was time to leave, many of the town residents accompanied them to the station, "seeming even more interested in us than before," noted Isaac Dickerson. His letter to AMA secretary Whiting described their departure: "As the train left the station…the people gave three cheers for *America.* Looking back as far as I could see I could see hats and handkerchiefs waving after us. Have we not much to thank God for! God bless the good people of England."[53]

Social invitations were as numerous in Scotland as they had been in England. One invitation the company gladly accepted was to a dinner party hosted by the Lord Provost of Edinburgh. Pike eagerly related a letter written by one of the guests, Reverend Dr. William Hanna, expounding on the good impression the Jubilee Singers made:

> …I found myself seated at table betwixt two of the female band of singers, and more intelligent or better-mannered companions at table no one could desire. After such an education as they had received at Fisk University, I was prepared for the intelligence; but I own that I was not prepared for the quiet, unassuming, cultured manner…. When after dinner, the health of the Jubilee Singers was given, one of their own number (Mr. Dickerson) in responding, said: "Ten years ago I was a slave: to-day I am not only enjoying all the privileges of a free man, but find myself sitting at such a table as this, surrounded by such kind friends, - ten years ago I was subject

to the auction-block and the lash: to-day there is no auction-block and no lash in all the United States."[54]

Isaac Dickerson, with eloquence honed through his speaking opportunities with the company, continued by telling the guests that he hoped the Jubilee Singers "would prove worthy of the deep sympathy and interest that their friends had taken in their enterprise, and that the negro race might yet be a people that no nation would be ashamed to own."[55]

During spring 1874, the Jubilee Singers completed the series of concerts in Scotland and began making their way back to London. Their crowded schedule of concerts and social activity did not subside. "Social invitations greeted us everywhere," wrote Ella Sheppard, and requests for their services at various Christian efforts were so great that they could not answer them all. The company formally closed its first British campaign with a concert in London's Exeter Hall on 31 March 1874 with Lord Shaftesbury presiding. According to the press, success had not tarnished the individual members' character, but only served to improve the company's overall musical excellence: "We need not characterize the singing; but recalling the first appearance of the singers, after their arrival in England, we could not but note that, although they must have been well-nigh surfeited with applause, they are as natural and unaffected now as at the commencement of their 'campaign'; while their execution appears to have gained in precision."[56] The Jubilee Singers had satisfied the musical and social expectations of audiences across Britain and Scotland, a triumphant conclusion to their first year overseas. "We captured the hearts of the Englishmen; we sang ourselves into their very souls," rejoiced Georgia Gordon.[57]

Return to Britain: 1875

The Jubilee Singers launched their final campaign abroad with an appearance in London at the annual meeting of the Freedmen's Mission Aid Society. They were greeted by an abundance of loyal supporters. "Our friends had heard that we would be there and packed both upper and lower halls, the corridors and streets so solidly that Lord Shaftesbury had difficulty in reaching the rostrum," wrote Ella Sheppard. "His Lordship welcomed our return 'in behalf of thousands and tens of thousands of British citizens, with joy.'"[58] America Robinson, new to the company, was instantly impressed with the display of public enthusiasm. "It is really wonderful how these English people do turn out to gatherings," she wrote her boyfriend, James Burrus, in amazement.[59] She was enthralled with the country immediately.

Once again, social invitations poured in and the Jubilee Singers found themselves thrust into the public limelight. "It was impossible to respond to all the invitations that came to us," said Sheppard.[60] With such fame came certain benefits, such as the power of their name alone. "I recall…how the singers when they got into restricted places did not hesitate to say, 'We are with the Jubilees.' For many doors that money could not open were thrown open to us by reason of our singing," wrote Maggie Porter.[61] Capacity crowds filled the halls, and within the first weeks of their arrival, Sheppard reported in her diary that they were having a "great time giving autographs."[62]

It was not long, however, before the Jubilee Singers learned how fame also brought its share of annoyances, most noticeably a loss of privacy. By the close of the first British campaign in 1874, Pike claimed that the Jubilees had become so accustomed to public notice that they were no longer especially flattered. In fact, such attentions were almost a "rather irksome addition to their labours."[63] When they returned to England in 1875, the Jubilee Singers found they were so well known that it was practically impossible to escape their public. Once after a performance at one of Moody's London revival meetings, Ella Sheppard reported that many people followed them home and stood around the gate outside their lodging. "Some even came into the yard which was exceedingly annoying," she confided to her diary.[64] In Kettering, vast crowds "swarmed the windows and doors" of their hotel, "waiting both our going to and from the concert." In their enthusiasm, citizens "outran the horses and class cars" that carried the company to and from the concert hall.[65]

Mabel Lewis recalled how crowds followed them as they strolled through town, especially if they took along Jennie Jackson, whose dark complexion fascinated the public: "We were great curiosities. Miss Jennie Jackson was very dark and she had no peace. She would take her umbrella and beat her way along with it. One time a crowd was following us and she went into a store and asked if she could go through the store and out the back door. We looked back and there they were, all following us into the store." In Ireland, Lewis described how people climbed trees to try and catch a glimpse of them as they rode into town, and so many had gathered at their hotel that the proprietor "had to take the hose to drive the crowd away." [66] It took only a few weeks for the independent America Robinson to grow weary of the public's attention. Illness forced her to leave one of their early London concerts before it was over, but she was "glad to get home," she wrote James, "for I did not want these English people to shake my hands off. Every one seems to think he must shake hands with me."[67]

When it came time to depart for an evening concert, the Jubilees found it preferable to sneak out the back door of their hotel rather than confront the crowds waiting for them at the front door. "The people were very kind here," Robinson told James, "almost too kind. They even invited themselves to supper and breakfast with us."[68] When she and Maggie Carnes left the hotel one morning, they were greeted by a crowd that shouted and cheered as they tried to make their way down the walk. The attention only irritated Robinson. "You are not allowed to slap any one on the street but you can pinch as much as you like," she wrote. "I felt strongly inclined to resort to the latter but knew I could not hurt them through their thick homespun." A gentleman came to their rescue and dispersed the crowds, said a grateful Robinson. "I could have knelt in the mud and thanked him for this unspeakable kindness but on second thought did not and too I had on a new dress."[69]

Managers set the Jubilees' concert and social calendars, accepting those invitations they felt would best advance the campaign and mission. Generally, the singers did not mind fulfilling these social obligations and many of them developed lasting friendships with several of their hosts. However, they were understandably offended when it appeared as if they were simply on display. Sheppard described staying with a family who thought nothing of inviting their close friends to constantly visit with her. "It doesn't seem to occur to them that these are company to us and therefore must take as much strength from us as any other strangers." The group members soon learned to accept an invitation to tea only on the condition "that there are to be no guests." Despite this sincere request, said Sheppard, often they would arrive to "find the house full of 'relations & particular friends'—who about kill us with conversation & singing."[70] Most of their hosts expected a mini-concert to accompany any visit with the Jubilee Singers, a fact that irked America Robinson. "It is very tiresome for us when we go visiting and have singing to do besides." She would rather forego the visit and just stay home, she told James.[71]

Sheppard considered one particular situation an egregious breach of etiquette. A Scottish minister asked if he could join the company members for their private evening worship held at the hotel. When the Jubilee Singers entered the designated room, they were surprised to find it filled with townspeople squeezed "shoulder to shoulder." "They had congregated at the church expecting that we would be there. They had been sent for to come to this room. The minister had his great bible and little pulpit from the church. He read and prayed and we sang several songs and then hastened to our rooms. I was disgusted but I suppose they meant well—but it did seem such an intrusion I could not worship with this crowd staring one in the face."[72] Though the public's desire to enter into their private lives sometimes crossed the boundaries of good taste, Sheppard was nonetheless grateful for the obvious welcome extended to the company throughout Europe, and agreed with those who felt their presence was God-ordained. "It almost makes me shudder to think of the power of the Jubilee Singers and its responsibility," she wrote.[73] Unlike America Robinson, who considered the public an irritating nuisance, Sheppard felt the inconveniences of fame were a necessary burden to bear for the sake of the company's Christian mission.

To their credit, the Jubilee Singers managed to overlook breaches of etiquette and enjoy the benefits of their status. Many of their hosts took special pains to show them the historical and cultural attractions of their towns, and in spite of a demanding concert schedule, the singers squeezed in time for long sightseeing jaunts, boat rides, carriage rides, and visits to museums and other cultural centers. Especially meaningful were the personal friendships developed with many of the people they met. "I have made some very dear friends here," America Robinson wrote to James. "They are what the people here call real ladies." James once accused her of considering Americans "below par." "Not at all," she retorted, "except those who consider me so. You quoted Cicero 'Old friends before new,' so think I. But I take special care to see who my old friends are. I am sorry to say I have few among the American whites."[74] In contrast, many friendships the singers made while in England seemed sincere.

In Wales, the Jubilees found themselves once again thronged by an adoring crowd. Townsfolk went out of their way to entertain and befriend the company, extending daily invitations "to tea or some amusement."[75] The company's gentlemen especially welcomed the young ladies' attention. America Robinson confided to James that the men sometimes "left some very sad ladies behind." Thomas Rutling, known for his flirtatiousness, was "enamored with the Belle of Builth," who seemed quite heartsick when the troupe left. Robinson, too, had developed a close friendship with a couple in town who told her they "fell in love" with her the first time they saw her and were quite sad to see her leave. "The people in Builth declared they could not get along without us," she informed James.[76]

By this time, the Jubilee Singers had become experts at discerning the motives of their various hosts. Those whose friendship and interest in them appeared genuine won the troupe's respect. Such was the case with Francis Alexander Keith-Falconer, the eighth earl of Kintore. His Lordship invited them to lunch with his family at Keith Hall and met them at the train station with his youngest son. Before lunch, he took them on a walking tour of his estate where the singers stopped to feed the swans and rest in garden chairs overlooking the lake.[77] Back at the hall, the singers spent some time poring over His Lordship's autograph album and admiring his collection of beautiful paintings. After they lunched, Lord Kintore proposed a toast:

> I wish to express to our American friends my earnest thanks for the pleasure which their visit has given me.... I welcome you not only as brother and sister in Christ, but as brothers and sisters indeed; for we are one blood, though it may be of different color. Whether we be Scythian, Parthian, English, American or Scotch, we are striving for the same home and serving the same master. May the Lord bless you for obtaining for others the privileges you enjoy, and may he transfer to your hearts, collectively and individually, the motto outside my door—"may grace and truth rest here in peace."

Sheppard recorded in her diary that His Lordship's gracious words brought tears to many eyes. Frederick Loudin rose to offer an eloquent reply on behalf of the troupe.

My lord, you can but little realize why and how your words have touched our hearts—we of the oppressed race, so unaccustomed to words of kindness and cheer. I repeat, you cannot realize how words such as we have just listened to, coming as they do from you, melt our hearts. I thank you for the evidence you have given us that you recognize so fully that great principle of truth, that God has made of one flesh and blood all the nations that dwell upon the face of the Earth. In the name of the millions of our race who were so long made mute by the chains they wore, and in the name of the cause we have come here to represent and labor for, and in the name of my associates, the Jubilee Singers, I thank you and yours, and the friends who are gathered here, more than I have language to express, for your sympathy and for the pleasure this occasion has afforded us.[78]

Ella interpreted Lord Kintore's hospitality as an expression of pure friendship and felt the day would remain one of her most "pleasant recollections." Buoyed in spirit, the company gave a good concert that evening to a crowded house. "It seems as tho our cup of blessings is running over today," Sheppard recorded in her diary.[79]

On return visits in and around Glasgow, Lord Kintore made a point of visiting his American friends. At the close of a concert in Aberdeen, he took the platform to praise the Jubilee Singers and their work. "I never was honored at Keith Hall by guests with whom I have had more real enjoyment and pleasure than the Jubilee Singers," he told the audience. He descended the platform and shook hands with each singer as he or she passed by. "Lord K said he loved us," Ella wrote in her diary. "It is returned."[80]

Invitations by Royalty

It is perhaps no surprise that invitations to appear before European royalty were prominent recollections for many of the Jubilee Singers. One particular performance before the crowned heads of Holland stood out in their memories because of its magnificence mixed with a sense of informality. The singers were awestruck by the "dazzling splendor of the reception given us at the palatial home of Baron van Wassenaer de Catwijck at the Hague," where they were asked to give a private concert for the royal family and about one hundred members of the nobility.[81] Though their hotel was across the street from the palace, court etiquette required that they be conveyed in carriages to the palace doorstep. A red carpet "stretched from the hall to the carriage so we did not touch the ground at all," marveled America Robinson, who was equally awestruck by the finery of court attire. Her Majesty the Queen, Sophia Fredericka Mathilde, was arrayed in a splendid diamond coronet. Diamonds and pearls adorned the bare necks of almost every lady in the room, and even the Baron's butler wore diamond studs. "Satins, silks and velvets, pearls and diamonds were dazzlingly set forth. I *never* beheld such splendor before," said an amazed Robinson. Ella Sheppard agreed: "The scene was beyond description in brilliancy and magnificence."[82]

The troupe's simple dress presented a sharp contrast to the vast display of wealth, thought Sheppard, but did not seem to dampen the enthusiasm with which they were greeted. Unlike Queen Victoria, who four years ago spoke to the Jubilee Singers only through one of her attendants, the Queen of the Netherlands "conversed freely" with the company. "There was not the least stiffness during the whole evening," claimed Robinson. Hinton Alexander recalled how the "Queen gave us pleasant individual greetings, asking each of us a separate question and telling us how much she enjoyed our singing." She was so taken by their performance that she later attended one of their public concerts. His Majesty, King William III, invited them to perform the following week at his country home. The King had a reputation of being cross and crabby, Robinson told James, and scheduled meetings only during certain times of the year. So the Jubilees were surprised to receive his impromptu invitation. His Majesty once again expressed his enthusiasm for the company and gave a large subscription to the Livingstone Hall fund.[83]

Another memorable visit with royalty was the Jubilee Singers' performance before Germany's Crown Prince Friedrich Wilhelm Nikolaus Karl and the Crown Princess Victoria, firstborn child of England's Queen Victoria. The princess had learned about the company from her mother, who had written a lengthy and enthusiastic letter after hearing the Jubilee Singers at Argyll Lodge four years earlier. Now she very much wanted to hear them herself, and wasted little time in extending an invitation for the singers to perform at the New Palace in Potsdam on a Sunday afternoon.

Arriving at the station, the company found the royal livery ready to transport them to the palace. They settled themselves in two roomy, plush carriages lined with white satin ("Now this is comfort," said Hinton

Alexander) and were delighted when a corps of soldiers stopped and saluted them as they passed. At the palace, they were ushered into a small room to dispose of their wraps, and then taken through a massive marble hall into an elegant salon chosen especially for its fine acoustics. Huge full-length mirrors hung between the frescos on the wall, and the polished floor glimmered. They had barely gotten settled when the Crown Prince and Princess entered, followed by their children and other members of the royal family, who rushed to greet their guests "with a hearty and cordial welcome." Cravath had sent ahead one of the Jubilee Singers' histories, which Prince Frederick had read, intently studying their photos in preparation for this visit. To their surprise, he knew several of the Jubilee Singers by name.

The troupe had just finished singing "Steal Away" and chanting "The Lord's Prayer" when the aging Emperor arrived. He had rearranged his schedule in order to hear the ensemble, and though offered a chair, chose to stand erect throughout their thirty-minute performance. Through an interpreter, he asked Cravath if all the members of the company were Christians and seemed satisfied to find that they were. He expressed great interest in the status of affairs for freedmen, especially in the effect of education upon their welfare. During "Nobody Knows the Trouble I See," Princess Victoria wept, and Sheppard speculated whether she was thinking of the recent loss of her child.[84] A "reliable source" later reported that the singing had so moved the princess that she could not rest all night and talked incessantly about their music. "Thank God for another evidence of the good results of our dear old sacred slave songs," said Sheppard.[85]

The ease and informality of the Crown Prince and Princess impressed the Jubilee Singers. In between songs, the royal family gathered around them and "talked as finely & socially as could possibly have been expected between equals," reported Sheppard.[86] "Crowned heads could not have been treated with more distinction than was shown us in Germany," noted Hinton Alexander.[87] "This was a great day," recalled Maggie Porter. "It was something of the splendor I was hungry for, yet we were cordially treated, spoken to, and lunched when we had sung."[88] "I shall never forget that one insight—without ceremony—into the home circle of the grandest royal house in the world," Sheppard confided to her diary that evening. "'Twas beautiful. Even in their dress there was simplicity yet elegance."[89]

After their mini-concert, the royal children came forward to shake the hand of each Jubilee. George White presented one of their linen-bound books of spirituals to the prince, who tucked it under his arm "as a child would a precious toy," promising he would sing them with his family. Pleased with the many complimentary remarks on their singing, the Jubilee Singers left the great hall, picked up their wraps, and then entered another room for a small lunch. "We had only five or ten minutes," said Sheppard, "but all King George's horses could not have pulled us away till we had drunk a cup of royal tea & a sandwich or cake from the royal tray & fruit & cake in my pocket to send to Rosa." Royal carriages took them back to their hotel where their own "plain tea awaited." "Oh my, what a difference in the flavors of the *tea!*" bemoaned Sheppard. The company gathered for their evening devotions with glad and grateful hearts, raising their voices in "Praise God from Whom All Blessings Flow." It was a fitting benediction, thought Sheppard, to a day "of the greatest & most peculiar honor to the Jubilee Singers."[90]

Benefits of Social Success

By the close of the last campaign, the Jubilee Singers could rightly boast that they had been invited into some of the most prestigious parlors known to the Western European world as well as the palaces of many of the crowned heads of Europe. The Jubilees interacted intimately with many Europeans and found themselves the darlings of British society. Members of royalty, families of nobility, and others persons of respected social standing entertained the Jubilee Singers individually and collectively in their private estates. Company members wrote personal letters, exchanged gifts, and forged close friendships with people from all stations of life. "Probably no private party of Americans was ever before treated with such distinguished attention as was this company of Jubilee Singers," declared Hinton Alexander.[91]

Traveling with the Jubilee Singers enterprise offered a dizzying array of experiences. The company had mingled with nobility, conversed with the American President, shared the platform with leading clergymen and politicians, and socialized with people from all walks of life. They had been in palaces as well as poor houses; they sang before kings and queens as well as orphans and the mentally ill. The troupe had given "Services of Song" in churches across the denominational spectrum and partnered with the era's most successful revivalist. Their concerts included performances before crowds that understood English, and those that understood not a word they sang. They had traveled between two continents, giving concerts throughout the Eastern United States and across several European countries.

Successfully navigating between these diverse worlds and through such a plethora of experiences required sophisticated social skills on the part of the ensemble's members. Each had to learn the proper rules of court etiquette, how to engage in small talk and also handle intellectual discourse, and how to fulfill the expectations required of them in various social arenas. They successfully dealt with denominational and pastoral idiosyncrasies and figured out how to manage an adoring but often annoying public. The male members of the company honed their public speaking skills as they mounted the platform to present the company's mission and the needs of their race. All learned how to champion the cause of freedom without violating the Victorian boundaries of good taste and proper decorum.

The members of the Jubilee Singers were keenly aware of the social burden prestige placed upon them. As famous African Americans, they represented their race to many whose knowledge of blacks was based largely on negative stereotypes. The hopes of many African Americans yearning for a share in the "American dream" were shaped in part by the ensemble's success. Each victory over prejudice, both publicly and privately, was a source of immense racial pride. In his 1881 history of notable African-American musicians, James Trotter described the Jubilee Singers as representing "perhaps the most picturesque achievement in all our history since the war." That a group of relatively young and inexperienced black musicians could gain international stature within a few short years was, to Trotter, an amazing feat.[92]

The freedom the Jubilee Singers felt in Europe affirmed their sense of self worth and empowered their voices for justice. In a letter published in the *New National Era*, Benjamin Holmes soundly denounced the racist practices adopted by the Baptists in Virginia and Illinois and stated that he "desired no fellowship with men whose hearts are so blackened with prejudice as to withhold from their fellow man the truth which God has given them to preach 'to every nation.'" While the Jubilee Singers were "enjoying all these blessings in this strange land," he declared, they would not fail to remember the struggles of their African-American brothers and sisters at home. "Therefore, let our young colored men be awakened to their duty, and neglect no opportunity which will make them bold to assert and strong to vindicate the rights of their people," Holmes fearlessly encouraged.[93] In time, other Jubilee Singers such as Frederick Loudin, Greene Evans, and Ella Sheppard added their voices to Holmes's to promote civil rights for African Americans.[94]

Perhaps the most significant outcome of the Jubilee Singers' social experiences abroad, however, was personal. One can only imagine the individual impact of living and working in a country where each member of the ensemble felt relatively free of racial prejudice. In England for the first time, noted Marsh, the company members lived daily lives as social equals: "In no way were they ever offensively reminded, through look or word— unless by some rude American who was lugging his caste conceit through a European tour, or by a vagrant Englishman who had lived long enough in America to 'catch' its color prejudices—that they were black."[95] The difference between the American and European social landscapes strongly affected the psyches of the young Jubilee Singers. One recalled: "While we were in England...we were not reminded of our colour. We almost forgot that we were anything but human beings. But we hardly landed on our native shores when we were made to feel very keenly that we belonged to a despised race."[96]

Working in an environment of relative freedom allowed each Jubilee Singer to mature and grow in self-awareness, self-confidence, and self-esteem. Their recollections indicate that touring with the company was a highlight experience of their lives. Thomas Rutling described his time spent with the Jubilee Singers as "the most pleasant epoch" of his life and an invaluable educational experience. "It not only enabled me to have glimpses into the homes of nearly all the kings, dukes, and great men of Protestant Europe, but also gave me a chance to see what refined, educated civilisation means."[97] Years later, Georgia Gordon recalled fondly her days as a Jubilee Singer. "I could go on writing of the beautiful things we saw, of the gracious and kindly words spoken to us, of the welcoming into the homes of the best people of England."[98] "I live daily in the sweet memories of those days," said an aging Maggie Porter. "God bless Fisk, through which I have had so many wonderful experiences."[99] Porter claimed England as her favorite spot in all of Europe, as did America Robinson. "I like England better than any country I ever was in, because there is not an atom of prejudice here," declared Robinson.[100]

Traveling outside of the United States gave the Jubilees an opportunity to experience the absence of social distinction based on race. In England, they found themselves admitted freely into public places, welcomed in churches and concert halls, socially entertained by friendly sympathizers, and invited into the private residences of royalty. Daily living as social equals strengthened each Jubilee's sense of identity and self-worth and, as a result, empowered their individual voices, which they exercised fiercely on behalf of their own rights and for the cause of freedom universally.

The Jubilee Singers' interaction with society's elite reassured the AMA and its like-minded members that education plus religion was indeed the pathway by which African Americans could enter mainstream society. The AMA wasted no time in trumpeting the ensemble's social success:

> It seems more appropriate to romance than reality that a little company of ex-slaves should, by their musical gifts, win the applause of large and cultured audiences,—that the rigid caste prejudice in America should break down before them, and that the traditional exclusiveness of British society should so far be overcome that its refined people, learned divines, titled nobility, and even royalty itself, should delight to hear them; that castle halls and grounds should be opened for their reception; that the Prime Minister should give them entertainment in his own house, and that imperial cities should officially welcome them as guests![101]

Few could claim such a reception by persons of the highest rank in British society, a fact the AMA felt was a "just rebuke to the miserable caste-prejudice that still lingers in this country." That the Jubilee Singers had gained such favorable attention in such a short time was a powerful tool with which AMA officials publicly denounced America's discriminatory practices. "Some of our pert hotel-clerks and self-important railroad conductors could only, by a fee to the servants, gain admission to the empty rooms in mansions where the titled owners have welcomed and feasted these colored people," the leaders stated.[102]

Each successive victory the company enjoyed on European soil fueled the AMA's attack on the American psyche regarding the inherent dignity of African Americans. If newly freed slaves could achieve such phenomenal musical and social success in the public and private spheres of life, argued the AMA, then who could deny their potential? The AMA pointed to the Jubilee Singers' fame, recognition as concert artists, and social acceptance by the Western world's most illustrious citizens as irrefutable proof that these young African-American men and women were indeed social equals.

Chapter 7

"Infinite Troubles":

Practical Application of American

Missionary Association Ideals

Most of the singers keep humble, but a few give me infinite trouble.[1]

The association's aims to "elevate, educate and evangelize" the freedmen were being realized to their fullest extent in the lives of the Jubilee Singers. So were the American Missionary Association's (AMA) hopes of raising leaders who could guide the race forward. The individual members of the company flourished in an atmosphere that granted them a measure of respect, independence, social acceptance, and educational enrichment. Moreover, what had begun as a student ensemble crusading for the cause of Fisk University had evolved into a professional, experienced company representing the AMA and its broader ministry goals. With the signing of contracts, each member accepted a commitment to the ideological goals of the AMA and a clear understanding of the demands of the work: missionary consecration, self-sacrifice, good health and physical energy, personal character, and respectable conduct.[2] In every way and at all times, the Jubilee Singers were not to lose sight that they were employees of the AMA.

Just how these expectations translated practically and personally became the source of internal tensions at various levels. The Jubilees' contracts stipulated that each member was "to work cheerfully and in harmonious cooperation" with their business managers.[3] However, in practice, the accountability structure and control of the Fisk Jubilee Singers enterprise was less defined and more difficult to maintain, due in part to the fact that the singers did not come empty-handed to the negotiation table.

Their vocal talent and artistic rendering of the spirituals were absolutely essential to any fundraising success. "We cannot sing without singers you know," America Robinson once remarked.[4] Moreover, the speeches and appeals made by many of the male singers on behalf of the race and the AMA's work with freedmen carried an authority unavailable to their white counterparts. The Jubilees understood their indispensable role in the business and wanted to function as valued partners rather than simply as hired workers, exercising some measure of control over the musical product and self-determination over their personal lives.

While all supported the stated goals of the AMA, not all agreed on the strategy for achieving these goals. Neither did everyone embrace or interpret "missionary service" alike, a fact that also contributed to internal friction. The AMA and its higher education institutions were founded by men and women who had made huge personal sacrifices, even risked their lives in some instances, for the causes of abolition and freedmen's education. The leadership expected no less from anyone participating in the Jubilee Singers enterprise. Data suggest that the company members wholeheartedly believed in the cause for which they labored and embraced the same codes of conduct as their managers. Singers and managers enjoyed the same comforts and suffered similar physical hardships. The Jubilee Singers business venture was a partnership from its inception with everyone sharing equally in the trials and victories the company experienced. At times, though, the singers felt that their interests were being ignored or denied. While company members recognized and accepted established lines of authority, they were unwilling to bow to the overlording of whites. They might accept advice and guidance, but ultimately demanded the freedom to determine their own destinies. Any suspicion of white domination or hint of unfair practices did not set well with the company members. Squabbles over salaries, complaints about the work schedule, and interpersonal clashes soured some relationships and brought to the forefront questions of control. Finding a proper balance between commitment to the AMA's ideology and personal sacrifice was a challenge for all those associated with the enterprise.

Recurring illnesses and a demanding work schedule that left little time for personal rest and relaxation exacerbated tensions. Pike had accurately predicted that there was no way to make the amount of money for which the AMA hoped without submitting to a non-stop performance schedule.

Therefore, the ensemble met every concert obligation regardless of whether or not all of the company members were in good health. They simply could not afford to cancel an engagement. Because Fisk University's needs were so great, there was a real sense that the Jubilees could never raise enough to satisfy the coffers. Once one need was met, another would surface, and this stark reality created an endless sense of urgency to the Jubilee Singers' fundraising efforts. The stress of such an unrelenting schedule contributed to raw nerves and short feelings between everyone associated with the company. Managers sometimes disagreed with the AMA executive leadership over campaign strategies and fiscal management. White wrangled with the temperaments and desires of individual singers, and personality clashes between participants were increasingly common.

These circumstances made the Jubilee Singers undertaking a living laboratory, in a sense, for the practical working out of the AMA's Christian Reconstruction's espoused ideals. The principles of freedom and full equality within the context of missionary service were tested on a daily basis. Imperfection characterized the actions and behaviors of all as each participant, regardless of race or position, struggled to reconcile the overarching aims of the association with daily living.

What follows here is a litany of the growing tensions that eventually culminated in the AMA's decision in July 1878 to disband the company. Though the Jubilee Singers were at the height of their concert success and enjoyed a relatively untainted public image, internal struggles had severely deteriorated company morale. Bickering escalated and George White resigned, leaving the ensemble in the hands of his brother-in-law, President Erastus Cravath. Ministry expectations and the demands of an exhausting fundraising schedule collided with the health, well-being, and personal desires of many individuals associated with the enterprise. For some, the sacrifice the AMA required was just too great.

Conflicts, as troublesome as they were to the overall morale of the company, also represent moments of growth for the Jubilee Singers. Traveling with the group had exposed the members to educational, social, and life experiences they never would have had as students at Fisk University. Being known as a Jubilee Singer was a title each wore with pride. As the members gained confidence and experience, they stepped forward to exercise their rights as equals in matters that pertained to them personally. They were ready to voice their opinions, challenge decisions, and attempt to make it on their own apart from the AMA's watchful care. In short, they matured into polished professionals with the self-confidence to function as equals with their white managers. It was an outcome the AMA leadership fully desired, but did not quite know how to handle when realized.

Given that the company lived together closely and had daily work obligations, they managed interpersonal relationships fairly well. The high standards of Christian behavior required civil discourse, impeccable conduct, and the complete yielding of one's will for the sake of the mission. More often than not, the Jubilee Singers and their managers met these lofty criteria. The relationship failures we find in their story simply illustrate that human beings do not always get along, even if they share common goals, beliefs, and lifestyles. As Sandra Graham reminds us, their personal foibles help us see the Jubilee Singers not as "sanitized role models but instead as multidimensional human beings."[5] We find that human beings can accomplish great good in spite of their individual weaknesses.

This was certainly the case with the Jubilee Singers. Almost single-handedly, the company ensured the survival of Fisk University. Had it not been for their concert success, the institution could have joined the ranks of many other small, struggling colleges that lived and died during this time.[6] Instead, their musical triumphs spread the names of Nashville and Fisk University throughout the world, and their fame inspired other gifted African-American musicians and entertainers to pursue professional careers. Most of the Jubilee Singers emerged from their tenure with the group as leaders of their race, some on the local level and others on the national and international scene. Though being a member of the Jubilee Singers had its share of ups and downs, the experience had enhanced the self-confidence and self-image of all. Catapulted to positions of fame, they remained positive role models and symbols of hope for all African Americans.

Frugality and Self-Sacrifice

By all accounts, the inaugural campaign of the Jubilee Singers was the most trouble-free internally. Perhaps the constant battles to establish identity, gain the endorsement of the AMA, and win the confidence of the Northern Christian community so consumed the troupe that the net result was a cohesive internal bonding. White and his small band of singers considered themselves crusaders on a common mission to save their institution from demise. With a sense of solidarity, they endured difficult trials during the first months of their campaign, all for the sake of the cause.[7]

The AMA issued contracts for subsequent campaigns stipulating that each member could expect "comfortable and reasonable board and transportation." The association further promised "to exercise a watchful care" over each singer's personal interests, safety, and health, and guaranteed each member a two-month summer vacation.[8] Meeting some of these contractual obligations was much easier for the managers to achieve in England than it had been in America, as they did not have to wrestle with prejudicial hotel managers. It took a while for Pike to establish a consistent concert schedule for the ensemble's first campaign in England as they arrived in London's "off-season." In the interim, the singers accepted more social invitations than concert gigs, which alarmed Pike, who feared they would grow accustomed to a lighter work load and a more extravagant lifestyle unbefitting a good missionary. In letters to Cravath, he hinted that the ensemble and its director needed to practice more economy. "The great success of last winter was very demoralizing," Pike wrote, referring to their previous tour of New England, "and it will take a little time to restore those concerned to industrial and economic ideas."[9]

As concert appearances increased, so did the company's popularity. However, the dedicated missionary spirit for which Pike yearned did not materialize to his satisfaction. In fact, it seemed to him that the company's commitment to Christian service was even more difficult to maintain while living in the lap of luxury and basking in the glow of public praise. "Consecration is not next door neighbor to great popularity," he complained, "and so we sometimes find uphill work."[10] He agonized over whether success would jeopardize their public persona and suggested to

Cravath that it would be far less expensive to send him out alone as a fundraiser than try to manage this unwieldy group.

> The Jubilee Singers enterprise grows more expensive and so more trying to me, as it grows popular and successful. And it is sometimes hard to convey an idea that you are consecrated to a missionary work unless you can show it—by a readiness to work—to economize—to deny yourself for the furtherance of the mission you have in hand. You know it. Ward wrote home to his folks in war time that he and his soldiers were suffering great hardship in New York—they had to "take their meals at Delmonico and to sleep at the St. Nicolas Hotel." When our mission gets so it gives religious people this idea respecting the hardships we are suffering I have no doubt the time will be near when it will be right for me to take some other way to serve my God and country than by trying to meet the expenses of an enterprise that never can be managed so that my judgement or conscience will be satisfied. We have one concert this week - so the Singers might rest—tho I have no knowledge that any of them are tired—and none of them make such a complaint. White is tired. He always will be tired—you can't rest him. He will do all manner of superfluous things if he has no legitimate thing on hand. I have said all these things to explain in some measure why I cannot at all consent to put myself under any obligation to do Jubilee Singers business after the £6000 is raised.[11]

Within a mere three months of their stay in England, Pike felt the company's understanding of missionary service had eroded to a level he could no longer support. Once he had fulfilled his commitment, he told Cravath, he intended to move on to other fields of service for the AMA.

The Reverend Dr. Healy, corresponding secretary of the Freedmen's Aid Society, also felt that the expense of the Jubilee Singers venture was beyond the normal realm appropriate for a charitable organization, and wasted no time telling Cravath so:

> The "Jubilee Singers" and their escort are our neighbors.... I can but feel—though not directly my business—that their attaché is far too numerous and expensive. British philanthropists who are our best admirers and friends, remark upon the employment of two clergymen in such a work. In addition, as you are aware, a business manager is employed by Bro. Pike, to whom they give 1/10 of the gross receipts. Pardon this intrusive information and *bear in mind that it is...not to be repeated.*[12]

Considering the "15 hours a day" he was giving to the work, Pike would have likely defended his need for even more help.[13] However, he certainly shared Healy's concern for their reputation. Should the religious community suspect their motives, he feared their mission was lost. One British minister to whom they appealed expressed his "fullest sympathy with the attempt to educate the emancipated Africans," but did not hide his disapproval of the company's fundraising methods. Their programs seemed to him "to partake of that sensationalism of which, I think, we have too much already in the religious world."[14] The managers knew that the troupe's public image had to square with the Christian community's expectations for a missionary endeavor if they hoped to achieve their fundraising goals.[15]

Aggravations and Negotiations

George White struggled with his own frustrations. He had fretted over sending the troupe to London in May, England's "off-season," suspecting that the company would have difficulty securing concert engagements. Adding to his worries was concern over Laura, his ailing wife. White hoped the trip abroad would improve her poor health, but she required a doctor's care almost from the moment they landed and never recovered completely. Her "old troubles" kept her confined to her bed and the medical bills mounted. "It is very hard for us both and we get almost discouraged," wrote White, "especially as we find that our salary barely supports us." He assured his brother-in-law that they were trying to be as "economical as possible but the money goes." White had to engage a nurse to assume care of the children and the house and left his family behind in Scotland to fulfill his obligations with the troupe. After an operation performed in mid-September, Laura attempted to join her husband in Ireland but found she could not endure the passage and had to return to Glasgow.[16]

Differences also began to arise within the company. By October 1873, most of the members had been with the Jubilee Singers for at least a year, and a few were beginning their third year of service. Time had honed their artistic skills, and for six months in England, they had been petted and adored by the British. No longer did they need the protective nurturing of White, and could probably do quite well as solo concert artists without the supervision of the AMA. A few members toyed with the idea of striking out on their own. Both Pike and White were alarmed at the potential crisis.

"Only last week Mr. Watkins demanded his pay intending to pull out and leave us," White informed Cravath. He scrambled to negotiate, using "every inducement" he could to entice several of the singers to stay on board until the close of the campaign. "I have no hope of keeping the singers together longer," he warned Cravath. "If anything more is done it will have to be a new venture."[17]

White's plan was to give concerts abroad through March 1874, and then return in April for a series of American performances. He negotiated with the faction of disgruntled company members and finally reached a compromise: each singer would receive a benefit concert at the close of the campaign as a "handsome bonus" to their year's salary. "I desire to do the best thing," he told Cravath, and urged him to push the completion of Jubilee Hall by the first of May so that the benefit concerts could occur on the verandah. He saw this as a fitting and glorious finale to the campaign. In the meantime, White encouraged Cravath to recruit a "reserve force" of musical talent from which he could draw at a moment's notice just in case "any of our singers drop out." "I ought to have one good tenor, soprano & bass within reach," he wrote. "Most of the singers keep humble, but a few give me *infinite trouble*."[18]

Much to his chagrin, White learned that construction on Jubilee Hall had lagged. Though the university had broken ground for its new building in early 1873 and laid the cornerstone in October, there would be no completed Jubilee Hall by May of the next year. Finances were tight for the AMA and Cravath had redirected some of their earnings from Europe to help carry the association through the hard times. White was distraught over the news. "Mr. White's nerves are weak," reported Pike, "and sometimes he is tortured with apprehensions that are painful to him and very difficult to manage."[19] The stress of his wife's sickness, strife in the ensemble, and his perceived misappropriation of their hard-earned funds began to take their toll on White. "He has been holding on so long and takes things so seriously that I really think on his account it would be best for him to let up at the close of the year and take a time for recuperation without the great anxieties which he certainly cannot shake off in his present state of health," Pike advised Cravath.[20]

In subsequent letters, Pike expressed his own thoughts about how this fundraising effort could be managed more effectively. He strongly urged that the AMA leadership reestablish clear guidelines for any new undertaking involving the singers:

> As for Jubilee Singing in the future—I tell Mr. White and adhere to it with a consistent conviction that the Singers in the future should be employed by you just as the teachers of Fisk or Atlanta are employed—that they should be taught they are doing missionary work—the same—that their accounts should be submitted to you just as the accounts of the teachers are submitted, and that Mr. White's relation to them should be the same as Mr. Ware's relation is to the teachers at Atlanta, and that such persons as can be secured to work in that way would in the long run promote missionary work more than it can be promoted just now. This plan would save Mr. White one half the ware and tare he now suffers, and it would be more likely to keep the cooperation of any man who might have sufficient ability to attend to the financial part of this work. I am very anxious that the movement of anything under the patronage of the AMA should keep up the missionary character of our great society, as more than a little cash in hand is needed. We must inspire confidence—our work must be such it will bear investigation from top to bottom. Everything should be so that if all good men knew about it they would be inspired to help.[21]

To Pike, the root of their difficulties was that the company had lost its spiritual footing. He felt strongly that a return to the ideals of Christian missionary service would restore the proper boundaries for how the troupe should operate.

It took a few weeks for White to "recover from his disappointment and find his equilibrium," said Pike.[22] White rearranged his plans and abandoned the idea of giving concerts in America, while Pike filled the singers' concert calendar through spring 1874, leaving time at the close of the campaign for the benefit concerts White had promised. Pike disapproved of this arrangement, feeling that giving concert proceeds directly to the Jubilees' pockets compromised the association's integrity. "I never felt that this would be quite safe after the pretenses we have made to the public of the voluntary offer of the students to build the Hall as a free will offering for the colored people," Pike stated.[23] Moreover, he felt the company's comfortable lifestyle and numerous social engagements were setting a precedent the AMA would be unable to continue. He pondered what White and his singers would do after the campaign closed now that they were accustomed to such ease. "I do not believe Mr. White and his singers can *come down* to any other work," Pike told Cravath. "I really do not see what else any of them can do and keep their position *and* anywhere near meet the demands of the habits they have formed."[24]

Pike believed their behavior revealed a lack of discipline that was already affecting other aspects of this campaign. "The Singers do not like to practice," he stated plainly, and he felt their concerts subsequently did not always rise to the high musical standards of which the ensemble was capable. "There is nothing to 'take them down occasionally' as there was in America," he said, hinting that the members were a lot easier to handle when they faced the daily hardships and sufferings caused by American prejudice. "White is bothered to do anything with some of them," continued Pike, while also admitting that his own hands were kept full just bolstering up the director's spirits.[25]

Pike took care never to expose his doubts publicly, instead expressing supreme confidence in the singers' ability to handle public acclaim. In his second book on the ensemble, he proclaimed that touring had contributed to the Jubilees' moral and character development: they were "neat in their habits, and careful in their use of language." Pike applauded their thrift, non-materialism, commitment to their studies, and complete lack of impropriety or decorum. He portrayed the Jubilee Singers as model citizens transformed under the influence of the AMA. Confidentially, he warned Cravath to guard against any business or lifestyle practices that might damage the association's image or jeopardize its ministry.[26]

"Sinking Down"

The unyielding concert schedule during spring 1874 began to exact a heavy toll on various members of the troupe. Extended illness forced Susan Gilbert, the chaperone, and Pike's assistant, J. H. Halley, to discontinue their work with the company. Sickness also kept Pike confined to his room where he tried to direct the company's business through mountains of correspondence. White had to carry the bulk of campaign responsibilities alone, though fatigue was affecting his own health. Nonetheless, he left his family behind in Glasgow and journeyed with the singers so as to prevent any disruption in the itinerary. Within a few short weeks, however, he received word that Laura's health was in a serious condition. Having no one to whom he could pass the reigns of leadership, White considered it his "duty" to remain with the company. A few days later, he got a second telegram urging him to return immediately as his wife had contracted typhoid fever and was not expected to recover. He reached her bedside two days before she died on 20 February 1874, leaving behind three small children. [27]

"Poor Mr. White!" wrote Adam Spence's mother. She could only imagine the added sorrow White must bear for how little time he had spent with Laura during her illness.[28] The bereavement seemed to drain what energy and physical stamina White had left. He was unable to sleep or eat and began hemorrhaging in his lungs. For days, his closest friends feared for his life. Christian supporters came to the company's aid, offering not only prayers for White's health, but practical help with concert details so that the Jubilees could fulfill their performance obligations for the next month.[29] On 31 March 1874, the company closed its campaign with a farewell concert in Exeter Hall.[30]

White was still too ill in April to pay much attention to the benefit concerts given by the singers. According to Pike, they were not well received by the British public and would little more than pay expenses. The disgruntled members assigned the failure of these concerts to Pike and threatened to remain in England to pursue engagements on their own. When White heard this news, he became completely prostrate, barely able to speak to visitors. "The Doctor says there is some great anxiety on his mind and until that is removed he *cannot recover*," a frantic Ella Sheppard wrote Adam Spence. She charged his anxiety to the actions of those recalcitrant singers whose plans could not be dissuaded even by the pleas of two of their staunchest allies, Lord Shaftesbury and Dr. Allon. "If they do not change their purpose soon I fear nothing can save him," Sheppard worried. "My heart bleeds while I write this.... I can tonight say from the depths of my soul—'Oh! Lord keep us from sinking down.'"[31]

Pike was not sure he should even try to reign in the faction, admitting "it would be a relief" simply to have them go: "If they do remain I shall try and utilize them for the AMA.... It does not look as tho Mr. White would have further use for these Singers, even if he should recover—as they make him infinite trouble—I hope for the best. God governs the world, our work is clearly in the line of his providence."[32] Most troubling was the fact that the press had gotten wind of the company's quarrels and printed news of the internal friction. Such news would travel quickly until "every village paper in the land has published it," warned their friend James Powell. "Such is the inconvenience of great fame. So much success and so much flattery has turned the young people's heads and they will find out to their grief by & by that they may have acted *unwisely* in seeking redress from wrong fancied or real by rushing into public with their grievances."[33] Powell's prediction was right. A letter from one of the members outlining their grievances found its way to the *Nashville Banner*. It accused White of intentionally using his influence against the proposed new troupe and claimed he had threatened to sue any singer who might try to appropriate the company's name. "Mr. White says that we are ungrateful for all that he has done for us, but I tell you, sir, that what has been done was done by us, and he cannot take it all to himself." The article further claimed that many African Americans joined in their disapproval of the chain of events, fearing that the Jubilee Singers venture was ending just as they had predicted: "badly for the singers."[34]

Fortunately for the AMA (providentially, according to Pike), the company received a missive from Cravath concerning Maggie Porter's mother that changed Porter's mind. Her decision to return home broke up the proposed quartet and saved Pike a "mountain of embarrassment." "I hope God will bless you for sending that dispatch," wrote a much relieved Pike to Cravath. Dickerson and Watkins chose to remain in England while the rest of the company departed for the States in early May.[35]

Pike stayed behind in London to settle business details. Though the AMA leadership encouraged him otherwise, he had firmly decided to resign as the Jubilee Singers' manager. Pike hesitated to offer a full explanation for his feelings: "It would take a week to review all the ins and outs of the past year, and the results of the review would not be worth the trouble."[36] He urged Cravath to pay White a $500 bonus equal to what each singer had received, saying "no man out of a mad house" would have endured willingly such personal sufferings. Besides, why should White go home penniless "while a girl like Minnie [Tate] clears $800 besides a very large number of goods?" Pike asked rhetorically.[37]

As to the possibility of future Jubilee Singers campaigns, Pike remained guarded. Perhaps another American tour followed by a second

British tour might turn a profit, but he thought the association first needed to give careful attention to its business practices. "Time has come when we should proceed cautiously that the AMA may be praised not only for its enterprise, but for its wisdom, prudence & efficiency in all its branches of work," wrote Pike.[38] Any further concert endeavor must be conducted in such a way as to avoid potential damage to the association's image. Money should be earned through effective methods that both benefited the AMA and established a "lasting name and fame [for] Mr. White as well," he urged.[39]

Pike was distressed to discover Jubilee Hall would not be finished until 1875, yet another year away, and two years from the completion date he had publicly announced. He could not see how he was going to explain this further holdup to their British supporters. "I hope you would not note me a croaker if I say that for many reasons I have felt of late that [the] AMA should proceed in its affairs with utmost caution," he told Cravath in a blunt letter offered, he claimed, in highest friendship. "There have been so many *investigations* of late. We ought to be especially warned lest we fail to meet the rightful expectations of our friends." Cravath needed to "exercise greater caution" in managing restricted funds, Pike said flatly. If "God graciously saves me from public reproach" for his part in a fundraising effort whose methods had begun to nag at his conscience, he vowed to "not be a party to the like again."[40]

Finally, Pike advised that White and the association must be extremely careful in their personal dealings with the Jubilee Singers. He related how White had grown so frustrated with the "rebellious" members of his company at the close of the campaign that he had threatened to withhold their salaries. This knee-jerk response would not work, argued Pike, as the "public were very sensitive" about how the Jubilee Singers were treated. Hostilities between the Jubilees and their director could lead to nothing but public disaster. Therefore, he had encouraged White to "recognize their civil rights" and end the campaign "in such a way as would lead them to esteem him as their greatest friend," Pike informed Cravath.[41] Too often, Pike found himself in the role of mediator between White and the Jubilees. The headstrong director considered the singers' demands almost mutinous, at the very least disloyal. His paternalistic, heavy-handed leadership style may have helped launch the company against overwhelming odds, but it was not as effective or as appreciated once the ensemble was established and successful.

Several of the Jubilee Singers began to consider their futures. There was no promise of lasting employment with the AMA, even if they wanted to subject themselves again to such arduous work. Those who had been students at Fisk left their studies mid-stream to become Jubilee Singers and only a few desired to return to student status at Fisk University.[42] Since there were strong indications that a concert career in England might prove lucrative, some felt they should test these waters even at the risk of irritating the AMA.

Thus, the "rebellious" singers and their managers found themselves at cross purposes. White interpreted the conflict as a personal attack against him; both he and Pike felt these singers' actions were disloyal to the aims of the AMA. The silence of the other female members who did not align themselves with the faction leaves us to speculate as to their true feelings about the matter. Ella Sheppard remained the staunch ally of her friend and mentor, George White. This incident was just the first of many in which her loyalty was tried. Perhaps the others were disinclined to risk something new or were simply ready to go home.

Most apparent is the degree to which the relationship between the Jubilees and the managers had changed in the course of a year. Time coupled with the life experiences "jubileeing" offered had strengthened the Jubilee Singers' self-confidence. Dickerson and Rutling had given scores of speeches and established themselves as eloquent spokespersons on behalf of the AMA.[43] All had benefitted from the sense of freedom they experienced abroad. Now, several had no qualms about expressing their personal interests.

Final Campaign Years, 1875–1878

The 1874 summer's rest helped everyone recover both physically and emotionally. When the AMA decided to dispatch a new company, White took special care in selecting singers. He knew it was critical to "get the best of the old company," for forming a completely new ensemble would prove time-consuming and expensive, but he felt it was unwise to pressure the others and risk turning their feelings "against the movement."[44] Only Ella

Sheppard and Mabel Lewis were ready to make a commitment. In early November 1874, White called a meeting with all the old members to discuss the terms of their contracts. Holmes negotiated on behalf of others, which offended Sheppard for she knew he had no intention of touring again. All agreed to sign on for another year except Holmes and Rutling. The salary offer had risen to $800 with a promised $200 bonus if net proceeds exceeded the target goal of $25,000. Rutling made a counter-offer, which was refused, and held out on accepting the AMA's contract terms until late December.[45]

The Jubilee Singers had made such a name for themselves as a professional musical ensemble that White could no longer afford to put anything less than a stellar group before the public. With old members pulling out, he was desperate to find replacements who did not have to be "worked up from the rough."[46] If he could not get the level of talent his ensemble required from among the Fisk student body, White decided to simply search elsewhere. He had heard it rumored that the Hamptons might disband, so he asked Cravath to try recruiting their bass to join the Jubilee Singers, especially as the young man would be "used to the style of singing" and type of concert work the two groups shared.[47]

Putting the new company together and working out campaign details were quickly wearing on White's physical reserves. He was further disturbed by the knowledge that Cravath had chosen a "raw hand" to assume the company's business affairs. Rather than get someone new, White suggested the wisest course of action would be to hire someone who already knew the business. He had his hands full trying to pull an ensemble together, he explained, and did not need to be saddled with having to attend to administrative matters as well. As White was still nursing his health, he feared that taking on so many responsibilities would land him right back in bed within six weeks of the campaign's start.[48]

The ensemble still had not come together by December and White was increasingly anxious. The new voices he had begun training disappointed him for one reason or another. They were either too weak to match the strength of the others or could not withstand constant rehearsing. "It is *very hard* to get a *combination* of voices & get them drilled up to anything like *Jubilee Singing*," he told Cravath. Just in time, he discovered and signed Frederick Loudin. Thomas Rutling finally "came to his senses," said White, and chose to accept the new contract terms. America Robinson, a senior in Fisk's first college class, also joined the company, even though she would have to make up her last few classes while on the road in order to graduate on time. "Our 'machine' is at last made," White reported thankfully, "and I have been so long in anxiety.... The waiting of the past few weeks has been like the holding of that line on the Peninsula under fire with no ammunition." Now, he felt they were squeezed for time to work the ensemble into one harmonious whole.[49]

The tensions of the previous campaign had not faded from White's memory. He continued to stress the need for solid musical instruction at Fisk so that he would have a pool of singers ready to replace any of the troupe "who might from sickness or refractory disposition have to drop out." Moreover, he hoped that having substitutes waiting in the wings would give him "command of the situation" and thereby prevent any possible repeat of their prior difficulties. Never again did White want to handle behaviors he considered insubordinate. Having a reserve of singers in readiness at Fisk gave him the leverage he thought he needed to maintain control. If forced, he could simply supplant any rebel. To ensure the quality of musical training at Fisk, White assumed the responsibility for hiring his replacement at the institution, informing Cravath that he could cancel the arrangement if he disapproved.[50]

The last campaign started off smoothly enough, with only the usual grumbling that happened when too many people were assigned to one room or managers scheduled an activity that interrupted the singers' "rest" day. As the weeks and months rolled by, however, sickness, cramped quarters, and the unrelenting work schedule once again put everyone's tempers on edge. Even the private and equable Ella Sheppard attributed her tense nerves to her inability to have any alone time. "Some nights I don't sleep at all before daybreak," she recorded in her diary, especially vexed that weariness was causing her to make small mistakes on stage.[51]

Illness beset everyone in the troupe. They often performed without the full roster of singers, but not without some complaints from the other members. "There is ever a fuss when one is absent and their work is to be divided," Sheppard once observed. Most everyone in the company took to their beds at one time or another. White had recovered in time to travel to England with the troupe in May 1875, but his health deteriorated quickly.

In August he announced he must leave the Jubileeing work altogether and was unlikely to see the troupe until they returned to America. Sheppard was heartsick and "perfectly dumb with surprise and grief." She could not imagine having anyone else in charge: "...it is impossible for any other leader to take his place. Morally we shall ever hold him as our leader. Others may come and do the leading but Mr. W [White] will always be '*the* leader of the Jubilee Singers'—any other will only be his substitute, temporarily too."[52] Perhaps Sheppard knew intuitively that White's departure would add to the musical burdens she would bear. Weeks earlier, she had added the task of transcribing the company's spirituals to her concert and social obligations, responsibility for onstage direction, and the job of keeping the ensemble's scrapbooks.[53] Sheppard managed to complete nine songs in about six weeks' time, all the while nursing severe ear infections.[54]

The fall 1875 concert season brought changes and unexpected tragedies. Erastus Cravath, who had recently retired as a field secretary for the AMA to assume the presidency of Fisk, decided to take charge of the ensemble, arriving sometime in October.[55] Unlike White, Cravath was not a musician and had little appreciation for how much the Jubilees worked physically and emotionally to pull off a good concert. He was also fresh to the business and had not yet experienced the wear and tear of "jubileeing." Consequently, he crammed as many performances into the week as he could in hopes of making more money. Almost nightly concerts interspersed with frequent appearances at religious meetings quickly wore the Jubilees to a complete frazzle. By November 1875, the company was "about worked down" from a schedule that included five to seven concerts a week. It felt to Sheppard like they were "pulling against the stream" and they still had a full season ahead of them. The winter months were especially taxing for her as she battled a recurring illness that puzzled the doctors. One told her to stay on her feet all the time and "work off the nervousness" while another said just the opposite: "Lie down just as much as possible. Use the back very little and don't even take much or usual exercise." Since she was thoroughly worn out, she decided to abide by the advice of the second doctor.[56]

Throughout winter and early spring 1876, Sheppard went from one physician to another, tried one medicine after another, and stayed in bed as much as possible in between concerts. Her diaries reveal her private concerns for her health: "I never was more worn out. It seems as though I would die." Sheppard had rarely missed a performance, but was so sick a few days later that Miss Gilbert, alarmed, asked Theodore Seward, White's replacement, to postpone his scheduled rest and help with the situation. The two decided Ella was too ill to attend the evening concert. "I was awfully annoyed and had a good cry," Sheppard wrote, bothered as much for the disruption in Seward's plans as the fact that Gilbert had recognized the seriousness of her illness. Despite her protestations, Sheppard was shipped off to London to recuperate.[57]

The rest of the singers coughed and sputtered their way through one performance after another, managing to earn public acclaim for their vocal proficiency despite the physical strain under which they performed. They watched as one member or another broke down, only to have the empty spot filled by one of the reserve singers from Fisk. When Cravath attempted that spring to rewrite their contract terms regarding vacation time, Loudin took the lead in protesting:

> Three years killed Mr Holmes and but for a miracle would have killed Mr White. Three years broke down Dickerson, but *rest* restored his voice. A less time broke down [Mabel] Lewis. Rest has built her up again. Ella is quite gone. Jennie Jackson is failing as all can see…. Still you seem determined to drive ahead as if we were all superhuman and in fact as we are killed, you put in a new one, while one of the managers rests while another keeps us a going until another takes his or her place. I know you will say this is a hard saying but I feel that the facts will verify what I have said…. I realize that I owe a duty to myself which forbids that I should break myself down in two or three years when with a *reasonable* amount of work I might last much longer.[58]

Cravath sought the opinions of the other singers and discovered that everyone agreed with Loudin. Their contracts clearly stipulated a three-month vacation. "We have had but one month and if you call that just then we dont agree," wrote Jennie Jackson. Porter warned that White would strongly object if he knew Cravath was trying to decrease their rest period. Rutling felt the singers had "*given* as much work as *any one*, connected with the work. I think we should have something. I am *not satisfied* and have not been."[59]

This was perhaps the first time all the Jubilee Singers were a united voice in protest against their managers. In time, other disputes would surface to possibly divide their loyalties, but here they all agreed: they were spent emotionally and physically and needed time off. All felt that sacrificing their health was too high a price to pay, regardless of how much they supported the mission. Sleep deprivation, seemingly endless traveling, and non-stop performances in drafty halls were taking their toll on their voices. Their vocal talent was an invaluable commodity they were unwilling to lay on the altar for the sake of the AMA. Concert demands did not allow anyone to coddle his or her voice. However, argued Loudin, no Jubilee Singer should allow his or her voice to be completely worn to the point of damaging it forever. If asked to do "light concert work" of two or three hours a day in exchange for an extended vacation offering real rest, the members unquestionably should receive extra pay. In the face of united opposition, Cravath acquiesced and granted the Jubilees a two-month vacation in Geneva.[60]

"Pride and Hauteur"

Control issues were not restricted to matters between singers and managers. At times, individuals within the ensemble jockeyed for positions of power. Loudin rose to claim the position vacated by Dickerson as the chief spokesperson, his commanding bass voice resonating through the vast halls in which the Jubilees performed. While Sheppard admitted the man spoke with eloquence, she felt that over time Loudin's speeches had begun to seem "more of a *boast* than a *plea* for this people."[61] His tendency to take the reins of leadership put Sheppard on guard and kept her quietly suspicious of his true motives, feelings that did not lessen with time. Near the end of their final campaign, Sheppard confided to her diary that she wished she had more confidence in him. "I seem to lose more & more each day instead of being charitably inclined toward his weaknesses." When chided about missing an entrance, Loudin replied that it did not matter, since "it was his singing & person" that carried the ensemble. His prideful reply so disgusted Sheppard that she publicly rebuked him.[62]

Harmonious cooperation between group members became more difficult to maintain as the campaign years ensued. The stress and strain of touring gnawed at everyone's emotions and often erupted in words or deeds that sometimes put the group's reputation at risk. Such was the case when Maggie Porter and Jennie Jackson got into an intense argument that escalated into a real fight. The fracas awoke the other members of the company, and Ella Sheppard ran to fetch Susan Gilbert White, fearing that the disturbance would wake the neighbors. The shameful behavior of her peers appalled Sheppard: "It seems to me I never felt such a *disgust* in my heart for anything human as I feel towards those two girls. I think of their acting so shamefully after all the advantages they have had for the past 4 years. I feel as tho' I could never forgive the creatures—certainly by their often repeated fussing etc. they have forfeited every right of respect from everyone."[63] Her feelings were shared by others in the company, especially when it came to judgments about Maggie Porter. Though everyone recognized that she had one of the best voices in the ensemble, Robinson reported that Porter's "haughty and insolent" manner toward all, managers and peers alike, had become almost unbearable. "They say in the class that she has every year grown worse and worse till now she has come to think herself the ruling power of the class. It matters not where we are James, she says the most cutting and uncalled for things. She has called the managers liars and fools in public. When we meet for a pleasant gathering she is sure to say something hurtful. And now we all feel as if we can no longer put up with it."[64] Robinson had been with the troupe for a shorter period of time than the others, and yet she, too, had "tasted the venom" of Porter's anger.

White's attempts to resolve the altercation were in vain. Rather than apologize, Porter turned in her resignation. "All the Singers were most indignant over her behavior and lack of repentance—we were indeed shocked," said Robinson. White, who had borne the brunt of his star soprano's histrionics, was at the end of his patience. "Indeed Mr. White says that if a white person had used the same language to him he would have slapped his or her face," Robinson wrote. He accepted her resignation on the spot and made arrangements for her departure, which caught Porter off guard. "She had no thought that she would ever be sent home," confided Robinson. "She thought herself of so much consequence she evidently felt her importance more than others. I hope that this sudden humbling of her pride and hauteur will do her good."[65]

Only Loudin and his wife were on hand to bid Porter goodbye; the rest seemed thankful to be rid of her. "She had the sympathy of the whole company but the approval of none," White told his field agent, J. H. Halley. "It is wonderful how the atmosphere has cleared up since her exit. I feel as if an *aching tooth* had been extracted." Robinson admitted that the company would miss her singing, but not her tongue. "It is very sad to see Maggie go home but we have all breathed freer since we knew that we were to be rid of our tyrant," she told James.[66]

Instead of going home, Porter went to London to lay her case before Matthew Henry Hodder, of Hodder and Stoughton, and an Englishman named Stone who had previously offered to help with her education. Stone was so incensed by Porter's version of her removal from the company that he wrote to White demanding the members be allowed to vote on readmitting her. To Sheppard, the letter revealed clearly that Stone was "totally blind as to the true state of affairs" and completely "ignorant of the fact that we *have been* consulted" about whether Porter should remain with the company. Sheppard felt the language of the letter illustrated that Maggie still had the "same defiant spirit of evil" and bore no guilt or regret for what had transpired.[67]

When White read the letter and put the vote to the class, however, the former unity between the company members against Porter dissolved. Whereas Loudin, Alexander, and Watkins once agreed "the class was better off without her," now they refused to vote either way and abstained from an otherwise unanimous vote of "no." White wrote a letter of reply that clearly outlined the history of the charges against Porter and gave the results of their class vote. Sheppard hoped this would "banish ever the very memory of that girl," but intuitively knew Porter had "no intention of letting us forget her."[68] She expected more trouble was on its way.

Another letter from Hodder and Stone arrived requesting that they and Porter meet with White and the company to settle the case. White confided to Sheppard that the dispatch had "seemed like a death wound," so weary was he of the whole affair.[69] The next day, the company met with Porter's representatives early in the morning and discussed the matter until past four in the afternoon. Ella Sheppard described their discussion in her diary:

Each singer expressed their dislike of M.L.P. [Maggie L. Porter] and said that while they felt the class and work were better off without her and certainly personally the Singers could not do their work as well in her presence yet if her absence from the company was going to cause public misunderstanding and trouble (unless her wickedness were exposed) that they would not *hinder* her return, but would never give their *consent* to her return and they wished M.P. to understand that their neither *invited* or *requested* her return. Mr W. said that he felt the same and that the door was open to her (as he told her in Geneva) when she chose to return providing she was a *changed being* that he would not allow her return unless she promised to live as the others, as he requested long ago and the refusal of which caused her dismissal.[70]

Hodder and Stone presented Porter's promise of compliance, but Sheppard insisted she appear in person and apologize.[71] Afterwards, she recorded in her diary: "...while her *words* expressed all we requested, her *manner* told us the old Maggie was still there and ever would be." None-theless, the troupe voted her back. However, none of the female company members wanted to room with her, so the managers decided she should stay with Ella Sheppard. "Lord help me!" cried Sheppard privately in her diary.[72]

The Final Year

Salary disagreements resurfaced during the last year the company was intact. In May 1877, Cravath approached each singer about remaining with the company for one more year. Everyone opted to resign except Loudin, Rutling, Alexander, and Porter—too few to think of keeping the ensemble together. America Robinson and Maggie Carnes refused to sing again unless they earned the same salary as the others. They had joined the troupe for a lesser salary with the promise from Cravath that they would "work their way up." "That we have done," stated Robinson flatly, "and now that we have reached the consummate point, when, according to his principle we would get the same amount he was unwilling to abide by it fearing the old singers would demand more." She suspected that the only company member to oppose her request was Maggie Porter, but felt the prima donna was so anxious to keep the company together "she would hold her tongue on that account." Cravath attempted to play to Robinson's guilt, asking how she could "let such a noble work hinge for the sake of a few hundred dollars." Robinson, however, would not be guilt-ridden about an issue of equity: "The reason I felt that I ought to get the same salary was because I have found out that I do the same amount of work."[73]

By the Jubilees' final touring year, friction within the troupe began to subtly find its way onstage. Angry with Cravath that his account had been mishandled, bass Edmund Watkins refused to attend one evening performance. The Jubilees felt Watkins's behavior was inappropriate, but were equally disturbed by Cravath's inept handling of the matter. Other company members confident of their superior vocal talent took to quibbling over musical and performance issues. During one concert, Sheppard hesitated before giving the "signal for rising," a slight nod of the head to tell the singers to rise and acknowledge an encore. By the time she did, the encore opportunity had passed, which caused some of her peers to ridicule her. On another occasion, Loudin and Rutling made a sudden program change in the middle of a concert that left Sheppard scrambling for music she could not locate. Slight mistakes such as these were enlarged, evoking judgmental looks onstage and jeers backstage. "I am sick at heart of the struggles which continually surround us," lamented Sheppard.[74]

The most contentious musical issue, though, concerned pitch. Sheppard was responsible for giving the pitch onstage before each selection. After enduring numerous complaints that the pitch was either too high or too low, she decided to use a tuning fork. The fussing continued until White finally called a meeting to discuss the issue. As usual, said Shep-pard, Loudin, Rutling, and Porter were the loudest voices of complaint. White suggested they choose their own opening pitch, which they did, and then tested them before and after the selection to see if they fell flat. Sheppard said the final pitch was worse than ever, yet they would not "believe in even the *tuning* fork." Porter continued to fume about pitches for the next week or so. Even when Sheppard felt she finally had the pitches "all fixed," she admitted there was still no peace in the group. "Lord have mercy upon us miserable sinners!" she wailed.[75]

White felt the internal bickering tainted their musical performances to the point of public embarrassment. "Matters have grown steadily worse…. Last night the people paid three marks for their tickets and were offered the veriest rubbish that could receive the name of music," he told Cravath. He felt their "singing was about as bad as it could be." Without a major reorganization that would give him more control, White considered it a duty to himself, the public, and Fisk University to resign as soon as their present commitments were filled.[76]

Tensions peaked in late April 1878 as health issues and petty arguments escalated. Finally, White told Cravath a decision over the company's future was imperative: neither he nor the ensemble could continue in its present condition. "The sacrifice is too great," he wrote, "I simply cannot endure the life we now live.... I have hoped against hope—and struggled against the constantly increasing tide of evil, until the mental suffering I have must be relieved or I must be sacrificed to a vain effort to accomplish an impossibility."[77] White was torn. To leave the group meant that Ella Sheppard would have to assume all musical responsibility, and he feared she would wilt "like a broken reed" if faced with difficulties. The best solution, he suggested, was to reorganize the company and put the onus of financial and musical success on the shoulders of the others:

> About the future, I see but one chance for me to continue, and I have but little faith in that. If we could put the knife right into the company & cut out three or four & send them *squarely home*—and throw the burden of making success onto the others—with the alternative of financial loss to themselves—and disgrace to themselves the University & their people. Modify the programme & make up for the loss of voice by an organ or piano accompaniment. We might keep our reputation sufficiently to pull through the remaining months.[78]

White was convinced he needed to get rid of several members for the overall good of the company. Audience response to their mission had been grand, but "the *stench* of the *dead corpse* that we carry with us is horrible beyond description," he claimed.[79]

Those White wanted to send home immediately included America Robinson, Maggie Carnes, and the pianist, Mrs. Swart, who had joined the company during Sheppard's leave of absence due to illness. His suggestion met with instant revolt. Robinson and Carnes refused to travel with Mrs. Swart, and Alexander and Rutling said if the girls were sent home, they would also leave. Rather than support White, Cravath crumbled and said he would keep them all. White was humiliated by this defeat and tendered his resignation. Cravath accepted it immediately and asked Sheppard to assume musical responsibility: "Mr. Cravath has asked me to stay. My very soul recoils from it. I can scarcely conceal the utter & indelible contempt I feel for today's proceedings. I *cannot* feel it right for me to remain yet to go would make matters worse. If I stay I must face probably *fatal* results! If I go I have hope of regaining my strength. O, Lord, show me my duty! I can only fall *mute* before Thee. My burden seems *too hard*."[80] Illness and fatigue had characterized Sheppard's last year with the troupe. Now, she was being asked to endure the work without the emotional and physical support of her two closest friends, George and Susan White.

After a night spent in prayer and reflection, Sheppard told Cravath she would commit to fulfilling only the company's present engagements. He did not take her response well:

> I had only said as much when he flew into a passion—said he would make no such agreement, would not beg me to stay. If I chose to *desert* I could—& then marched from the room & did not even listen to Mr White's protest at his evil word "desert." Tho' I live to be an old woman—the scar of that word "*Desert*" will remain upon my heart. As hard as I worked for *seven* years—late & early doing *extra* work—to at last be called a deserter!!![81]

Not wanting to be labeled a "deserter" by the president of Fisk, Sheppard felt she had no choice but to remain with the troupe. What little concern she had left for her own welfare drained away. Though they traveled to cities with tempting tourist attractions, Sheppard said she had "no more heart to do more than *duty* required." Her only consolation was that she was henceforth given a private room, apparently her one demand to which Cravath yielded.[82]

For the Whites, the next few weeks were spent in agonized reflection over just what had gone wrong. They felt compelled to offer Cravath their perspective on their apparent "failure":

> During the past two days and nights, Mrs. White and I have been carefully over the experiences of the past fifteen months beginning with our sudden protraction in Leeds. We cannot feel that all our decisions have been wise, or that all our work has been as earnest & faithful as it should have been—but this we *do feel*, that in no year of our work for Fisk University, have we been more thoroughly consecrated to the work, or have labored more incessantly or faithfully for the accomplishment of success than this year.

Neither of us *believed* in the wisdom of undertaking the Continental campaign with the conditions of the company what they were, and with the material we could command to supply the vacancies. But we yielded to your judgement and have kept nothing back in our effort to make the year successful. I do not mention this as wanting praise. We simply did our duty. I refer to it only as throwing light on what I write after –

The principal causes of our *apparent* failure, and of our being obliged to leave the work at this time, have been before you ever since our return - The intimacy of the four young persons began in Holland - Poor Mr. Seward wrote me of his trouble and grief over it. The combination, or "ring" has grown and strengthened with each month. After fully discussing the matter with you, and using our best effort to either stop it, or neutralise its effect we have endured it, until the evil purpose centered in it was used to thwart our effort to correct other wrongs in the class, and had actually succeeded in rendering us powerless to secure the good order and right living necessary to preserve the character and good name of the company—and further, for many weeks past the evil influence has reached into our public work, and to a great extent has nullified every effort I could make to permanently improve the concerts. You saw the effect of it in Frankfort and Dresden.

The statement of Mr. Rutling that we have been influenced by likes and dislikes is wholly false. We have been repelled in our effort to influence them, and opposed in our work, because we sought to raise the standard of living, and character of the company. In doing this, we had to take hold of their personal conduct & practice—Hence the combination and strife.

White felt disgraced by his departure from the company, especially as the real cause could not be revealed to the public. Without some explanation, the public could impute that White had deserted the troupe "in its hour of need" and forget his "long weary struggle for good order and right living in the company" or his "jealousy for its honor and good name." He was devastated to think his seven years of service had come to this dismal ending.[83]

The company continued giving concerts for a few more weeks, but profits waned and the Jubilee Singers' spirits were deflated. Moreover, company debts had mounted and the AMA leadership did not want to commit to another campaign without first settling all accounts. Cravath finally agreed it was time for the company to disband. At their last concert on 1 July 1878, Rutling refused to sing, causing Sheppard much embarrassment and a hasty rearrangement of the program order. Regrettably, she wrote, there was "trouble to the last."[84]

Chapter 8

The Fruit of Christian Reconstruction:

Leaders of the Race

> Fisk University was founded in 1866 in recognition of the principle that to elevate any race, leaders are needed, and that these leaders must be far above the majority of their fellows in character and ability.[1]

The American Missionary Association (AMA) considered leadership development among African Americans a desired major outcome of its "duty to Christian culture." Throughout the turbulent changes of the Reconstruction years, Fisk steadfastly maintained the belief "that the very best possible training of the intellectual and moral natures with a sound, self-controlled body is essential for those who are to be the leaders of their people." By the turn of the century, the alumni encapsulated the institution's educational philosophy in a short phrase: the "Fisk idea."

> The rudiments of learning for all, manual training for those that are adapted to it and will use it in their after life, the best of culture for those who are capable of receiving and employing it. In a word, capacity not color, Christianity not caste, is to decide the question as to the kind of education a youth is to receive, whether he dwell in the North or South, whether he be an Ethiopian or an Anglo-Saxon. Exceeding few in comparison with the vast multitude of their race will be those who receive their diploma at Fisk; but they are to be the leaders of a people sorely needing leadership. And Fisk's determination to rear such leaders is an abiding protest against the spirit which denies to any human being a chance, and a declaration that the Church, like its divine Master, is to minister to those who most need help.[2]

Fisk officials reasoned that strong spiritual and intellectual leaders were vital to racial uplift. "It is the purpose of the Faculty to send forth no one who is unworthy of confidence or incapacitated to be a leader of those who have never had the opportunities afforded at Fisk," stated one of the institution's promotional brochures.[3] Annually, the university proudly published a list of its graduates and their various accomplishments as visible proof of Fiskites' leadership potential.[4]

Shaping "Christian men and women" involved more than just academic rigor. Teachers were not satisfied with simply improving intellects, but sought also to instill a sense of Christian duty to humankind. Each graduate was expected to leave Fisk fully prepared to meet the challenges of the world and imbued with a "distinct and avowed purpose to bless his race." By the turn of the century, the school had developed an informal tradition of having each graduate present his or her plan to promote the Fisk principle of "not to be ministered unto but to minister."[5] Fisk graduates were encouraged to make positive, lasting changes in the world.

How these ideals were internalized and transformed in the lives of the individual men and women who participated as Jubilee Singers lends insight into the extent to which the AMA's Christian Reconstruction goals were accomplished. Considering the many detours and roadblocks before them, it is inspiring to note the multifarious achievements of those who participated as Jubilee Singers. Unfortunately, spotty data exist for many of these individuals, rendering a thorough group analysis impossible. The appendix provides brief summaries of their life activities.[6] Two of the Jubilee Singers—Frederick J. Loudin and Ella Sheppard Moore—left written legacies revealing their efforts to forge lives worthy of honor. Their concise biographies, presented here, illustrate how two dissimilar personalities allowed their experience as Jubilee Singers to enrich and inform their lives in positive ways. Though Loudin was never enrolled at Fisk University, he remained a staunch supporter of the ideals for which the institution stood and a respected voice for civil rights. Ella Sheppard married a Fisk graduate, George W. Moore, and the couple spent the remainder of their lives in active ministry with the AMA.

Loudin and Sheppard exemplify the type of leaders for which the AMA labored. Though their lives took different vocational paths, each found avenues of expression for his or her personal faith and convictions, demonstrating in part how the values to which they had been exposed while working for the AMA had been internalized. In the face of racism, ignorance, and hostility, these two exceptional people not only survived, but thrived to become educated, accomplished professionals ready to use their knowledge and experience in socially responsible ways.[7]

Frederick J. Loudin (1846?–1904), Bass

Frederick Loudin's parents, free blacks Jeremiah and Sybil Loudin, immigrated to the Western Reserve in Ohio from Connecticut in search of cheap land, as farming was one of the most lucrative professions a free African-American male could pursue. They arrived in the Charlestown Township in Portage County, Ohio in time to be counted in the 1830 census. Loudin's obituary lists his birth as 27 June 1842, but other documents suggest that 1846 is more likely correct.[8]

When Loudin grew old enough to attend school, his mother moved with the five children to Ravenna, Ohio in order to provide them with a better education. Though free, the Loudin family still battled racism. Sources state that Loudin's father had given generously to endow an unnamed college close to his Ravenna home, but when he sought entrance for one of his children, college officials coolly told him the institution did not accept "colored" students. Taxes from his farm helped support the public schools, but it was only by special exception that officials allowed the Loudin children to attend. Frederick proved to be a diligent scholar and quickly advanced in his studies. When white parents discovered that young Loudin had earned academic distinction above their own children, they withdrew their children in protest.[9]

Frederick Loudin recognized even as a child that he had a fine singing voice and that exceptional musical talent was part of his heritage. Many called his mother's voice extraordinary, his father sang bass, and some of his distant relatives were noted pianists. Loudin also claimed to be a cousin of the Luca family, who toured widely in the mid-1800s. Few opportunities for cultivating vocal talent were available to sons of African-American farmers. He once attended a local singing school where a man told him, "I would give everything I had did I possess your voice." Loudin was only seventeen and paid little attention to the compliment. Later, he began to take his talent seriously and approached his mother about going to a Boston conservatory for study. She deflated his dream quickly: "With the prejudices against you as a black man, you would never be able to make any headway."[10]

Loudin then turned his attention to developing a trade. He became a printer's apprentice under Abraham Pryme, publisher of Ravenna's *The Reformer*. He made forty-five dollars a year and contributed five dollars annually to his home church. Pryme was an enthusiastic abolitionist who wanted Loudin to take over the literary department of the newspaper. However, Loudin did not share all of Pryme's political and social views, and therefore graciously declined the offer. During this time, he joined the local Methodist church but was refused choir membership because of his color. Loudin also discovered that local white printers would not do business with a black compositor. Disillusioned with his church experience and disappointed in the printer's trade, he eventually decided to leave Ravenna and start anew.[11]

In his early twenties, Loudin moved to Pittsburgh where he remained until 1874. He met and courted Harriet Johnson of Philadelphia and on 12 May 1870 the couple married. They joined the Grace Presbyterian Church and kept their membership for over thirty years. In 1874 the couple moved to Memphis where Loudin began teaching music, playing the organ, and leading the choir for Avery Chapel. A friend who had heard the Jubilee Singers suggested that Loudin write the university and inquire about participating with the company. He complied, hardly expecting to receive an answer, and was therefore quite surprised when George White responded that he would make the 250-mile trip to hear Loudin sing. The following Sunday, Loudin performed "Free as a Bird" during the church service as his audition. Afterwards, White approached him enthusiastically and said, "Yes, it is all there."[12] To Cravath, White wrote excitedly, "I think I have found a first rate man as bass singer. If he proves to be as good as he appears to be at first sight he will be far superior to Watkins. He is an Ohio man—is a musician naturally & professionally."[13]

Loudin seemed to make a favorable first impression on all who met him. One observer described him as a "finely proportioned man" who carried himself with dignity. "His full, clear eye, well-balanced head, and firm chin indicate that he would have risen to distinction in any line of life he chose to adopt."[14] Ella Sheppard remarked that he seemed a "man of some experience" and was initially impressed by the seriousness with which he responded to White's question of whether or not he could "stand being flattered & praised for one year." After a moment of reflection, he answered that "he didn't know but hoped so." Sheppard considered his response not only appropriate, but far different from the other members of the company.[15]

The strength and beauty of Loudin's voice startled the group gathered to hear him when he was introduced for the first time to the Jubilees. "I never heard such power," wrote one. "Mr. Seward said there were few such voices black or white. I was in when he first sang before the class and it was very amusing to see the excitement.... Mr. White asked if I did not think he had 'struck oil.'"[16] Loudin later remarked that he did not initially share their confidence in his abilities. When he first heard the Jubilee Singers perform, he said his "heart sank," for he had never received vocal training and recognized his limitations. "What voice I had was purely natural," Loudin later confided.[17] Despite his initial reservations about his lack of training, Loudin emerged as a featured soloist after a few short weeks with the company.

Loudin was older than the other Jubilees and a married man. Perhaps because of his age, bearing, and excellent oratorical skills, White often cast him in the role of spokesperson for the company. His magnificent speaking voice commanded the audience's attention as effectively as his singing did. One newspaper account of a speech given at a concert in Scotland reveals how talented Loudin was at wooing the audience with his words:

> Mr. Louden on behalf of the singers, thanked the audience for their presence. He believed that those present were not only friendly towards the singers, but also to the cause of humanity, which they had come to represent. (Applause.) Amongst the Scotch people they had met with the warmest friends, and they felt almost at times as if the spirit of Livingstone pervaded the whole. (Loud applause).... They were endeavouring to raise funds for the building of the Livingstone Missionary Hall, and he hoped that it would be one worthy to bear his name. (Applause.)[18]

At the 1875 Annual Meeting of the Freedmen's Mission Aid Society, Loudin's "felicitous address" won him the credit of being "the speaker of the night."[19]

While his stage presence earned the crowd's respect, Loudin's "brilliant singing," capable of filling the large halls in which the company sang, generated kudos by the press:

> The sonorous power of the deep notes, the wonderful melodious, rounded, soft and sure falsetto in high tones, the splendid intonation, the firm delivery, this in all is superb, and Mr. Loudin, if he understood, or was trained to sing European musical works of art (concert pieces), which we do not know, and which we do not consider impossible, would be one of our leading concert singers.[20]

One critic said he had a "rattling bass voice…with very good taste and force of expression." Others described his voice as powerful and superb, possessing a "true bass register" capable of effective expression.[21] The generous praise of his vocal production suggests that Loudin had a rich, resonant tone spanning several octaves. His solos during concerts often elicited a demand for an encore.[22]

Traveling with the Jubilee Singers developed Loudin's self-confidence in his ability as both a performer and a speaker. These skills were further nurtured by the sense of freedom he felt once the troupe arrived overseas:

> When I first visited England it seemed to me as if I had always been walking about blind before. We were astonished to find such freedom there, such an entire absence of race prejudice. I was astonished when I gradually realized that I could do what anybody else could do, if I had capacity enough; and I could go where I pleased and do what I pleased, without any prohibitions on the ground of my color. I am an enthusiastic American, but there is no place for perfect freedom like England.[23]

Empowered by the welcome he received abroad, Loudin honed his oratorical skills to a high degree.[24] One reviewer called his speech of the evening a "genuine oratorical treat."[25] A master performer, Loudin easily commanded his audience, whether singing or speaking.

Though initially impressed with Loudin, Ella Sheppard seemed to grow less trustful of her peer over time. By the end of the campaign, she found him egotistical and was somewhat suspicious of his motives. Her growing distrust may have been fanned by his alleged inappropriate behavior toward another group member, soprano Georgia Gordon. According to America Robinson, the two had formed an attachment that was a source of much grief for the managers and led to a decision to send the young soprano home.

> Mr. White and Mr. Seward have tried to stop Mr. Loudin's going with Georgia and at one time they thought they had succeeded but of late they are together more than ever. Mr. S [Seward] would get Mr. Loudin out of the class if he could for he believes him to be almost a demon. He worked his meshes around her until he has her just where he wishes. Every one can see that she loves him. Whenever his wife comes around—you know she does not stay with us—it is pitiable to see how cool he treats her. He gets furious he does not like to have her come.… He lavishes his smiles and soft words on Georgia and cuts his wife up at every turn.

America had little compassion for Georgia's foolishness. "She is no more the same girl she used to be," she wrote to James. "She ought to be with her mother."[26] Whatever misgivings the managers may have had about Loudin's behavior did not result in his removal from the company or prevent his continuing as its leading spokesperson. He remained with the company until it disbanded in 1878.

A year later, George White reorganized a company of Jubilee Singers that operated independently of Fisk University and the AMA. The ensemble, which included both Loudin and Sheppard, embarked on a concert tour from fall 1879 to 1882 in support of the Civil Rights Act of 1875.[27] The troupe, also called the Fisk Jubilee Singers, continued earning accolades for its "sincere, truthful, emotional" singing that went "straight to the hearts of the audience, as no achievement of chilly, high art could have done, and won them unreservedly." Loudin's talent was the star attraction: "…and when that gentleman descended right down to the lowest subterranean dungeons of the bass clef and liberated melodious thunders imprisoned there, they one and all decided that he was indeed a Loud-'un." Another review stated that his voice of "wonderful power, compass and beauty" had been "likened to the tones of the tuba" by European critics. Yet another remarked, "Mr. Loudin's voice seems to range from high C to the basement, and is musical on all the landings."[28]

The civil rights tours of White's Jubilee Singers presented multiple opportunities for Loudin to address racial inequities in America. Years of traveling abroad had sharpened his political awareness and speaking before diverse crowds had polished his eloquence.[29] He delivered his speeches with fearless passion that carried authority. "But I believe that we are not so unlike other people," he told a crowd gathered at Chautauqua for a reunion of the United States Christian Commission.

> Here, my dear friends, are four millions of our race that you and I, and I emphasize the word you, must educate; or the result—who can tell? But with education, with education, who fears as to the result of the future of this race of which I am.... We want an equal chance, and we ask for nothing more; and we shall be able to work out for ourselves as glorious and noble a future as that which marks the onward march of any other race upon the earth. The question that I have to ask you in a word is this: Will you help us in this onward march? Christian men and women, do you not feel that you owe to us something in this direction?

The Jubilee Singers were the main attraction of the Chautauqua meetings and they carried the conference "by storm." Certain speeches blended religious and political issues, to the disapproval of some attendees. Others argued for the land to "ring with such speeches, until the heart and conscience of the nation are regenerated and enlightened." On one evening, the speaker took Loudin's hand, claiming it symbolically represented the nation's three million blacks. "I take this other hand to say that the ballot in it ought to be as sacred as the ballot in mine. And so say you, and so says the nation. So too says the church, and why is not the national will executed?"[30]

While at the 1880 Chautauqua conference, George White accidentally fell from the platform and suffered severe injuries. He was forced to leave the troupe temporarily while he convalesced at his father-in-law's house in nearby Fredonia.[31] The troupe continued its concert itinerary with Loudin acting as the chief spokesperson for the company, a leadership role that further sealed his authority. The Reverend Theodore L. Cuyler of New York called Loudin the "hero of the troupe—an educated Ohio negro with something of the electricity of Fred. Douglass in him.... But when he makes a speech, as he did the other night on presenting a framed picture of the troupe, he did it with a grace and a richness of voice that any Caucasian orator might covet. Spurgeon's voice is no match for his baritone."[32]

In October 1880, the Jubilee Singers visited with General James A. Garfield and his wife at their home in Ohio. After they had sung, silence filled the room. Then General Garfield offered his thanks for their singing and expressed his support in their fight to eradicate injustice: "You have sung to the hearts of your people, and I hope and believe that your voices are heralding the great liberation which education will bring to your lately enslaved brethren. You are fighting for light and for the freedom it brings; and in that contest I would rather be with you and defeated than against you and victorious."[33] "You know how we have been looking to the future," Loudin replied, "how the wheels have seemed to roll backward for the past few years.... You do not know how we cling to every word that you utter, and especially to the sentiments that you have just expressed touching the rights of our people." Loudin and his fellow Jubilee Singers had high hopes for the civil rights advancements General Garfield might accomplish as President. His assassination four months after securing office abruptly ended their hopes. Expressing his own grief and that of other African Americans, Loudin wrote:

> Do you ask why that sable throng of mourners from the lowliest cabins of the south land come, most of them unlettered, to bring their tribute of tears, as with aching hearts they gather round our nation's sainted dead? "Why," do you ask? I answer because experience has taught us that our friends are few, and as well, that these changes at the nation's head are more dangerous to us than to all the other forty-three millions of this nation's mourners, who gather around his bier. We have learned by sad experience that 'tis a rare thing to elevate to that lofty seat a man who believes in the "Universal brotherhood of man," and believing in it dares to act upon it. Such a one was he whom we mourn today.[34]

Garfield had been a true friend of the Jubilees. When he discovered that no hotel in Springfield, Illinois would grant the company lodging, he sent a telegram announcing that the White House would always be open to them.[35] Loudin added his own condemnation of the incident during the ensemble's concert at Chicago's Music Hall. He publicly thanked George Pullman who "demanded that the Jubilee Singers should have the same rights in the Pullman car as other people who paid their money." In contrast, he found the Springfield citizens' behavior disgraceful when hotels refused them accommodations "in sight of the tomb of the man who had given liberty to most of the members of their company." Loudin proclaimed his love for his native land, but refused to mince his words when telling audiences that "in all their journeys in despotic lands they had never experienced such indignities as these at the Capital of the great free commonwealth of Illinois."[36]

In 1882, Loudin assumed full control of the Jubilee Singers. George White had never fully recovered from his accident at Chautauqua, and feeling that the company's ability to turn a profit had reached its limit, announced his decision to disband the group. Loudin, however, disagreed with White's assessment and felt the company still had a future. He also knew he had the managerial talent to run the enterprise himself and decided to take action. "In September, 1882, a Negro steps to the helm and henceforth directs the now famous Jubilee Craft," wrote Loudin after he had taken control. In recalling that moment, he acknowledged how aware he was that should the troupe fail, "it would greatly damage the cause of the Negro" and "thousands, who have no confidence in the leadership of the Black Man would say significantly, 'I told you so,' or 'I knew it.'"[37] Undaunted, Loudin dared to take on the challenge.

Loudin reorganized his troupe and spent the next two years touring the United States and Canada. In April 1884, he launched what would become a six-year worldwide tour encompassing England, Ireland, Australia, New Zealand, and the Orient.[38] Loudin's management of his own company reflected the degree to which he had been trained by White and influenced by AMA ideals. He carefully chose members not only for their talent, but also for their character and public demeanor:

> I know of one in America who has a voice equal to, if not superior to Patti, but she would not do for us. We make the most particular inquiries as to moral character and previous life. We are very careful also as to deportment and manners and general culture, otherwise a member might unpardonably offend when we are invited out to Government-house, Mr. Balfour's or Mr. Berth's. Even amongst the 6,000,000 of black people in the South, and the 3,000,000 in the North, it is difficult to find the necessary culture, accompanied by voice, and the musical ability and sympathy, for they have only been free about twenty years.[39]

Loudin set high standards for his company members. "Good strong sweet voices and none but ladies or gentlemen," he once told a friend, "...nice looking and reasonably good disposition no drinkers or gamblers or profane people wanted."[40] Remarks made at his memorial service suggest that

Loudin conducted daily devotions with his company, a practice White inaugurated in his management of the original Jubilee Singers.[41]

Loudin also relied on vocal technical training similar to what he had received as a Jubilee Singer thirteen years ago, claiming his artistry had always "been appreciated in the most highly cultured musical circles." He stressed perfection in blend and harmony to produce "one grand whole—one beautiful volume" and drilled his ensemble daily. "A new singer is not worth much to us for about six months—until he becomes initiated into our method, which is our own," Loudin stated. Constant practice was necessary before the group felt there was not a stranger among them.[42]

From 1884 to 1886, Loudin's company performed throughout England and Ireland. The Earl of Tankerville invited them to appear at Chillingham Castle in the North of England during October. Loudin expected a crowd of perhaps five or six hundred, but when they opened the castle gates, in streamed nearly two thousand people from across the countryside. In February, they sang at Hengler's Circus in Liverpool to an audience of nearly seven thousand who demanded encore after encore. The original Jubilees had appeared only in principle Northern Ireland towns because of fear that Roman Catholicism might be so strong in other places as to prevent an audience from patronizing their concerts. Loudin decided to risk concerts in outlying areas and found that Catholic audiences were as enthusiastic about their singing as Protestant ones.[43]

Though he had never enrolled as a student, Loudin remained loyal to Fisk University and promoted the institution throughout his travels. He believed in the university's mission and spoke with deep feeling about the relationship the Jubilee Singers would always have with the institution: "From the loins of Fisk University we have sprung; we are a part of you and you are a part of us.... And so our hearts turn homeward wherever our feet carry us. Although debarred from working for you actively, there is a tie which shall strengthen as the years go on, which bind us more closely together."[44] As he traveled the world, Loudin kept Fiskites informed of the company's many successes, solicited subscribers to the university's publications, and appeared on campus whenever possible.[45]

In spring 1886, Loudin's company set sail for Australia and landed in Williamstown, the port of Melbourne.[46] The troupe's first appearance was a private concert for the city's select citizens. Leota Henson, Loudin's niece, described how the local newspapers gave a "fine account of the program and after that our concert dates came in thick and fast."[47] Their first public concert created a furor of excitement. "The singers...warble with all their soul," exclaimed one critic. "And then the earnestness with which they one and all sing is perhaps the most captivating thing of all about their performance," claimed another. "I came away after spending the most enjoyable musical evening that has ever fallen to my lot."[48] For three weeks, the company packed the 3,200-seat Town hall, turning hundreds away. Before leaving, the Jubilee Singers gave over eighty successful concerts, setting a record for any musical troupe that had appeared in the city. Comparable success was repeated in cities across Australia: sixty concerts in Sidney, forty in Adelaide, and thirty in Brisbane.[49]

The troupe's encounter with the Australian aborigines and the New Zealand Maori people left an unforgettable impression upon Loudin. A missionary invited the ensemble to his Meloga mission station to sing for the aborigines. When they arrived, the Jubilee Singers found the people shy and somewhat suspicious. As the troupe began to sing "Steal Away to Jesus," they noticed a subtle transformation upon the faces before them:

> Up to this time they seemed like unwilling children forced to go to Sabbath School; but what a change of expression the tones of the old slave songs awoke! First, wonder, which seemed to say, "What strange sounds are these which for the first time fall upon our ears?" then joy, as the full volume of the melody filled the humble little church.... they were weeping like children, tears of joy; and when we had finished they gathered about us, and, with tears still flowing, they clasped our hands and in broken accents exclaimed, "Oh! God bless you! we have never heard anything like that before!" As we drove off, they climbed upon the fences and up in the trees, and until our carriages were lost to view, they waved us good-bye.[50]

A similar experience happened with the Maoris of New Zealand. After hearing the Jubilees, many Maoris followed them from concert to concert. "It was evident that a strong sympathetic feeling exists between these people of color," noted one observer. When asked why, an old tattooed Maori warrior explained, "Oh! all the same the Maori." Though the company was delighted with this enthusiastic response and felt at ease with the people, Loudin later admitted he found the Maori customary greeting of rubbing noses somewhat awkward.[51]

Loudin's Jubilee Singers traveled for three and a half years throughout Australasia, introducing the spiritual to some of the area's most remote sections. People of all classes scrambled to gain a seat at their concerts and money poured in. Perhaps their greatest financial triumph occurred in Wellington where a series of ten concerts earned fifteen hundred pounds, causing one critic to state: "The people who are really making the money in New Zealand are the Fisk Jubilee Singers."[52]

From Australia, the Fisk Jubilee Singers departed for the Orient. They spent three days in Ceylon and then set sail for Calcutta, enduring a rough voyage caused by a fierce storm. Concerts throughout India were successful, but mostly attended by Europeans and Eurasians. They appeared in Bombay where crowds were so large that many sat on the stage behind them. At Agra, the custodian of the Taj-Mahal offered to take them on a personal tour of the tomb, and at Loudin's request, allowed them to gather around the sarcophagi and sing three spirituals: "Steal Away to Jesus," "I've Been Redeemed," and "We Shall Walk Through the Valley." It was perhaps the first time Christian songs were ever heard in the sacred tomb, thought Loudin.[53]

The tour continued with concerts in the Methodist church of Rangoon in Lower Burma and an appearance in a mission school where they met Miss Henrietta Matson, a former Fisk teacher who was then serving in a foreign field.[54] They next traveled along the coast of the Malay Peninsula to Penang and Singapore. Unfortunately, their booking agent had scheduled their concerts in Hong Kong and Shanghai during race-week, an annual event that consumed public attention. Consequently, concerts in these two cities were not as successful as Loudin had hoped.

About two weeks later, the company sailed to Japan for concerts in Nagasaki, Kobe, and Yokohama. Large audiences eagerly paid the one and two-dollar admission fees to hear the ensemble, often erupting in vigorous hand clapping and deep, drawn sighs (Japanese expressions of the highest degree of delight, explained Loudin). After several weeks of concerts, the troupe departed for America on 3 April 1890, exactly six years to the day from the time they set sail from New York on their worldwide tour. "We looked with longing eyes back to this beautiful land where our stay had been much too short, either for profit or pleasure," wrote Loudin.[55]

The return voyage was a rough seventeen days at sea before reaching San Francisco's Golden Gate. For the next two months, the performers literally "sang their way" from the West Coast to their homes in the East. Throughout his world travels, Loudin reported that he had rarely battled discrimination, but back in America it met them squarely in the face. After a concert in Pueblo, the company headed to its next stop, Colorado Springs, forty-two miles away. To their chagrin, no hotel would admit them and they were compelled to return to Pueblo. The next concert was east of Colorado Springs, but as they were still unable to find accommodations, the troupe had to return once again to Pueblo. In America, his homeland, Loudin was forced to pay the passage for twelve to go eighty-four miles just to find a place to sleep.[56]

The company arrived home by June, having circled the globe in six years and two months. To those who had predicted their failure, Loudin was able to point with pride to an impressive list of accomplishments. Many of the singers had earned enough money to be able to purchase comfortable homes, one indicator of middle-class status in America. Patti Malone built a beautiful home for herself and her mother in Athens, Alabama. Loudin purchased the lot next to his mother's in Ravenna, Ohio, and built an impressive home he called "Otira," named after a famous gorge he visited in New Zealand. He furnished it with wood, antiques, art objects, tapestries, and brocades collected from his travels.[57]

Though Ravenna citizens had once snubbed Frederick Loudin because of his race, they eagerly welcomed home their accomplished world traveler. His company appeared in Kent, Ohio on 29 September 1891 to an enthusiastic audience. The troupe's advanced billing touted their recent return from a six-year world trip where they appeared in seventeen countries before six crowned heads of Europe, four United States presidents, two governor generals of Canada, six governors of Australian colonies, the viceroy of India, and the governor of Bombay. The people from his boyhood home lauded him as a fine and cultured gentleman and crowded into Reed's Opera House for the return concert.[58]

Though Loudin was grateful for Ravenna's welcome, he found America's ingrained prejudice a bitter pill to swallow after the success of his worldwide tour, as an article in the Detroit *Plaindealer* reveals:

Mr. F. J. Loudin…comes back from his last trip abroad bereft of all his patriotism and love for the American flag. He has had more indignities heaped upon him in one day in the land of his birth than in all the six years that he as [sic] spent abroad…. His travels have extended all through Europe, parts of Asia and all Australia, and he has been brought into contact with all classes of society, and nowhere save in this country does an Afro-American have to stop and consider where he may get a meal without insult, where he may go to church without reproof. Mr. Loudin met many Afro-Americans who are engaged in successful businesses, some of whom fought manfully for the Union cause, but who have foresworn all allegiance to their inhuman mother country; and while he himself returns to the United States from a sense of duty, he does not blame them in the least….[59]

The battle for recognition of human dignity and civil rights for African Americans was one Loudin fought the rest of his life.

In October 1892, the Detroit *Plaindealer* announced a new business in Ravenna that could not help but "have its influence on the Afro-American throughout the country." Loudin had opened the F. J. Loudin Shoe Manufacturing Company, which employed both blacks and whites and produced almost 3,000 pairs of shoes daily. The *Plaindealer* appealed to its readers to support the African-American company: "We feel sure that the greater part of the help will be furnished by the Afro-American, and in view of this fact every colored man in the land should pledge himself to wear the F. J. Loudin shoe."[60] So successful was this business that Loudin eventually was able to purchase another shoe factory. His creative talents extended to two small inventions, which he patented in the 1890s.[61]

In 1893, Loudin joined forces with Ida B. Wells and Frederick Douglass to demand African-American involvement in the upcoming World's Columbian Exposition scheduled to be held in Chicago. The United States government invited nations from around the world to participate in this event celebrating the discovery of America, but refused African Americans' request for representation. In an open letter to *The Cleveland Gazette*, Loudin suggested the publication of a pamphlet that would inform readers about racial oppression in America. Ida B. Wells authored the pamphlet, which appeared in English, French, and German, and was distributed for no charge at the fair.[62] Though the three activists appealed to African-American newspapers across the country to open a subscription list in their columns to help raise funds for the project, they received little support. The *Freeman* was openly opposed both to the idea of the pamphlet as well as a "Colored Folks Day" at the fair: "Few homes but what contain their 'skeletons'; but does it follow that the guest at the family circle must be regaled with the history of the same? For the reason therefore that we are opposed to a 'nigger day' at the Columbian Exposition, we are opposed to this contemplated issue of a 'nigger' pamphlet, and hence cannot do as we have been so gracefully requested, run the advertisement of, or contribute to the same."[63] Despite this lack of support, the trio forged ahead with their plans. Loudin contributed one hundred dollars to the project; Wells and Douglass gave fifty dollars each and arranged a series of meetings to help raise more money. Though the pamphlet's final form failed to meet their initial hopes, Douglass and Wells managed to circulate ten thousand copies. Wells later reported that "echoes from that little volume have been received by me from Germany, France, Russia, and faraway India."[64]

Loudin's efforts for racial uplift found practical expression when he and Harriet decided to invite a young man by the name of Alexander L. Turner to live with them in Ohio. Though the Loudins had no children of their own, they parented young Turner and financed his education. Alexander Turner earned a degree from the University of Michigan in 1908 and then pursued medical studies. That same year, Turner married Loudin's niece, Leota Henson. Eventually, the couple moved to Detroit where Dr. Turner practiced medicine and Leota remained active in social and benevolence work. For twenty-six years she served as the treasurer of the Phyllis Wheatley Home Association in Detroit, the place where Maggie Porter Cole spent her last years.[65]

Loudin interspersed his business activities with more concert tours throughout the latter 1890s and the early years of the new century. In 1902 Loudin's company was in Scotland when he was suddenly "stricken with a complete nervous collapse." Leaving the management to his niece, Loudin recovered sufficiently to return to his beloved "Otira" in October 1902. Alexander Turner helped care for Loudin as his health steadily declined. He died on 3 November 1904. His last words were spoken to his wife: "God is calling me; God is calling me home."[66]

Many friends gathered to pay tribute to Frederick Loudin. His funeral service was resplendent with the spirituals he had shared around the world.

The officiating minister spoke of a company of jubilee singers that had formed in Scotland as a result of Loudin's influence. "What a beautiful memorial to the man and his work," he remarked.[67]

Ella Sheppard Moore (1851–1914),
Soprano, Accompanist, Musical Assistant

Ella Sheppard was born on 4 February 1851 in Nashville, Tennessee to Sarah Hannah and Simon Sheppard. Various accounts of Ella Sheppard's childhood exist, some apocryphal in nature, thus contributing to the romanticism surrounding her early life.[68] Her mother, Sarah Hannah Sheppard, was a determined woman whose small frame and delicate features masked the strength of character that lay within. Slavery had forced her to yield to the master's orders, yet she had an iron will that surfaced when needed. Ella Sheppard ascribed her mother's strength to faith in a supernatural God who heard and listened to the prayers of his children. "Telling it all to Jesus" throughout the night was a practice Sarah shared with other slaves who joined in their small quarters to pray and sing, bodies swaying in time, the moaning voices blended by the unity of suffering: "*Nobody knows the trouble I see Lord, nobody knows but Jesus.*"[69]

Perhaps Sarah also came by this strength of character genetically, for she had royalty in her blood. Her high cheekbones and angular face bore testimony to the Cherokee ancestry of her grandmother, Rose, the full-blooded daughter of a chief of a tribe settled near Nashville. Rose met and married an African slave, the son of an African chief, who was owned by the Donelson family in Nashville. Captain John Donelson, the brother of General Andrew Jackson's wife, had property adjacent to Jackson's Hermitage plantation. Many regarded the Hermitage neighborhood as the best land in all of Davidson County because the soil was so well suited for growing cotton. All the planters who worked the land in that part of Davidson County reaped a rich reward from cotton.[70]

Though legally free, Rose chose to serve the white Donelson family in order to remain with her enslaved husband with whom she bore fourteen children, slaves by law. But whenever she encountered the white masters' harsh criticism, or worse, dark anger, Rose's fierce pride coursed through her veins and she defiantly left the plantation to return to her tribe, threatening revenge on any who dared harm her children during her absence. Until her death at the ripe old age of 109, Rose Donelson shared with other slave mothers the abuses and cruelty of slavery.

Rebecca Donelson, one of Rose's offspring, married Jimmie Sheppard, a fellow family slave. From this union came twelve children, one of whom was a daughter, Sarah Hannah, Ella Sheppard's mother. Sarah belonged to Pheribee R. Donelson, who married Major Benjamin Harper Sheppard in 1838. Their union brought the couples' inherited slaves, both bearing the surname of Sheppard, into one "family" of Sheppards. Counted among Major Sheppard's slaves was his own half-brother, Simon, who for a time held the position of coachman at the Hermitage. Simon was an enterprising and hardworking man, managing a livery stable with four carriages and eight horses as a side business. Though legally a slave and the property of his half brother, Simon was allowed to hire himself out in Nashville and eventually earned $1,800 with which he bought his freedom.[71]

Sarah Hannah Sheppard was the head nurse and housekeeper for her mistress, an esteemed position for a slave. As such, she was generally treated kindly and was highly valued by Pheribee. In their old age, Sarah and Pheribee exchanged affectionate letters, having developed a comfortable relationship based on years of shared joys and sorrows that eventually softened the distinction between mistress and slave. Upon Sarah's heart "hung the secrets of the white family as the keys of the great house, and its treasures hung upon her body," Ella later recounted.[72]

Since she had complete responsibility for Pheribee's children, Sarah's room was adjacent to that of her mistress. At seventeen, Sarah married Simon Sheppard in the parlor of the mansion. Apparently, Major Sheppard, like many other plantation owners, allowed and even encouraged slave marriages, even though they held no legal status and the family was a nonentity in the law. Many plantation owners, however, believed that such unions fostered contentedness and therefore productivity and discipline.[73] Though married, data suggest that Sarah resided at the Sheppard plantation while Simon lived at the Hermitage, his probable birthplace.

Within their first year together, Simon and Sarah bore and buried their first child. Six years passed before a second child was born, a frail daughter named Samuella (Ella). For almost seven years, Simon and Sarah feared the separation that almost inevitably came to slave families. In speeches delivered in her later years, Ella reminded audiences that "the sanctity of the home and family was neither respected nor protected, and was made or broken as the wishes or circumstances of the master dictated; this condition pertained to and permeated every class and degree of master and slave." By the time she was old, Sarah Hannah had witnessed countless violations of young female slaves, tales of horror she confided to her eldest daughter: "From the cradle to the grave, the Negro woman lived in constant dread; no matter how favorably situated with kind and intelligent owners, there was no assurance that on tomorrow she would not be torn from her children and loved ones and sold to the coarsest and most illiterate master, and subjected to that from which only death could release her."[74] It was quite common to have children of mixed parentage throughout the slave quarters. "Friends of mine have looked into the faces of colored children whose white father was also their grandfather," Ella noted. Many plantation landowners easily took slaves as concubines but rarely openly acknowledged the offspring as their own. Young slave mothers were left alone to deal with personal shame and degradation while also enduring the hostility of a jealous and angry white mistress. According to one slave, "[you] had no chance to run off or ever get off; you had to stay and take what come."[75] An astute child, Ella internalized the sorrow that filled the life of a female slave, particularly that of her own mother. Her earliest memories were of her "mother's tears over the cruelties of slavery, as she realized that its degradation fell heaviest upon the young Negro girl."[76]

Simon had purchased his freedom, but Sarah remained the property of her mistress. Pheribee repeatedly promised to sell Sarah to Simon once he accumulated $1,300, and the young couple steadfastly held to this glimmer of hope. In this uncertain world devoid of privacy or power, young Sarah Hannah Sheppard clung fiercely to her newborn daughter, Ella. Since Sarah was a house servant, little Ella had the best life possible for a slave, playing in the master's house and receiving frequent attention from the mistress. Every day with her child was precious to Sarah, for all slaves knew that young females were often traded sooner than young boys to serve in adult domestic positions, sometimes as early as age ten. However, the daily chores required of a house slave were so time-consuming that constant care of one's own young children was difficult, leaving a frail child vulnerable to neglect or illness. One account of Ella's childhood suggests that she, too, suffered from being deprived of the constant physical attention and care of a mother.[77]

According to Ella Sheppard, her mother suffered a cruel blow when she discovered the mistress had taught her daughter how to spy on her own mother. Pheribee Sheppard had eagerly received little Ella's childish report, then magnified it and threatened Sarah with punishment. Spying was a common practice in slavery, encouraged by white owners who relished the reports they received while apparently oblivious to the fact that the "spies" they trained were capable of acting as "double agents." Sarah knew her mistress might continue to use Ella as a pawn against her and eventually the bond between mother and child could be broken.

So, says one legendary version of Ella's childhood, Sarah Hannah Sheppard settled her young daughter upon her hip and set out for the Cumberland River with a set jaw and grim determination. A watery grave would be a better outcome, she surmised, than the curse of slavery: "Before I'd be a slave, / I'd be buried in my grave." So absorbed was Sarah in her thoughts that she was genuinely startled by the voice that cried, "Stop!" Old Mammy Viney was painstakingly making her way to the frenzied mother. The look on Sarah's face betrayed her intent, but Mammy Viney had "seen" a different future. "Don't you do it, Honey, don't take that that you cannot give back," Mammy Viney counseled. She slowly lifted her eyes heavenward and instructed Sarah to do the same. "Look, Honey, don't you see the clouds of the Lord as they pass by? The Lord has got need of this child."[78] The old mammy's words stirred something in Sarah's heart. She slowly turned from the banks of the Cumberland River, abandoned her fatal plan, and made her way back to the big house.

When Ella was three years old, Major Sheppard announced he had purchased a plantation in Okalona, Mississippi and intended to relocate his family and property. Simon reminded Pheribee Sheppard of her promise to sell Sarah to him, but she refused. There would be no kept promise; rather, the day of separation had finally come.[79]"*Mississippi*" was a dreaded word to all slaves and certainly was not the future Sarah had hoped for her young daughter.[80] Empowered by a boldness undoubtedly borne from intense desperation, Sarah approached Mistress Pheribee with a threat: "If you will sell Ella to her father immediately, I will remain your slave; if you do not you lose both of us. My baby shall never be a slave." Sarah braced herself for the whipping she expected to receive. Instead, Pheribee relented and allowed Simon to purchase Ella for $350. Soon afterwards, mother and child said goodbye to each other, a painful separation that Sarah bore all her life.[81] "My back was never struck," she later told Ella, "but my heart is like a checkerboard with its stripes of sorrow."[82]

Knowing his wife would never return, Simon later married Cornelia, another slave in Nashville, whose freedom he purchased for $1,300. Freedom was an ambiguous term for freed blacks in the antebellum South as there was the constant danger of being kidnapped and resold into slavery. Without the protection of a white patron, a freed slave's status was precarious. The situation for African Americans grew tense when a race riot erupted in Nashville in December 1856, causing whites to tighten the reins on their control and releasing an onslaught of repressive measures by white vigilantes. They expressed their anger in part by forcing Daniel Wadkins's free black school on Line and High Street to close. Simon had sent little Ella to learn under the aging Wadkins, a teacher with a dramatic yet effective educational style she recalled fondly:

> He was a typical "John Bull" in appearance and an "Uncle Sam" in vivacity. He used the old Webster blue back spelling book. Each class stood up against the wall, head erect, hands down, toes straight. I recall only three classes, the Eb, Ib, Ob class; the Baker, Maker, Taker class, and the Republication, Replication class. They spelled in union with a musical intonation, swaying their bodies from side to side, with perfect rhythmical precision on each syllable, which we thought grand. Mr. Watkins [sic] gave out each word with such an explosive jerk of the head and spring around of the body, that it commanded our profound respect. His eyes seemed to see every one in the room, and woe be to the one who giggled or was inattentive, whether pupil or visitor, for such a one instantly felt a whack from his long rattan. We little visitors soon learned to spell many of the words of each class and sang them at our homes.[83]

Wadkins had managed to keep the school operating since 1837 despite numerous attempts by local whites to shut it down. This time, however, the school doors closed.[84]

Complicating the tense race relations was a downturn in Nashville's economy in 1857. Simon Sheppard's business waned as a result and debts mounted. He had been so preoccupied with his business that he had yet to secure free papers for his new wife. They could be obtained only in a free state (the nearest was Ohio) and Simon had not had time to make the trip. Legally, Cornelia was his property and could be claimed by creditors to pay off his debts. Warned by a white friend that this was exactly what his creditors intended to do, Simon immediately gathered his wife, secretly trekked through the woods to meet a midnight train, and sent her to Cincinnati. He and Ella followed a few days later, leaving behind all of their possessions for the creditors in Nashville. Though penniless, the Sheppard family remained intact and began anew in a free state.

Simon took whatever work he could find in Ohio, and Cornelia took in washing and ironing and ran a small boarding house off and on. Little by little, the family gathered bits and pieces of furniture with which to make a home. Accustomed to hard work and sacrifice, Simon eventually helped his family gain a semblance of financial stability and was even able to splurge a little and buy Ella her own piano.[85]

Simon's educational desires for Ella had not dimmed, so as soon as he was able, he sent her to Cincinnati's Seventh Street Colored School.[86] Ella was a small-framed girl with delicate features and thin lips that graced her oval face. Perhaps her most compelling feature was her large eyes, which reflected a tinge of sorrow and wisdom beyond her years. She was reserved and somewhat shy, intently serious, and painstakingly conscientious. Ella was determined to succeed, prone to self-reflection, God-fearing, and concerned with exactness and propriety. These personal qualities would later serve her well in her position as musical assistant of the Fisk Jubilee Singers. At this juncture in her young life, these traits nourished her thirst for an education.

Unfortunately, Ella was plagued with frequent illnesses, which prevented her from pursuing her studies consistently. In 1863, at the age of twelve, she became so sick she had to drop out altogether and did not resume her studies for two years. Around this time, Ella began taking piano lessons with a German woman for a year and a half. Though physically unable to withstand the rigors of daily classroom instruction, she nonetheless was able to devote time to periodic music lessons and no doubt filled her empty days with constant practice on the piano her father had given her. Her musical talent quickly blossomed.[87]

Simon's enterprising skills soon earned him a respectable amount of property and the means for Ella and her stepmother to enjoy time at nearby

Tawawa Springs. Formerly a popular health resort, Tawawa Springs had been purchased in 1856 by concurrent action of the Methodist Episcopal and African Methodist Episcopal Conferences of Ohio for a proposed university. A 200-room building on the property was ideally suited for the main campus, and faculty and staff occupied the several cottages surrounding it. They named the institution Wilberforce University after the noted English statesman and abolitionist, William Wilberforce. Because of its commitment to equality regardless of race or creed in its student body, faculty, and governance structures, the institution quickly became a wellspring of hope for all African Americans. Ella and her stepmother spent portions of several summers at Tawawa Springs, which afforded Ella ample opportunity to practice piano at Wilberforce's music department.[88]

Ella was fourteen when the Civil War came to a close and the long-cherished dream of emancipation became a reality. Four million former slaves began the search to locate and reunite displaced family members scattered across the nation. Ella was one of them. Fortunately, her mother had remained with the Sheppard family after the war. Simon located her and arranged for Ella to meet her mother in Nashville. "I did not even know her face," Ella said when she recalled the bittersweet reunion.[89] The visit lasted for several weeks and not only rekindled the relationship, but introduced Ella to three-year-old Rosa, her half-sister and the offspring of a white father. Their time together was interrupted by the arrival of an unexpected telegram bearing the news that Simon Sheppard had died in a cholera epidemic that swept through Cincinnati. Ella needed to return home immediately. Once again, mother and daughter bid farewell, "one back to the North and the other again to the far South," initiating another long period of separation between the two. When they next met face to face, Ella had achieved a measure of fame and fortune of which Sarah could hardly dare to dream, fulfilling Mammy Viney's prophecy

A lawsuit followed Simon's death, forcing Cornelia Sheppard to sell all of the family's possessions, including Ella's piano, to cover expenses. Ella and her stepmother found themselves in dire straits without protection or provision. To help bring in money, Ella took in washing and ironing, worked for a local family, taught a few private piano students, and offered her services as pianist at festivals and local functions. A bright note in an otherwise bleak life occurred when James Presley Ball, a free African-

American photographer, offered to underwrite vocal lessons for Ella on the promise that she would pay him back when possible. Ella gladly agreed and began her studies with Madame Caroline Revé, a prominent white teacher employed at the exclusive Glendale Female College.[90] However, Madame Revé had strict guidelines by which she would accept a black student: "I took twelve lessons in vocal music of Madame [Revé]; was the only colored pupil; was not allowed to tell who my teacher was: and, more than all that, I went in the back way, and received my lessons in a back room up stairs, from nine to quarter of ten at night."[91] J. P. Ball was unable to continue his patronage, and after one quarter of study, Ella was forced to suspend her lessons.

Since her prospects for a secure financial existence were dim and she had little hope of furthering her musical study, Ella decided to take a subscription school in Gallatin, Tennessee. She had thirty-five scholars under her supervision who were as eager to receive an education as Ella was to impart it. Unfortunately, very few of them could pay. After five months of teaching, she had saved a mere six dollars. Ella hungered for more training herself, so in September 1868 she went to nearby Fisk University, hoping to persuade Fisk officials to let her work her way through school. She arrived with all of her possessions in a trunk so small that the young men of Fisk teasingly called it her "pie box." Ella later admitted her small trunk was not even fully packed. She asked to speak with someone in charge and came face to face with a man who would become her musical director, friend, and mentor: George Leonard White.

Ella Sheppard's small frame was dwarfed by White's towering stature and her quiet, reserved nature stood in stark contrast to his forcefulness. The conversation they exchanged on the day of her arrival set events in motion that would impact the lives of many. Ella announced she had only six dollars to her name, to which White replied that the amount would keep her at Fisk just a little more than three weeks. Perhaps Ella paused and her lips grew thinner. She had come a long way and could not be deterred so easily, so she asked if she could work at the school in exchange for an education. White replied that many students asked for work; in fact, there was a waiting list of potential students with similar aspirations. Undoubtedly, Ella's spirits fell at this announcement, and yet she had no other place to go or alternative plan to pursue. She announced that she would stay anyway until her money ran out.[92] It was the beginning of a long friendship built on shared beliefs and mutual admiration, and a musical partnership that would ultimately command the attention of the Western world.

Sheppard managed to secure three music students in Nashville who each paid four dollars per month for music lessons. She traveled to their homes on Wednesdays and Saturdays, returning to the campus long after the evening meal had passed. On other days, she waited on tables and washed dishes, and thereby managed to remain at Fisk. In her little bit of free time, she joined with other Fisk students to rehearse music with George White. He quickly noticed her skill, and a year later offered her the position of assistant music teacher, making her the first African American to serve on Fisk University's faculty.[93]

Ella Sheppard's role in the musical life of Fisk and the success of the Jubilee Singers was invaluable. Her talent was first noticed by a Nashville critic reviewing the *Cantata of Esther*, a production she both rehearsed and provided organ accompaniment for during the performance. "Miss Shepard [sic] who presided at the organ, played with true artistic touch, showing consummate skill and taste, as well a thorough knowledge of musical rules, as to progression or modulations, for it must be remembered, that where the vocal pieces followed each other abruptly, this lady much improved the effect, by improvising interludes that were correct and tasteful."[94] Another critic noted her decorum as well as her artistry: "Miss Ellen Shepard [sic], pianist and soprano, is not only excellent in her capacity as an artist, but makes as favourable [an] impression for her modest yet self-possessed manners as almost any one that we remember."[95] As a Jubilee Singer, Sheppard assisted in musical training, sang with the ensemble, accompanied on the piano and guitar, arranged medleys, transcribed spirituals, gave onstage direction, and kept the ensemble's scrapbooks. Though she was not the most gifted singer of the troupe, she was perhaps the most valuable member because of her broad musical skills, dependability, and quiet leadership.

Of all the female members of the Fisk Jubilee Singers, Sheppard was by far the most committed to the AMA's Christian Reconstruction ideology.

She was a devout Christian and a firm supporter of the missionary service required of a Jubilee Singer. She shared with her mentor, George White, a strong sense of duty and a willingness to sacrifice her personal interests for the sake of the mission. Her writings and her actions testify to her sincere piety and intense interest in spiritual things, and she spent her life in various forms of service to others. In many ways, her life served as an excellent model for those women committed to pursuing the Victorian ideals of "true womanhood."[96]

Sheppard needed no convincing that the Jubilee Singers were engaged in a worthy missionary cause. Shortly after the company's launch in 1871, she wrote home rejoicing how their singing had "changed the hearts of men":

> O I could write for hours if I had time of many such meetings when old men shed tears of gladness some of sorrow.... Surely God is with us and leading us. I feel we are in his hands doing his work. We are comforted through our many difficulties when we remember "we are prayed for at *home*." We are succeeding in reaching the people far beyond our expectations. In many matters our expenses have been and are very heavy. It may be difficult for us to go sometimes yet when it seems dark we receive *help*. We should, and do feel very thankful for our work so far.

Sheppard, well acquainted with sacrifice and tribulation, considered the struggles they faced as normal battles confronting anyone working for good. "It is a very tiresome work yet we are not tired or weary nor discouraged," she told Spence, believing the company's devotionals each morning and night coupled with the prayers of their friends at Fisk would see them through: "We are all well and praying and hoping for better times."[97]

A second letter followed within a month continuing the theme of thanksgiving for the reception they were enjoying in churches. In it, Sheppard reveals her pleasure at being a participant in Christian ministry, and an understanding similar to White's of the sacrificial requirements of missionary service:

> Dear friend just behold for one minute—*Your students* in the *grand old churches* conducting a meeting of hundreds of persons—and *I*—poor Ella—doomed to sit at the organ and lead them. The first word Mr. Ogden said was "Ella I have watched and kept close trace *of your work* and now my heart is to overflow to see you leading *your* people to the light by music."

That one word cheered me and lifted my poor heart to say *"work on and try to do good."* After that through many sad and discouraging hours if could *hope*—for I am conscious I have worked not for self but for *Jesus*—I have not even allowed my health to stop my work.

This letter also reveals Ella's mixed emotions concerning the failure of many without and within the company to acknowledge her contribution to the ensemble's success. She confided her thoughts to Spence:

The people up north (only a few) don't know I have had anything at all to do with the class. I am glad they don't for I am afraid I should be made vain. If what I hear said to others, was said to me, I listen with perfect satisfaction. I think the general impression is that "I am only playing for them" very well—I am many times pained with the different in my position—I have not been very happy concerning such. Miss W[ells] is very kind and loving to the girls—Yet often misunderstands me—and oftener when I do my duty as of yore "reminds me I am getting a little above myself"—or position or something of the kind. You know how I have worked with this class. Yet all the praise is carried to others. I wish I could sit and tell you many things.

Ella hoped to have shared her concerns with Spence prior to the troupe's departure, looking for a "confiding friend to open my heart to for comfort," but time had not permitted the conversation. "Did you ever think I had a secret sorrow hidden beneath my seemingly happy countenance?" she inquired. "Well such is the case. How often have I wanted to lay my weary heart to *rest* in the quiet grave—but I must work and try to make others happy—I am young & weary of life." She begged Spence to keep this portion of her letter private for she "would not have the world to know" of her unhappiness.[98]

It was rare for Sheppard to reveal her inner thoughts. She was an intensely private and introverted woman who generally kept her emotions carefully masked. Years later in Germany, when each member had his or her portrait made in pencil for wood cuts, Dönig, the artist, remarked that Sheppard's face and mouth were particularly difficult to catch. White retorted in jest that there was no expression to catch.[99] Her leadership role and the fact that she was older than the other females in the company may explain in part why she remained aloof. Perhaps her distaste for conflict and unwillingness to enter into the disputes that surfaced during the campaigns also reinforced her behavior.

Sheppard often appropriated spiritual language to assess the company's success or failure, describing the troupe's early victories as a miraculous answer to prayer: "We are now where you and all our friends have for four months prayed that we might be—'How good is He the giver whose mercies fail us never.' I can not only thank him for our success in always meeting the *best Christian* people but for the bounteous gifts of presents and *money*." Though she feared success might adversely affect some, Sheppard assured Spence she was the "same *humble* Ella" who preferred to be out of the spotlight. "In the midst of applause and flattery I often wish to be back in some little secluded spot where I can be from every eye—in the presence of my God and pour out my soul in thanksgiving."[100] Solitude was precious to Sheppard, but she was denied the luxury of a private room until the last few months of the final campaign. Forsaking her privacy for the cause was one of her greatest personal sacrifices as a Jubilee Singer.

Sheppard's diary entries from 1874 through 1878 contain numerous references to the scores of sermons she heard. She listened carefully, analyzed what she heard, and afterwards engaged in self-reflection. After one of the Moody revival services, Sheppard wrote: "It seemed that the whole sermon was just suited to my case. How often have these things troubled me. How often have I wept because I could not *feel* a greater sense of my sins and doubted my acceptance of the Father simply because of trusting to feeling."[101] Her diary includes sermon notes, biblical citations, and contemplation of theological ideas she considered odd:

One thing he said struck me as very peculiar, that if he was taught anything at all from the Bible it was that in heaven there were different courts...and that each soul after death works its place in the society according to its spiritual standing. I did not like the idea at first—nor can I now only as I associate with it the idea that even there the soul has a chance of being "promoted." Even this idea does not satisfy me. It sounds too earthly. Is it possible for the soul to be ambitious and not sin, even in heaven?[102]

To one who knew intimately the debilitating effects of social caste, the notion that heavenly saints still experienced rank was unappealing and theologically suspicious.

Sheppard's keen sense of Christian duty sometimes conflicted with her timid, reserved nature. The company had been working with the Moody revival team for more than a month before she got up the nerve to volunteer her services at the inquiry meetings held after the services. Moody considered these meetings the most important part of his revival services, for here the "personal work" of salvation and sanctification took place. Trained workers were on hand to counsel and pray for seekers. They were instructed to listen carefully, take their time, seek the Holy Spirit's guidance in all they said, and offer an appropriate scriptural response. Most of all, they were to win souls to Christ.[103] Sheppard's experience left her with mixed feelings about her ability to meet Moody's expectations for volunteers:

> I went into the Enquiry Room for the first time. Had not been present but a moment when a young face behind me in tears moved me to speak to her. We talked of Christ's power to save her soul. She had been ignorant of these meetings until two evenings before. Her husband, a Christian, had said to her that if she "wished to hear some most beautiful singing" to go with him and she came and for the first time sought peace. Our songs had fairly melted her stony heart. She seemed so anxious—I tried to lead her but somehow I could not or seemed not to make the way plain for her. I wanted to help her oh so much. She looked so thirsty and clung to my hand with such a nervous grasp I became nervous and confused and ashamed of my weakness and could do nothing. Just then a woman behind us began to have hysterics and screamed so loud that I could stay no longer, but I promised to pray night and day for her, and with God's help I will.[104]

The demands of personal counseling in a revival atmosphere stretched Sheppard's comfort zone, and there is no evidence that she ever volunteered in the inquiry room again. Nonetheless, such experiences as these broadened her understanding of other forms of ministry and human expressions of spirituality.

The variety of religious services in which the Jubilee Singers participated also sharpened Ella's sense of social consciousness and improved her unique ministry skills. The "breakfast for the poor" in Edinburgh placed her before "seven or eight hundred...of the most wretched poor" she had ever seen. "I could not help weeping," she confided as she acknowledged her own blessings. "I never received such a rebuke—it seemed that I could never murmur again." A visit to the bedside of one who had been an invalid for forty years made Sheppard pause and offer thanks for her own health. "I could but praise the Lord for my health - as I gazed at him and prayed for *my* life to be buried in Christ till I should become a fountain of pure living water to hungry souls."[105] At another meeting in Glasgow, she agreed to give an impromptu speech about American prejudice and became so immersed in recounting her experiences that she continued for almost an hour. "I was very much surprised that I should have done so—and a little mortified for fear that I had used too much time till Mr F kindly put away my trouble by saying how much he had enjoyed hearing it—that he was not at all wearied."[106] Contrary to the discomfort she had felt in Moody's Inquiry Room, this opportunity to speak about issues that affected her personally seemed to empower her. This informal speaking engagement was a prelude to the impassioned speeches Sheppard would give in her lifetime.

Sheppard's faith and concern for the disenfranchised found practical expression in other ways. She adopted a group of girls in Scotland that she referred to as her "class" and with whom she maintained close contact. She visited one dying from consumption and left the visit with a "sweet peace" in her soul. When Ella and America Robinson visited the Royal Infirmary intending to see only one patient, they became so engrossed in their work that they spent over two hours visiting five wards. "I came home very weary but O so happy," Sheppard wrote. Her visit the following day to an orphanage also taxed her physically but renewed her spiritually. "It is such pleasant work to use one's strength helping encourage such work," she said. After attending a missionary service, she wrote, "I almost wished I was going as a *Christian missionary*. My heart goes out to Africa."[107]

Though Sheppard made it a practice to extend kindness generously to others, she shared her inner thoughts with only a few chosen people.[108] She was close to Susan Gilbert but careful of how she handled the friendship lest she aggravate the envy already brewing within the company. Ella was therefore surprised when the Jubilees encouraged her to travel ahead of them to assist Gilbert on her wedding day to George White. "Mr S[eward] had suggested it before to me and I had hesitated because some of the Singers are so jealous of Miss G[ilbert] and my friendship and were fussed because I went off with her last Thursday."[109] Sheppard was intensely fond of the Whites, yet she seemed somewhat shocked to find the affection returned. On one occasion after their marriage, Susan Gilbert White was ill and could rest comfortably only once Ella arrived. "She told me how she had suffered alone, and how she longed to have some one with her last night especially - & how bitterly she wept over it." Realizing her importance to this woman evoked a self-effacing response from Sheppard: "O, if *I* can ever be such an unselfish, loving & lovable creature as she I could see a reason for existence. I sometimes think it strange that God should crowd so many blessings upon worthless & unlovable me."[110] Another time, she wrote, "Oh that I deserve such a friend! I might live up to this standard."[111]

Sheppard's inclination towards self-reflection may have also contributed to her tendency to bear the company's troubles personally. She grieved over every slight against White and attempted to act as peacemaker between feuding company members. The troubles of the 1877–1878 campaign year caused her endless worry. She had difficulty with Mrs. Swart during rehearsals and Minnie Butler during concerts.[112] To make matters worse, Maggie Porter committed a major offense: "Satan is about & MP [Maggie Porter] did something worse, accepting an invitation *personally* which was intended *generally* & then *lied* out of it!"[113] The constant fussing between company members taxed her peacemaking abilities. "This afternoon Jennie [Jackson] & Mr W[hite] had it very hotly—the cause I do not know…. Jennie was all packed & replied to me that she was going home today if she could start…. I tried to cheer her out of her anger but failed."[114] It seemed to Sheppard that "just as soon as we have a day of unusual success or honor & special rejoicing it is followed [by] almost unparalled[ed] trouble & perplexity."[115] Everyone's frazzled nerves made life in the company almost unbearable and the Jubilees' coolness toward her wounded her deeply. "I have a great sorrow, yet must bear it *alone*," she confided to her diary. "There are moments when I wish death might have come instead."[116]

Only her keen sense of duty kept Sheppard going during the last few weeks of the campaign. On the final voyage home, the company sang the "Star-Spangled Banner" and "John Brown's Body" for the passengers on board. "Many wept during the evening & one lady followed me to my room weeping—threw her arms around my neck & kissing me cried, 'I never thought I would or *could* kiss a negro before! I do thank you. I never *felt* such music before!'" Such a proclamation was bittersweet for Sheppard as she considered what effective change agents the Jubilee Singers could be if unfettered by their own weaknesses. Her last diary entry reads: "How much good we might do not only for others but for our own people & hearts! May our Father forgive us!"[117]

Sheppard returned to Nashville for a season before joining White's reorganized company bearing the same name as the original ensemble. It was perhaps during this time that she first met George Washington Moore, a native of Nashville born on 9 November 1854 to slave parents Rice Moore and Elizabeth Corry. Young George and his mother were sold to a surgeon in the Confederate Army in 1861 with whom they traveled throughout the South. After the Civil War, they returned to Nashville and reunited with his father, where his parents were legally married. George Moore completed the normal course of study by the age of sixteen and then concluded he had enough education. His father could not persuade him otherwise, so one morning decided to try a new tactic. He asked George to take a walk with him, and together they began a 3,000-mile journey across the country through territories the father had traveled as a fugitive slave. They took on small jobs to meet expenses and camped at night in the woods. The journey ended at the county jail in Bowling Green, Kentucky, the place where George's father had finally been captured.

George Moore later recalled how the three-month object lesson changed his life. With a newfound appreciation for the value of an education, he eagerly enrolled at Fisk University, eventually graduating in 1881 from the college and theological departments. After a period he described as "much perplexity and struggle," he consecrated his life to Christian service while at Fisk and began preaching in a mission church in Nashville for no pay. In 1876, the AMA commissioned Moore to preach at Fisk's newly constructed Howard Chapel for a monthly salary of twenty dollars, which he shared with three other struggling students.[118] "The work is still small but I am not discouraged because I know that I am trying to work for the Master," he reported to the AMA. Conversions were few, but "those who attend the meetings seem to be interested in their salvation" and some demonstrated conviction.[119]

The following year found Moore loving the work "more and more." He and his fellow ministerial students had established a chapter of the

YMCA and were holding open-air meetings. "The Lord has blessed my labor both in the church and out door work," he reported. "I long to be a winner of souls."[120] In 1878 Moore sent a lengthy report to AMA headquarters. "I endeavor to teach that vital Christianity is the work of Christ Church, no denomination will save a person, nothing but the blood of Christ can do this." He stressed how the people needed Bibles in their homes and "missionaries to go from house to house teaching the word." "If they are industrious, economical and prudent and trust in the Lord He will supply all their wants," he claimed. The "Christian work has been encouraging," Moore reported, with around fifty conversions during the term. He had also been elected as president of the Society for the Evangelization of Africa, which he considered "a great honor, greater than I deserve," and prayed that God would make the organization "a power for good."[121]

During his last year at Fisk, Moore worked as hard as he could to "build up the work" at Howard Chapel "in number and firmness."[122] He felt there was much to be done in the South and the fact that his studies kept him from giving his full attention to the needs of the church weighed heavily on him. After graduating from Fisk University in May 1881, Moore entered the theological department of Oberlin College for seminary studies where he earned the Bachelor of Divinity degree in 1883.[123]

It is little wonder that Ella Sheppard and George Moore were attracted to each other. Both shared similar values, a commitment to the AMA, and the missionary qualities of self-sacrifice and service to others. They somehow managed a courtship while Ella was touring with White's independent troupe of Jubilee Singers and George was completing his education. During summer 1882, Moore served three white churches in Southern Ohio as an employee of the Ohio Home Missionary Society, including the First Congregational Church of Sullivan, whose congregation requested that he remain as their full-time pastor. However, he felt the need to work among his own people and graciously declined.[124]

On 20 December 1882, Ella Sheppard and George W. Moore were married in the Whites' parlor in Fredonia, New York.[125] Six months later, on 1 June 1883, the couple began their pastoral ministry at the Lincoln Memorial Church of Washington, DC, located in one of the most notorious sections of the city. Seventeen saloons and several gambling establishments within blocks of the church contributed to the flourishing criminal activity. The Moores rolled up their sleeves and got to work. Within two years they established the first Young People's Society of Christian Endeavor and led a successful temperance crusade against the saloons near their church, transforming the neighborhood known as "Hell's Bottom" into a desirable residential section of the city.[126] The crusade was not without its critics. Some remarked that for every saloon closed down, three "speakeasies" opened up around the corner and the grand effect was that a few "colored men" were deprived of their liquor licenses to the benefit of the white liquor store owners. Nonetheless, the Christian social gospel advocates were delighted with the success of the campaign.[127]

Lincoln Memorial quickly became known throughout Washington, DC for its social and benevolence work among the needy. On its sixth anniversary, the *Washington Bee* contained a brief sketch of Rev. Moore's impact upon the church and the city: "It began with only eleven and now has an enrollment of over eighty members. Rev. Moore, and the officers of the church deserve great credit for the fine condition in which the church has been put. Rev. Moore, is an energetic and Christian gentleman, who is entitled to the respect and confidence of the entire community. Much success to this young divine."[128] Reverend Moore was one of a long line of highly educated ministers who helped establish a tradition at Lincoln Memorial of exercising a practical Christianity. During his tenure, the church became a launch pad for the careers of many African-American Congregational ministers and societies such as the American Negro Academy. Prominent African-American leaders such as Booker T. Washington, A. P. Miller, and Mary Church Terrell were associated with the church's history.[129]

While filling the pulpit at Lincoln Memorial, Reverend Moore also completed his Master's degree at Howard University and served as a professor of biblical history and literature from 1887–1892. In 1908, Howard University awarded him the Doctor of Divinity degree.[130] Meanwhile, Ella Sheppard Moore busied herself with church work and rearing a family. George Sheppard was born on 27 September 1883, followed by a daughter named Sarah Elizabeth (Sadie) on 11 June 1885 who died in 1893 at the age of seven.[131] A third son, Clinton Russell, was also born to the Moore family. Both sons graduated from Fisk University.

George Sheppard Moore received his diploma in 1906 and pursued studies in medicine at the Northwestern Medical School, graduating in 1910. He became a physician and surgeon and served as the chair of the Mental and Nervous Diseases Department of Nashville's Meharry Medical College. Clinton Russell Moore graduated in 1914 and became the proprietor of a cafeteria in New York City.[132]

Ella Sheppard first began caring financially for members of her family while touring with the Jubilee Singers. In 1876, she brought her mother and half-sister, Rosa, from their log cabin home in Okolona to live in Nashville. She provided a home for them close to the campus and financed Rosa's education at Fisk University. Rosa graduated in 1883 from the normal department and pursued a successful teaching career, later marrying W. A. Caldwell who became the principal for all of the "colored schools" in Mobile, Alabama. Sarah Hannah Sheppard lived for many years under her daughter's protective care. Ella and her husband also provided materially for her stepmother and mother-in-law and helped raise George Moore's niece, Elizabeth, from the time the child was four years old. They financed Elizabeth's education at Fisk and celebrated her graduation from the normal department in 1889.[133] Though Ella had sacrificed her own hopes of receiving a college diploma, she was instrumental in ensuring a college education for four of her loved ones.[134]

Ella Sheppard Moore was deeply concerned about the spiritual and intellectual development of her people and strived to advance their status. Her travels in America gave her invaluable experience facing and fighting prejudice and exposure to some of the nation's most prominent African Americans. Traveling abroad and interacting with persons of intellect and power in a climate of social acceptance introduced her to a world far different from the one American society attempted to force upon her. The respect granted her overseas was life-changing, informing her understanding of equality and strengthening her voice for justice. She used her status as a former Jubilee Singer and the wife of the Reverend George W. Moore to speak authoritatively on social issues relevant to African Americans. A speech delivered in 1889 reveals the passion with which she attacked the prejudice still confronting black women:

Have they had a fair chance in the race of life? No. They have met caste-prejudice, the ghost of slavery, at every step of their journey during these years of freedom. They have been made to feel that they are a separate species of the human family. The phrases "Your people" and "Your place," do not so much designate their race identity, as the fixed status in the sisterhood of races. This idea, as harmless as it may appear, or as much as it is used, with varied phrases of meaning, according to the attitude of the speaker, has been one of the greatest barriers to the progress of the Negro, especially of the women and girls.

Ella Sheppard Moore argued vehemently that a black female should rise "just as high as she has the ability to reach and sustain." "My five years' experience in Europe as a Jubilee Singer gave me a taste of the sweets of true womanhood, unfettered by caste-prejudice and by a low estimate of my position," she pronounced. The time to extend the same privilege to African-American women was long overdue. "It is said that the 'hand that rocks the cradle,' rules the world. It matters not whether that hand be black or white, but it does matter whether that hand be intelligent or ignorant. They not only need the education of the schools to develop their minds, and industrial training to prepare their hands for the practical duties of life, but Christian education, such as is given in the schools of the Association."[135]

In 1892, George W. Moore resigned his pastorate after ten years of service at Lincoln Memorial Congregational Church to become a field missionary for the AMA. His church had grown tremendously and was known throughout the capital city as a "great power for good." Observers suggested that Rev. Moore's success was "due in no small measure to the personality of his wife, Ella Sheppard Moore." Rev. Moore's new assignment involved giving counsel to regional churches and pastors, planting new churches, and assisting in evangelical work. He also served as a trustee of Fisk University until his death. The couple moved to Nashville and lived in a house they built across from Fisk's Livingstone Hall.[136]

Ella continued her work for the AMA by performing or speaking at various religious meetings and helping to prepare new vocal talent at Fisk University.[137] In 1890, she trained a company of university-sponsored singers who began a seven-month fundraising tour on 16 October 1890 under the management of Reverend Charles Shelton.[138] Thomas Talley, a talented bass who later became a noted educator, recalled how the young students at Fisk had rehearsed with Mrs. Moore only a few short hours before they realized that "the Lord had laid His hands on her."[139] In 1899, Fisk University developed a touring male quartet bearing the celebrated Jubilee name. The "Fisk Jubilee Quartette," under the leadership of John Wesley Work II, toured for several years to much acclaim.[140] Meanwhile, Ella trained and directed the Jubilee Club on the Fisk campus.[141] In 1902, the ensemble had a surprise performance before Prince Henry of Prussia. The prince, who was touring the United States, had sent a telegram ahead to Fisk University asking to hear the famous Jubilee Singers when he stopped in Nashville. As there was no time to bring the male quartet back to campus, Ella Sheppard Moore fulfilled the request by having her Jubilee Club ready at the train station to sing a few spirituals. The prince was delighted to discover she was one of the original singers he had heard years before in Berlin.[142]

While fulfilling these musical services to Fisk University, Ella Sheppard Moore maintained her activity in social and religious causes. In 1893, she presented a paper before the World's African Congress entitled "Missionary and Temperance Work in the District of Columbia" and another entitled "What Congregational Women Have Done for the Uplift-ing of the Negro" before the Women's Congregational Congress. She represented Fisk University in 1898 at the Conference of Congregational Churches in Tennessee and was also the state president of the Woman's Missionary Union for eighteen years. Mrs. Moore also authored pamphlets published by the AMA on the effects of slavery, and on several occasions delivered lectures and performed for Fisk audiences.[143]

Mrs. Moore was as willing to fight injustice levelled against one person as she was the indignities suffered by her entire race. Thomas Talley remarked that "God was the staff of her life and she was fearless": "I remember on one occasion when she thought a young man was about to be wronged by his superiors, unsolicited she went to them and declared that she would walk the by-paths at midnight and arouse every righteous-minded individual in the community against them, unless the action was withheld. It was withheld."[144] With her life, her music, and her words, Ella Sheppard Moore fought for what she considered to be right, sought to promote understanding between the races, and worked tirelessly to effect social change in America.

Ella gave special attention to advancing the educational opportunities for African Americans. She was a member of the National Federation of Afro-American Women, an organization that touted among its ranks such notables as Mrs. Booker T. Washington and Ida Wells-Barnett. In 1896, Mrs. Moore joined with Mary Church Terrell, Ida Wells-Barnett, Charlotte Forten Grimke, Alice Moore Dunbar, and others to create the National Association of Colored Women (NACW), formed from the merger of the National Federation of Afro-American Women and the National League of Colored Women.[145] Ella had first given practical expression to her desire to see young African Americans educated when she sent scholarship assistance to a musically gifted student named Rebecca Wickle at Fisk University in 1875. "I had Miss Wells select such a pupil," she informed Secretary Whiting while on tour, and sent money designated for Miss Wickle's educational expenses. Twenty-one years later, her educational aspirations for her race had only intensified. Mrs. Moore joined the ranks of other African-American female leaders dedicated to the "elevation of mankind and womankind especially" and welcomed them to their first annual meeting held on the Fisk University campus.[146]

Time only strengthened Ella Sheppard Moore's belief in the AMA's ideological stance that religion and education were the keys to racial uplift. If "better training" of young African-American boys and girls began at the cradle, and if their intellects were nurtured throughout infancy and childhood, "there could be but one result, viz., a more perfect and stronger girlhood, which was bound to produce a wiser and better prepared womanhood," she wrote. Her heart, she said, yearned for "every Negro mother and daughter that they might for once get out of the narrow radius which has closed in their entire vision of life and its opportunity, morally, mentally, spiritually, even physically for generations."[147]

In June 1914, Ella Sheppard Moore traveled to Trinity School in Athens, Alabama, to deliver the commencement address.[148] Afterwards, she became quite ill and had to return immediately to Nashville where doctors determined that she had acute appendicitis. Medical attention came too late, and on 9 June 1914, Ella Sheppard Moore died at the age of sixty-three.[149] A few days later, her youngest son, Clinton, graduated from Fisk University.

Reverend C. W. Morrow, Bishop I. B. Scott, and Reverend H. H. Proctor conducted her stirring funeral service in Fisk's Memorial Chapel on 11 June 1914. Local newspapers hailed her as "one of the most noted women of the negro race in the entire world."[150] "Her life had shared the want and squalor of the humblest slave cabin, and then also it had gathered around the festal beard with the jewelled heads of princes," wrote one of her admirers.[151] Ella Sheppard Moore was buried in Nashville's City Cemetery close to the mother whom she had honored and dearly loved, and beside her friend and fellow singer, Mabel Lewis.

George W. Moore carried on his work for the AMA and Fisk University for several years. After his death, Fisk President Fayette Avery McKenzie recalled fondly the time he spent with this "gentle, but true, servant of God, servant of man, servant of his race." He noted that age had diminished Moore's body, but could not mute his passion for his beloved alma mater. "He wanted Fisk right, he wanted Fiskites true, he wanted Fisk strong in resources," reflected McKenzie. It was a dream Moore had shared with his wife, Ella Sheppard Moore. Together, they influenced countless lives in their quest for spiritual, intellectual, and social uplift for all African Americans.[152]

Afterword

Let us not despise the day of small things.[1]

On 1 January 1876, a throng of people trudged up the hill for the dedication of Fisk University's newly constructed Jubilee Hall. Faculty, administrators, students, dignitaries, and visiting guests, both blacks and whites, joined together to consecrate the new facility "to the good cause of Christian culture." Swags of magnolia leaves wound around the American and British flags hung proudly over the door leading to the platform, representing the two countries united in purpose to elevate, educate, and evangelize the freedmen. Speeches, prayers, and congregational singing interspersed with special performances of spirituals filled the celebration.

As the Fisk Jubilee Singers were still on tour in England, they sent their greetings by telegram: "Hitherto hath the Lord helped us. May Fisk University be inspiration to struggling humanity in America, and light to Africa's millions. May Great Britain and America ever thus unite to extend Christ's kingdom." Fisk University responded: "To the Jubilee Singers, to their friends at home and in the land of Wilberforce and Sharpe, we owe what God hath wrought. May the two flags floating to-day from Jubilee Hall ever symbolize the united purpose of both lands to fit the struggling Freedmen of America to carry light to Africa."[2]

Reverend J. B. McFerrin, D.D., Secretary of the Missionary Society of the Methodist Episcopal Church South, rose to offer his congratulatory remarks, reminding the audience that all "intelligent, patriotic and Christian people of the South" rejoiced in what this day represented. He further cautioned the faculty and American Missionary Association (AMA) officials gathered that all their efforts to educate the mind and bestow culture should ultimately result in one's spiritual enrichment. "Your Sunday-schools, churches, seminaries, and your colleges, are worth nothing unless you bring those taught to Jesus." General Clinton B. Fisk's dedicatory prayer echoed the sentiment:

Here within these walls may there ever be taught that which will mature into noble manhood and womanhood the thousands of youth, who, we trust, will throng these halls in seeking wisdom that they may be properly fitted for positions of responsibility and usefulness. Let there be laid, broad and deep, the foundations of virtue, truth and honesty in every character here moulded. But, above all else, may they who herein enter be made "wise unto salvation through faith which is in Christ Jesus,"... Lift up your eyes and behold the outstretching, whitening harvest, which invites you who will go forth from this institution with the Divine benediction upon you, to teach and preach among the millions of our land...and the unnumbered millions more, who from the heart of Africa are inviting the means of religious renovation of that mysterious land from which—thanks be to God—the pall of barbarism is being lifted.[3]

The audience rose and lifted their voice with the choir in heartfelt response, singing "The Year of Jubilee."

The remarks made on that day of celebration encapsulate the underlying beliefs of Christian Reconstruction that characterized both Fisk University and its celebrated ensemble, the Jubilee Singers. "Elevate, educate, and evangelize" were the fundamental goals the AMA embraced in its quest to change its world. Those associated with the association shared a common understanding that intellectual, economic, and social attainment for African Americans would be imperfect if Christianity did not govern their souls. The political health and well-being of America, as well as the civilization and Christianization of Africa, depended on equal accomplishment in all three areas. These inseparable, codependent goals flavored every missionary activity under the sponsorship of the AMA, from its colleges and schools in the South to its mission bases abroad. With the Jubilee Singers' worldwide fame, the association's work achieved international exposure upon a public platform. The Jubilees were ambassadors of Christian Reconstruction, whose success or failure would either validate or render null the ideology's principles.

In relating the days' events to its constituents in its monthly journal, the AMA chose to follow the article about Jubilee Hall's dedicatory festivities with British newspaper extracts about the Jubilee Singers' most recent appearances. The first extract focused on the crowded audience who showed their appreciation of the company's extraordinary talent by demanding frequent encores. The second gave an account of the troupe's time spent with Lord Kintore at his private residence. A speech against the Fugitive Slave Circular given by Loudin during one concert was the feature of the third extract, while the fourth short article told of the Jubilee's visit to the Royal Albert Idiot Asylum.[4]

Perhaps the AMA chose these particular newspaper extracts randomly with no conscious intention. They nonetheless represent four ways in which the AMA upheld the Jubilee Singers as tangible evidence of the ultimate supremacy of its Christian Reconstruction beliefs. The troupe's concert success before audiences of thousands confirmed the Jubilees' mastery of the divine art of music and thus demonstrated their educability and cultural attainment. Lord Kintore's invitation to his home was but one illustration of the company's victory in the social arena. Such societal acceptance affirmed their human dignity before the world and became ready ammunition with which the AMA chided Americans whose minds and attitudes were still ensnared by prejudice. Loudin's speech was indicative of the Jubilees' powerful voice raised on behalf of all struggling humanity. The Jubilee Singers' fight for civil rights often gained public attention and represented the daily battles on many less visible fronts in which AMA personnel were engaged. Finally, the Jubilees' asylum visit served as evidence that the company was committed to ongoing Christian ministry to those less fortunate than themselves, seeking every opportunity to spread the gospel through music, words, and good deeds. As representatives of Fisk University and the AMA, the Fisk Jubilee Singers were living tributes to how attention to intellectual, social, and spiritual growth produced educated, upstanding Christian citizens equipped to serve others.

Such diverse success indicators placed great demands upon any participant in the Jubilee Singers enterprise. Each one found him or herself engaged in entertainment and ministry simultaneously. Business demands coexisted with expectations for benevolence work, and political activism rested alongside evangelical fervor. Achieving balance between these oft-competing interests was not easy, especially with the eyes of the world constantly watching and evaluating. Whatever company members said or did, onstage and off, individually or collectively, reflected upon the AMA and the race as a whole. Triumphs were validations of what African Americans could accomplish, while interpersonal and management feuds were quietly tucked away as much as possible from public scrutiny.

Despite the hardships and internal problems they endured, those associated with the Jubilee Singers and Fisk University maintained an intense pride for the work they had done in behalf of the institution. With only a few exceptions, personality clashes were kept out of the public limelight and the ensemble emerged from its seven years of campaigns relatively free of scandal or public embarrassment. In short time, the troubles that had surfaced between participants seemed buried and forgiven, if not completely forgotten. For example, an altercation between Georgia Gordon and George White that occurred shortly before his initial launch in October 1871 was so severe that he refused to let her travel with the company. The two patched up their differences and Gordon joined the troupe after nine months. Years later, she referred to the heated argument simply as a "misunderstanding." And though Maggie Porter's prima donna behavior had been the source of major friction within the group, Gordon described her female peers as models of Fisk University's ideals:

> I wish to leave with those who read this that the Christian training which we received from Prof. John Ogden, George L. White, A. K. Spence, E. M. Cravath, and others has been uppermost in our hearts. We have never grown haughty. We are still the simple, unassuming children grown to matured women. We still cling to our childhood faith, trusting God, standing up for all that is good and pure, and maintaining the Christian spirit which from the beginning has pervaded Fisk University.[5]

Gordon's alleged affair with Loudin indicated in America Robinson's letters to James Burrus was never exposed publicly. Like many of her peers, Gordon chose to preserve the image of nobility, Christian service, and self-sacrifice the AMA had nurtured during the Jubilee Singers' tenure.

The transformation of the Jubilee Singers' story from historical event to legendary status produced several notable outcomes. First, it established the university's distinctive identity as an institution committed to developing African-American leaders. Traveling with the Jubilee Singers had prepared each member to assume positions of leadership within their respective chosen fields. Fisk officials were able to point to the Jubilees' collective and individual achievements as standards for other students. Richardson notes how well Fisk graduates rose to meet these standards, especially in the field of education. Within a few decades, the university had a wide reputation for producing excellent teachers, principals, and college professors.[6]

Second, the fact that the ensemble had succeeded despite overwhelming odds gave credence to the missionary spirit, religious faith, and self-sacrifice endorsed by Fisk employees and solidified the university's reputation as an institution dedicated to fighting racial injustice. The Jubilee Singers modeled a warrior spirit tempered by religious faith and personal integrity that in turn permeated the campus atmosphere.

The celebrated exploits of the Jubilee Singers also generated an intense loyalty to Fisk University among its faculty, students, and alumni. Even Frederick Loudin, who never enrolled at Fisk, wore his association with the institution with pride and maintained strong ties to the institution. In his travels across the globe, his troupe upheld Fisk's commitment to education, racial uplift, and civil rights, spreading the fame and reputation of the institution. Original company members became respected figures in the institution's memory and Fisk officials made special efforts to bring them back to the campus for Jubilee Day observances. Mabel Lewis Imes, who outlived many of her peers, often traveled from her Cleveland home to the campus to celebrate Jubilee Day. Upon her death in 1935, Fisk's President Jones lauded her as "an outstanding example of all that Fisk University has stood for throughout the years."[7] She was buried in Nashville in a special plot set aside for those who had given exemplary service to the institution.[8]

The Jubilee Singers' rags-to-riches story formed the substance of Fisk University's institutional mythology, which, over time, became increasingly romanticized. Remarks made by Professor H. S. Bennett at an 1886 Jubilee Day ceremony, less than ten years after the original troupe had disbanded, indicate how the Jubilees' travails had assumed legendary status: "The story of the Jubilee singers reads like a tale of romance. That a company of young ex-slaves should sing as they sang and make money to build such a building as Jubilee Hall is one of the most astonishing facts of history. That history would grow more precious as it grew older. We are too close to it to estimate it at its true value. It is like old wine, it must have the flavor of age to give it aroma and taste."[9] Fisk President George E. Gates echoed this sentiment in 1911. He acknowledged that other colleges for blacks had noble histories grounded in the leadership of charismatic personalities, such as General Samuel Chapman Armstrong's connections with Hampton and

Booker T. Washington's founding of Tuskegee. However, Fisk University held a special claim to the power of music and the tenacious determination of songsters to rescue and establish an institution. "The romance of Fisk's early beginnings will always be associated in the popular mind with the Jubilee Singers and Jubilee songs," he claimed.[10]

The story of the Jubilee Singers formed an institutional saga that remains at the center of the university's identity to this day.[11] In 1996, the current group of Jubilee Singers commented on how they saw themselves as the keepers of a sacred tradition. "It's a symbol," said one of the singers. "Once you're a Jubilee Singer, people will always know you as a Jubilee Singer, even after you graduate." In addition to being an effective public relations tool for the institution, the current Jubilee Singers keep the Fisk community linked to its past. "Many times, when I sing, I feel an inner connection—not just only with the Jubilee Singers, but with our forefathers," expressed a current group member. "There is a connection of the spirit and a great sense of freedom that ties me to slaves, and my ancestors, and Jubilee Singers."[12]

In the final analysis, one might ask whether or not the AMA's Christian Reconstruction ideology accomplished what it intended. Was it the recipe for freedom that the AMA proclaimed? Looking at the individual lives of those who participated with the Jubilee Singers enterprise lends some insight. Certainly, the AMA personnel with whom the singers interacted held high standards for how blacks and whites must live together that was nothing less than radical. Though their actions were often paternalistic and imperfect, they nonetheless reflect a genuine desire to instill in others the attitudes and values they felt were necessary for any person, regardless of race, to achieve social and political success in America. AMA teachers and officials lived lives of sacrifice and service that suggest a willingness to share power with those for whom power had long been denied.

Evidence indicates that company members were willing participants in the acculturation process of Christian Reconstruction. In general, they understood that being a Jubilee Singer meant accepting the mantle of a missionary and adhering to the AMA's Christian interpretation of prevailing Victorian standards. Each member affirmed the Protestant ethic of Victorian America, though not all were as ardent in their devotion to

Christian evangelicalism as Ella Sheppard and her husband. Every participant recognized and affirmed the middle-class criteria by which they were judged and usually employed the same standards to judge others. At times, though, the Jubilees reinterpreted and reshaped prevailing white values and attitudes to fit the realities of the dual worlds—black and white—in which they lived. They used their experience as Jubilee Singers to form lives worthy of honor, empower their voices for justice, and crack open the door to the Western concert stage for future generations of aspiring African-American artists. In short, they changed their world for the better.

The arduous quest for freedom was somehow sweetened by the power of music. Throughout their travels, the Jubilee Singers carried with them the lyrical melodies of the Negro spiritual. The simple but profound texts of these freedom songs delivered with quiet dignity challenged the intellects and emotions of Westerners. "These songs…are the pure waters of our affliction," Loudin told an audience at one of Moody's revival services at Bow Road Hall.

> They gushed forth from us when we were smitten by the hand of man, as the waters gushed from the rock in the wilderness when smitten by the rod of Moses. These songs came to us, as it were, fresh from the hand of God, as He gave them to us, in order to give utterance sometimes to our woes, and sometimes to our joys. Sometimes it was –
>
> *Nobody knows the trouble I see, Lord;*
> *Nobody knows but Jesus.*
> Sometimes it was –
> *You may bury him in the east,*
> *You may bury him in the west,*
> *But I'll hear the trumpet sound in that morning.*
>
> Glory be to God for what these songs have furnished us—how they lightened the burden of our affliction as we passed through a long night of sorrow![13]

After hearing the Jubilee Singers in concert, most agreed with Loudin's claim that the spirituals were God-given. In short time, these religious sorrow songs of slavery became the trademark of Fisk University as well as the theme song of the Jubilee Singers' lives.

"Let us not despise the day of small things," General Fisk reminded the audience gathered for the dedication of Jubilee Hall. What began as a seemingly harebrained scheme of one man had evolved into a finely tuned campaign strategy for raising funds and promoting the AMA's ideology. A nine-member fledgling vocal group had developed into a high-caliber, professional musical ensemble of international repute whose members personified the AMA's aspirations for all African Americans. Jubilee Hall stood as a witness to the Western world of what faith and sacrificial hard work could accomplish. AMA personnel and the Jubilee Singers had labored together in a unique partnership to open closed doors, tear down walls, and throw up highways for newly freed blacks wanting their share in the American dream.

The Year of Jubilee had come, but full freedom was not yet fully realized. For many decades, Americans would struggle to define freedom and set the criteria for who would get to taste its fruits. With their golden liquid tones, the Jubilee Singers had propelled the movement for freedom along, adding their sweet harmonies to the oft-harsh cacophony of voices engaged in the debate. The songs born in the darkness of slavery would continue to inspire generations seeking a more just world.

Appendix

Brief Biographies of the
Fisk Jubilee Singers, 1871–1878

(Excluding Frederick J. Loudin and Ella Sheppard Moore)

Hinton D. Alexander (1853–1925; tenor) Alexander came to Fisk in 1871 and advanced to the College Preparatory class in 1873. He joined the Jubilee Singers in 1875 and remained with the company until it disbanded in 1878. Alexander settled in Chattanooga where he was a mail carrier for the U.S. Postal Service and director of a musical group called "The Band of Hope."

Phebe Anderson Jones (1853–?; contralto) Anderson remained with the inaugural company of 1871 for only a few weeks due to her father's impending death. At his request, she did not rejoin the troupe. She later married, settled in Knoxville, and had a daughter who graduated from the city's high school.

Minnie Butler (?–?; voice part unknown) Butler's tenure with the Jubilee Singers was short. She joined the troupe in fall 1877 but was sent home by White in early 1878.

Margaret (Maggie) A. Carnes (?–?; soprano) Carnes arrived at Fisk in 1871 and advanced to the college preparatory class in 1873. She joined the Jubilee Singers in 1874 and remained with the company until it disbanded in 1878.

Isaac P. Dickerson (1850—1900; bass) Dickerson came to Fisk in 1869 and was a member of the 1871 inaugural company. He had a reputation for being fun-loving and somewhat flirtatious. While abroad in 1873, he accepted the offer of the Reverend Dean Stanley to finance his ministerial studies at Edinburgh University. In 1878, he began evangelistic work in

France then returned to England where he conducted a small mission in Plumstead.

Greene Evans (1848–?; bass) Evans traveled with the Jubilee Singers only during the company's first year. He then pursued work as a mail agent in Memphis and also engaged in the wholesale coal and wood business. Evans eventually capitalized on his interest in politics, serving as the Memphis deputy wharf master (1876–1877), Memphis city councilman (1879), state representative from Shelby County (1885–1887), and census enumerator for Shelby County (1880).

Georgia Gordon Taylor (1855–1913; soprano) Gordon enrolled at Fisk in 1867 and joined the Jubilees in 1872. When the company disbanded, she returned to Nashville and married Preston Taylor, a prominent businessman who owned and operated a funeral parlor, worked as a realtor, and was the minister of Lea Avenue Christian Church. Her only son died at the age of seven months. Georgia was active in the National Association of Colored Women and appeared often at Fisk University functions.

Ella M. Hildridge (?–?; soprano) Hildridge joined the Jubilees in 1876 to replace Maggie Porter but remained with the troupe for only a few months. She married Andrew E. Jackson, and together they served as two of the first four missionaries to Africa to come from the Fisk University student body.

Benjamin M. Holmes (1846 or 1848–1875; tenor) Holmes toured with the Jubilee Singers from 1871–1874 before returning to Nashville. He succumbed to tuberculosis in mid-1875.

Jennie Jackson DeHart (1852–1910; soprano) A member of the first touring ensemble, Jackson was involved in the altercation with Maggie Porter that led to Porter's resignation from the troupe. Jackson suffered an illness in April 1877 that made her unable to continue with the company on its excursion into Germany. She returned to the States in November 1877. Jackson toured again with the Jubilees under White and Loudin until 1884, then returned to Nashville and married the Reverend A. J. DeHart of Knoxville, a local pastor who eventually became the principal of the city's Colored High School. In 1891 she organized her own vocal sextet called the "Jennie Jackson DeHart Jubilee Club."

Julia Jackson (?–?; contralto) In 1871–1872, Julia Jackson was a member of the first-year class of Fisk University's normal school. She joined the Jubilees for the company's second trip abroad in 1874. A sudden paralytic stroke in June 1876 left one side of her body powerless. After several months of recuperation, she returned to the States.

Mabel R. Lewis Imes (1860?—1935; contralto) Lewis, who never enrolled at Fisk, auditioned for the Jubilees in 1872 while the company was near her home in Massachusetts. She was converted to Christianity during a Moody revival service in 1873. Illness prevented her from going with the Jubilees on their third campaign, but she rejoined the ensemble in August 1876. She toured with White's private group of Jubilee Singers, retiring in 1882. Lewis later married Martin Imes, settled in Cleveland, and led an active life in the community.

Patti J. Malone (?—1897; mezzo-soprano) Miss Wells, the chaperone for White's inaugural tour, met Patti Malone in Athens, Alabama, and sent her to study at Fisk in 1873. Malone replaced the ill Jennie Jackson in 1877 and remained with the company thereafter. She remained single, touring with Loudin's troupe until her death.

Josephine Moore (1857–?; pianist) Moore served as pianist for one of the two groups White formed in fall 1872. She also participated at the great World's Peace Jubilee festivities held in Boston in summer 1872. When White reorganized the company in 1873, her services were no longer needed.

Henry Morgan (?–?; voice part unknown) Morgan sang with the Jubilee Singers at the World's Peace Jubilee in summer 1872. He remained with the ensemble for three months, possibly until White reorganized the company in January 1873 in preparation for the first European campaign.

Gabriel E. Ousley (?–?; bass) Ousley's name appears in the potential roster of singers White was considering when he began reassembling his company for the second trip overseas. The 1874–1875 *Fisk University Catalog* lists Ousley as a student in the college preparatory division "currently absent with the Jubilee Singers." Data suggest Ousley remained with the troupe for only a short time.

Maggie Porter Cole (1853–1942; soprano) Porter held the lead role of "Queen Esther" in White's 1871 production of the cantata. She was a founding member of the Jubilee Singers, touring with the company without interruption save for the three months in 1876 when she resigned from the troupe and left in anger. She rejoined in October 1876 and remained with the ensemble until it disbanded in 1878. Porter next sang with Loudin's troupe for a short period before marrying Daniel Cole in 1884. The couple formed their own company (also bearing the name "Fisk Jubilee Singers") and toured under the management of Charles Mumford. Loudin considered them a rival in the field. Porter eventually settled in Detroit and bore three children, two of whom died. In her old age, she lived at the Phyllis Wheatley Home in Detroit, a situation made possible through the generosity of Leota Henson Turner, Loudin's niece, who was on the board of the organization. Porter was the oldest surviving member of the Fisk Jubilee Singers.

America Robinson Lucas (1855–?; contralto) Robinson was the only Jubilee Singer to graduate with a college diploma from Fisk University. She joined the Jubilees in 1875 for the company's third tour, replacing the ill Mabel Lewis. When the company disbanded, she remained in Germany for language study, eventually returning to the States where she married Ed Lucas and settled in Macon, Mississippi. Both she and her husband were well-respected educators.

Thomas Rutling (1854–1915; tenor) Rutling participated with the Jubilee Singers throughout their entire existence. When the company disbanded, he decided to remain on the continent for language study. He later returned to England to pursue a concert career, giving a debut solo performance at the Crystal Palace. Illness forced him to change his concert plans, and he eventually settled in Harrogate, Yorks, where he worked as a vocal instructor and a visiting master to a local boys' school.

Minnie Tate Hall (1857–1899; contralto) Only fourteen when the company left Fisk in 1871, Minnie Tate was one of the youngest of the Jubilee Singers. She toured with the troupe until 1875, returning to Fisk to resume her studies for a short time. She joined White's reorganized private company in 1878 where it is likely that she met her future husband, R. A. Hall. In 1884, she toured with Maggie Porter's company.

Benjamin W. Thomas (?–1892; bass) White recruited Thomas for the Jubilees in 1874. His name does not appear in any Fisk University catalog, suggesting he was never enrolled. He sang for a short time with White's private company of Jubilee Singers.

Lucinda Vance (?–?; contralto) A native of Washington, DC, Vance joined the Jubilee Singers in September 1877 along with Minnie Butler and Mrs. Swart.

Eliza Walker Crump (1857–?; contralto) Walker entered Fisk when it first opened as a student in the grammar school, and by 1871, had advanced to the first year of the normal school. She left to tour with the first company of Jubilees in 1871 but did not sing again with the troupe beyond the first campaign. A 1911 Fisk publication states that Walker resided in Chicago, Illinois where she was engaged in concert work with her husband.

Edmund Watkins (1850–1929; bass) Watkins attended Talladega College prior to coming to Fisk in 1871 as a student of the College Preparatory Division. He joined the Jubilees in time to embark on the England campaign of 1873 and remained in London in 1874 to pursue musical studies. He returned to New York City some years later where he resided until his death in 1929. Paul Cravath, son of Erastus Cravath, cared for Watkins in his old age.

Sources

Archives and Special Collections

America Robinson Letters (ARL), 1875–1878. Fisk University Franklin Library, Special Collections. Fisk University, Nashville, Tennessee (FU).

American Missionary, 1866–1901. Amistad Research Center, Tulane University, New Orleans (AMAA). Also available on microfilm.

American Missionary Association Archives (AMAA). Amistad Research Center, Tulane University, New Orleans.

Ella Sheppard Diaries (FJS), 1874–1876 and 1877–1878. Fisk University Franklin Library, Special Collections. Fisk University, Nashville, Tennessee (FU).

The Fisk Expositor, 1878–1881. Fisk University Franklin Library, Special Collections. Fisk University, Nashville, Tennessee (FU).

The Fisk Herald, 1884–1905. Fisk University Franklin Library, Special Collections. Fisk University, Nashville, Tennessee (FU).

Fisk News, 1928–1939. Fisk University Franklin Library, Special Collections. Fisk University, Nashville, Tennessee (FU).

Fisk University Catalog, 1867–1918. Fisk University Franklin Library, Special Collections. Fisk University, Nashville, Tennessee (FU).

Fisk University News, 1911–1958. Fisk University Franklin Library, Special Collections. Fisk University, Nashville, Tennessee (FU).

The Greater Fisk Herald, 1927–1938. Fisk University Franklin Library, Special Collections. Fisk University, Nashville, Tennessee (FU).

Jubilee Singers Collection (FJS), 1873–1878. Fisk University Franklin Library, Special Collections. Fisk University, Nashville, Tennessee (FU).

The Jubilee Singers European Tour (JSET), 1873–1878. Fisk University Franklin Library, Special Collections. Fisk University, Nashville, Tennessee (FU).

Jubilee Singers Scrapbooks (JSS), 1867–1881. Fisk University Franklin Library, Special Collections. Fisk University, Nashville, Tennessee (FU).

Limestone County Archives. Athens, Alabama. Various documents on Trinity High School and biographical information on Patti Malone.

Minutes of the First Annual Convention of the National Federation of Afro-American Women, 1896. Auburn Avenue Research Library, Atlanta, Georgia.

Minutes of the National Association of Colored Women, 1897. Auburn Avenue Research Library, Atlanta, Georgia.

Moorland-Spingarn Research Center, Washington, DC. Various documents on
   Lincoln Memorial Congregational Temple and biographical information on
   George W. Moore.
Portage County Historical Society, Ravenna, Ohio. Various manuscripts and
   documents on Frederick J. Loudin.
Reed Memorial Library, Ravenna, Ohio. Various manuscripts and documents on
   Frederick J. Loudin.
Spence Family Collection (SFC), 1812–1961. Fisk University Franklin Library,
   Special Collections. Fisk University, Nashville, Tennessee (FU).

Newspapers

Most newspaper extracts are from the following two sources: The Jubilee Singers
   Scrapbooks, The Fisk University Franklin Library, Special Collections. Fisk
   University, Nashville, Tennesee (cited as JSS); and the British Library
   Newspaper Library, Colindale, London (cited as BNL). Other newspapers
   cited include:
The Bee (Washington, DC)
Cleveland Call and Post (Cleveland, Ohio)
The Freeman (Indianapolis)
Nashville Tennessean and the Nashville American (Nashville)
New National Era (Washington, DC)
The Ravenna Republican (Ravenna, Ohio)
The Record Courier (Ohio)

Books, Dissertations, Journals, and Other Documents

Abbott, Lyman. *The Life of Henry Ward Beecher: A Sketch of His Career: With
   Analyses of His Power as a Preacher, Lecturer, Orator and Journalist, and
   Incidents and Reminiscences of His Life.* 1887. Reprint, Honolulu HI:
   University Press of the Pacific, 2002.
Abbott, Lynn, Ray Funk and Doug Seroff. "100 Years From Today: A Survey of
   Afro-American Music in 1890 as Recorded in the Black Community Press."
   78 Quarterly 6: 51–63.
Abbott, Lynn, and Doug Seroff. "100 Years from Today: A Survey of African-
   American Music in 1892 and 1893 as recorded in the Black Community
   Press." *78 Quarterly* 9: 105–17.
———. *Out of Sight: The Rise of African American Popular Music 1889–1895.*
   Jackson: University Press of Mississippi, 2002.
Alexander, Hinton D. "Reminiscences of Jubilee Singers." *Fisk University News* 2/5
   (October 1911): 38–41.

Allen, William Francis, Charles Pickard Ware and Lucy McKim Garrison, editors. *Slave Songs of the United States.* 1867. Reprint, New York: Peter Smith, 1951.

Anderson, James D. *The Education of Blacks in the South, 1860–1935.* Chapel Hill and London: The University of North Carolina Press, 1988.

Anderson, Paul Allen. *Deep River: Music and Memory in Harlem Renaissance Thought.* Durham and London: Duke University Press, 2001.

Anderson, Toni Passmore. "The Fisk Jubilee Singers: Performing Ambassadors for the Survival of an American Treasure, 1871–1878." Ph.D. dissertation, Georgia State University, 1997.

Armstrong, Mrs. M. F., and Helen W. Ludlow. *Hampton and Its Students.* 1874. Reprint, New York: AMS Press Inc., 1971.

Baillie, Albert Victor, and Henry Hector Bolitho, editors. *Later Letters of Lady Augusta Stanley 1864–1876.* London: Jonathan Cape, 1929.

Beard, Augustus Field. *A Crusade of Brotherhood: A History of the American Missionary Association.* 1909. Reprint, New York: Kraus Reprint Co., 1970.

Berman, Edward H. *African Reactions to Missionary Education.* New York and London: Teachers College Press, 1975.

Berry, Mary Frances, and John W. Blassingame. *Long Memory: The Black Experience in America.* New York and Oxford: Oxford University Press, 1982.

Blassingame, John W. *The Slave Community: Plantation Life in the Antebellum South.* New York: Oxford University Press, 1972.

Bohlman, Philip V., Edith L. Blumhofer and Maria M. Chow, editors. *Music in American Religious Experience.* New York: Oxford University Press, 2006.

Booth, Catherine. "Worldly Amusements and Christianity." *Papers on Practical Religions (1879).* Victorian Women Writers Project; an Electronic Collection. Bloomington, Indiana: Indiana University, 1996. *http://www.indiana.edu/~letrs/vwwp/booth/practrel.html* (accessed June 26, 2006).

Botkin, B. A., editor. *Lay My Burden Down: A Folk History of Slavery.* Chicago: University of Chicago Press, 1945.

Botume, Elizabeth Hyde. *First Days Amongst the Contrabands.* 1893. Reprint, New York: Arno Press and The New York Times, 1968.

Bullock, Henry Allen. *A History of Negro Education in the South, From 1619 to the Present.* Cambridge MA: Harvard University Press, 1967.

Butchart, Ronald E. *Northern Schools, Southern Blacks, and Reconstruction: Freedmen's Education, 1862–1875.* Westport CT: Greenwood Press, 1980.

Carnes, Mark C., editor. *Invisible Giants: Fifty Americans Who Shaped the Nation But Missed the History Books.* Oxford and New York: Oxford University Press, 2002.

Clark, Burton R. "Belief and Loyalty in College Organization." *The Journal of Higher Education* 42/6 The Invitational Seminar on Restructuring College and University Organization and Governance (June 1971): 499–515.

————. "The Organizational Saga in Higher Education." *Administrative Science Quarterly* 17/2 (June 1972): 178–84.

Clark, Clifford E., Jr. *Henry Ward Beecher: Spokesman for a Middle-Class America.* Urbana: University of Illinois Press, 1978.

Clayton, W. W. "George L. White," *History of Davidson County, Tennessee 1780–1880.* 1880. Reprint, Nashville TN: Charles Elder, 1971. Tennessee State Archives.

Cole, Maggie Porter. "The Jubilee Singers on the Ocean and in Europe." *Fisk University News* 2/5 (October 1911): 33–35.

Crosthwaite, Mrs. M. L. "A Résumé." *Fisk University News* 2/5 (October 1911): 6–10.

Cuny-Hare, Maud. "The Source." *Musical America* (September 1930): 19–30.

Davis, Elizabeth Lindsay: introduction by Sieglinde Lemke. *Lifting As They Climb.* New York: G. K. Hall & Co., an Imprint of Simon & Schuster Macmillan, 1996.

DeBoer, Clara Merritt. *Be Jubilant My Feet: African American Abolitionists in the American Missionary Association 1839–1861.* New York and London: Garland Publishing, Inc., 1994.

————. *His Truth Is Marching On: African Americans Who Taught the Freedmen for the American Missionary Association 1861–1877.* New York and London: Garland Publishing, Inc., 1995.

DeVenney, David P., comp. *Source Readings in American Choral Music.* Monographs and Bibliographies in American Music Series, no. 15. Missoula MT: The College Music Society, 1995.

Dorsett, Lyle W. *A Passion for Souls: The Life of D. L. Moody.* Chicago: Moody Press, 1997.

Douglass, Frederick. *My Bondage and My Freedom.* 1855. Reprint, Los Angeles CA: Milligan Books, 1999.

Drake, Richard Bryant. "The American Missionary Association and the Southern Negro 1861–1888." Ph.D. dissertation, Emory University, 1957.

DuBois, W. E. B. *Black Reconstruction in America: An Essay toward a History of the Part Which Black Folk Played in the Attempt to Reconstruct Democracy in America, 1860–1880.* 1935. Reprint, Cleveland: World Publishing Co., 1964.

————. *The Souls of Black Folk.* 1903. Reprint, New York: The New American Library, Inc., 1969.

Dwight, John Sullivan. "The Fisk Jubilee and Hampton Singers." *Dwight's Journal of Music* (5 April 1873). In *Source Readings in American Choral Music,* compiled by David P. DeVenney. Monographs and Bibliographies in American Music Series, no. 15. Missoula MT: The College Music Society, 1995.

Eaton, John. *Grant, Lincoln and the Freedmen; reminiscences of the Civil War, with special reference to the work for the contrabands and freedmen of the Mississippi*

Valley. 1907. Reprint, New York: Negro Universities Press, 1969. Quoted in Paul David Phillips, "Education of Blacks in Tennessee During Reconstruction, 1865–1870." *Tennessee Historical Quarterly* 46 (1987): 98–109.

Epstein, Dena J. "Black Spirituals: Their Emergence into Public Knowledge." *Black Music Research Journal* 10 (Spring 1990): 58–64.

———. *Sinful Tunes and Spirituals: Black Folk Music to the Civil War.* Urbana and Chicago: University of Illinois Press, 1977.

———. "The Story of the Jubilee Singers: An Introduction to its Bibliographic History." In Josephine Wright and Samuel A. Floyd, Jr., editors. *New Perspectives on Music: Essays in Honor of Eileen Southern.* Michigan: Harmonie Park Press, 1992.

Evans, W. R. "George L. White." *The Greater Fisk Herald* 11/4 (January 1927): 26–27.

Findlay, James D., Jr. *Dwight L. Moody: American Evangelist, 1837–1899.* Chicago and London: The University of Chicago Press, 1969.

Flemming, Cynthia Griggs. "The Effect of Higher Education on Black Tennesseans After the Civil War." *Phylon XLIV* (1983): 209–16.

Flexner, Abraham. *Funds and Foundations; Their Policies, Past and Present.* New York: Harper & Brothers Publishers, 1952.

Floyd, Samuel A., Jr. *The Power of Black Music: Interpreting its History from Africa to the United States.* New York and Oxford: Oxford University Press, 1995.

Foner, Eric. *The Story of American Freedom.* New York and London: W. W. Norton & Company, 1998.

Graham, Sandra. "The Fisk Jubilee Singers and the Concert Spiritual: The Beginnings of an American Tradition." Ph.D. dissertation, New York University, 2001.

———. "On the Road to Freedom: The Contracts of the Fisk Jubilee Singers." *American Music* (Spring 2006): 1–29.

Hall, Robert L. "Dedication to Industry, the Useful Arts and Christian Education: A Brief History of Lincoln Congregational Temple—United Church of Christ, 1868–1960." Paper presented at the Twelfth Annual Conference on Washington, DC Historical Studies, 22 February 1985. Vertical file: "Lincoln Memorial Congregational Temple," Moorland-Spingarn Research Center, Washington, DC

Higginson, Thomas Wentworth. "Negro Spirituals." *Atlantic Monthly* 19 (June 1867): 685–94.

Hill, Adelaide Cromwell, and Martin Kilson, editors. *Apropos of Africa: Sentiments of Negro American Leaders on Africa from the 1800s to the 1950s.* London: Frank Cass & Co. Ltd., 1969.

History of the American Missionary Association: Its Churches and Educational Institutions Among the Freedmen, Indians, and Chinese. New York: S. W. Green, Printer, 1874.

Hodder, Edwin. *The Life and Work of the Seventh Earl of Shaftesbury.* Volume 3. London: Cassell & Company, Limited, 1886.

Howe, Daniel Walker, editor. *Victorian America.* University of Pennsylvania: University of Pennsylvania Press, 1976.

Hubbard, G. W. *A History of the Colored Schools of Nashville, Tennessee.* Nashville: Wheeler, Marshall & Bruce, 1874.

Imes, Mabel Lewis. "Some Hotel Experiences." *Fisk University News* 2/5 (October 1911): 31–32.

Ingalls, Zoë. "From Slavery to Celebrity: The 125-Year Success of the Fisk Jubilee Singers." *The Chronicle of Higher Education* (3 May 1996): B7.

Johnson, Clifton H. "The American Missionary Association, 1846–1861: A Study of Christian Abolitionism." Ph.D. dissertation, University of North Carolina at Chapel Hill, 1958.

Lotz, Rainer E. "The Black Troubadours: Black Entertainers in Europe, 1896–1915." *Black Music Research Journal* 10/2 (Fall 1990): 253–73.

Loudin, F. J. "Supplement." In J. B. T. Marsh. *The Story of the Jubilee Singers by J. B. T. Marsh, with Supplement Containing an Account of the Six Year's Tour around the World, and Many New Songs, by F. J. Loudin.* Cleveland: The Cleveland Printing & Publishing Co., 1892.

Lovell, John, Jr. *Black Song: The Forge and the Flame.* New York: Paragon House Publishers, 1972.

Lovett, Bobby L. *The African-American History of Nashville, Tennessee, 1780–1930.* Fayetteville: The University of Arkansas Press, 1999.

MacDonald, M.D., Greville. *George MacDonald and His Wife.* 1924. Reprint, New York: Johnson Reprint Corporation, 1971.

Marsh, J. B. T. *The Story of the Jubilee Singers by J. B. T. Marsh, with Supplement Containing an Account of the Six Year's Tour around the World, and Many New Songs, by F. J. Loudin.* Cleveland: The Cleveland Printing & Publishing Co., 1892.

———. *The Story of the Jubilee Singers; With Their Songs.* Revised edition. Boston: Houghton, Osgood and Company; Cambridge: The Riverside Press, 1880.

Marshall, Gloria J. "The Survival of Colleges in America: A Census of Four-year Colleges in the United States 1636–1973." Ph.D. dissertation, Stanford University, 1995.

Mather, Frank Lincoln, editor. *Who's Who of the Colored Race: A General Biographical Dictionary of Men and Women of African Descent.* 1915. Reprint, Detroit: Gale Research, 1976.

Matthew, H. C. G., editor. *The Gladstone Diaries vol. VIII (July 1871–December 1874).* Oxford: Clarendon Press, 1982.

McClellan, B. Edward. *Moral Education in America: Schools and the Shaping of Character from Colonial Times to the Present.* New York: Teachers College Press, 1999.

McLoughlin, William G., Jr. *Modern Revivalism: Charles Grandison Finney to Billy Graham.* New York: The Ronald Press Company, 1959.

———. *The Meaning of Henry Ward Beecher: An Essay on the Shifting Values of Mid-Victorian America, 1840–1870.* New York: Alfred A. Knopf, 1970.

McPherson, James M. *The Abolitionist Legacy from Reconstruction to the NAACP.* Princeton NJ: Princeton University Press, 1975.

———. "The New Puritanism: Values and Goals of Freedmen's Education in America." In Lawrence Stone, editor. *The University in Society vol. II: Europe, Scotland, and the United States from the 16th to the 20th Century.* Princeton NJ: Princeton University Press, 1974.

Meier, August. *Negro Thought in America, 1880–1915.* Ann Arbor: The University of Michigan Press, 1969.

Moore, Ella Sheppard. "Before Emancipation." New York: American Missionary Association, undated.

———. "Historical Sketch of the Jubilee Singers." *Fisk University News* 2/5 (October 1911): 41–58.

———. "Negro Womanhood: Its Past." New York: American Missionary Association, undated.

———. "Victoria, the Gracious Queen, and the Jubilee Singers." *The Fisk Herald* 18/9 (June 1901): 9–10.

Morgan, Edmund S. "Charles Grandison Finney," in Mark C. Carnes, editor. *Invisible Giants: Fifty Americans Who Shaped the Nation But Missed the History Books.* Oxford and New York: Oxford University Press, Inc., 2002.

Morgan, Helen C. "Fisk University Before the Jubilee Singers Went Forth." *Fisk University News* 2/5 (October 1911): 14–17.

The Nation Still in Danger; or Ten Years After the War. A Plea by the American Missionary Association. American Missionary Association: 1875.

Nieman, Donald G., editor. *African Americans and Education in the South, 1865–1900.* Volume 10. New York and London: Garland Publishing, Inc., 1994.

Patterson, Joseph Norenzo. "A Study of the History of the Contribution of the American Missionary Association to the Higher Education of the Negro—With Special Reference to Five Selected Colleges Founded by the Association, 1865–1900." Ed.D. thesis, Cornell University, 1956.

Peeps, J. M. Stephen. "Northern Philanthropy and the Emergence of Black Higher Education—Do-Gooders, Compromisers, or Co-Conspirators?" In Donald G. Nieman, editor. *African Americans and Education in the South, 1865–1900.* Volume 10. New York and London: Garland Publishing, Inc., 1994.

Peirce, Paul Skeels. *The Freedmen's Bureau: A Chapter in the History of Reconstruction.* 1904. Reprint, New York: Haskell House Publishers, Ltd., 1971.

Phillips, Paul David. "Education of Blacks in Tennessee During Reconstruction, 1865–1870." *Tennessee Historical Quarterly* 46 (1987): 98–109.

Pierson, Arthur T. *Evangelistic Work in Principle and Practice.* New York: Baker and Taylor, 1887. Quoted in Lyle W. Dorsett. *A Passion for Souls: The Life of D. L. Moody.* Chicago: Moody Press, 1997.

Pike, G. D. *The Jubilee Singers, and Their Campaign for Twenty Thousand Dollars.* Boston: Lee and Shepard, Publishers; New York: Lee, Shepard and Dillingham, 1873.

———. *The Singing Campaign for Ten Thousand Pounds; or, The Jubilee Singers in Great Britain.* New York: The American Missionary Association, 1875.

Proceedings of the National Conference of Colored Men of the United States Held in the State Capitol at Nashville, Tennessee, May 6–9, 1879, Afro-American History Series, edited by Maxwell Whiteman, no. 231. Washington, DC: Rufus H. Darby, Steam Power Printer, 1879.

Proctor, Henry Hugh. *Between Black and White: Autobiographical Sketches.* 1925. Reprint, Freeport NY: Books for Libraries Press, 1971.

Radano, Ronald. "Denoting Difference: The Writing of the Slave Spirituals." *Critical Inquiry* 22/3 (Spring 1996): 506–44.

Richardson, Joe M. *Christian Reconstruction: The American Missionary Association and Southern Blacks, 1861–1890.* Athens and London: The University of Georgia Press, 1986.

———. *A History of Fisk University, 1865–1946.* University AL: The University of Alabama Press, 1980.

Rutling, Thomas. "My Life Since Leaving the Jubilee Singers." *Fisk University News* 2/5 (October 1911): 36–37.

———. *"Tom": An Autobiography, with Revised Negro Melodies.* Bradford: Wm. Byles & Sons Ltd., Printers, 1907.

Sammons, Vivian Ovelton. *Blacks in Science and Medicine.* New York: Hemisphere Publishing, 1990.

Scott, Anne Firor. "Most Invisible of All: Black Women's Voluntary Associations." *The Journal of Southern History* 56/1 (February 1990): 3–22.

Seroff, Doug. "Gospel Arts Day. Nashville." June 19, 1988. Booklet provided courtesy of the author.

———. "A Voice in the Wilderness: The Fisk Jubilee Singers' Civil Rights Tours of 1879–1882." *Popular Music & Society* 25. Part 1/2 (2001): 131–78.

Seroff, Doug, and Lynn Abbott. "Black Music in the White City (African-Americans at the 1893 World's Columbian Exposition)." *78 Quarterly* 1/9: 47–60.

Shaw, Lacy. *Not a Slave! Free People of Color in Antebellum America, 1790–1860*. New York: American Heritage Custom Publishing Group, 1995.

Shaw, Stephanie J. *What a Woman Ought to Be and to Do: Black Professional Women Workers During the Jim Crow Era*. Chicago and London: The University of Chicago Press, 1996.

Slaughter, Linda Warfel. *The Freedmen of the South*. 1869. Reprint, New York: Kraus Reprint Co., 1969.

Smith, Amanda. "An Autobiography: The Story of the Lord's Dealings with Mrs. Amanda Smith, the Colored Evangelist." New York: The Digital Schomburg, The New York Public Library. File number 1997wwm97264.sgm.1997. *http://digilib.nypl.org/dynaweb/digs/wwm97264* (accessed April 25, 2002).

Southern, Eileen. "The Antebellum Church." *Black American Literature Forum*. 25/1, The Black Church and the Black Theatre (Spring 1991): 23–26.

———. *The Music of Black Americans: A History*. 2nd edition. New York and London: W. W. Norton & Company, 1983.

———. "An Origin for the Negro Spiritual." *The Black Scholar* (Summer 1972): 8–13.

Spence, Mary E. "A Character Sketch of George L. White." *Fisk University News* 2/5 (October 1911): 2–5.

Spencer, Jon Michael. "African American Religious Music from a Theomusicological Perspective." In Philip V. Bohlman, Edith L. Blumhofer, and Maria M. Chow, editors. *Music in American Religious Experience*. New York: Oxford University Press, 2006.

———. *Protest and Praise: Sacred Music of Black Religion*. Minneapolis: Fortress Press, 1990.

Stevenson, Louise L. *The Victorian Homefront: American Thought & Culture, 1860–1880*. Ithaca and London: Cornell University Press, 1991.

Stone, Lawrence, editor. *The University in Society vol. II: Europe, Scotland, and the United States from the 16th to the 20th century*. Princeton NJ: Princeton University Press, 1974.

Stuckey, Sterling. *Slave Culture: Nationalist Theory and the Foundations of Black America*. New York and Oxford: Oxford University Press, 1987.

Talley, Thomas W. "Appreciation of Mrs. Ella Sheppard Moore by a Fellow Student." *Fisk University News* (1914): 11.

Taylor, A. A. "Fisk University and the Nashville Community, 1866–1900." *The Journal of Negro History* 39/2 (April 1954): 111–26.

Taylor, Georgia Gordon. "Reminiscences of Jubilee Singers." *Fisk University News* 2/5 (October 1911): 28–30.

Thorpe, Earl E. "African Americans and the Sacred: Spirituals, Slave Religion and Symbolism." Unpublished paper (1980?). Quoted in Jon Michael Spencer, "African American Religious Music from a Theomusicological Perspective," in Philip V. Bohlman, Edith L. Blumhoffer and Maria M. Chow, editors.

Music in American Religious Experience. (New York: Oxford University Press, 2006) 47.

Trotter, James M. *Music and Some Highly Musical People*. New York: Charles T. Dillingham, 1881. Reprint, New York: Johnson Reprint Corporation, 1968.

Veysey, Laurence R. *The Emergence of the American University*. Chicago and London: The University of Chicago Press, 1965.

Ward, Andrew. *Dark Midnight When I Rise: The Story of the Jubilee Singers Who Introduced the World to the Music of Black America*. New York: Farrar, Straus and Giroux, 2000.

Washington, Booker T. "A University Education for Negroes," *Independent* 68 (24 March 1910): 613. Quoted in Joe M. Richardson, *A History of Fisk University, 1865–1946 (*University AL: The University of Alabama Press, 1980) 7.

Waterbury, Maria. *Seven Years Among the Freedmen*. 1890. Reprint, Freeport NY: Books for Libraries Press, 1971.

Wells, Ida B. *Crusade for Justice: The Autobiography of Ida B. Wells*, edited by Afreda M. Duster. Negro American Biographies and Autobiographies Series, edited by John Hope Franklin. Chicago and London: The University of Chicago Press, 1972.

Wells, S. M. "Character Sketch of Professor Adam Knight Spence." *Fisk University News* 2/5 (October 1911): 17–19.

Welter, Barbara. "The Cult of True Womanhood: 1820–1860." *American Quarterly* 18/2 (Summer 1966): 151–74.

Whittier, John Greenleaf. *Anti-Slavery Poems: Songs of Labor and Reform*. 1888. Reprint, New York: Arno Press & The New York Times, 1969.

Wilkinson, Frederick D., editor. *Directory of Graduates: Howard University, 1870–1963*. Washington: the University, 1965.

Woodson, Carter G. *The Mis-Education of the Negro*. 1933. Reprint, Trenton NJ: Africa World Press, Inc., 1990.

———. "The Negroes of Cincinnati prior to the Civil War." In Lacy Shaw, *Not a Slave! Free People of Color in Antebellum America, 1790–1860*. New York: American Heritage Custom Publishing Group, 1995.

Work, John Wesley. *Folk Song of the American Negro*. Nashville TN: Press of Fisk University, 1915.

———. "Jubilee Music." *The Fisk Herald* 15/6 (March 1898): 5–6.

Wright, Josephine, and Samuel A. Floyd, Jr. *New Perspectives on Music: Essays in Honor of Eileen Southern*. Michigan: Harmonie Park Press, 1992.

Wyatt-Brown, Bertram. *Lewis Tappan and the Evangelical War Against Slavery*. Cleveland: The Press of Case Western Reserve University, 1969.

Notes

Chapter One

[1] "Education and Religion," *American Missionary* (September 1866): 203, 204, AMAA.

[2] Deboer, *Be Jubilant My Feet,* 4.

[3] William G. McLoughlin, Jr., *Modern Revivalism: Charles Grandison Finney to Billy Graham* (New York: Ronald Press Company, 1959) 67–73, 105–12; Edmund S. Morgan, "Charles Grandison Finney," in Mark C. Carnes, ed., *Invisible Giants: Fifty Americans Who Shaped the Nation But Missed the History Books* (Oxford and New York: Oxford University Press, 2002) 89–95.

[4] Bertram Wyatt-Brown, *Lewis Tappan and the Evangelical War Against Slavery* (Cleveland: The Press of Case Western Reserve University, 1969) 126–32.

[5] Richard Bryant Drake, "The American Missionary Association and the Southern Negro 1861–1888" (Ph.D. diss., Emory University, 1957) 3, 4. For a brief synopsis of Oberlin's role in the antislavery movement, see Joseph Norenzo Patterson, "A Study of the History of the Contribution of the American Missionary Association to the Higher Education of the Negro—With Special Reference to Five Selected Colleges Founded by the Association, 1865–1900" (Ed.D. thesis, Cornell University, 1956) 74, 75.

[6] Augustus Field Beard, *A Crusade of Brotherhood: A History of the American Missionary Association* (1909; rep., New York: Kraus Reprint Co., 1970) 23–32; *History of the American Missionary Association,* 4.

[7] Beard, *A Crusade of Brotherhood,* 31, 32; Wyatt-Brown, *Lewis Tappan and the Evangelical War Against Slavery,* 292, 293.

[8] Richardson, *Christian Reconstruction,* 37.

[9] DeBoer, *Be Jubilant My Feet,* 10. The most prominent "voices" in the antislavery movement were those of William Lloyd Garrison and the Tappan brothers. As DeBoer notes (xi-xii), both Garrison and the Tappans were radical activists who worked for the same cause, yet differed in their ultimate aim. The Garrisonians sought the dissolution of slavery while the Tappans and the "evangelical abolitionists" sought an egalitarian, caste-free society. Thus, when Congress passed the Thirteenth Amendment, the Garrisonians could rightly claim their work was done. The evangelical abolitionists, however, felt the battle had barely begun.

[10] Clifton H. Johnson, "The American Missionary Association, 1846–1861: A Study of Christian Abolitionism" (Ph.D. diss., University of North Carolina at Chapel Hill, 1958) 98–115.

[11] Wyatt-Brown, *Lewis Tappan and the Evangelical War Against Slavery*, 287–300. By the time of Tappan's death, a new generation of reformers dominated the landscape led by the noted Bostonian preacher Henry Ward Beecher. The abolitionist crusade was then decades old, and Tappan felt it seemed to have lost some of its fire and passion. Tappan was troubled over this new generation of abolitionists, men he considered far more interested in material gain than in "the sick, the imprisoned, the ignorant, the vicious, and the unconcerned" (341). Abolitionist ideals remained a part of the AMA, although somewhat muted and less abrasive. Richardson's work *Christian Reconstruction* addresses this point, concluding that while the "momentum for full integration had been slowed, the AMA never abandoned its original goals" (260).

[12] Joe M. Richardson, *A History of Fisk University, 1865–1946* (University AL: University of Alabama Press, 1980) 2; "Memorial Service," *The Fisk Herald* 18/2 (November 1900): 6–20, Fisk University Franklin Library. Special Collections (hereafter cited as FU).

[13] "Memorial Service," *The Fisk Herald* 18/2 (November 1900): 17, FU.

[14] "To the Editor of the Tribune," *American Missionary* (January 1868): 3, AMAA; "Who Shall Educate the Freedmen?" *American Missionary* (September 1866): 193–95, AMAA. For many Americans, the goal of moral education in both private and public schools was to establish a common moral code that promoted social harmony and order. See B. Edward McClellan, *Moral Education in America: Schools and the Shaping of Character from Colonial Times to the Present* (New York: Teachers College Press, 1999) 22, 23. For Christian abolitionists, the highest aim of moral education was personal salvation, which would in turn lead to a stable society. Also see James M. McPherson, "The New Puritanism: Values and Goals of Freedmen's Education in America," in Lawrence Stone, ed., *The University in Society vol. II: Europe, Scotland, and the United States from the 16th to the 20th Century* (Princeton NJ: Princeton University Press, 1974) 611–39.

[15] "Our Duty to the Freedmen," *American Missionary* (May 1866): 115, 116, AMAA.

[16] The issue of land redistribution advanced by other abolitionists was rarely addressed by any of the missionary agencies working in the freedmen's education movement. Ronald Butchart holds that the missionary societies shortsightedly adopted education as the panacea for America's ills and held doggedly to this belief even in the face of failure. He writes: "The more education failed to alter conditions in the South, the more education was called upon to alter the conditions and the less likely were the societies to suggest other or additional modes of reaching their

ends. Continued failure led to theories of gradual assimilation and racial weakness that further deflected pressure for change and further lowered black aspirations." See Ronald E. Butchart, *Northern Schools, Southern Blacks, and Reconstruction: Freedmen's Education, 1862–1875* (Westport CT: Greenwood Press, 1980) 207.

[17] "Education and Religion," *American Missionary* (September 1866): 202, AMAA.

[18] "Our Duty to the Freedmen," *American Missionary* (May 1866): 155, AMAA; "Education and Religion," *American Missionary* (September 1866): 203, AMAA.

[19] "Twenty-sixth Annual Report of the American Missionary Association— 1872," 112–16. The speaker's use of the phrase "Mene Tekel" refers to the story in the biblical book of Daniel of the handwriting on the wall warning of the impending downfall of King Belshazzar's kingdom. Daniel divinely interpreted the handwriting: "mene" meant that God had numbered the days of the king's reign and brought it to an end; "tekel" meant that God had weighed the king and found him wanting.

[20] Butchart, *Northern Schools, Southern Blacks, and Reconstruction*, 99.

[21] Abraham Flexner, *Funds and Foundations: Their Policies, Past and Present* (New York: Harper & Brothers Publishers, 1952) 1–8; Paul Skeels Peirce, *The Freedmen's Bureau: A Chapter in the History of Reconstruction* (1904; rep., New York: Haskell House Publishers, Ltd., 1971) 44, 47; Richardson, *Christian Reconstruction*, 75–84. General Howard was considered such a friend of the AMA that the society named one of its prominent historically black institutions, Howard University, after him.

[22] *History of the American Missionary Association*, 18, 19.

[23] Clara Merritt DeBoer, *His Truth is Marching On: African Americans Who Taught the Freedmen for the American Missionary Association 1861–1877* (New York and London: Garland Publishing, Inc., 1995) 4–6. DeBoer's research shows that four out of twelve men on the AMA's policy-making board were African Americans, and she identified almost 500 African-American abolitionists connected with the association. Many of the black missionaries who traveled into the South were educated at Oberlin through financial assistance by the Tappans.

[24] Richardson, *Christian Reconstruction*, 37.

[25] Ella Sheppard Moore, "Before Emancipation," pamphlet published by the American Missionary Association, no date, 8, Jubilee Singers Collections, 1873–1878, Fisk University Special Collections (hereafter cited as FJS). The Sunday-school model was imported from England in the 1790s and was intended to teach reading, writing, and moral values to poor children in Eastern cities. Most American Protestants saw public school and Sunday-school education as complementary. However, as the public school movement grew in the mid-1800s,

offering nonsectarian moral education to all classes, Sunday schools were free to become more doctrinally specific in their educational approaches. See McClellan, *Moral Education in America*, 22, 33–35. For African Americans, Sunday or Sabbath schools became a primary venue through which to address the problem of illiteracy.

[26] *History of the American Missionary Association*, 21, 22. Also see "Twenty-fifth Annual Report of the American Missionary Association—1871," 19, AMAA.

[27] DeBoer, *Be Jubilant My Feet*, 4.

[28] Booker T. Washington, "A University Education for Negroes," *Independent* 68 (24 March 1910): 613, quoted in Richardson, *A History of Fisk University*, 7. Northern missionaries to the South discovered that African Americans had many educational efforts already in place. See James D. Anderson, *The Education of Blacks in the South, 1860–1935* (Chapel Hill and London: University of North Carolina Press, 1988).

[29] Paul David Phillips, "Education of Blacks in Tennessee During Reconstruction, 1865–1870," *Tennessee Historical Quarterly* 46 (1987): 98–99. The term "contrabands" was first applied to slaves by General Butler, commanding officer at Fortress Monroe, Virginia. He arrived to his assignment on 22 May 1861, and the following day, three slaves of a confederate officer came into the camp. General Butler labeled them contraband of war, borrowing the analogy from international law. Soon the "contrabands" appeared with their wives and children, and kept coming, until the number of contrabands was so great that it forced the government to devise a system for their care.

[30] John Eaton, *Grant, Lincoln and the Freedmen; reminiscences of the Civil War, with special reference to the work for the contraband and freedmen of the Mississippi Valley* (1907; rep., New York: Negro Universities Press, 1969) 208, quoted in Phillips, "Education of Blacks in Tennessee During Reconstruction," 98.

[31] Quoted in W. E. B. DuBois, *Black Reconstruction in America: An Essay toward a History of the Part Which Black Folk Played in the Attempt to Reconstruct Democracy in America, 1860–1880* (1935; rep., Cleveland: World Publishing Co., 1964) 641–42.

[32] "Teachers; Their Qualifications and Support," *American Missionary* (July 1866): 152, AMAA.

[33] Linda Warfel Slaughter, *The Freedmen of the South* (1869; rep., New York: Kraus Reprint Co., 1969) 131.

[34] Quoted in ibid., 148–49.

[35] "Teachers; Their Qualifications and Support," *American Missionary* (July 1860): 151, AMAA.

[36] Richardson, *Christian Reconstruction*, 177–82; W. E. B. DuBois, *The Souls of Black Folk* (1903; rep., New York: The New American Library, Inc., 1969) 71.

[37] When not faced with human hostility, the missionary teachers had to contend with animals peculiar to the South that they especially feared, such as snakes or the numerous fierce dogs that guarded Southern plantations. For firsthand accounts by missionary teachers working in freedmen's education, see Elizabeth Hyde Botume, *First Days Amongst the Contrabands* (1893; rep., New York: Arno Press and The New York Times, 1968) and Maria Waterbury, *Seven Years Among the Freedmen* (1890; rep., Freeport NY: Books for Libraries Press, 1971).

[38] Louise L. Stevenson describes how Victorians defined "civilization" as a world based on moral law where good and bad were rewarded or condemned accordingly. This standard of judgment provided Victorians the basis for assessing not only their own culture, but the cultures of others. See Louise L. Stevenson, *The Victorian Homefront: American Thought & Culture, 1860–1880* (Ithaca and London: Cornell University Press, 1991) xxix, 77.

[39] In recalling Fisk's early days, Helen Morgan, one of the institution's matriarchal teachers, noted the "buildings and grounds were scrupulously neat, for with Professor Ogden cleanliness and order were cardinal virtues." See Helen C. Morgan, "Fisk University Before the Jubilee Singers Went Forth," *Fisk University News* 2/5 (October 1911): 15, FU.

[40] Henry Allen Bullock, *A History of Negro Education in the South, From 1619 to the Present* (Cambridge MA: Harvard University Press, 1967) 30.

[41] DuBois, *The Souls of Black Folk*, 132.

[42] "Twenty-fifth Annual Report of the American Missionary Association–1871," 21, AMAA.

[43] James M. McPherson, *The Abolitionist Legacy from Reconstruction to the NAACP* (Princeton NJ: Princeton University Press, 1975) 52.

[44] J. M. Stephen Peeps sees two distinct chapters in the history of white philanthropic support of black higher education: "The first one, written by Reconstruction's egalitarian-minded missionaries, proved short-lived but inspirational. It embraced the ideal of liberal education for the freedmen, and based it on true faith in black educability." The second chapter, says Peeps, involved white philanthropic support of industrial education for African Americans that "proved pragmatic but repressive." See J. M. Stephen Peeps, "Northern Philanthropy and the Emergence of Black Higher Education—Do-Gooders, Compromisers, or Co-Conspirators?" in Donald G. Nieman, ed., *African Americans and Education in the South, 1865–1900,* vol. 10 (New York and London: Garland Publishing, Inc., 1994) 310.

[45] *The Nation Still in Danger; or Ten Years After the War. A Plea by the American Missionary Association* (American Missionary Association: 1875) 3, 4.

[46] A. A. Taylor, "Fisk University and the Nashville Community, 1866–1900," *The Journal of Negro History* 39/2 (April 1954): 112.

[47] Richardson, *A History of Fisk University*, 4.

[48] G. W. Hubbard, *A History of the Colored Schools of Nashville, Tennessee* (Nashville: Wheeler, Marshall & Bruce, 1874) 21–22; Richardson, *A History of Fisk University*, 3, 4.

[49] The institution was named for General Clinton B. Fisk to acknowledge his help in acquiring the buildings and for his continued financial support amounting to approximately $30,000 (Richardson, *A History of Fisk University*, 4).

[50] Hubbard, *A History of the Colored Schools of Nashville, Tennessee*, 22.

[51] (Helen C.) Morgan, "Fisk University Before the Jubilee Singers Went Forth," 15.

[52] "The African Woman in America. Her Mission," *American Missionary* (May 1869): 108, 109, AMAA. Also see Daniel Walker Howe, ed., *Victorian America* (University of Pennsylvania: University of Pennsylvania Press, 1976) 25–27.

[53] "The African Woman in America. Her Mission," *American Missionary* (May 1869): 108, 109, AMAA; Richardson, *A History of Fisk University*, 16, 17; *History of the American Missionary Association*, 27; "Twenty-fifth Annual Report of the American Missionary Association—1871," 38, AMAA.

[54] "Rules and Regulations of Fisk University," 4 April 1868, AMAA.

[55] Laurence R. Veysey, *The Emergence of the American University* (Chicago and London: University of Chicago Press, 1965) 32. Veysey's chapter entitled "Discipline and Piety" lends insight into the twin emphases of morality and religion in American higher education during this time. Institutions maintained firm codes and regulations designed to encourage moral and socially acceptable behavior.

[56] Hubbard, *A History of the Colored Schools of Nashville, Tennessee*, 22; "Twenty-fifth Annual Report of the American Missionary Association—1871," 38, AMAA.

[57] Richardson, *A History of Fisk University*, 10–12, 21.

[58] "A Biographical Sketch of Prof. Chase," *The Fisk Herald* 17/8 (May 1900): 2–7, FU.

[59] America Robinson to James Burrus, 26 September 1876, America Robinson Letters, Fisk University Special Collections (hereafter cited as ARL).

[60] Spence relinquished his leadership role to Cravath in 1875 and returned to the Fisk classroom as a professor of Greek until his death in 1900.

[61] A. K. Spence to Elizabeth Spence, 26 December 1870, The Spence Family Collection, Fisk University Special Collections (hereafter cited as SFC).

[62] Fisk's college department was organized in 1869 and accepted its first four students in 1871 (Richardson, *A History of Fisk University*, 15).

[63] A. K. Spence to Mr. and Mrs. Dickerson, 3 January 1871, SFC.

[64] A. K. Spence to Elizabeth Spence, 29 September 1870; 7 November 1870; 20 December 1870, SFC.

[65] Even in the late 1890s, a time when Fisk students began to shun the religious music of their heritage, Spence insisted on singing spirituals during chapel services whether or not the students joined in, unwilling to let the music fade from memory. See "A Biographical Sketch by Prof. Chase," *The Fisk Herald* 17/8 (May 1900): 5, 6, FU. John W. Work, a professor at Fisk University and a scholar of the spiritual, also worked to perpetuate the singing of spirituals. See "Jubilee Music," *The Fisk Herald* 15/6 (March 1898): 5, 6, FU.

[66] A. K. Spence to Elizabeth Spence, n.d. April 1871, SFC.

[67] W. W. Clayton, "George L. White," *History of Davidson County, Tennessee 1780–1880* (1880; rep., Nashville TN: Charles Elder, 1971) 442; G. D. Pike, *The Jubilee Singers, and their Campaign for Twenty Thousand Dollars* (Boston: Lee and Shepard, Publishers; New York: Lee, Shepard and Dillingham, 1873) 43–45.

[68] "Teachers; Their Qualifications and Support," *American Missionary* (July 1866): 152, AMAA; W. R. Evans, "George L. White," *The Greater Fisk Herald* 11/4 (January 1927): 26, FU.

[69] Mary E. Spence, "A Character Sketch of George L. White," *Fisk University News* 2/5 (October 1911): 5, FU.

[70] Ibid.

[71] Richardson, *A History of Fisk University*, 22; Spence, "A Character Sketch of George L. White," 5.

[72] G. L. White to E. M. Cravath, 7 April 1871, AMAA. Adam Spence described the poor quality of the food in a letter to his mother: "The tea and coffee are generally cold and weak and not well sweetened. The steak is tough and potatoes are often not well cooked. The gravy is poor and the butter wretched. The bread is often poor or indifferent; I use the coarse bread." See A. K. Spence to Elizabeth Spence, 30 September 1870, SFC.

[73] G. L. White to E. M. Cravath, 21 September 1871, AMAA. Though Spence admitted that there had been more "friction…since the beginning of the school," he felt by spring 1871 that he was beginning to grow accustomed to his leadership position. "I am getting in the habit of making decisions," he told his mother. "I make them by the scores daily, hit or miss. I say to this one go and he goeth and to another come and he cometh, etc." See A. K. Spence to Elizabeth Spence, April 1871, SFC.

[74] A. K. Spence to Elizabeth Spence, 9 April 1872, SFC.

Chapter Two

[1] Margaret A. Carnes (Maggie) signed contract, November 1874, FJS.

[2] Clayton, *History of Davidson County, Tennessee*, 442.

[3] Ella Sheppard Moore, "Historical Sketch of the Jubilee Singers," *Fisk University News* 2/5 (October 1911): 42, FU.

[4] Hubbard, *A History of the Colored Schools of Nashville, Tennessee*, 22. Hubbard suggested that this concert helped sway Nashville's City Council to open the city schools to African-American children.

[5] G. L. White to E. P. Smith, 7 November 1868 and 21 November 1868, AMAA.

[6] G. L. White to E. P. Smith, September 1869 and 30 September 1870, AMAA. Sheppard's regular duties included playing for the family worship services morning and night, and helping to drill the choir. Until 1875, Ella Sheppard was the only African American on the Fisk teaching staff. When she left to tour with the Jubilee Singers, Adam Spence wrote Cravath requesting that he "hire another black during Ella's absence lest the students rebel." See Beth Howse, "Leaders of Afro-American Nashville: Ella Sheppard (Moore) 1851–1914," publication produced as a project for the 1987 Nashville Conference on Afro-American Culture and History. Printed by the Metropolitan Historical Commission, available FU.

[7] G. L. White to E. M. Cravath, 13 February 1871, AMAA.

[8] "The Cantata of Esther," *Tennessee Tribune*, undated, Jubilee Singers Scrapbooks, 1867–1881, Fisk University Special Collections (hereafter cited as JSS). For an in-depth discussion of this production, see Sandra Graham, "The Fisk Jubilee Singers and the Concert Spiritual: The Beginnings of an American Tradition" (Ph.D. diss., New York University, 2001) 81–87. Graham's research correctly attributes this work to William Bradbury.

[9] Clinton B. Fisk to G. L. White, 25 April 1871, AMAA.

[10] A. K. Spence to Elizabeth Spence, 13 March 1871, SFC.

[11] Richardson, *A History of Fisk*, 22–24; G. L. White to E. M. Cravath, 8 February 1871, AMAA.

[12] Moore (Sheppard), "Historical Sketch of the Jubilee Singers," 43.

[13] G. L. White to E. M. Cravath, 1 October 1870, AMAA.

[14] G. L. White to E. M. Cravath, 7 April 1871, AMAA.

[15] A. K. Spence to Elizabeth Spence, April 1871, SFC.

[16] G. L. White to E. M. Cravath, 31 February 1871, AMAA. By all accounts, the food served at Fisk University left much to be desired. Mrs. P. R. Burrus, one of Fisk's earliest students, recalled her impressions as a young ten-year-old student sitting down to her first meal at Fisk: "…as I went into the supper table, and seeing the table held only light bread, molasses and water, as my light refreshments were passed to me, I could not control my feelings. I broke down and wept aloud." Spence and the other teachers thought she was just homesick, but Burrus said that in her first letter home to her mother, she wrote, "Please send me something to eat." See *Notes by Mrs. P. R. Burrus on Jubilee Day, October 6, 1927*, FJS

[17] G. L. White to E. M. Cravath, 26 April 1871, AMAA. The Hutchinson family recorded a visit to Fisk University in which they heard White's ensemble sing. "I suggested to the professor that he bring a choir of his freedmen to the North, for I was sure it would prove a great financial as well as musical success. The result of the suggestion was a tour of the Fisk University Jubilee Singers, which so soon followed," recalled John Hutchinson (quoted in Graham, "The Fisk Jubilee Singers and the Concert Spiritual," 95). Perhaps the Hutchinsons were some of the "friends" to whom White refers. Another friend of the troupe included the Reverend William B. Brown of the Clinton Street Congregational Church, who heard White's company while attending an examination at Fisk University and "was completely carried away with the singing." He entered into the conversation regarding the financial backing of a Northern tour. See "Music Extraordinary. Jubilee Concert Troupe of ex-Slaves at the First Congregational Church," *Newark Evening Courier*, ca. January 1872, JSS.

[18] (Helen C.) Morgan, "Fisk University Before the Jubilee Singers Went Forth," 16.

[19] G. L. White to E. M. Cravath, 26 April 1871, AMAA.

[20] G. L. White to E. M. Cravath, 7 April 1871 and 26 April 1871, AMAA.

[21] G. L. White to Clinton B. Fisk, 3 July 1871, AMAA.

[22] In his speech at the dedication of Jubilee Hall in 1876, General Fisk recounted his reply to White's request: "I wrote an answer and told him not to think of such a thing; that he would bring disgrace upon us all, and told him to stay at home and do his work." See "Fisk University: History, Building, and Site, and Services of Dedication at Nashville, Tennessee, January 1, 1876," 22. Brochure ca. 1876, FJS.

[23] Eileen Southern, *The Music of Black Americans: A History*, 2nd ed. (New York and London: W. W. Norton & Company, 1983) 92–93.

[24] Pike, *Campaign for Twenty Thousand Dollars*, 107. Also see Andrew Ward, *Dark Midnight When I Rise: The Story of the Jubilee Singers Who Introduced the World to the Music of Black America* (New York: Farrar, Straus and Giroux, 2000) 120.

[25] E. M. Cravath to G. L. White, 14 April 1871, AMAA.

[26] A. K. Spence to E. M. Cravath, 6 April 1871, AMAA. Sandra Graham includes a generous portion of this letter in her dissertation, "The Fisk Jubilee Singers and the Concert Spiritual," 96–98.

[27] G. L. White to E. M. Cravath, 21 August 1871, AMAA.

[28] G. L. White to E. M. Cravath, 9 September 1871, AMAA.

[29] G. L. White to E. M. Cravath, 4 August 1871, AMAA.

[30] G. L. White to E. M. Cravath, 21 August 1871, AMAA.

[31] G. L. White to E. M. Cravath, 12 September 1871, AMAA.

[32] E. M. Cravath to G. L. White, 24 August 1871, AMAA.

[33] G. L. White to E. M. Cravath, 26 April 1871 and 9 September 1871, AMAA; Moore (Sheppard), "Historical Sketch of the Jubilee Singers," 42, 43.

[34] E. M. Cravath to G. L. White, 24 August 1871, AMAA.

[35] A. K. Spence to Catherine Spence, 11 September 1871, SFC.

[36] A. K. Spence to Elizabeth Spence, 3 October 1871, SFC.

[37] A. K. Spence to Elizabeth Spence, 8 October 1871, SFC.

[38] G. L. White to E. M. Cravath, 29 September 1871, AMAA.

[39] G. L. White to Clinton B. Fisk, 3 July 1871, AMAA.

[40] Moore (Sheppard), "Historical Sketch of the Jubilee Singers," 45.

[41] Richardson, *A History of Fisk University*, 26.

[42] S. M. Wells, "Character Sketch of Professor Adam Knight Spence," *Fisk University News* 2/5 (October 1911): 17, FU. Spence confided his private thoughts about White's concert scheme to his mother: "I am glad at all events that this music is to be tested and the thing settled in one way or the other. I don't care much which. If that is the Lord's way may it succeed; if not may it fail." See A. K. Spence to Elizabeth Spence, 8 October 1871, SFC. Two years later, Spence credited White for daring to embark on such a doubtful mission: "In justice, it must be said that, humanly speaking, without the courage, determination, and faith of Mr. George L. White, the 'Jubilee Singers' would never have gone forth." See *History of the American Missionary Association*, 28.

[43] G. L. White to E. M. Cravath, 21 September 1871, AMAA.

[44] "The Cantata of Esther," *Tennessee Tribune*, ca. 1871, JSS.

[45] J. B. T. Marsh, *The Story of the Jubilee Singers; With Their Songs*, rev. ed. (Boston: Houghton, Osgood and Company; Cambridge: Riverside Press, 1880) 103–19.

[46] Moore (Sheppard), "Historical Sketch of the Jubilee Singers," 46; "The Jubilee Singers. Some Account of Little Georgie Wells," ca. 1871, JSS.

[47] Pike, *Campaign for Twenty Thousand Dollars*, 75.

[48] Moore (Sheppard), "Historical Sketch of the Jubilee Singers," 46; Pike, *Campaign for Twenty Thousand Dollars*, 79–80.

[49] Moore (Sheppard), "Historical Sketch of the Jubilee Singers," 46.

[50] Pike, *Campaign for Twenty Thousand Dollars*, 81–82.

[51] Ibid., 107. Also see Southern, *The Music of Black Americans*, 92–93.

[52] Marsh, *The Story of the Jubilee Singers; With Their Songs*, 21–23. The identity of J. B. T. Marsh, author of the 1875 abridged history of the ensemble, remains unclear. Dena Epstein notes several letters and routine reports sent to the AMA between 1877 and 1882 from a J. B. T. Marsh, who was the secretary of Oberlin College in Ohio from 1877–1878. See Dena J. Epstein, "The Story of the Jubilee Singers: An Introduction to its Bibliographic History," in *New Perspectives*

on Music: Essays in Honor of Eileen Southern, ed. Josephine Wright with Samuel Floyd, Jr. (Michigan: Harmonie Park Press, 1992) 157. A 1911 article by Mrs. M. L. Crosthwaite, Registrar of Fisk University, lists Marsh as one of the agents or managers who assisted in the Jubilee Singers' campaigns. See Crosthwaite, "A Résumé," *Fisk University News* 2/5 (October 1911): 10, FU. Ella Sheppard also refers to Mr. Marsh in several diary entries throughout 1875.

[53] Pike, *Campaign for Twenty Thousand Dollars*, 82, 100.

[54] Maggie Porter Cole, "Maggie Porter-Cole, interview by W. Barton Beatty," *Fisk News* 13/1 (November 1939): 5, FU.

[55] Moore (Sheppard), "Historical Sketch of the Jubilee Singers," 43; Program for concert given at Mozart Hall, 17 October 1871, JSS. The program contains twenty musical selections from standard concert choral repertoire, but also contains this statement: "As occasion offers during these concerts many of the old plantation melodies and genuine 'spiritual songs,' that gave hope and comfort to the hearts of the colored people through the dark and sad years of bondage, will be introduced."

[56] "Fisk Celebrates Jubilee Day," *Fisk News* 5/2 (December 1931): 3, 4, FU.

[57] Unsigned, handwritten note, ca. 1874, found on the back of a monthly statement dated 26 March 1873, most probably an impromptu speech made by one of the Jubilee Singers, FJS.

[58] "Jubilee Day," *The Fisk Herald* 4/3 (November 1886): 3, FU.

[59] Pike, *Campaign for Twenty Thousand Dollars*, 77.

[60] Ibid., 85–86; Ella Sheppard to A. K. Spence, 21 October 1871, SFC.

[61] Pike, *Campaign for Twenty Thousand Dollars*, 97.

[62] Quote found on a program from a concert in Akron, Ohio, 1871, JSS.

[63] A. K. Spence to Elizabeth Spence, n.d. October 1871, SFC.

[64] Moore (Sheppard), "Historical Sketch of the Jubilee Singers," 48.

[65] Untitled Springfield Ohio newspaper, November 1871, JSS.

[66] Ella Sheppard to A. K. Spence, 21 October 1871, SFC.

[67] Untitled, *Daily Republic*, Springfield, Ohio, 21 October 1871, JSS; "A Troupe of Colored Singers," *American Missionary* (December 1871): 282, AMAA; Pike, *Campaign for Twenty Thousand Dollars*, 84; A. K. Spence to Elizabeth Spence, 24 October 1871, SFC.

[68] Ella Sheppard to A. K. Spence, 12 November 1871, SFC.

[69] Pike, *Campaign for Twenty Thousand Dollars*, 95; Marsh, *The Story of the Jubilee Singers; With Their Songs*, 28.

[70] Pike, *Campaign for Twenty Thousand Dollars*, 96.

[71] Ibid., 97–99.

[72] Moore (Sheppard), "Historical Sketch of the Jubilee Singers," 47.

[73] G. L. White to E. M. Cravath, 26 November 1871, AMAA.

[74] Moore (Sheppard), "Historical Sketch of the Jubilee Singers," 47.

[75] B. M. Holmes to A. K. Spence, 23 November 1871, SFC.
[76] G. L. White to E. M. Cravath, 26 November 1871, AMAA.
[77] Pike, *Campaign for Twenty Thousand Dollars*, 92.
[78] G. L. White to E. M. Cravath, 6 December 1871, AMAA.
[79] Pike, *Campaign for Twenty Thousand Dollars*, 99; Ella Sheppard to A. K. Spence, 5 December 1871, SFC.
[80] G. L. White to E. M. Cravath, 6 December 1871, AMAA.
[81] A. K. Spence to Elizabeth Spence, 13 December 1871, SFC.
[82] G. L. White to E. M. Cravath, 6 December 1871, AMAA.
[83] Pike, *Campaign for Twenty Thousand Dollars*, 102–105; "The Jubilee Singers Concert," *Elmira Daily Advertiser*, December 1871, JSS.
[84] G. L. White to E. M. Cravath, 8 December 1871, AMAA.
[85] G. L. White to E. M. Cravath, 6 December 1871, AMAA; G. L. White to A. K. Spence, 8 December 1871, SFC.
[86] G. L. White to A. K. Spence, 8 December 1871, SFC.
[87] (S. M.) Wells, "Character Sketch of Professor Adam Knight Spence," 19.
[88] A. K. Spence to Elizabeth Spence, 13 December 1871, SFC.
[89] Moore (Sheppard), "Historical Sketch of the Jubilee Singers," 48.
[90] "Henry Ward Beecher's Lecture, delivered in Lincoln Hall on the evening of Jan. 23, 1874," *New National Era*, 29 January 1874.
[91] Lyman Abbott, *The Life of Henry Ward Beecher: A Sketch of His Career: With Analyses of His Power as a Preacher, Lecturer, Orator and Journalist, and Incidents and Reminiscences of His Life* (1887; rep., Honolulu HI: University Press of the Pacific, 2002) 223.
[92] Moore (Sheppard), "Historical Sketch of the Jubilee Singers," 48; Pike, *Campaign for Twenty Thousand Dollars*, 108.
[93] Pike, *Campaign for Twenty Thousand Dollars*, 109.
[94] Cole (Porter), "Maggie Porter-Cole, interview by Beatty," 5.
[95] Pike, *Campaign for Twenty Thousand Dollars*, 109.
[96] "Henry Ward Beecher and the Fisk Jubilee Singers," *The Fisk Herald* (March 1888): 9–10, FU.
[97] Cole (Porter), "Maggie Porter-Cole, interview by Beatty," 5.
[98] Ibid., 5.
[99] Pike, *Campaign for Twenty Thousand Dollars*, 108–10.
[100] Cole (Porter), "Maggie Porter-Cole, interview by Beatty," 5.
[101] Abbott, *The Life of Henry Ward Beecher*, 285–302. For more on how Beecher's theology and preaching appealed to Victorian Americans, see Clifford E. Clark, Jr., *Henry Ward Beecher: Spokesman for a Middle-Class America* (Urbana: University of Illinois Press, 1978).

[102] William G. McLoughlin's chapter entitled "White Supremacy and Anglo-Saxon Destiny" explores how Beecher "spoke for the majority of Northern white Americans who were willing to grant a minimum of political freedom to the slaves because they felt that such a backward, childish, irresponsible race would never be serious competitors to the Anglo-Saxons" (221). The worse aspects of Beecher's deep beliefs of white supremacy, says McLoughlin, were tempered by his "commitment to Christian brotherhood and…commitment to the American democratic faith" (240). Beecher's fascination with the Jubilee Singers represents the complicated mix of convictions that motivated the seemingly altruistic actions of Victorian Christians. See William G. McLoughlin, *The Meaning of Henry Ward Beecher: An Essay on the Shifting Values of Mid-Victorian America, 1840–1870* (New York: Alfred A. Knopf, 1970).

[103] "The Nashville Colored Musicians," *Morning Call, Brooklyn*, ca. December 1871, JSS.

[104] "Jubilee Singers," untitled newspaper, ca. December 1871, JSS.

[105] "Beecher's Negro Minstrels," *New York Herald*, 28 December 1871, JSS; Pike, *Campaign for Twenty Thousand Pounds*, 111, 112. The quote from *The New York Herald* is also included in Pike's account. Also see "The Jubilee Singers," *New York Tribune*, 28 December 1871, JSS; "The Jubilee Singers," *Days Doings, New York*, December 1871, JSS.

[106] Moore (Sheppard), "Historical Sketch of the Jubilee Singers," 48.

[107] Pike, *Campaign for Twenty Thousand Dollars*, 115.

[108] "A Troupe of Colored Singers," *American Missionary* (December 1871): 282, AMAA.

[109] Moore (Sheppard), "Historical Sketch of the Jubilee Singers," 48; "A Troupe of Colored Singers," *American Missionary* (December 1871): 282–83, AMAA; "The Jubilee Singers of Fiske [sic] University, Nashville, Tenn.," *American Missionary* (January 1872): 14, AMAA.

[110] A. K. Spence to Elizabeth Spence, 26 December 1871, SFC.

[111] G. L. White to A. K. Spence, 21 December 1871, SFC. Also see Pike, *Campaign for Twenty Thousand Pounds*, 112.

[112] G. L. White to A. K. Spence, 21 December 1871, SFC. Also see A. K. Spence to Elizabeth Spence, 26 December 1871, SFC.

[113] Lyceums were a form of organized adult education that flourished in the United States during the nineteenth century, established to improve the social, intellectual, and moral fabric of society. Lyceums sponsored a variety of activities in concert and town halls across America, including lectures, dramatic and concert performances, and debates. The "lyceum circuit" touted such notables as Ralph Waldo Emerson, Henry Thoreau, William Lloyd Garrison, Mark Twain, and Susan B. Anthony.

[114] Pike, *Campaign for Twenty Thousand Pounds*, 116. Beecher's quote was also included in promotional material used to launch the Jubilee Singers' first European campaign in 1873.

[115] Ibid., 115–20. Throughout this research, I use quotes from press reviews received by the Jubilee Singers during their seven years of tours to demonstrate the company's popularity and the AMA's interpretation of their concert success. Many scholars have examined how the language used to describe or interpret the spiritual reveals racial undertones that fostered a misinterpretation of African-American culture. See chapter 5 for more on this subject.

[116] A. K. Spence to Elizabeth Spence, 30 January 1872, SFC.

[117] Ella Sheppard to A. K. Spence, 12 February 1872, SFC.

[118] G. L. White to A. K. Spence, 21 December 1871, SFC.

[119] "The Jubilee Singers," *American Missionary* (February 1872): 37, AMAA.

[120] A. K. Spence to Elizabeth Spence, 23 January 1872, SFC.

[121] G. L. White to A. K. Spence, 13 January 1872, SFC.

[122] A. K. Spence to Elizabeth Spence, 13 February 1872, SFC.

[123] G. L. White to A. K. Spence, 19 January 1872, SFC.

[124] A. K. Spence to Elizabeth Spence, 30 January 1872 and 13 February 1872, SFC.

[125] G. L. White to A. K. Spence, 13 January 1872, SFC.

Chapter Three

[1] "The Jubilee Singers of Fisk University: Their past success and their plans for the coming year," *American Missionary* (September 1872): 208, AMAA.

[2] Mary E. Spence Notes, SFC, quoted in Ward, *Dark Midnight When I Rise*, 162. Pike wrote that the public attention the young man received was "injurious not only to him but to his associates" (*Campaign for Twenty Thousand Dollars*, 120).

[3] Pike, *Campaign for Twenty Thousand Dollars*, 125, 139. Susan Gilbert, who became one of Ella Sheppard's closest friends, married the widowed George White in April 1876.

[4] G. L. White to A. K. Spence, 20 February 1872, SFC.

[5] The AMA commissioned Pike to author two historical accounts of the Jubilee Singers' campaigns, written contemporaneously with the singers' immense popularity. The AMA printed various editions with slight revisions as membership in the company changed.

[6] Pike, *Campaign for Twenty Thousand Dollars*, 85, 86.

[7] Pike valued wealth and prestige in a Christian life, seeing its practical usefulness in advancing ministry and good works. "From my earliest manhood I entertained the idea that if a person would accomplish a successful life, it would be

fortunate for him to possess three things: the first was a renewed heart, the second, a liberal education, and the third, wealth. I argued that with these attainments he would become philanthropic, and gain a useful position among men; moreover, I believed that the education furnished by schools would be enlarged and made more valuable by travel." See G. D. Pike, *The Singing Campaign for Ten Thousand Pounds; or, The Jubilee Singers in Great Britain* (New York: The American Missionary Association, 1875) 1. Because of this personal philosophy, Pike had no compunction about appealing to the wealthy elite, thus making him an effective fundraiser.

[8] Pike, *Campaign for Twenty Thousand Dollars*, 142.

[9] Endorsements on a Jubilee Singers program from Tremont Temple Concert, 12 March 1872, and St. Paul's M. E. Church, Newark, 8 March 1872, JSS.

[10] Pike, *Campaign for Twenty Thousand Dollars*, 122.

[11] Ibid., 123–25, 130, 144.

[12] Moore (Sheppard), "Historical Sketch of the Jubilee Singers," 48.

[13] A. K. Spence to Elizabeth Spence, 19 February 1872, 27 February 1872, and 19 March 1872, SFC.

[14] Pike, *Campaign for Twenty Thousand Dollars*, 147, 148.

[15] Ibid., 126.

[16] "The Jubilee Singers," untitled newspaper, ca. April 1872, JSS.

[17] "The Jubilee Singers," *Boston Daily Advertiser*, ca. March 1872, JSS.

[18] Untitled article, *The Congregationalist*, 21 March 1872, JSS.

[19] Pike, *Campaign for Twenty Thousand Dollars*, 142, 143.

[20] "The Jubilee Singers in Newark," untitled newspaper, February 1872, JSS.

[21] G. L. White to A. K. Spence, 25 March 1872, SFC.

[22] Thomas Rutling, "*Tom*": *An Autobiography, with Revised Negro Melodies* (Bradford: Wm. Byles & Sons Ltd., Printers, 1907) 20.

[23] Pike, *Campaign for Twenty Thousand Dollars*, 147.

[24] Untitled New York newspaper, ca. April 1872, JSS.

[25] "The Jubilee Singers," untitled newspaper, ca. May 1872; "Missionary Meeting," untitled newspaper, ca. May 1872. These clippings are attached to Elizabeth Spence to A. K. Spence, 22 May 1872, SFC.

[26] "The Jubilee Singers," *Waterbury Daily American*, 6 February 1872, JSS.

[27] Pike, *Campaign for Twenty Thousand Dollars*, 122–27.

[28] Moore (Sheppard), "Historical Sketch of the Jubilee Singers," 48; Unidentified Jubilee Singer to A. K. Spence, 1 March 1872, SFC.

[29] Pike, *Campaign for Twenty Thousand Dollars*, 130.

[30] Ella Sheppard to A. K. Spence, 12 February 1872, SFC.

[31] "We were well indorsed, well supplied with working force, and pretty well posted concerning 'how to do it,' when we started for Boston to finish up the New England campaign," Pike claimed (*Campaign for Twenty Thousand Dollars*, 139).

[32] G. D. Pike, "How to do It," 1872, JSS.

[33] Letters of request from towns whose churches or halls seated only 600 have notes in the margins that read, "Can't accept." See various letters in The Jubilee Singers European Tour 1873–1878, Fisk University Special Collections (hereafter cited as JSET). Beth Howse, archivist at Fisk, discovered this collection of letters in a trunk during one of my research visits. She allowed me access to this material before it had been catalogued.

[34] Pike, *Campaign for Twenty Thousand Dollars*, 148, 149.

[35] Proverbs 20:1 states, "Wine is a mocker and beer a brawler; whoever is led astray by them is not wise."

[36] Pike, *Campaign for Twenty Thousand Dollars*, 148, 149.

[37] Quoted in ibid., 130. Also see "The Jubilee Singers in Newark," untitled New Jersey newspaper, ca. February 1872, JSS.

[38] Pike, *Campaign for Twenty Thousand Dollars*, 131, 132; Moore (Sheppard), "Historical Sketch of the Jubilee Singers," 48; "Civilization in Newark," untitled newspaper, ca. February 1872, JSS.

[39] Moore (Sheppard), "Historical Sketch of the Jubilee Singers," 46.

[40] Pike, *Campaign for Twenty Thousand Dollars*, 131–32.

[41] "The Jubilee Singers," *New York Independent*, 4 March 1872, JSS.

[42] Unidentified Jubilee Singer to A. K. Spence, March 1872 (fragment), SFC.

[43] Untitled New York newspaper, 7 December 1871, JSS.

[44] Pike, *Campaign for Twenty Thousand Dollars*, 132–35; Ella Sheppard to A. K. Spence, 6 March 1872, SFC.

[45] "The Jubilee Singers in Steinway Hall," *American Missionary* (April 1872): 87–90, AMAA.

[46] Pike, *Campaign for Twenty Thousand Dollars*, 153, 154.

[47] Patrick Sarsfield Gilmore was an Irish-American bandmaster who settled in Salem, Massachusetts. He gained popularity for the mammoth musical festivals he held in Boston: the *National Peace Jubilee* (1869) and the *World's Peace Jubilee* (1872). Gilmore claimed to be the composer of "When Johnny Comes Marching Home" (*Baker's Biographical Dictionary of Musicians*, s.v. "Patrick Sarsfield Gilmore").

[48] Moore (Sheppard), "Historical Sketch of the Jubilee Singers," 49.

[49] The Hyers Sisters, soprano Anna Madah and contralto Emma Louise, eventually formed the Hyers Sisters Concert Company. Historian Eileen Southern credits them among the first African Americans to enter the post-war concert world (*The Music of Black Americans*, 240).

[50] Moore (Sheppard), "Historical Sketch of the Jubilee Singers," 49, 50.

[51] Marsh, *The Story of the Jubilee Singers; With Their Songs,* 41, 42.

[52] "The Jubilee Singers of Fisk University; Their past success and their plans for the coming year," *American Missionary* (September 1872): 206–208, AMAA.

[53] "Fisk University. The New Jubilee Hall to be Erected at Fort Gillem," *American Missionary* (February 1873): 30, AMAA. In February 1873, the institution broke ground for the new multi-purpose facility, Jubilee Hall. Fisk University was originally housed in the Union hospital complex west of the Chattanooga depot on a parcel of land about 310 feet by 320 feet. Fisk's new site was an eight-acre plot on which had sat the former Union fortification of Fort Gillem (Richardson, *A History of Fisk University,* 3; Ward, *Dark Midnight When I Rise,* 188). The AMA informed its readers that the new Jubilee Hall would be a two-story building, 128 feet across the south front and 145 feet across the east front. It was to be heated by steam and have "all the modern appliances for such buildings" ("Fisk University. The New Jubilee Hall to be Erected at Fort Gillem," 30).

[54] "The Jubilee Singers of Fisk University: Their past success and their plans for the coming year," *American Missionary* (September 1872): 208, AMAA. The belief in the providential guidance of the Jubilee Singers remained central to the association's public rhetoric. In its 1873 annual report, the AMA proudly touted the Jubilee Singers' "wonderful career, awakening so much popular attention, and securing so much aid in erecting a Hall for Fisk University." The leadership interpreted the troupe's remarkable success in part as evidence of "a hand divine" encouraging them to continue the AMA's work in the South: "The inspiration of success is an impulse to greater zeal. What God doth bless and good men favor should be pushed forward to finished results." See "Twenty-seventh Annual Report of the American Missionary Association - 1873," 21, 22, AMAA.

Chapter Four

[1] Pike, *The Singing Campaign for Ten Thousand Pounds,* x-xi.

[2] G. L. White to G. D. Pike, 19 October 1872 and 21 October 1872, AMAA. Spurious groups capitalizing on the fame of the original Jubilee Singers plagued the company throughout its tenure. In 1875, the AMA printed a handbill entitled "Caution to the Public" warning of a group claiming to be the original company: "We do not question in the least, the right of these persons to give Concerts, but when they use the title, and unblushingly publish themselves as the 'Troupe which created such a furore in this Country, and in Europe,' and even go so far as to quote, as their own, the testimonials formerly given to the Jubilee Singers of Fisk University, Nashville, Tenn., we deem their exposure due to the public" ("Caution to the Public," 30 January 1875, JSS). Despite such attempts, copycat groups

continued to flourish. "We have rivals in the field now right good earnest," America Robinson wrote to James Burrus (22 December 1876, ARL). "These Wilmington Jubilee Singers are imitating us in everything—our poster, programs, etc." In 1877, a Baptist minister wrote the managers questioning the authenticity of yet another group holding concerts in his town. "From the general tone of the enclosed bill, some Friends here think those who are about to visit us are not those who have been through the country singing for the above; for nothing is said as to how 'the proceeds' will be devoted. Some well known names are missing. We however see that of Lord Shaftesbury, who is also counted with your Society, & we see many names strange to us. Would you kindly tell us by return of post if you know these singers? Whether your Society gives them sympathy? Or if they be purely a private affair" (Joseph Jones to E. M. Cravath, 4 January 1877, JSET). Also see Toni Passmore Anderson, "The Fisk Jubilee Singers: Performing Ambassadors for the Survival of an American Treasure, 1871–1878 (Ph.D. diss., Georgia State University, 1997) 162, 163.

[3] In the *American Missionary* (April 1873, AMAA), the AMA announced that the Hampton Singers were in New York after a concert tour that included appearances in Washington and Philadelphia. "Following in the line of their popular predecessors, the Jubilee Singers, they give a somewhat different, though perhaps, equally pleasing rendering of the peculiar songs of the slaves" (88).

[4] The son of George MacDonald, the Scottish novelist, credited his parents with encouraging the idea of a British tour: "My parents persuaded them to visit England, which they did, and very successfully, the following year." See Greville MacDonald, M.D., *George MacDonald and His Wife* (1924; rep., New York: Johnson Reprint Corporation, 1971) 442. Another proponent of the tour was Mark Twain (Ward, *Dark Midnight When I Rise*, 199).

[5] Though the AMA's largest work was in antislavery and freedmen's education through its home department, the association had supported foreign missionaries from its inception. In 1854, the AMA had seventy-nine missionaries in its Foreign Department, some who served in West Africa at the Mendi Mission. This station was established in 1841 by three missionaries and several of the freed Amistad captives (*History of the American Missionary Association*, 3, 4).

[6] Marsh, *The Story of the Jubilee Singers; With Their Songs*, 42; Crosthwaite, "A Résumé," 6, 7.

[7] White wrote Georgia Gordon's mother outlining her daughter's offenses and stating that she must "apologize for her rude treatment" if she expected to stay with the class. "I have done all that I could to avoid this trouble. I have offered every inducement that could be offered. Georgia is young as you say but she is old enough not to trample on kindness—and children must not undertake to control the affairs of older people," (G. L. White to Mercy Gordon, 10 August 1871,

AMAA). For more on the altercation, see Anderson, "The Fisk Jubilee Singers," 72–74.

[8] Watkins remained in London at the end of the 1874 concert season to pursue musical studies. White's attempts to persuade him to rejoin the 1875 company failed. He was replaced by Frederick Loudin. See G. L. White to E. M. Cravath, 13 October 1874, 27 November 1874, and 13 December 1874, AMAA.

[9] *Fisk University Catalog*, 1871–1872 and 1874–1875, FU.

[10] J. E. Jackson to E. M. Cravath, 3 December 1874, AMAA. In June 1876, while on tour, Jackson suffered a paralytic stroke that left one side of her body powerless. She failed to recover and had to return to the States. See America Robinson to James Burrus, 23 June 1876, 26 September 1876, 28 October 1876, and 30 October 1876, ARL.

[11] Mabel Lewis Imes, "Reminiscences," personal interview, ca. 1920, FJS. Lewis was also one of the most mischievous members of the group. "I can be dignified a little while but not too long," she once said. When observers of the troupe described her as the "little quiet one," the other Jubilees groaned. "You don't know her as we do," they retorted (M. L. Imes to "My Dear Friends," 1 October 1934, FJS).

[12] Signed contract for Margaret A. Carnes (Maggie), November 1874, FJS. The contract calls for two months of vacation in the summer, or three to four months of lighter concert work. In comparison, Ira Sankey, famed soloist of the Moody and Sankey revival duo, earned $500 above expenses for himself and his wife while traveling with Moody in 1873. His salary was for eight to ten months of work.

[13] Ella Sheppard diary, 10 November 1874, FJS.

[14] Ella Sheppard diary, 10 November 1874, FJS; Various financial records, JSET; Account statement for Maggie Porter, FJS.

[15] Richardson, *A History of Fisk University*, 19, 79; Richardson, *Christian Reconstruction*, 179, 180.

[16] Signed contract for Margaret A. Carnes (Maggie), November 1874, FJS.

[17] "The Expiation for Slavery," *American Missionary* (April 1872): 84, AMAA.

[18] G. D. Pike to E. M. Cravath, 30 January 1873, AMAA.

[19] Pike, *Singing Campaign for Ten Thousand Pounds*, 13, 14.

[20] Henry Ward Beecher to Rev. Henry Allon, 13 March 1873 promotional leaflet, "Jubilee Singers: Correspondence Between Rev. Henry Ward Beecher and the Rev. Henry Allon, D.D.," FJS.

[21] George MacDonald to Henry Allon, 6 March 1873, in *American Missionary* (April 1873): 88, AMAA.

[22] G. D. Pike form letter for promotional purposes, 1873, FJS.

[23] G. D. Pike to E. M. Cravath, 16 April 1873, AMAA. The AMA had long held to the idea that freedmen's education was inextricably linked to African missions. An article in the 1866 issue of the *American Missionary* declared: "Africa also will feel the effects of the Christian elevation of the colored race here, for if the people are cultured and enlightened they will be the bearers of a Christian civilization to their fatherland. The elevation then of this people involves the welfare of two races and extends its influence over two continents" ("Education and Religion," 202, AMAA). Pike enlarged and emphasized this aspect of the vision to prospective British audiences.

[24] England sent missionaries to Africa in the early 1700s and established colonies in many of its coastal regions. According to Edward H. Berman, the era of missionary expansion spurred by Livingstone "did not end until the nations of western Europe effectively spread their colonial nets, often with missionary support, at century's end." Most often, states Berman, the missionaries "actively encouraged the extension of imperial control." Edward H. Berman, *African Reactions to Missionary Education* (New York and London: Teachers College Press, 1975) xiv, 3, 4, 12.

[25] Richardson, *Christian Reconstruction*, 104–105; Pike, *Singing Campaign for Ten Thousand Pounds*, 18–22, 30.

[26] Pike, *Singing Campaign for Ten Thousand Pounds*, pref.; G. D. Pike to E. M. Cravath, 16 April 1873, AMAA.

[27] "Jubilee Singers," *American Missionary* (May 1873): 110, AMAA.

[28] Maggie Porter Cole, "The Jubilee Singers on the Ocean and in Europe," *Fisk University News* 2/5 (October 1911): 33, FU.

[29] Marsh, *The Story of the Jubilee Singers; With Their Songs*, 57–59; Pike, *Singing Campaign for Ten Thousand Pounds*, 44, 45, 54.

[30] Edwin Hodder, *The Life and Work of the Seventh Earl of Shaftesbury*, vol. III (London: Cassell & Company, Limited, 1886) 264.

[31] "The Coloured Jubilee Singers," *The Christian World*, 9 May 1873, British Newspaper Library (hereafter cited as BNL).

[32] J. W. Healy to E. M. Cravath, 17 May 1873, AMAA.

[33] "The Jubilee Singers of Fisk University," untitled newspaper, May 1873, JSS.

[34] Pike, *Singing Campaign for Ten Thousand Pounds*, 29; G. D. Pike to E. M. Cravath, 13 May 1873, AMAA.

[35] Ella Sheppard Moore, "Victoria, the Gracious Queen, and the Jubilee Singers," *The Fisk Herald* 18/9 (June 1901): 9, 10, FU.

[36] "Jubilee Singers. England's Welcome. Press Notices," *American Missionary* (July 1873): 146, AMAA.

[37] Pike, *Singing Campaign for Ten Thousand Pounds*, 40, 41.

[38] Ibid., 82–89.

[39] W. E. Shipton to Clinton B. Fisk, 26 May 1873, AMAA.

[40] J. W. Healy to E. M. Cravath, 25 June 1873, AMAA.

[41] Curwen to "Dear Sir," 27 June 1873, AMAA; G. L. Costen to G. D. Pike, 14 July 1873, AMAA; Common to G. D. Pike, 21 July 1873, AMAA.

[42] Pike, *Singing Campaign for Ten Thousand Pounds*, 94–102.

[43] Ibid., 50.

[44] "Jubilee Singers. England's Welcome. Press Notices," *American Missionary* (July 1873): 147, AMAA.

[45] Pike, *Campaign for Ten Thousand Pounds*, 48–50; *The Baptist*, n.d., quoted in Pike, *Singing Campaign for Ten Thousand Pounds*, 54.

[46] Moore (Sheppard), *Historical Sketch of the Jubilee Singers*, 51.

[47] "National Temperance Soiree," *The Temperance Record*, 7 June 1873, BNL.

[48] "The Jubilee Singers," *The Temperance Record*, 10 May 1873, BNL; "The Annual Conversazione of the National Temperance League," *The Temperance Record*, 31 May 1873, BNL.

[49] Marsh, *The Story of the Jubilee Singers; With Their Songs*, 56, 57. Also see "Our Temperance Column," *The Baptist*, 30 May 1873, BNL; "Crystal Palace Fête," *The Temperance Record*, 26 July 1873, BNL.

[50] G. D. Pike to E. M. Cravath, 23 July 1873 and 28 July 1873, AMAA.

[51] G. D. Pike to E. M. Cravath, 16 April 1873, 23 July 1873, 28 July 1873, and 20 August 1873, AMAA; "Jubilee Singers," *American Missionary* (November 1873): 254, AMAA.

[52] Pike, *Campaign for Twenty Thousand Dollars*, 126. For a brief history of the "service of song," see Graham, "The Fisk Jubilee Singers and the Concert Spiritual," 142–44.

[53] Of the scores of newspaper clippings in the 1867–1872 Jubilee Singers Scrapbooks, only a few use the term "praise" in their titles or descriptions: "Remarkable Praise Meetings," untitled Ohio paper, November 1871; "Praise Concert" and "The Praise Meeting Last Evening," untitled New York newspapers, December 1871, JSS. An 1871 flyer advertising a performance in Akron, Ohio uses the term "Praise Service" and an 1872 review states that the group presented a "praise service" (see "The Jubilee Singers from Fisk University, untitled newspaper, ca. 1872, JSS). An untitled Detroit, Michigan newspaper uses the title "Missionary Meeting" for its review (ca. March 1872, JSS).

[54] Promotional material from G. D. Pike, 1873, JSS. Many press notices from the early months of the 1873 European campaign on indicate that the Jubilee Singers conducted a "Service of Song." By the launch of the second British campaign in 1875, this description for the Jubilee Singers' work was well intact. See

"The Jubilee," promotional pamphlet, ca. 1875, British National Library at St. Pancras.
[55] G. D. Pike to E. M. Cravath, 11 September 1873, AMAA.
[56] Moore (Sheppard), *Historical Sketch of the Jubilee Singers,* 52. "In accordance with their usual practice in the towns which they visit, they offered to hold an evangelistic service for Sunday scholars," reported the *Liverpool Mercury.* "They (the Jubilee Singers) were not altogether satisfied with giving concerts, and whenever they had a chance they always liked to get the children of the town together to sing to them those hymns which they sung in the dark days of slavery." See "The Jubilee Singers: Immense gathering of Sunday-school Children," *Liverpool Mercury,* ca. 1876, rep. in *American Missionary* (April 1876): 89, 90, AMAA.
[57] Quoted in "The Jubilee," promotional pamphlet, ca. 1875, British National Library at St. Pancras. Also see Marsh, *The Story of the Jubilee Singers; With Their Songs,* 67–68.
[58] W. E. Shipton to G. D. Pike, 28 October 1873, AMAA.
[59] Pike, *Singing Campaign for Ten Thousand Pounds,* 101.
[60] "The Jubilee Singers in Sunderland," *The Sunderland and Durham County Herald,* 15 August 1873, BNL.
[61] I. P. Dickerson to W. E. Whiting, 13 August 1873, AMAA.
[62] Lyle W. Dorsett, *A Passion for Souls: The Life of D. L. Moody* (Chicago: Moody Press, 1997) 130, 131, 173.
[63] Ibid., 179–81.
[64] Pike, *Singing Campaign for Ten Thousand Pounds,* 150.
[65] Dorsett, *A Passion for Souls,* 187.
[66] Arthur T. Pierson, *Evangelistic Work in Principle and Practice* (New York: Baker and Taylor, 1887), 252, quoted in Dorsett, *A Passion for Souls,* 185.
[67] *Christian* (6 December 1883): 9, quoted in James D. Findlay, Jr., *Dwight L. Moody: American Evangelist, 1837–1899* (Chicago and London: University of Chicago Press, 1969) 211.
[68] Dorsett, *A Passion for Souls,* 184. Findlay's work discusses how Moody benefited from other historical developments, especially in Scotland, which created a climate whereby old traditions were being challenged and people were ready to receive the novelty and freshness of his message and preaching style. See Findlay, *Dwight L. Moody: American Evangelist,* 159–63.
[69] Pike, *Singing Campaign for Ten Thousand Pounds,* 150, 151.
[70] Imes (Lewis), "Reminiscences," FJS.
[71] "Messrs. Moody and Sankey's Meetings," *The Weekly Review,* 27 December 1873, BNL.
[72] "The Jubilee Singers," *American Missionary* (March 1874): 62, AMAA.

[73] Moore (Sheppard), "Historical Sketch of the Jubilee Singers," 52; Marsh, *The Story of the Jubilee Singers; With Their Songs,* 67–68.

[74] "Notes by the Way," untitled newspaper clipping, ca. February 1874, JSS.

[75] Prepared statement published in the press at the beginning of the second campaign, ca. 1873, JSS.

[76] "The Jubilee Singers at Exeter Hall," handbill printed by the AMA and the Freedmen's Aid Society, ca. 1874, FJS.

[77] Ibid. Also see "Freedmen's Mission & The Jubilee Singers," *The English Independent,* 28 May 1874, BNL. This article reflects the depth to which the Freedmen's Aid Society was committed to freedmen's education in America as a means to African evangelization: "…mention was made of the wonderful providence of God in emancipating the millions of negroes in America, and in inspiring thousands of them to become the spiritual emancipators of their race in their fatherland, at a time when exploration and commerce are opening up Africa to missionary enterprise. This Divine co-relation of demand and supply is without a parallel in the history of Christian Missions, and plainly indicates the duty of the Christian Church. Without native agency Africa can never be evangelised. The method by which this society seeks to promote the work is by specially training young freedmen in the colleges and universities which have been established in America for the education of the coloured race in general, and thus furnishing the various missionary societies with prepared agents" (586).

[78] G. L. White to E. M. Cravath, 12 March 1875, AMAA.

[79] Initially, White opposed returning to England until Jubilee Hall was complete. When it became clear that the building would not be finished, he suggested the idea of working in cooperation with Moody. White was most likely encouraged in this decision by a letter from Isaac Dickerson, a Jubilee Singer who left the company to pursue ministerial studies at Edinburgh University in 1874 . "The letter which you forwarded was from Mr. Dickerson—he writes that there is much enquiry in regard to the return of the Singers—people want to hear them." G. L. White to E. M. Cravath, 24 February 1875 and 12 March 1875, AMAA.

[80] "Mr. Loudin's Speech," *The Christian,* quoted in *American Missionary* (September 1875): 200, AMAA. Loudin quickly rose as one of the chief spokespersons for the troupe. His brief biography is presented in chapter 8.

[81] For the London meetings, Moody divided the city into four sections and held revival meetings simultaneously in rented or newly constructed large buildings. In the fashionable West End, he held meetings at the Agricultural Hall and the Royal Opera House. He constructed two large temporary buildings in Camberwell Green and on the Bow Road in the East End, the working class section of the city (Findlay, *Dwight L. Moody: American Evangelist,* 171). Moody relied on the help of local ministers to keep these multiple services operational. He put Rev. Aitken and

Mr. Henry Varley in charge of the Bow Road Hall meetings in which the Jubilee Singers provided the music. The September 1875 edition of the *American Missionary* included an excerpt from *The Christian* with news of the Jubilees' participation in the London revivals: "After Messrs. Moody and Sankey had closed their services at Bow Road Hall to go to Camberwell, the meetings were continued at the former place with very effective preaching each night by the Rev. Mr. Aitken or Mr. Henry Varley, and singing by the Jubilee Choir. The attendance was so large, on week-day as well as on Sunday evenings, that hundreds were sometimes turned away, even after a congregation of ten or twelve thousand had crowded into the hall" (200, AMAA).

[82] Ella Sheppard diary, 13 June 1875 and 10 July 1875, FJS.

[83] Moore (Sheppard), "Historical Sketch of the Jubilee Singers," 54.

[84] Ella Sheppard diary, 14 June 1875, FJS.

[85] Ella Sheppard diary, 15 June 1875, FJS.

[86] "Meetings with Mr. Moody," *American Missionary* (September 1875): 200, AMAA.

[87] Marsh, *The Story of the Jubilee Singers; With Their Songs,* 82.

[88] "Mr. Moody and the Jubilee Singers," *American Missionary* (September 1875): 201, AMAA.

[89] Ella Sheppard diary, 17 July 1875, FJS.

[90] "Mr. Moody and the Jubilee Singers," *American Missionary* (September 1875): 201, AMAA.

[91] Handbill advertising the concert at Guildhall, Plymouth, 18 August 1875, FJS.

[92] Frederick Loudin said that the Jubilees proposed the idea of Livingstone Hall after a chance meeting with Dr. Livingstone's daughter, Mrs. Bruce, while in Edinburg. She introduced herself to the Jubilees at the close of their concert: "Pardon me, but I was born in Africa, and I wish to tell you how I feel toward the African race, and also of the deep interest my father has in that country." The singers were amazed to discover who she was and accepted her invitation to visit the following day. They later "conceived the idea of extending their school" and broached the idea to Mrs. Bruce, who expressed her delight "and gave £25 toward the project, the first money that was raised towards it." See "The Jubilee Singers. A Short account of their Labors and Travels. Interesting Chat with the Basso," *London Advertiser,* 28 October 1880, JSS.

[93] "Visit of the Jubilee Singers to Crieff," *Strathearn Herald,* 7 October 1876, JSS. The newspaper extract quotes the New York Journal, *Harper's Weekly* (no date given).

[94] "The Jubilee Singers in Barhead," *Barhead Independent,* 28 October 1876, JSS.

⁹⁵ "The Jubilee Singers," *The Banbury Guardian*, 31 May 1877, JSS.
⁹⁶ The letter was signed by Georgia Gordon, Frederick Loudin, and B. W. Thomas. See *American Missionary* (June 1878): 180, AMAA.
⁹⁷ A. P. Miller to Catherine Spence, broadside, 10 January 1879, MES, quoted in Ward, *Dark Midnight When I Rise*, 371.
⁹⁸ *Evangelisch-Kirchlicher Anzeiger*, 9 November 1877, JSS. Translation by Christiane Price.
⁹⁹ "Die Jubiläumssänger in Deutschland," *Daheim*, ca. February 1878, JSS. Translation by Christiane Price.
¹⁰⁰ "The Jubilee Singers of Fisk University," *American Missionary* (September 1872): 208, AMAA.
¹⁰¹ Six of the Jubilee Singers are known to have engaged in some form of Christian ministry after leaving the company. As noted in this chapter, Ella Hildridge and her husband became missionaries to the Mendi Mission in Sierra Leone. Georgia Gordon, Jennie Jackson, and Ella Sheppard each married ministers. Hinton Alexander became the music director for Chattanooga's Congregational Church and led his own ensemble called "The Band of Hope," known as a "great financial as well as a great spiritual power among the members" (Crosthwaite, "A Résumé," 6). Isaac Dickerson traveled as an evangelist in France for several years. He then spent time in Italy and Palestine before returning to England where he was known as a popular evangelist/speaker and the chaplain of a small mission in Plumstead. For more biographical details, see Anderson, "The Fisk Jubilee Singers," 201–331.

Chapter Five

¹ "Concert der Jubiläums-Sänger," *Courier (Hannover)*, 6 January 1878, JSS. Translation by Christiane Price.
² In its appeal for missionary teachers to aid its work in the South, the AMA declared that God had providentially placed emancipated slaves "at our feet with the command to fit them for the new position in society they are to occupy." See "Teachers; Their Qualifications and Support," *American Missionary* (July 1866): 153, AMAA.
³ Howe, "Victorian America," 5–9. For this discussion, I rely on Howe's definition of culture as an "evolving system of beliefs, attitudes, and techniques, transmitted from generation to generation, and finding expression in innumerable activities people learn: religion, politics, child-rearing customs, the arts and professions, *inter alia*" (5).
⁴ The AMA's twenty-sixth annual report includes a sermon delivered by the Rev. E. P. Goodwin that illustrates this point: "Harmony can only come when the two races out of whose antagonism the conflict grew come to have a mutual respect

for each other. The colored man must demonstrate by his intelligence, his character, his achievements, that he is competent to take care of himself, and capable of being a white man's equal. More; he must demonstrate by what he is and what he does that the interests of the two races are identical; that, as a matter of fact, as respects muscle, brain, government, religion, every thing, his old master can not spare him out of the social compact" ("Twenty-Sixth Annual Report of the American Missionary Association—1872", 114, 115, AMAA). How the reform efforts of missionaries engaged in freedmen's education can be characterized as mere attempts to recreate Northern Protestant culture has been the subject of many scholars. In her work, Flemming states that white missionaries attempted to transform former slaves into "carbon copies of white Americans" by imposing their own code of ethics and insisting on conformity to rigid codes of behavior. See Cynthia Griggs Flemming, "The Effect of Higher Education on Black Tennesseans After the Civil War," *Phylon XLIV* (1983): 209–16. Carter G. Woodson agrees: "Their aim was to transform the Negroes," he wrote, "not to develop them." See Carter G. Woodson, *The Mis-Education of the Negro* (1933; rep., Trenton NJ: Africa World Press, 1990) 17.

[5] Veysey, *The Emergence of the American University*, 184–91.

[6] In its self-published history, the association described its first school established prior to the grand movement for freemen's education as "the harbinger of the hundreds that have followed, and of the thousands that are yet to come, that are to give an intelligent Christian culture to the colored race in America" (*The History of the American Missionary Association*, 12). By the end of the century, Fisk University articulated its commitment to "liberal culture" in its 1899 promotional material: "The student body honors scholarship, awakens ambitions, cultivates good manners, frowns upon untidyness of appearance, while by firmly sustained legislation the faculty forbids any display of extravagance in attire." See "Fisk University," promotional brochure, ca. 1899, AMAA.

[7] Dubois, *The Souls of Black Folk*, 129. Fisk University resisted the path taken by other historically black colleges in the late 1800s to adopt industrial education as the modus operandi of the institution. W. E. B. DuBois was the champion of classical education and a respected voice against Booker T. Washington, the proponent of agricultural and mechanical training for African Americans. For how this debate impacted the policies and practices at Fisk University, see Richardson, *A History of Fisk University*, 55–70.

[8] "Education and Religion," *American Missionary* (September 1866): 204, AMAA.

[9] Richardson, *Christian Reconstruction*, 53; Richardson, *A History of Fisk University*, 15. Examiners at the close of the 1869 spring semester gladly described the twenty-five Fisk students of the Normal Class as exhibiting "good teaching

talent, which bore evidence of having been well cultivated." See "Colored Education. Examination at the Fisk University," ca. June 1869, JSS.

[10] White intended to expose his young students to musical repertoire he considered as the best Western culture had to offer, especially songs containing moral or inspirational messages. He therefore introduced his students to a generous sampling of popular religious songs, sentimental ballads, and patriotic tunes typically used in schools and churches throughout the North. He pulled from this repertoire when choosing selections for his earliest concerts at Fisk, knowing that the tunes would be familiar to the general public and considered appropriate material for any collegiate group, whether black or white. For a review of the tunes presented on White's early public performances, see Graham, "The Fisk Jubilee Singers and the Concert Spiritual," 63–75, 103–11.

[11] William Francis Allen, Charles Pickard Ware, and Lucy McKim Garrison, eds. *Slave Songs of the United States* (1867; rep., New York: Peter Smith, 1951). Returning army officers and travelers often reported hearing slaves singing at their prayer meetings, but comparatively few in the North had heard this religious folk music. Personal narratives appeared in a few periodicals with references to the music of the South, and a few spirituals had been arranged and published for commercial sale. Thirty-six spirituals transcribed by Thomas Wentworth Higginson appeared in the 7 June 1867 issue of the *Atlantic Monthly*, and the same year saw the publication of the historic collection *Slave Songs of the United States*. While such publications made printed transcriptions of spirituals obtainable, the general public of the North had little opportunity to actually hear this religious music presented live. This situation changed shortly after the Jubilee Singers began touring. In 1873, Hampton Institute launched its own student choral ensemble, and by 1875, numerous copycat groups had also entered the field as rivals, helping to spread the popularity of spirituals. Public awareness of spirituals increased significantly with the release of Pike's book, *The Jubilee Singers and Their Campaign for Twenty Thousand Dollars,* which included Theodore Seward's transcriptions of many spirituals in the Jubilee Singers' repertoire. The book sold over 30,000 copies by 1875, and in its wake, many "Jubilee clubs" and societies sprang up, proliferating the spiritual throughout America and Europe. See John Lovell, Jr., *Black Song: The Forge and the Flame* (New York: Paragon House Publishers, 1972) 414, 415.

[12] Southern, *The Music of Black Americans,* 167–72. Also see Eileen Southern, "The Antebellum Church," *Black American Literature Forum* 25/1, The Black Church and the Black Theatre (Spring 1991): 23–26; Eileen Southern, "An Origin for the Negro Spiritual," *The Black Scholar* (Summer 1972): 8–13; and Dena J. Epstein, *Sinful Tunes and Spirituals: Black Folk Music to the Civil War* (Urbana and Chicago: University of Illinois Press, 1977) 278–87.

¹³ During slavery, religious meetings were held in a variety of places, from slave cabins to a designated "praise house," or in secret meeting spots in the woods on those plantations where the overseer attempted to prevent slave assemblies. Ritual dancing and singing of both long-meter hymns that slaves had learned from whites and spirituals of their own invention were components of these religious gatherings. Spirituals were "sacred to our parents," recalled Ella Sheppard, "who used them in their religious worship and shouted over them." See Moore (Sheppard), "Historical Sketch of the Jubilee Singers," 43.

¹⁴ Sterling Stuckey, *Slave Culture: Nationalist Theory and the Foundations of Black America* (New York and Oxford: Oxford University Press, 1987) 27. The first chapter in this work, "Slavery and the Circle of Culture," discusses how the shout connected slave culture with its African ancestry. "The repetition of stanzas as the dancers circled around and around with ever greater acceleration reinforced and deepened the spirit of familiar attachment, drawing within the ancestral orbit slaves who may not have known either a father or a mother, their involvement being an extension of that of others, the circle symbolizing the unbroken unity of the community" (29).

¹⁵ Rutling, "*Tom*," 21.

¹⁶ John Wesley Work, *Folk Song of the American Negro* (Nashville TN: Press of Fisk University, 1915) 20.

¹⁷ Frederick Douglass, *My Bondage and My Freedom* (1855. rep., Los Angeles CA: Milligan Books, 1999), quoted in Lovell, *Black Song*, 228.

¹⁸ Earl E. Thorpe, 1980? "African Americans and the Sacred: Spirituals, Slave Religion and Symbolism," unpublished paper, quoted in Jon Michael Spencer, "African American Religious Music from a Theomusicological Perspective," in Philip V. Bohlman, Edith L. Blumhoffer, and Maria M. Chow, eds., *Music in American Religious Experience* (New York: Oxford University Press, 2006) 47.

¹⁹ Spencer, "African American Religious Music from a Theomusicological Perspective," 43–56.

²⁰ Samuel A. Floyd, Jr., *The Power of Black Music: Interpreting its History from Africa to the United States* (New York and Oxford: Oxford University Press, 1995) 9.

²¹ "The Jubilee Singers in Calcutta," *The Fisk Herald* 7/6 (February 1890): 3, FU. Frederick Loudin established his own touring company of Jubilee Singers in 1882. See chapter 8 for more details.

²² Paul Allen Anderson, *Deep River: Music and Memory in Harlem Renaissance Thought* (Durham and London: Duke University Press, 2001) 5. Throughout their travels, singing the spirituals kept the Jubilee Singers connected to each other and their people. The spiritual represented a common bond, a shared cultural memory that these young songsters translated into musical sound. Once in a private

Christmas celebration while on the road, the company members spontaneously began to sing an old Christmas carol they had learned as youngsters. "How many happy days that one verse brought to my memory!" sighed Sheppard. "It seems so many years ago. It was though I was sixty years old calling to mind some of early childhood." Though not all knew the words, each Jubilee joined in and improvised a part to create a beautiful whole and a powerfully emotional moment that was felt by everyone in the room. It was, to Sheppard, "one of the happiest evenings we ever had." See Ella Sheppard diary, 6 December 1877, FJS.

[23] Sometimes coded messages called slaves to actions contrary to the master's wishes. According to Thomas Rutling, "Steal Away to Jesus," the signature piece of the Jubilee Singers, functioned as a signal to slaves to cross the Red River into Indian territory where missionaries were holding prayer meetings. Since plantation masters and overseers forbade these meetings, slaves would have to literally "steal away to Jesus." See Rutling, "*Tom*," 20–21.

[24] Jon Michael Spencer, *Protest and Praise: Sacred Music of Black Religion* (Minneapolis: Fortress Press, 1990) 13.

[25] W. E. B. DuBois suggested that "a faith in the ultimate justice of things…that sometime, somewhere, men will judge men by their souls and not by their skins," resonated in each spiritual (*The Souls of Black Folk*, 274).

[26] Spence, "A Character Sketch of George L. White," 4.

[27] Pike, *Singing Campaign for Ten Thousand Pounds*, 3, 4.

[28] Spence, "A Character Sketch of George L. White," 4.

[29] White trained his singers to keep intensity in the core of the sound, regardless of dynamic level. To illustrate this idea, he was known to say: "If a tiger should step behind you, you would not hear the fall of his foot, yet all the strength of the tiger would be in that tread" (Spence, "A Character Sketch of George L. White," 4).

[30] "The Jubilee Singers," *The Tonic-Sol-fa Reporter* (15 May 1873): 153, AMAA.

[31] Spence, "A Character Sketch of George L. White," 4.

[32] Georgia Gordon Taylor, "Reminiscences of Jubilee Singers," *Fisk University News* 2/5 (October 1911): 30, FU.

[33] Cole (Porter), "The Jubilee Singers on the Ocean and in Europe," 34.

[34] Floyd, *The Power of Black Music*, 61.

[35] "The Jubilee Concert," untitled newspaper, ca. December 1871, JSS.

[36] John Sullivan Dwight, "The Fisk Jubilee and Hampton Singers," *Dwight's Journal of Music* (5 April 1873), in *Source Readings in American Choral Music*, compiled by David P. DeVenney. Monographs and Bibliographies in American Music Series, no. 15 (Missoula MT: The College Music Society, 1995) 66.

[37] Mrs. M. F. Armstrong and Helen W. Ludlow, *Hampton and Its Students* (1874; rep., New York: AMS Press Inc., 1971) 128.

[38] Dwight, "The Fisk Jubilee and Hampton Singers," 66.

[39] "The Voice of Ethiopia," *Church Union*, quoted in *American Missionary* (April 1875): 90, AMAA.

[40] "The Jubilee Singers," *Syracuse Journal*, October 1872, JSS.

[41] "The Jubilee Singers," *The Town Crier*, November 1873, JSS.

[42] "The Gentle Shepherd Again," *New York Musical Gazette*, April 1872, JSS. The writer of the *New York Musical Gazette* article responded to this charge with a tongue-in-cheek statement acknowledging the musical ignorance of the many college professors, ministers, and other "educated people" of New Haven who had thoroughly enjoyed the Jubilee Singers. He, like other ardent supporters of the Jubilee Singers, scorned those who failed to appreciate the "true inspiration" of the ensemble and their music.

[43] Ronald Radano, "Denoting Difference: The Writing of the Slave Spirituals," *Critical Inquiry* 22/3 (Spring 196): 508. Radano further writes: "Inscribed as an evanescent difference of formidable power, the songs would subsequently acquire international significance, becoming aural signifiers of late-nineteenth-century Western conceptions of race" (517).

[44] "The Jubilee Singers," *The Newcastle Daily Chronicle*, 11 November 1873, BNL.

[45] Catherine Booth, "Worldly Amusement and Christianity," *Papers on Practical Religion (1879)*. Victorian Women Writers Project: an Electronic Collection, Bloomington, Indiana: Indiana University, 1996, http://www.indiana.edu/`letrs/vwwp/booth/practrel.html (accessed July 26, 2006).

[46] "Music Extraordinary," *Newark Evening Courier*, ca. January 1872, JSS.

[47] Southern, *The Music of Black Americans,* 91.

[48] "The Jubilee Singers," *The Tonic-Sol-fa Reporter* (15 May 1873): 152, AMAA.

[49] "The Jubilee Singers in Brighton," untitled newspaper, 9 March 1874, JSS.

[50] Pike, *Campaign for Twenty Thousand Dollars*, 109.

[51] Untitled newspaper from Dumfries, 20 December 1873, JSS.

[52] "The Jubilee Singers," *The Tonic Sol-fa Reporter* (15 May 1873): 152, AMAA.

[53] White applied this standard to himself. He did not conduct the Jubilees, choosing rather to stand close by offstage or seat himself behind the piano. "During the performance," stated one German critic, "Mr. White had chosen to remain modestly seated behind the piano, as to give the impression that the accomplished Singers did not need a director. This only reinforced the impression of the immediate flowing natural expression of the heart which characterized most of the

songs performed." See "Concert der Jubiläums-Sänger," *Courier (Hannover)*, 6 January 1878, JSS. Translation provided by Christiane Price.

[54] Quote from the *Delaware Gazette* found on a broadside entitled "Praise Service," ca. 1871, JSS.

[55] Quote from the Rev. J. E. Rankin, D. D. of Washington, DC included in "The Jubilee Singers," untitled newspaper, ca. December 1871, JSS; Quote from Dr. William Adams, in "The Jubilee Singers," untitled newspaper, ca. March 1872, JSS.

[56] Untitled Hamburg newspaper, 8 January 1878, JSS.

[57] "Speech of Mr. Seward," *American Missionary* (April 1872): 90, AMAA. Also found in Theodore F. Seward, "Preface to the Music," in Marsh, *The Story of the Jubilee Singers; With Their Songs*, 121–22.

[58] Pike, *Singing Campaign for Ten Thousand Pounds*, 14, 15.

[59] Quote contained in promotional material used to launch the Jubilee Singers' first European campaign, ca. 1873, JSS. Also see Pike, *Campaign for Twenty Thousand Dollars*, 116.

[60] "Amusements. The Jubilee Singers," *Detroit Michigan Tribune*, 21 May 1872, JSS.

[61] "The Jubilee Singers," untitled Connecticut newspaper, February 1872, JSS. Radano reflects on how the Jubilee Singers' presentation of the spiritual was concurrent with the emergence of nationalism and an interest in folk authenticity. While some held that German concert music was representative of the highest cultural expression, others argued that spontaneous folk music was the best expression of "nature's power." See Radano, "Denoting Difference: The Writing of the Slave Spirituals," 515–17.

[62] "Our Native Music—The Jubilee Singers," letter to the editor, *Newark Evening Courier,* 17 January 1872, JSS. Swedish soprano Jenny Lind gained popularity in America through the efforts of P. T. Barnum, who sponsored her American concert tour in 1850 (*Baker's Biographical Dictionary of Musicians*, s.v. "Jenny Lind").

[63] "The Jubilee Singers," *New York Independent,* 4 March 1872, JSS. Swedish soprano Christine Nilsson made her operatic debut in Paris in 1864, then gained worldwide renown for her roles sung in opera houses in London, Vienna, St. Petersburg, and New York (*The New Grove Dictionary of Music and Musicians*, 2nd ed., s.v. "Christine Nilsson"). Euphrosyne Parepa-Rosa, a Scottish soprano with a huge voice, was born in Edinburgh, Scotland in 1836 and made her first American concert tour in 1865, quickly gaining popularity with the American public (*Baker's Biographical Dictionary of Musicians*, s.v. "Euphrosyne Parepa-Rosa"). The reviewer may have been referring to the German operatic tenor Theodor Wachtel, known for his powerful high notes, who made his London debut in 1862 at Covent

Garden (*The New Grove Dictionary of Music and Musicians,* 2nd ed., s.v. "Theodor Wachtel"). English baritone Sir Charles Santley made his USA tour in 1872, joining the Carl Rosa company in 1875 (*The New Grove Dictionary of Music and Musicians,* 2nd ed., s.v. "Sir Charles Santley).

[64] "The Jubilee Singers. Letter to the Editor," *The Union,* ca. March 1872, JSS; "The Jubilee Singers," *Brooklyn Daily Eagle,* December 1871, JSS.

[65] "The Jubilee Singers," *New York Independent,* 4 March 1872, JSS.

[66] "Books and Exchanges—Jubilee Songs," *New York Musical Gazette,* April 1872, JSS.

[67] "The Jubilee Singers," *Tonic-Sol-fa Reporter* (May 1873): 154, AMAA.

[68] "The Jubilee Singers," *The Lancaster Guardian,* 11 December 1875, BNL.

[69] Ella Sheppard diary, 28 August 1876, FJS.

[70] Marsh, *The Story of the Jubilee Singers; With Their Songs,* 86; Ella Sheppard diary, 28 August 1876, FJS.

[71] Marsh, *The Story of the Jubilee Singers; With Their Songs,* 87–89.

[72] G. L. White to E. M. Cravath, ca. 1878, AMAA.

[73] Ella Sheppard diary, 4 November 1877, FJS.

[74] Marsh describes the Sing-Akademie as "a music hall into which nothing but entertainments of high tone and the best character are admitted" (*The Story of the Jubilee Singers; With Their Songs,* 94).

[75] Following the concert, a friend reported to Sheppard details about the important music critics in the audience: "He told us that the critic who wrote such a fine criticism on our first singing at the Sing Academy [*sic*] is *the* authority for Germany musically and that all the finest teachers must pass an examination from him & when they have succeeded with him they are perfect. At the concert...the teacher here in charge of the largest & best ladies school for music arose during the intermission & ran to him to know his opinion which created quite a sensation throughout the hall as she is known to be a fine scholar & his opinion would do much toward our success or failure & her excitement showed satisfaction & great pleasure." See Ella Sheppard diary, 13 November 1877, FJS.

[76] Moore (Sheppard), "Historical Sketch of the Jubilee Singers," 56.

[77] *Vossische (Privilegierte) Zeitung,* ca. 8 November 1877, quoted in "The Jubilee Singers at the Imperial Court of Germany," *The Fisk Expositor* (January 1878): 3, FU. Also in *Berliner Musik-Zeitung,* ca. 1877, JSS, quoted in Marsh, *The Story of the Jubilee Singers; With Their Songs,* 95.

[78] "Die Jubiläumssänger in Berlin," *Leipziger Tageblatt,* 16 November 1877, JSS; Untitled article, *Mainzer Journal,* 19 December 1877, JSS. Translation by Christiane Price.

[79] "Dortmund," *Dortmunder Zeitung,* 30 January 1878, JSS. Translation by Christiane Price.

[80] "Concert der Jubiläumssänger," untitled newspaper, 10 March 1878, JSS; "Mussikalisches," *Unzeiger,* 5 February 1878. Translation by Christiane Price.

[81] "Concert der Jubiläumssänger," *Zwickauer Wochenblatt,* 19 March 1878, JSS. Translation by Christiane Price.

[82] "Die Jubiläums-Sänger," *Morgen-Zeitung,* 18 April 1878, JSS. Translation by Christiane Price.

[83] "Die Jubiläumssänger," *Neuen Preussischen Kreuz-Zeitung,* 14 November 1877, JSS. Translation by Christiane Price.

[84] Taylor (Gordon), "Reminiscences of Jubilee Singers," 29.

[85] Moore (Sheppard), "Historical Sketch of the Jubilee Singers," 56, 57.

[86] "The Jubilee Singers," *American Missionary* (February 1875): 28, AMAA.

[87] Marsh, *The Story of the Jubilee Singers; With Their Songs,* 100.

[88] "Thirty-second Annual Report of the American Missionary Association—1878," 26, 27, AMAA.

Chapter Six

[1] Pike, *Campaign for Twenty Thousand Dollars,* 79.

[2] Eric Foner's *The Story of American Freedom* (New York and London: W. W. Norton & Company, 1998) is an excellent discussion of how the term "freedom" has evolved throughout American history. In particular, see his chapter entitled "A New Birth of Freedom" for various interpretations of freedom during Reconstruction.

[3] From its inception, the AMA affirmed the ideal of full social equality for African Americans. The association appointed black trustees to its institutions, operated integrated schools (when whites could be persuaded to attend), sanctioned dances and other forms of social interaction, and worshipped with African Americans. Several AMA institutions adopted official stances on social equality that infuriated local whites. For example, Berea College had a policy allowing mixed race marriages among its students, and some of the AMA's missionary teachers were interracial couples. While some AMA teachers were cautious about violating Southern racial etiquette, others flagrantly challenged prevailing attitudes in an ongoing effort to secure social rights for African Americans, believing that their actions carried far greater influence than could mere rhetoric. Their deliberate tactics at times received reluctant affirmation from Southern whites. Upon inspection of the Atlanta University faculty, the Georgia State Superintendent of Instruction noted disapprovingly that "although social equality between the races is not taught formally at the college, it is taught by example, in the most effective way." See Richardson, *Christian Reconstruction,* 222–24.

[4] According to Louise Stevenson, African Americans during the Reconstruction era may have entered public life, but they "never entered the parlors

of white Americans as equals." This physical space essential to all middle-class homes served symbolically as the gateway into the private lives of Victorians. Welcome into this room extended graciousness to another and indicated a degree of intimacy that bespoke friendship, commonality, and true acceptance as equals (Stevenson, *The Victorian Homefront*, 97–100). Stevenson's review of the contents of the *Freedmen's Readers* used in schools across the South suggests that even white supporters of freedmen's education never anticipated a fully integrated American society.

[5] Imes (Lewis), "Reminiscences," FJS.

[6] Stevenson, *The Victorian Homefront*, preface to the Cornell Paperbacks Edition, xvii, xviii. Also see the two newspaper cartoons included in this book. Both artist renderings are gross caricatures of the Jubilee Singers in concert.

[7] Mabel Lewis Imes, "Some Hotel Experiences," *Fisk University News* 2/5 (October 1911): 31, FU.

[8] "Fisk Celebrates Jubilee Day," *Fisk News* 5/2 (1931): 3, FU. The incident that so traumatized Porter could have been one of many the company endured. Ella Sheppard describes one early mishap at the train station in "Historical Sketch of the Jubilee Singers," 43. A statement made by the Jubilee Singers in 1880 indicates that the company had lawsuits pending in Tennessee for "assault upon some of the ladies of our company while trying to enter one of the general cars" within the past year ("From the Jubilee Singers," unnamed newspaper, ca. August 1880, JSS). Though Maggie Porter was not traveling with the company at that particular time, trouble with Southern railways seems to have been a problem whenever the company traveled into the South.

[9] Cole (Porter), "Maggie Porter-Cole, interview by Beatty," 5.

[10] Moore (Sheppard), "Historical Sketch of the Jubilee Singers," 46–48.

[11] Cole (Porter), "Maggie Porter-Cole, interview by Beatty," 5.

[12] Imes (Lewis), "Reminiscences," FJS.

[13] Imes (Lewis), "Some Hotel Experiences," 32.

[14] Ella Sheppard diary, 24 January 1874; 3 February 1875; 15 February 1875; 19 February 1875; and 20 February 1875, FJS.

[15] A. W. Robinson to J. D. Burrus, 4 March 1875, ARL.

[16] Hinton D. Alexander, "Reminiscences of Jubilee Singers," *Fisk University News* 2/5 (October 1911): 38, FU.

[17] Pike, *Campaign for Twenty Thousand Dollars*, 132, 133.

[18] "The Jubilee Singers," *American Missionary* (March 1873): 60, 61, AMAA.

[19] Pike, *Campaign for Twenty Thousand Dollars*, 150–51.

[20] Untitled newspaper article, ca. March 1872, JSS.

[21] Pike, *Campaign for Twenty Thousand Dollars*, 126; Moore (Sheppard), "Historical Sketch of the Jubilee Singers," 48.

²² Pike, *Campaign for Twenty Thousand Dollars*, 128–29.
²³ B. M. Holmes to A. K. Spence, 23 November 1871, SFC.
²⁴ Moore (Sheppard), "Historical Sketch of the Jubilee Singers," 50.
²⁵ B. M. Holmes to L. H. Douglass, 14 May 1873, in *New National Era*, 5 June 1873.
²⁶ Pike, *Singing Campaign for Ten Thousand Pounds*, 170–71.
²⁷ Moore (Sheppard), "Historical Sketch of the Jubilee Singers," 50.
²⁸ Pike, *Singing Campaign for Ten Thousand Pounds*, 37, 38. Lady Stanley was one of Queen Victoria's closest friends. They exchanged letters frequently and she was the only person to visit and eat with the Queen during the first trying weeks of her widowhood. The Dean and Lady Stanley were famous for their ability to entertain royalty, politicians, ecclesiastical associates, and others of noteworthy accomplishment (all at the same time) in elaborate dinner parties with a graciousness and ease that became legendary. One of the canons once asked if Lady Stanley's cordial manner was genuine, to which the Duchess of Buccleuch replied, "Yes, it is the echo of her heart." See Albert Victor Baillie and Henry Hector Bolitho, eds., *Later Letters of Lady Augusta Stanley 1864–1876* (London: Jonathan Cape, 1929) 31. It was not unusual for the couple to host over thirty people at meals for several days in a row, members of the royalty mixing with Tennyson or Browning, renowned singers Christine Nilsson or Jenny Lind, or scientists such as Tyndall and Owen.
²⁹ Baillie and Bolitho, *Later Letters of Lady Augusta Stanley*, 173.
³⁰ B. M. Holmes to L. H. Douglass, *New National Era*, 5 June 1873.
³¹ Pike, *Singing Campaign for Ten Thousand Pounds*, 64.
³² B. M. Holmes to L. H. Douglass, *New National Era*, 10 July 1873.
³³ Ibid.
³⁴ MacDonald, *George MacDonald and His Wife*, 442.
³⁵ Pike, *Singing Campaign for Ten Thousand Pounds*, 71–73; Moore (Sheppard), "Historical Sketch of the Jubilee Singers," 51.
³⁶ Pike considered this event as providentially given for the advancement of their mission and spent the day before this appearance in earnest prayer. "To scale the Alpine heights of society needs much of the consecration of a soldier," noted Pike, "and when the business is for Christ's sake, the Holy Ghost must help our infirmities" (*Singing Campaign for Ten Thousand Pounds*, 74, 75).
³⁷ Pike, *Singing Campaign for Ten Thousand Pounds*, 76.
³⁸ "John Brown's Body" was as popular with audiences as were the spirituals. The tune was used by William Steffe as a camp meeting song in the 1850s. An anonymous Civil War soldier added the stanza about John Brown, investing the tune with new meaning for black soldiers who adopted it as their unofficial theme song. Even after Julia Ward Howe wrote the text for "The Battle Hymn of the

Republic" in 1862, African Americans continued to prefer their own version. Graham notes that British audiences considered the song almost comical until they heard the Jubilee Singers' passionate performance (see Graham, "The Fisk Jubilee Singers and the Concert Spiritual," 217–18).

[39] B. M. Holmes to the Editor, *New National Era*, 14 August 1873.

[40] Ibid.

[41] Quoted in Pike, *Singing Campaign for Ten Thousand Pounds*, 77, 78. Also see H. C. G. Matthew, ed., *The Gladstone Diaries* vol. VIII July 1871-December 1874 (Oxford: Clarendon Press, 1982) 362.

[42] Pike, *Singing Campaign for Ten Thousand Pounds*, 78.

[43] B. M. Holmes to Editor, *New National Era*, 14 August 1873. The italics are Holmes's.

[44] Moore (Sheppard), "Historical Sketch of the Jubilee Singers," 51.

[45] Newman Hall to the *New York Independent*, 21 August 1873, quoted in Pike, *Singing Campaign for Ten Thousand Pounds*, 79–82; also quoted in the "Twenty-seventh Annual Report of the American Missionary," 1873, AMAA.

[46] Pike, *Singing Campaign for Ten Thousand Pounds*, 81. Rev. Hall also noted the special significance of this invitation to the Jubilee Singers as guests and not entertainers. Referring to a previous visit to the prime minister's, he said: "But, on that occasion, they came to entertain the guests. Yesterday, they were themselves the guests" (79).

[47] Newman Hall to the *New York Independent*, 21 August 1873, quoted in Pike, *Singing Campaign for Ten Thousand Pounds*, 81. Gladstone invited the Jubilee Singers to another meal when they returned to England in 1875. The Gladstones first sat down at the table with their company, but to the singers' surprise, dismissed the servants and rose to wait on the Jubilees themselves. "Mr. Gladstone explained to us that he and Mrs. Gladstone wanted the honor of serving us to show us how greatly we and our mission were esteemed," recalled Sheppard. "This was a special honor indeed—one that we shall long be proud to remember." Afterwards, the party retired to the drawing room where the ensemble offered to sing a few selections. When Loudin performed "The Standard of the Free," Gladstone stood "like a statue," his eyes brimming with tears. "That song is *thrilling* and will *stir the heart of England*," he enthusiastically told the troupe. Their rendition of "John Brown's Body" evoked a similar response: "No song can equal that one," claimed Gladstone sincerely. His wife added her own heartfelt thanks. "I have prayed God to spare me long enough to hear that song again and now my prayer is answered. I do so thank you." For Sheppard, "those two remarks were worth all the strength and efforts spent to accept their invitation." See Moore (Sheppard), "Historical Sketch of the Jubilee Singers," 51; and Ella Sheppard diary, 6 December 1875, FJS.

[48] Pike, *Singing Campaign for Ten Thousand Pounds*, 86.

[49] J. D. Douglas and Philip W. Comfort, eds., *Who's Who In Christian History* (Wheaton IL: Tyndale House Publishers, Inc., 1992) s.v. "Charles Haddon Spurgeon."

[50] Pike, *Singing Campaign for Ten Thousand Pounds*, 84, 85.

[51] Ibid., 88–89; B. M. Holmes to L. H. Douglass, *New National Era*, 25 September 1873.

[52] Pike, *Singing Campaign for Ten Thousand Pounds*, 98.

[53] I. P. Dickerson to W. E. Whiting, 13 August 1873, AMAA.

[54] Pike, *Singing Campaign for Ten Thousand Pounds*, 137.

[55] Ibid., 138. Dickerson so enjoyed the personal freedom he experienced throughout England and Scotland that he decided to remain behind when the company closed its campaign, accepting the patronage of Dean Stanley to support his education at Edinburgh University for ministerial studies.

[56] "Jubilee Singers at Exeter Hall," *English Independent*, 2 April 1874, JSS.

[57] Taylor (Gordon), "Reminiscences of Jubilee Singers," 29.

[58] Moore (Sheppard), "Historical Sketch of the Jubilee Singers," 54.

[59] A. W. Robinson to J. D. Burrus, 2 June 1875, ARL. Robinson maintained regular correspondence with her boyfriend and Fisk peer, James Burrus, throughout her tenure as a Jubilee Singer. The courtship ended abruptly in 1878 and Robinson remained in Germany to pursue further study before returning to the States. She married Ed Lucas and settled in Macon, Mississippi where both she and her husband pursued careers as educators. For more biographical detail, see Anderson, "The Fisk Jubilee Singers," 238–47.

[60] Moore (Sheppard), "Historical Sketch of the Jubilee Singers," 54.

[61] Cole (Porter), ""The Jubilee Singers on the Ocean and in Europe," 34.

[62] Ella Sheppard diary, 16 June 1875, FJS.

[63] Pike, *Singing Campaign for Ten Thousand Pounds*, 186–87.

[64] Ella Sheppard diary, 25 June 1875, FJS.

[65] Ella Sheppard diary, 1 September 1875, FJS.

[66] Imes (Lewis), "Reminiscences," FJS.

[67] A. W. Robinson to J. D. Burrus, 2 June 1875, ARL.

[68] A. W. Robinson to J. D. Burrus, 24 March 1877, ARL.

[69] A. W. Robinson to J. D. Burrus, 27 March 1877, ARL.

[70] Ella Sheppard diary, 10 June 1876, FJS. Another diary entry records the company's visit with the Gilbert family, which she described as "very pleasant except that we were asked to sing or play about every half hour during the day which not only wearied but made the visits similar to all others." See Ella Sheppard diary, 2 March 1875, FJS.

[71] A. W. Robison to J. D. Burrus, 12 October 1876, ARL.

[72] Ella Sheppard diary, 16 September 1875, FJS.

[73] Ella Sheppard diary, 30 August 1875, FJS.

[74] A. W. Robinson to J. D. Burrus, 16 August 1875, ARL.

[75] Ella Sheppard diary, 29 July 1875 and 30 July 1875, FJS.

[76] A.W. Robinson to J. D. Burrus, 2 August 1874, ARL. "The crowd about devoured us," Sheppard wrote of the Builth citizens who greeted the Jubilee Singers upon their arrival (Ella Sheppard diary, 20 July 1875, FJS).

[77] When Ella Sheppard asked the name of his lake, he replied that it had none and offered her the "privilege of naming it." She suggested "Jubilee Loch," but as "loch" was a highland word and His Lordship was a "lowlander," he changed it to "Jubilee Lake" (Ella Sheppard diary, 4 October 1875, FJS).

[78] Ella Sheppard diary, 4 October 1875, FJS.

[79] Ibid.

[80] Ella Sheppard diary, 12 October 1876, FJS.

[81] Moore (Sheppard), "Historical Sketch of the Jubilee Singers," 55.

[82] A. W. Robinson to J. D. Burrus, n.d. February 1877, ARL; Moore (Sheppard), "Historical Sketch of the Jubilee Singers," 55.

[83] A. W. Robinson to J. D. Burrus, n.d. February 1877, ARL; Alexander, "Reminiscences of Jubilee Singers," 40.

[84] Ella Sheppard diary, 4 November 1877, FJS.

[85] Ella Sheppard diary, 5 November 1877, FJS.

[86] Ella Sheppard diary, 4 November 1877, FJS.

[87] Alexander, "Reminiscences of Jubilee Singers," 40.

[88] Cole (Porter), "The Jubilee Singers on the Ocean and in Europe," 34.

[89] Ella Sheppard diary, 4 November 1877, FJS.

[90] Ibid.

[91] Alexander, "Reminiscences of Jubilee Singers," 38.

[92] James M. Trotter, *Music and Some Highly Musical People* (New York: Charles T. Dillingham, 1881; rep., New York: Johnson Reprint Corporation, 1968) 255.

[93] B. M. Holmes to L. H. Douglass, *New National Era*, 16 August 1873 and 25 September 1873.

[94] The civil rights efforts of Frederick Loudin and Ella Sheppard Moore are discussed in chapter 8. Greene Evans pursued a political life in his efforts to secure rights for African Americans. See Appendix: Brief Biographies of the Jubilee Singers.

[95] Marsh, *The Story of the Jubilee Singers; With Their Songs*, 73.

[96] Untitled article, *The English Independent*, 2 July 1874, BNL.

[97] Rutling, "*Tom*" 18.

[98] Taylor (Gordon), "Reminiscences of Jubilee Singers," 30.

[99] Cole (Porter), "The Jubilee Singers on the Ocean and in Europe," 33, 35.

[100] Cole (Porter), "Maggie Porter Cole, interview by Beatty," 5; A. W. Robinson to J. D. Burrus, 2 July 1875, ARL. Robinson chose to remain in Europe after the company disbanded in 1878. She returned to Strasbourg, Germany and pursued language studies and further musical training.

[101] "Book Notice," *American Missionary* (November 1874): 260, AMAA.

[102] "Twenty-eighth Annual Report of the American Missionary Association—1874," 17, AMAA.

Chaper Seven

[1] G. L. White to E. M. Cravath, 13 December 1873, AMAA.

[2] "Teachers; Their Qualifications and Support," *American Missionary* (July 1866): 152, AMAA. The sixth qualification for prospective missionary teachers was teaching experience. These requirements are discussed in chapter 1.

[3] Signed contract for Margaret A. Carnes (Maggie), November 1874, FJS.

[4] A. W. Robinson to J. D. Burrus, 18 April 1877, ARL.

[5] Sandra Graham, "On the Road to Freedom: The Contracts of the Fisk Jubilee Singers," *American Music* (Spring 2006): 26.

[6] According to Marshall, 510 colleges, both black and white, were founded between 1860–1906. By 1973, approximately 100 years later, 377, or 74%, still existed. A larger percentage of black institutions than non-black institutions survived. See Gloria J. Marshall, "The Survival of Colleges in America: A Census of Four-year Colleges in the United States 1636–1973" (Ph.D. diss., Stanford University, 1995) 84–88.

[7] Shortly after joining the company, Pike wrote to Cravath: "Prof. White is winning golden opinions and I find him a very noble soul & Christian—we are living at peace among ourselves and the blessing of God is upon us" (G. D. Pike to E. M. Cravath, 29 January 1872, AMAA).

[8] Signed contract for Margaret A. Carnes (Maggie), November 1874, FJS.

[9] G. D. Pike to E. M. Cravath, 28 July 1873, AMAA.

[10] G. D. Pike to E. M. Cravath, 20 August 1873, AMAA. "I am sometimes fearful that there is a wrong in holding up to the people the idea that ex slaves are showing great virtue and promise by their sacrifices to endow an institution," Pike explained to Cravath. He was grateful for the "growing disposition on Mr. White's part—to have the young men attend S. S. [Sunday School] meetings—and others" and hoped that some in the troupe might be "encouraged to do missionary work as years advance."

[11] G. D. Pike to E. M. Cravath, 30 September 1873, AMAA.

[12] J. H. Healy to E. M. Cravath, 25 June 1873, AMAA.

[13] G. D. Pike to E. M. Cravath, 24 October 1872, AMAA.

[14] W. Kingsland to G. D. Pike, 12 November 1873, AMAA.

[15] In 1877, a correspondent for the *New York Observer* wrote an article charging the Jubilee Singers with living an extravagant lifestyle of wealth and privilege. George White wrote a rebuttal: "They 'put up,' when possible, at Temperance hotels, where they get good comfortable board at a reasonable price.... Occasionally, through the generosity of friends...they are treated to a ride in a turnout which they could not themselves afford. They never appear in fine carriages with elegant equipage and horses...*at the expense of the enterprise.* As to the 'thoroughly good time' they are having in raising money for the University, I will only state that, during the present year's work, six members of the company and management have been seriously ill from the effects of the fatigue and exposure incident to their concert work, and on June 10th the Singers were all together for a concert for the first time since January." See "Jubilee Singers in England," and White's letter to the editor, untitled newspaper, 12 July 1877, JSS.

[16] G. L. White to E. M. Cravath, 10 September 1873 and 23 September 1873, AMAA.

[17] G. L. White to E. M. Cravath, 29 October 1873, AMAA.

[18] G. L. White to E. M. Cravath, 13 December 1873, AMAA.

[19] G. D. Pike to E. M. Cravath, 1 December 1873, AMAA. Pike did not share White's frustration over the reallocation of funds. "Personally, it is a pleasure to me to know that money sent from Europe can tide you over the hard times instead of pushing up the walls of J. Hall," he told Cravath. See G. D. Pike to E. M. Cravath, 11 December 1873, AMAA.

[20] G. D. Pike to E. M. Cravath, 27 October 1873, AMAA.

[21] G. D. Pike to E. M. Cravath, 11 December 1873, AMAA.

[22] G. D. Pike to E. M. Cravath, 1 December 1873, AMAA.

[23] Ibid.

[24] G. D. Pike to E. M. Cravath, 6 January 1874, AMAA.

[25] G. D. Pike to E. M. Cravath, 6 January 1874, AMAA.

[26] Pike, *Singing Campaign for Ten Thousand Pounds*, 187. "I never heard an immodest word from one of them," he wrote, "or observed an impropriety of deportment in the intercourse between the gentlemen and ladies of the party, during the two years I was associated with them; and this, I think, is as much as could be said of any eleven young people born *out* of slavery. The most of them were careful of their clothing, and saving of money, while their great ambition seemed to be for advancement in their studies. Few, if any of them, were content with their attainments, and I think none of them would knowingly do anything to weaken the confidence of their many thousand generous friends" (187, 188).

[27] Marsh, *The Story of the Jubilee Singers; With Their Songs*, 70, 71; *American Missionary* (April 1874): 84, AMAA; Untitled newspaper, ca. 21 February 1874, JSS.

[28] Elizabeth Spence to A. K. Spence, 7 April 1874, SFC.

[29] Pike, *Campaign for Twenty Thousand Dollars*, 175–177.

[30] Ibid., 196–200.

[31] Ella Sheppard to A. K. Spence, 26 April 1874, SFC.

[32] G. D. Pike to E. M. Cravath, 20 April 1874, AMAA.

[33] James Powell to E. M. Cravath, 15 May 1874, AMAA.

[34] "Troubles of the Jubilee Singers," *New York Times*, 11 May 1874, quoted in Graham, "On the Road to Freedom," 9.

[35] G. D. Pike to E. M. Cravath, 4 May 1874, AMAA.

[36] G. D. Pike to E. M. Cravath, 28 May 1874, AMAA.

[37] G. D. Pike to E. M. Cravath, 5 May 1874 and 28 May 1874, AMAA.

[38] G. D. Pike to E. M. Cravath, 3 June 1874, AMAA.

[39] G. D. Pike to E. M. Cravath, 2 July 1874, AMAA.

[40] G. D. Pike to E. M. Cravath, 8 June 1874, AMAA.

[41] Ibid.

[42] The only Jubilee Singer to receive a college diploma from Fisk University was America Robinson, and she was unable to return for the commencement exercises because of her touring obligations. Of all the Jubilees who traveled abroad between 1873 and 1878, it appears that Minnie Tate, Benjamin Holmes, and Alexander Hinton may have resumed their studies at Fisk (*Fisk University Catalog*, 1874–1875 and 1879, FU). However, none seem to have pursued collegiate-level training. America Robinson, Isaac Dickerson, Thomas Rutling, and Edmund Watkins remained in Europe after the company disbanded. Perhaps they and other company members shared Rutling's view that they were "too old to do the hard study necessary to get a B.A. at Fisk University." See Thomas Rutling, "My Life Since Leaving the Jubilee Singers," *Fisk University News* 2/5 (October 1911): 36, FU. The institution awarded baccalaureate degrees posthumously to the original members at its commencement ceremonies in 1978, 100 years after the ensemble disbanded (see "Honorary Degrees Conferred," an article found in the display case of memorabilia located in Jubilee Hall on the Fisk campus).

[43] Both Dickerson and Rutling often gave speeches at the Jubilee Singers' concerts and other religious services at which the company appeared, such as Sunday schools, prayer meetings, and revivals. Dickerson's speaking experience led in part to his decision to enter into the ministry. See Marsh, *The Story of the Jubilee Singers; With Their Songs*, 68.

[44] G. L. White to E. M. Cravath, 13 October 1874, AMAA.

[45] Ella Sheppard diary, 10 November 1874 and 18 December 1874, FJS. Holmes remained in Nashville and resumed his studies for a while at Fisk University.

[46] G. L. White to E. M. Cravath, 30 November 1874, AMAA.

[47] G. L. White to E. M. Cravath, 27 November 1874, 30 November 1874, and 1 December 1874, AMAA.

[48] G. L. White to E. M. Cravath, 7 December 1874 and 10 December 1874, AMAA.

[49] G. L. White to E. M. Cravath, 13 December 1874; 16 December 1874; and 18 December 1874, AMAA.

[50] G. L. White to E. M. Cravath, 28 December 1874, AMAA. "We are getting a pretty strong feeling in the company now that two or three singers can't control the movement any longer,"White reported confidently.

[51] Ella Sheppard diary, 1 July 1875, FJS.

[52] Ella Sheppard diary, 2 August 1875; 13 August 1875; 18 August 1875, FJS.

[53] Ella Sheppard diary, 27 June 1875 and 2 August 1875, FJS. Theodore Seward, White's musical assistant, had surprised Sheppard by handing over the task of transcribing the spirituals, claiming his hand had given out. He left soon after for a short rest. Robinson told Burrus that Seward suffered from "nervous prostration" and thought he should relinquish his duties as musical director and simply attend to business matters. "He seems to think a change will do him good," she wrote. "I would advise him to rest entirely from any labor whatever." A. W. Robinson to J. D. Burrus, 2 August 1875, ARL.

[54] Ella Sheppard diary, 29 June 1875; 30 June 1875; 2 July 1875; 17 July 1875; 27 July 1875; 30 July 1875; 3 August 1875; and 7 August 1875. Seward returned to the company and remained with them until fall 1876.

[55] "Rev. E. M. Cravath," *American Missionary* (September 1875): 201, AMAA; A. W. Robinson to J. D. Burrus, 31 October 1875, ARL.

[56] Ella Sheppard diary, 27 January 1875; 12 March 1875; 1 July 1875; 30 October 1875; 12 November 1875; 26 February 1876; and 29 February 1876, FJS.

[57] See Ella Sheppard diary entries from 15 December 1875 through 29 February 1876, FJS.

[58] F. J. Loudin to E. M. Cravath, 20 February 1876, quoted in Ward, *Dark Midnight When I Rise*, 310. As manager of his own company, Loudin held to the rule of singing "only five times a week, the rest of the time being necessary for relaxation, in order to enable them to endure the constant strain on their voices" ("The Fisk Jubilee Singers," unnamed Toronto newspaper, ca. November 1880, JSS).

[59] J. Jackson to S. Gilbert, n.d.; M. Porter to S. Gilbert, n.d.; T. Rutling to E. M. Cravath, 24 February 1876, quoted in Ward, *Dark Midnight When I Rise*, 311.

[60] Ward, *Dark Midnight When I Rise*, 312.

[61] Ella Sheppard diary, 6 March 1876, FJS.

[62] Ella Sheppard diary, 12 December 1877, FJS.

[63] Ella Sheppard diary, 8 June 1876, FJS.

[64] A. W. Robinson to J. D. Burrus, 19 August 1876, ARL.

[65] Ibid.

[66] G. L. White to J. H. Halley, n.d., ca. August 1876, JSET; A. W. Robinson to J. D. Burrus, n.d. August 1876 and 19 August 1876, ARL.

[67] Ella Sheppard diary, 11 September 1876, FJS.

[68] Ella Sheppard diary, 11 September 1876, FJS.

[69] Ella Sheppard diary, 28 September 1876, FJS.

[70] Ella Sheppard diary, 29 September 1876, FJS.

[71] Porter's dismissal from the company was for "no other cause than a desire on her part to improve her education," claimed Hodder. "I believe it was of great importance that Maggie should be restored to the work for its sake & for her," he told Cravath, "& I rejoice most heartily that God has answered prayer & put all right again" (M. H. Hodder to E. M. Cravath, 3 October 1876, FJS).

[72] Ella Sheppard diary, 29 September 1876, FJS.

[73] A. W. Robinson to J. D. Burrus, n.d. May 1877, ARL. Robinson had a keen business sense, a fact her boyfriend, James, would soon find out. When he wrote and asked to borrow money for graduate studies, she willingly agreed but was appalled at his suggestion that he pay nine percent interest. "Now about the money, I shall charge you 50 per ct for every dollar I send you!" (A. W. Robinson to J. D. Burrus, 24 May 1877, ARL).

[74] Ella Sheppard diary, 6 November 1877 and 7 November 1877, FJS.

[75] Ella Sheppard diary, 4 February 1878; 5 February 1878; 7 February 1878; 10 February 1878; and 11 February 1878, FJS.

[76] G. L. White to E. M. Cravath, ca. April 1878, AMAA.

[77] G. L. White to E. M. Cravath, 5 April 1878, AMAA.

[78] G. L. White to E. M. Cravath, 6 April 1878, AMAA.

[79] G. L. White to E. M. Cravath, 5 April 1878 and 6 April 1878, AMAA.

[80] Ella Sheppard diary, 23 April 1878, FJS.

[81] Ella Sheppard diary, 24 April 1878, FJS.

[82] Ella Sheppard diary, 26 April 1878 and 28 April 1878, FJS.

[83] G. L. White to E. M. Cravath, 26 April 1878, AMAA. After 1878, White managed an independent troupe also bearing the name of "Jubilee Singers," which was comprised of many of the original members. An accident suffered at Chautauqua in 1880 forced him to leave the group temporarily. See "Prof. Geo. L. White," *The Fisk Expositor* 4/1 (January 1881): 3, FU. White moved in with his in-laws in New York and relinquished control of the musical ensemble to Frederick Loudin in 1882. In 1894, he wrote to Adam Spence: "I should be glad to see the old friends again but I have no desire to ever go back, and probably never shall" (G. L. White to A. K. Spence, 20 September 1894, SFC). White never returned to Fisk. A massive stroke claimed his life on 9 November 1895 at the age of fifty-

eight. "The news of your father's death meant to me the passing of the most ardent spirit I have ever known," a friend wrote to White's daughter, Georgia Laura White. See "Jubilee Day," *Fisk News* 8/1 (November/December 1934): 6, FU. The memorial service at Fisk included several spirituals and short remarks by Ella Sheppard Moore. The faculty expressed sorrow in his passing, noting "that in him the colored people have lost one of their warmest friends, who was instant in pleading their cause at all times and places, and also a great benefactor in that he made their name and their genius for music known in all lands." See "White's Memorial Service," *The Fisk Herald* 15/2 (December 1895): 8, 9, FU.
[84] Ella Sheppard diary, 1 July 1878, FJS.

Chapter 8

[1] "Fisk University and Some of its Graduates," promotional brochure published by Fisk University, ca. 1900, AMAA.
[2] "Fisk University," promotional brochure, ca. 1899, AMAA.
[3] "Fisk University," promotional brochure, ca. 1905, AMAA.
[4] "Fisk University," promotional brochure, ca. 1899, AMAA. Henry Hugh Proctor, an 1891 Fisk graduate who would become the first African-American minister of the First Congregational Church in Atlanta, felt the institution drew the "best youth of the race." He praised his alma mater for holding firm to a "full college course for the training of the leaders of a people. As a result Fisk built up an institution with a spirit that took deeper hold on the talented tenth of the race than any other school." See Henry Hugh Proctor, *Between Black and White: Autobiographical Sketches* (1925; rep., Freeport NY: Books for Libraries Press, 1971) 28.
[5] "Fisk University," promotional brochure, 1905, AMAA.
[6] For more biographical detail on the individuals who participated with the Jubilee Singers, see Anderson, "The Fisk Jubilee Singers," 201–331. Biographies of the singers are also embedded in Andrew Ward's work, *Dark Midnight When I Rise*.
[7] Stephanie Shaw's research shows how the educational process for black females fostered an orientation toward achievement. Strong family and community support for aspiring black women created psychologically and intellectually independent females while also developing a sense of mutual obligation between them, an ethic she terms "socially responsible individualism." See Stephanie J. Shaw, *What a Woman Ought to Be and to Do: Black Professional Women Workers During the Jim Crow Era* (Chicago and London: University of Chicago Press, 1996). Fisk University's leadership development rhetoric illustrates a similar ethic applied to both females and males.
[8] Historical accounts disagree on the year of Loudin's birth, ranging from 1836 to 1847. Doug Seroff's research suggests the most convincing date is 1846.

See Doug Seroff, "A Voice in the Wilderness: The Fisk Jubilee Singers' Civil Rights Tours of 1879–1882," *Popular Music & Society* 25 Part 1/2 (2001): 135. For other biographical accounts, see "A Man of Strong Friendship," *Ravenna Republican*, 10 November 1904, Portage County Historical Society and "Notes on the Life of Frederick J. Loudin by his niece Leota Henson Turner," Portage County Historical Notes, Reed Memorial Library.

⁹ Mary Folger, "Frederick Loudin: one of Ravenna's most illustrious citizens," *Record Courier*, 3 November 1871, Portage County Historical Society; "An Interview with Mr. Loudin," *The Fisk Herald* 4/2 (October 1886): 3, FU; Marsh, *The Story of the Jubilee Singers; With Their Songs*, 1883 edition, 112–13.

¹⁰ "An Interview with Mr. Loudin," *The Fisk Herald* 4/2 (October 1886): 3, FU. The Lucases were a black singing family who often performed alongside the white singing family troupe, the Hutchinsons, at abolition conventions.

¹¹ "A Man of Strong Friendship," *The Ravenna Republican*, 10 November 1904, Portage County Historical Society. See also Norman C. Stikes, Sr., "Frederick Loudin…A Man For All Times," photocopy of undated essay, Reed Memorial Library. Loudin told how he was refused choir membership to a minister in Scotland who replied, "If he comes here we will take him into our's, and be glad to get him" (see "The Jubilee Singers in Crieff," *Strathearn Herald*, 21 October 1876, JSS).

¹² "An Interview with Mr. Loudin," *The Fisk Herald* 4/2 (October 1886): 3, FU; "A Man of Strong Friendship," *Ravenna Republican*, 10 November 1904, Portage County Historical Society.

¹³ G. L. White to E. M. Cravath, 16 December 1874, AMAA.

¹⁴ "An Interview with Mr. Loudin," *The Fisk Herald* 4/2 (October 1886): 3, FU.

¹⁵ Ella Sheppard diary, 16 November 1874, FJS.

¹⁶ Unknown to Fred, 18 December 1874, SFC. Ella Sheppard confided to her diary: "He [Loudin] sang this evening in the sitting room—his name should be Mr. Loud-man, has a wonderful voice" (16 November 1874, FJS).

¹⁷ "An Interview with Mr. Loudin," *The Fisk Herald* 4/2 (October 1886): 3, FU.

¹⁸ *The Eastbourne Standard*, 9 September 1876, JSS.

¹⁹ "Reports from England," *American Missionary* (August 1875): 177, AMAA.

²⁰ "The Jubilee Singers at the Imperial Court of Germany," *The Fisk Expositor* (January 1878), FU.

²¹ "The Jubilee Singers at the Music Hall," *The Daily Review*, 31 October 1876, JSS; "The Jubilee Singers," *Ballymena Observer*, 9 December 1876, JSS; "The Jubilee Singers," *The Newry Reporter*, 14 December 1876, JSS.

[22] "The Jubilee Singers," *Western Times,* 20 August 1875, JSS; "The Jubilee Singers," *Sunderland Daily Echo,* 21 December 1875, JSS; "The Jubilee Singers," *The Lancaster Guardian,* 11 December 1875, JSS. Loudin's delivery of "The Standard of the Free," a patriotic ballad composed especially for him, almost always earned an encore and special notice by the critics. The ballad condemned the Admiralty Circular, an order demanding the return of fugitive slaves to their masters, and commemorated how Britons had responded to the order with active opposition.

[23] "An Interview with Mr. Loudin," *The Fisk Herald* 4/2 (October 1886): 3, FU.

[24] Loudin sometimes downplayed his speaking abilities. He opened a speech given at the Chatauqua conference of 1880 by saying: "Were I accustomed to speak and possessed of a tongue far more eloquent than that I am possessed of, and with an ability to speak even equal to the one who has just taken his seat, I think all this would fail me to express a tithe of what I feel and have felt since I have been privileged to visit Chautauqua.... I feel I can sing well and do one thing well, I am quite content with that and I always feel, every time people ask me to say something, that I may do it, or attempt to do it, and fail, and thus throw somewhat of a blur upon what I hope and attempt to do in the way of singing" ("After Service," *Assembly Herald,* 11 August 1880, JSS).

[25] *The Conservator* (Chicago), 30 April 1881, JSS.

[26] A. W. Robinson to J. D. Burrus, 24 March 1877, ARL.

[27] For a detailed chronology of these tours, see Seroff, "A Voice in the Wilderness: The Fisk Jubilee Singers' Civil Rights Tours of 1879–1882." During these touring years, Loudin frequently addressed audiences and authored articles protesting America's discriminatory practices that violated the Civil Rights Acts of 1875.

[28] *Chautauqua Farmer,* 29 September 1880, JSS; *The Fredonia Advertiser,* 1 October 1880, JSS; *Daily Journal,* Ithaca NY, 22 March 1881, JSS.

[29] In 1879, Loudin was a delegate to the National Conference of Colored Men of the United States held in Nashville. These state and national conventions became significant events primarily because so many distinguished African-American leaders attended, thereby providing a powerful collective voice for the race. The meeting's proceedings indicate that the conference body hoped to test the effectiveness of the Civil Rights Bill by prosecuting a case brought by the Jubilee Singers. Loudin was appointed a member of the prosecuting committee. See *Proceedings of the National Conference of Colored Men of the United States Held in the State Capitol at Nashville, Tennessee, May 6–9, 1879,* Afro-American History Series, ed. Maxwell Whiteman, no. 231 (Washington, DC: Rufus H. Darby, Steam Power Printer, 1879) 40–41. August Meier called the convention movement the "most

representative vehicle of thought among the articulate masses" during the Reconstruction period. See August Meier, *Negro Thought in America, 1880–1915* (Ann Arbor: University of Michigan Press, 1969) 4.

[30] *Assembly Herald,* 11 August 1880, JSS; Untitled article, 2 September 1880, JSS.

[31] C. C. Painter, financial agent of Fisk University, traveled with the troupe during White's absence. See Seroff, "A Voice in the Wilderness," 154.

[32] "The Jubilees," *The New York Evangelist,* ca. October 1880, JSS.

[33] "Garfield and the Freedmen," *New York Daily Tribune,* 4 October 1880, quoted in Seroff, "A Voice in the Wilderness," 155.

[34] *Fredonia Censor,* 28 September 1881, quoted in Seroff, "A Voice in the Wilderness," 166, 167.

[35] "Notes. The Fisk Singers. Special Dispatch to The Chicago Tribune," untitled newspaper, 29 April 1881, JSS.

[36] "Chicago's Condemnation," untitled Chicago newspaper, 29 April 1881, JSS. Also see "The Jubilee Singers and the Hotels," *The Inter Ocean,* 30 April 1881; "They are 'Niggers,'" *The Chicago Tribune,* 29 April 1881; "A Dastard Disgrace," untitled newspaper, 29 April 1881; "Music and the Drama," *The Times: Chicago,* 30 April 1881, JSS.

[37] F. J. Loudin, "Supplement," in J. B. T. Marsh, *The Story of the Jubilee Singers by J. B. T. Marsh, with Supplement Containing an Account of the Six Year's Tour around the World, and Many New Songs, by F. J. Loudin* (Cleveland: The Cleveland Printing and Publishing Co., 1892) 123.

[38] Ibid., 124. The first leg of the new company's journey was through England, where their novice booking agent had scheduled concerts in the South rather than the North and hot weather made it too warm for indoor entertainment. Audiences were slim and by the end of the season, Loudin was several thousand dollars in debt. The troupe took six weeks of vacation and revised their strategy for the upcoming season. During this time, a former agent approached some of Loudin's singers about forming their own company called "The Original Fisk Jubilee Singers," luring them with the promise of higher salaries. It appears as if Maggie Porter left the company around this time. In 1884, she married tenor Daniel Cole and the two formed their own company of singers also bearing the name "Fisk Jubilee Singers" under the management of Charles Mumford. The troupe toured the United States and Canada throughout the late 1880s and early 1890s, and appeared in Sweden in 1895. See "Personals," *The Fisk Herald* 2/2 (October 1884) FU; Rainer E. Lotz, "The Black Troubadours: Black Entertainers in Europe, 1896–1915," *Black Music Research Journal* 10/2 (Fall 1990): 253; personal correspondence with Doug Seroff, January 1998.

[39] "An Interview with Mr. Loudin," *The Fisk Herald* 4/2 (October 1886): 3, FU. The singer to whom he refers was Patti J. Malone, soprano, who joined the original Jubilee Singers in 1877 to replace the ailing Jennie Jackson. Malone remained with White's troupe of Jubilee Singers in 1878, and then with Loudin's troupe until her death in 1897. See Frederick J. Loudin, "One of the World Renowned Singers of the Race Gone," *The Fisk Herald* 14/5 (March 1897): 5, FU.

[40] F. J. Loudin to Mr. Bruce, 29 April 1900, in *Apropos of Africa: Sentiments of Negro American Leaders on Africa from the 1800s to the 1950s*, compiled and edited by Adelaide Cromwell Hill and Martin Kilson (London: Frank Cass & Co. Ltd., 1969) 125.

[41] "A Man of Strong Friendships," *The Ravenna Republican*, 10 November 1904, Portage County Library. Dr. E. E. Whittaker, the officiating minister at Loudin's funeral, stated: "Not many managers find it convenient to conduct worship with their company in the morning, but I am told that this was Mr. Loudin's custom. Many of us here who are living a less public life than he know what it means to keep a time in the morning for prayer."

[42] "An Interview with Mr. Loudin," *The Fisk Herald* (October 1886): 3, FU.

[43] Loudin, "Supplement," 130–32.

[44] "Gift of the Bell," *The Fisk Expositor* 3/2 (June 1880): 3, FU.

[45] Fisk University also kept its student body informed of Loudin's travels, frequently publishing accounts of his troupe's success in its world travels. For example, see "The Fisk Jubilee Singers," *The Fisk Herald* 5/4 (December 1887) FU; "The Jubilee Singers," *The Fisk Herald* 6/9 (May 1889) FU; "The Jubilee Singers in Calcutta," *The Fisk Herald* 7/6 (February 1890) FU.

[46] Loudin's troupe consisted of sopranos Mattie Lawrence (prima donna soloist), Belle Gibbons, Maggie Carnes, and Pattie Malone; contraltos Georgie Gibbons and Maggie E. Wilson; tenors R. B. Williams and John T. Lane; bassos Loudin and Orpheus M. McAdoo; and pianist Leota Henson (Loudin's niece). See Lynn Abbott and Doug Seroff, *Out of Sight: The Rise of African American Popular Music 1889–1895* (Jackson: University Press of Mississippi, 2002) 4.

[47] Leota Henson quoted in Mary Folger, "Frederick Loudin: One of Ravenna's Most Illustrious Citizens," *Record Courier*, 3 November 1871, Portage County Historical Society.

[48] *Melbourne Daily Telegraph*, 8 June 1886, and *Christian World*, 11 June 1886, quoted in Abbott and Seroff, *Out of Sight*, 5, 6.

[49] Loudin, "Supplement," 140; "Personals," *The Fisk Herald* 4/4 (December 1886) FU.

[50] Loudin, "Supplement," 141.

[51] Ibid., 141, 142; *Detroit Plaindealer*, 20 July 1888; *Wairarapa Standard*, 21 February 1877; and *Wanganni Chronicle*, 31 April 1889, quoted in Abbott and

Seroff, *Out of Sight*, 7, 12, 13. The Maoris' response of kinship with the Jubilee Singers led Loudin to reflect on the role of music in missionary work. "I could see that my theory was confirmed that missionaries to the heathen could make more progress if they made more use of music and singing," he stated. See "The Fisk Jubilee Singers," *The Fisk Herald* 5/4 (December 1887): 2, FU.

[52] *L'Entre Act*, 12 March 1887, quoted in Abbott and Seroff, *Out of Sight*, 8.

[53] Loudin, "Supplement," 144–46.

[54] Henrietta Matson joined the Fisk faculty in 1870 and was a religious force at the university. She was a devoted champion of Adam Spence and considered the AMA's decision to replace him as president with Erastus Cravath as evidence that the "evil one had triumphed" (A. K. Spence to Elizabeth Spence, 3 April 1872, SFC). After seventeen years at Fisk, she went to Burma as a missionary (Ward, *Dark Midnight When I Rise,* 392).

[55] Loudin, "Supplement," 143–53. Loudin's niece, Leota Henson, wrote a series of articles describing their travels that were published in the *Cleveland Gazette*. See "Through India," 28 November 1896, 5 December 1896, 12 December 1896, Portage County Historical Society, courtesy of Doug Seroff.

[56] Loudin, "Supplement," 153.

[57] "Personals," *The Fisk Herald* 10/9 (August 1892) FU; "Notes on the life of Frederick J. Loudin by his niece Leota Henson Turner," Portage County Historical Notes, Reed Memorial Library; Norman C. Stikes, Sr., "Frederick Loudin…A Man for All Times," Reed Memorial Library. Loudin's house still stands on the corner of Walnut and Riddle streets in Ravenna, Ohio.

[58] Mary Folger, "Frederick Loudin: one of Ravenna's most illustrious citizens," *Record Courier*, 3 November 1871, Portage County Historical Society.

[59] *The Detroit Plaindealer*, 11 March 1892, quoted in Lynn Abbott and Doug Seroff, "100 Years from Today: A Survey of African-American Music in 1892 and 1893 as recorded in the Black Community Press," *78 Quarterly* 9: 107.

[60] *The Detroit Plaindealer*, 7 October 1892 and 2 December 1892, quoted in Abbott and Seroff, "100 Years from Today," 112, 113. Also see Loudin, "Supplement," 153.

[61] Mary Folger, "Frederick Loudin: one of Ravenna's most illustrious citizens," *Record Courier*, 3 November 1871, Portage County Historical Society. Folger reports that Loudin patented "a fastener for meeting rails of window sashes and another for a key fastener."

[62] Doug Seroff and Lynn Abbott, "Black Music in the White City (African-Americans at the 1893 World's Columbian Exposition)," *78 Quarterly* 1/9: 51; Ida B. Wells, *Crusade for Justice: The Autobiography of Ida B. Wells*, ed. Afreda M. Duster. Negro American Biographies and Autobiographies Series, ed. John Hope Franklin (Chicago and London: University of Chicago Press, 1972) 115–17.

[63] "No 'Nigger Day,' No 'Nigger Pamphlet,'" *The Freeman* (Indianapolis, Indiana), 25 March 1893.

[64] Wells, *Crusade for Justice,* 117.

[65] "Notes on the life of Frederick J. Loudin by his niece," Portage County Historical Society.

[66] "A Man of Strong Friendship," *Ravenna Republican,* 10 November 1904.

[67] "One of the World Renowned Singers of the Race Gone," *The Fisk Herald* (March 1897) FU; "A Man of Strong Friendship," *The Ravenna Republican,* 10 November 1904.

[68] The details of Ella Sheppard's ancestry and early childhood are culled from the following sources: Moore (Sheppard), "Historical Sketch of the Jubilee Singers"; Unsigned, handwritten document in the Ella Sheppard file, February 1934, FJS; Rosa Sheppard Caldwell, untitled manuscript, n.d., SFC; Ella Sheppard Moore, "Negro Womanhood: Its Past" (New York: American Missionary Association, undated) AMAA; Moore (Sheppard), "Before Emancipation," AMAA; Genealogical information courtesy of Marsha A. Mullin, curator of The Hermitage; Pike, *Campaign for Twenty Thousand Dollars,* 49–53; Marsh, *The Story of the Jubilee Singers; With Their Songs,* 104, 105; "Leaders of Afro-American Nashville: Ella Sheppard (Moore) 1851–1914," in unpublished bound collection courtesy of Beth Howse, Fisk University Special Collections.

[69] Moore (Sheppard), "Historical Sketch of the Jubilee Singers," 4.

[70] Clayton, *History of Davidson County,* 72, 73.

[71] According to Lovett, Nashville's elite whites sometimes allowed their slaves to earn an income with which to purchase their own freedom and/or that of their spouses or children. Nashville's population in 1950 included 5.9 percent free blacks, representing more than 20 percent of the city's African-American population. See Bobby L. Lovett, *The African-American History of Nashville, Tennessee, 1780–1930* (Fayetteville: University of Arkansas Press, 1999) 7, 15.

[72] Ella Sheppard Moore, "Negro Womanhood: Its Past" (New York: American Missionary Association, undated) 4, AMAA. Lovett discusses how the harsh conditions of frontier life resulted in a separation of the races that "seemed more invisible than visible, more metaphysical than physical, and more psychological than social." The "task system" characteristic of Nashville's plantation life, wherein each person completed assigned daily tasks, fostered a "family" atmosphere and also granted certain slaves greater independence (Lovett, *The African-American History of Nashville,* 7). Friendly relationships, albeit complex and peculiar, sometimes developed between slaves and their owners.

[73] John W. Blassingame, *The Slave Community: Plantation Life in the Antebellum South* (New York: Oxford University Press, 1972) 85–89.

[74] Moore (Sheppard), "Negro Womanhood: Its Past," 4, 5.

[75] B. A. Botkin, ed., *Lay My Burden Down: A Folk History of Slavery* (Chicago: University of Chicago Press, 1945) 54.

[76] Moore (Sheppard), "Negro Womanhood," 5.

[77] Moore (Sheppard), "Before Emancipation", 2, AMAA; Pike, *Campaign for Twenty Thousand Dollars*, 50.

[78] Moore (Sheppard), "Before Emancipation," 2. The prophetic element of this story tends to place it in the category of family folklore. Nonetheless, Sheppard's retelling and inclusion of it in printed form indicates that she heard and received it as a factual part of her life history. Another version of this event is found in Work, *Folk Song of the American Negro*, 78–82. Work's account of Ella's childhood was informed through his friendship with the Sheppard family. In it, Mammy Viney reached up, took an imaginary scroll, unrolled it, and read: "God's got a great work for dis baby to do; she's goin' to stand befo' kings and queens. Don't do it, honey" (80). Work also claimed that the well-known spirituals "Swing Low, Sweet Chariot" and "Before I'd be a Slave" had their origin in this experience of Sarah Hannah Sheppard's and evolved through oral transmission over time into their present forms. Another possible explanation for the origin of "Swing Low, Sweet Chariot" is found in Maud Cuny-Hare, "The Source," *Musical America* (September 1930): 2.

[79] There was no legal protection for a slave family as they were a nonentity in the law. Descendants of slaves were in bondage for life and masters could separate family members at will. See Mary Frances Berry and John W. Blassingame, *Long Memory: The Black Experience in America* (New York and Oxford: Oxford University Press, 1982) 8.

[80] John Wesley Work claimed that life for a slave was better in Tennessee than in any other state in the South, with the possible exception of Virginia. He wrote, "To be sold 'South' was, to the slave, to make the journey from which no traveler ever returned" (*Folk Song of the American Negro*, 80).

[81] Moore (Sheppard), "Before Emancipation," 2, 3.

[82] Moore (Sheppard), "Negro Womanhood," 4. Ten years passed before Sarah Hannah Sheppard saw her daughter again. After the Civil War, Sarah remained in Mississippi but never gave up hope that she would see Ella's face once again. Her hope, according to Ella Sheppard, was nurtured by Ella's grandfather, who claimed that "the Lord had promised him that she would be free and that she should yet join her daughter, and spend her last days under her own vine and fig tree" ("Before Emancipation," 4).

[83] Moore (Sheppard), "Before Emancipation," 7, 8.

[84] Lovett, *The African-American History of Nashville, Tennessee*, 36.

[85] Marsh, *The Story of the Jubilee Singers; With Their Songs*, 103–105.

[86] Pike, *Campaign for Twenty Thousand Dollars,* 51. According to Carter G. Woodson, Cincinnati's African-American community prior to the Civil War benefitted from a relatively peaceful relationship with local whites that enabled the rise of African-American businesses, educational institutions, and churches. By 1844, African Americans had established six schools, and elementary education was supplemented in the Sunday schools of many black churches. White philanthropy helped support two private high schools, the most successful being Gilmore High School, which attracted African Americans across the country. See Carter G. Woodson, "The Negroes of Cincinnati prior to the Civil War," in Lacy Shaw, *Not a Slave! Free People of Color in Antebellum America, 1790–1860* (New York: American Heritage Custom Publishing Group, 1995) 61–75.

[87] Pike, *Campaign for Twenty Thousand Dollars,* 51–53; "Struggles and Victories of Mrs. Ella Sheppard Moore," article found in an unpublished bound collection compiled by Beth Howse, FU.

[88] Wilberforce University opened in October 1856 but had to close its doors three months before the Emancipation Proclamation due to fiscal restraints. Daniel A. Payne, one of four African Americans serving on the original board of trustees, agreed to take charge of the institution in March 1863 in exchange for assuming the school's $10,000 debt. The doors reopened in summer 1863 with Payne at the helm, thus giving him the distinction of being the nation's first African-American college president.

[89] Rosa Sheppard Caldwell, untitled manuscript, n.d., SFC; Moore, "Negro Womanhood," 5. The facts regarding this time of Ella Sheppard's childhood do not concur. In Pike's version, Major Sheppard's family returned to Nashville for a visit, giving Ella the opportunity to see her mother briefly when she was five or six years old. Sarah Hannah got permission to see her daughter, but the second separation was so emotionally traumatic that her master vowed to never let her see Ella again. Sheppard's own account of her childhood disagrees with Pike's. "I never saw her again until after freedom, when a girl of fifteen I found her," states Moore (Sheppard) in "Negro Womanhood," 5.

[90] Ward, *Dark Midnight When I Rise,* 72.

[91] Pike, *Campaign for Twenty Thousand Dollars,* 52.

[92] Moore (Sheppard), "Historical Sketch of the Jubilee Singers," 41, 42.

[93] The *1869–1870 Fisk University Catalog* lists Sheppard as a Teacher of Instrumental Music (FU).

[94] "The Cantata of Esther," *Tennessee Tribune,* ca. 1871, JSS.

[95] "The Jubilee Singers," untitled newspaper, ca. 1872, JSS.

[96] Barbara Welter lists piety, purity, submission, and domesticity as the four cardinal virtues of "true womanhood." See "The Cult of True Womanhood: 1820–1860," *American Quarterly* 18/2 (Summer 1966): 151.

[97] Ella Sheppard to A. K. Spence, 21 October 1871, SFC.

[98] Ella Sheppard to A. K. Spence, 12 November 1871, SFC. Sheppard's candid letters to Adam Spence indicate that she did not share White's misgivings about Fisk's principal. Rather, she appreciated both men for their different strengths, and each was a strong father figure to whom she turned for guidance. The family atmosphere of Fisk University endeared the institution to Sheppard, perhaps filling the void in her life left by the death of her father and separation from her mother. Touring with the Jubilee Singers provided her with a sense of belonging and meaningful work.

[99] Ella Sheppard diary, 6 December 1877, FJS.

[100] Ella Sheppard to A. K. Spence, 12 February 1872, SFC.

[101] Ella Sheppard diary, 22 June 1875, FJS.

[102] Ella Sheppard diary, 7 November 1875, FJS.

[103] Dorsett, *A Passion for Souls,* 193, 194.

[104] Ella Sheppard diary, 11 July 1875, FJS.

[105] Ella Sheppard diary, 5 September 1875 and 11 October 1875, FJS.

[106] Ella Sheppard diary, 19 September 1875, FJS.

[107] Ella Sheppard diary, 16 October 1875; 7 November 1875; and 2 April 1876, FJS.

[108] Sheppard did not allow her timidity to keep her from extending graciousness. A story told by Amanda Smith, an African-American evangelist, sheds some light on how she put this virtue into action. Smith was a Christian singer the Jubilees most likely met while holding concerts at Boston's Music Hall in early 1872. At White's invitation, she performed a few numbers with them in their evening concert. At the close of the campaign, the singers returned to Nashville where Ella met Miss Smith by chance when she was in town for General Conference. Smith stated that she was snubbed by other prominent Christian women attending the conference, but welcomed with sincere joy when she happened to meet Ella Sheppard. Though Smith recognized Sheppard's smiling face, she could not recall her name. Sheppard, however, knew her immediately: "I'm so glad to see you. We just got home a few days ago, and we were talking about you last night; we were all in the parlor having a little sing, and we were speaking of the piece you sang with us in Music Hall, Boston." Amanda Smith realized with whom she was speaking and was grateful that someone in town had finally spoken to her. Ella invited her to the singers' performance scheduled for the evening conference meeting. When Smith arrived, Ella pointed her out to White, who asked her to join them onstage to repeat the selection they had performed together in Boston. Those at the conference who had previously slighted her were "surprised and astonished" at her singing and afterwards issued invitations to come to their churches. Smith credited Sheppard's kindness as initiating an event that

proved to be a turning point in her ministry. See Amanda Smith, "An Autobiography: The Story of the Lord's Dealings with Mrs. Amanda Smith, the Colored Evangelist," New York: The Digital Schomburg, The New York Public Library. File number 1997wwwm97264.sgm.1997, *http://digilib.nypl.org/dynaweb/digs/wwm9726* (accessed April 25, 2002).

[109] Ella Sheppard diary, 11 April 1876, FJS.

[110] Ella Sheppard diary, 12 June 1876, FJS.

[111] Ella Sheppard diary, 7 December 1877, FJS.

[112] Ella Sheppard diary, 24 November 1877, 8 January 1878, 10 January 1878, 14 January 1878, and 22 April 1878, FJS. Because of Sheppard's recurring illnesses, White engaged Mrs. Swart as assistant musical director during the last campaign year.

[113] Ella Sheppard diary, 8 January 1878 and 13 February 1878, FJS.

[114] Ella Sheppard diary, 7 November 1877, FJS. Also see Ella Sheppard diary, 21 November 1877, FJS.

[115] Ella Sheppard diary, 7 November 1877, FJS.

[116] Ella Sheppard diary, 25 January 1878, FJS.

[117] Ella Sheppard diary, 16 July 1878, FJS.

[118] George W. Moore, "Bondage and Freedom—The Story of a Life," publication by the 1987 Nashville Conference on Afro-American Culture and History, provided courtesy of Beth Howse, FU. Also see "Fisk University and Some of Its Graduates," ca. 1900, 8, AMAA.

[119] G. W. Moore to M. E. Strieby, 4 April 1876, AMAA.

[120] G. W. Moore to M. E. Strieby, 14 May 1877, AMAA.

[121] G. W. Moore to M. E. Strieby, 6 April 1878, AMAA.

[122] G. W. Moore to M. E. Strieby, 4 November 1878, AMAA.

[123] George W. Moore, "Bondage and Freedom—The Story of a Life," FU; Frank Lincoln Mather, ed., *Who's Who of the Colored Race: A General Biographical Dictionary of Men and Women of African Descent* (1915, rep., Detroit: Gale Research, 1976) 196; Alumni Register of Fisk University for Period 1875–1921, in *Fisk University News* 11/7 (April 1922): 67, FU.

[124] Moore, "Bondage and Freedom—The Story of a Life," 4, FU.

[125] Wedding invitation for Ella Sheppard and G. W. Moore, FJS.

[126] George Moore regularly reported the religious progress at Lincoln Memorial Church in the *American Missionary*. In January 1888, he wrote: "We have succeeded in closing two saloons near our church, and are hopeful of closing another notorious den about a square away" ("Religious Interest at Lincoln Memorial Church, Washington, DC, *American Missionary*, January 1888, 7, AMAA).

[127] Geo. W. Moore, "Christian Endeavorers in the A.M.A. Churches and Schools," *American Missionary* 54/4 (October 1900): 175–76, AMAA; "Hell's Bottom Liquor Traffic," *The Washington Bee*, 3 September 1892.

[128] "Dedication of Lincoln Memorial Church," *The Washington Bee*, 8 January 1887.

[129] Robert L. Hall, "Dedication to Industry, the Useful Arts and Christian Education: A Brief History of Lincoln Congregational Temple—United Church of Christ, 1868–1960." Paper presented at the Twelfth Annual Conference on Washington, DC, 22 February 1985, Moorland-Spingarn Research Center (vertical file: Washington Churches—Lincoln Memorial Congregational Temple).

[130] Frederick D. Wilkinson, ed. *Directory of Graduates: Howard University, 1870–1963* (Washington: the University, 1965) xxii. Courtesy of Moorland-Spingarn Research Center.

[131] "Personals," *The Fisk Herald* 1/3 (October 1883) and 1/4 (November 1883) FU; "Exchanges," *The Fisk Herald* (July 1885) FU; Crosthwaite, "A Résumé," 7. Shortly before her death, Sarah Elizabeth said to her father, "Papa, I want to be a missionary to preach to the people that do not know that the Lord sees us every day" (see unsigned letter from George W. Moore to AMA offices, ca. 1893, FJS).

[132] Vivian Ovelton Sammons, *Blacks in Science and Medicine* (New York: Hemisphere Publishing, 1990) 175; Mather, ed. *Who's Who of the Colored Race*, '196; "Alumni Register," *Fisk University News* 12/7 (April 1922): 82, 91, FU.

[133] S. H. Sheppard to "My Dear Daughter," 10 May 1875, AMAA; S. H. Sheppard to W. E. Whiting, 10 April 1876, AMAA; *Fisk University Catalog* 1876–1877 and 1883–1884, FU; "Struggles and Victories of Mrs. Ella Sheppard Moore," article found in an unpublished bound collection compiled by Beth Howse, FU.

[134] Fisk University awarded a baccalaureate degree posthumously to Ella Sheppard Moore at its commencement ceremonies of 1978.

[135] Mrs. G. W. Moore, "Needs of the Colored Women and Girls," *American Missionary* (January 1889): 22–25, AMAA.

[136] "Rev. Geo. W. Moore" and "Church Work," *American Missionary* (November 1892): 356–75, 364, AMAA.

[137] See the following for just a few examples of Ella Sheppard Moore's work for the AMA and Fisk University: "The South Anniversary Exercises," *American Missionary* (August 1893): 245, AMAA; "Forty-Seventh Annual Meeting of the American Missionary Association," *American Missionary* (December 1893): 379, 381, AMAA; "Personals," *The Fisk Herald* 10/4 (December 1892) FU; and *The Fisk Herald* 15/4 (November 1896) FU.

[138] *Detroit Plaindealer*, 31 October 1890, in Lynn Abbott, Ray Funk, and Doug Seroff, "100 Years From Today: A Survey of Afro-American Music in 1890

as Recorded in the Black Community Press," 78 *Quarterly* 6, 60. Seroff also writes: "A cardboard placard exists in the Fisk Special Collections which pictures 'The Jubilee Singers of 1896,' apparently organized to sing at an AMA Conference in Boston in October of that year." Ella and George Moore are photographed with the group, which remained on tour until around March 1897 (correspondence with Doug Seroff, 10 January 1998). Also see *The Washington Bee*, 8 October 1887; "The Jubilee Singers Home Again," *Fisk Herald* 8/10 (June 1891) FU.

[139] Prof. Thomas W. Talley, "Appreciation of Mrs. Ella Sheppard Moore by a Fellow Student," *Fisk University News* (1914): 11, FU.

[140] Information courtesy of Doug Seroff.

[141] "Musical Notes," *The Fisk Herald* 19/3 (January 1902) FU.

[142] "Prince Henry of Prussia, in Nashville," *The Fisk Herald* (April 1902) FU. This story is related by Doug Seroff in the booklet "Gospel Arts Day: A Special Commemoration," June 19, 1988. The booklet was provided courtesy of Doug Seroff.

[143] "Personals," *The Fisk Herald* 11/1 (September 1893) FU; "Local," *The Fisk Herald* 15/8 (May 1898) FU; "Commencement Week at Fisk University," *The Fisk Herald* 1/1 (June 1882) FU; "Fisk Anniversary Exercises," *The Fisk Herald* 15/4 (February 1896) FU; "Personals," *The Fisk Herald* 14/8 (June 1897) FU; "Jubilee Day," *The Fisk Herald* (November 1890) FU; "Jubilee Exercises," *The Fisk Herald* 19/8 (June 1902) FU; "Jubilee Day," *The Fisk Herald* 23/1 (November 1905) FU.

[144] Prof. Thomas W. Talley, "Appreciation of Mrs. Ella Sheppard Moore by a Fellow Student," *Fisk University News* (1914): 11, FU.

[145] Anne Firor Scott's research demonstrates how educated, cultured black women of this era joined forces to establish various volunteer organizations aimed at benefiting their race. She writes that by 1910, the number of voluntary associations organized and operated by black women rivaled that of their white counterparts. See Anne Firor Scott, "Most Invisible of All: Black Women's Voluntary Associations," *The Journal of Southern History* 56/1 (February 1990):12. For a history of the NACW, see Elizabeth Lindsay Davis: introduction by Sieglinde Lemke, *Lifting As They Climb* (New York: G. K. Hall & Co., an Imprint of Simon & Schuster Macmillan, 1996).

[146] Ella Sheppard to W. E. Whiting, 6 April 1875, AMAA; Minutes of the First Annual Convention of the National Federation of Afro-American Women, 1896, Auburn Avenue Research Library, Atlanta; Minutes of the National Association of Colored Women, 1897, Auburn Avenue Research Library, Atlanta; "The National Association of Colored Women," *The Fisk Herald* 15/1 (October 1897): 7, 8, FU; "The National Association of Colored Women Meet in Nashville, Tennessee," *The Indianapolis Freeman*, 2 October 1897.

[147] Moore (Sheppard), "Bureau of Woman's Work," *American Missionary* (August 1894): 303–304, AMAA.

[148] Trinity High School was founded in 1865 by Mary Frances Wells of Ann Arbor, Michigan, and supported by the AMA. Wells had been a nurse for Union soldiers during the Civil War and remained in Athens, Alabama, after emancipation to work with the freedmen. She served as the school's principal for twenty-seven years, leaving temporarily to travel as preceptress with White's inaugural company in 1871. Pattie J. Malone, one of the school's most celebrated graduates, attended Fisk University and joined the Jubilee Singers ("Trinity High School," typewritten, unpublished note in Limestone County Archives, Athens, Alabama).

[149] "Mrs. Ella Sheppard Moore—Biographical Sketch," *Fisk University News* (1914): 8, FU.

[150] "Ella Sheppard Moore, Jubilee Singer, Dies," *Nashville Tennessean and the Nashville American*, 10 June 1914.

[151] Prof. Thomas W. Talley, "Appreciation of Mrs. Ella Sheppard Moore by a Fellow Student," *Fisk University News* (1914): 11, FU.

[152] "The President's Page," *Fisk University News* (April 1920): 7, 8, FU.

Afterword

[1] "General Fisk's Address," *American Missionary* (February 1876): 33, AMAA.

[2] "Cable Telegram From England" and "Response From Nashville," *American Missionary* (February 1876): 35, AMAA.

[3] "Remarks of Rev. Dr. McFerrin," *American Missionary* (February 1876): 36, AMAA.

[4] "Jubilee Singers," *American Missionary* (February 1876): 37, 38, AMAA.

[5] Taylor (Gordon), "Reminiscences of Jubilee Singers," 30.

[6] Richardson, *A History of Fisk University*, 53. Four hundred students graduated from Fisk by 1900 and were employed in the following professions: education (college, high school, normal school, and grammar school), ministry, law, business, and government. Sixteen were in professional schools. These are impressive numbers when one realizes that only one percent of U.S. blacks (less than 23,000 persons) were in professional service by 1900. Also see *Fisk University and Some of its Graduates*, ca. 1900, AMAA.

[7] "Mabel Lewis Imes," *Fisk News* (September 1935): 4, FU. Also see "Music," *The Greater Fisk Herald* 3/2 (November 1927): 12, FU; "Jubilee Day," *Fisk News* 2/1 (October 1928): 4, FU; "Jubilee Day," *The Greater Fisk Herald* 4/1 (October 1938): 8, 9, FU; "Mabel Lewis Imes," *Fisk News* 2/8 (May 1929): 1, FU.

[8] "Notables Attend Imes Funeral. Burial in Nashville," *Cleveland Call and Post* (8 August 1935): 1, 8.

[9] "Jubilee Day," *The Fisk Herald* 4/3 (November 1886): 3, FU.

[10] "Foreword," *Fisk University News* 2/5 (October 1911): 2, FU.

[11] Burton Clark assigns the term "organizational saga" to the phenomenon of a historical event shaping the collective understanding and shared memory of a formally established group. He further explains: "With a general emphasis on normative bonds, organizational saga refers to a unified set of publicly expressed beliefs about the formal group that (a) is rooted in history, (b) claims unique accomplishment, and (c) is held with sentiment by the group." Burton R. Clark, "The Organizational Saga in Higher Education," *Administrative Science Quarterly* 17/2 (June 1972): 178–84. Also see Burton R. Clark, "Belief and Loyalty in College Organization," *The Journal of Higher Education* 42/6 The Invitational Seminar on Restructuring College and University Organization and Governance (June 1971): 499–515.

[12] Zoë Ingalls, "From Slavery to Celebrity: The 125-Year Success of the Fisk Jubilee Singers," *The Chronicle of Higher Education* (3 May 1996): B7.

[13] "Mr. Loudin's Speech," *American Missionary* (September 1875): 200, 201, AMAA.

Index

219, 240n17, 250n7, 250n8,
270n10, 270n15, 273n53,
277n31, 283n108; background
of, 23, 24; relationship with
Spence, 24, 25, 34, 36; as
treasurer, 28, 29, 33, 46; as
music teacher, 258n10; and
concert scheme, 29, 30-36,
241n22, 242n42; and Ella
Sheppard, 27, 41, 193, 194, 195,
196, 199, 200, 203, 283n98,
284n112; and the *Cantata of
Esther*, 27-29; first campaign, 27,
37-43, 147, 287n148; and
spirituals, 39, 40, 99, 101, 102;
and T. K. Beecher, 42; names
the ensemble, 43, 44; advertising
ideas of, 44, 45; and troubles of
first campaign, 37-40, 43, 45,
46, 273n15; and Henry Ward
Beecher, 49-51, 54; choral
methods of, 50, 103, 260n29;
missionary beliefs of, 24, 53, 54;
and AMA support, 52, 55, 57,
70, 71; and Jubilee Hall, 55; and
Pike, 58, 270n7, 271n19; and
campaign strategies, 60-62, 64,
69, 85; at World's Peace Jubilee,
68, 69; and rival groups, 73;
second campaign of, 74-76; in
England, 82, 89, 90, 148; and
"Service of Song," 84; and
Moody, 91, 93, 254n79; stage
presence of, 106, 108, 261n53;
in Germany, 112, 137; and
discrimination, 118; and
ensemble tensions, 145, 149,
150-156; and Laura, 149, 153;
and singer selection for final
campaign, 156-158; marriage to
Susan Gilbert, 246n3; altercation
with Porter, 162, 163;

resignation of, 165-168; and
Loudin, 173, 174, 176, 180; and
independent group, 176, 201,
202, 218, 219, 220, 221,
278n39; accident at Chautauqua,
177, 179; death of, 274n83
White, Georgia Laura, 274
White, Laura A. Cravath, 23
Whiting, W. E., 129, 207
Wickle, Rebecca, 207
Wilberforce, William, 192, 209
Wilberforce University, 192, 282n88
Williams, R. B., 279n46
Wilson, Maggie E., 279n46
Work, John Wesley II, 99, 206,
282n80
World's African Congress, 206
World's Columbian Exposition,
184, 185
World's Peace Jubilee, 68, 219,
248n47
Women's Congregational Congress,
206
"Year of Jubilee," 43, 44, 52, 210,
216
YMCA, 72, 79, 81, 85, 86, 202
Young People's Society of Christian
Endeavor, 203